William Edmondson
"Grumble" Jones

William Edmondson "Grumble" Jones

The Life of a Cantankerous Confederate

JAMES BUCHANAN BALLARD

McFarland & Company, Inc., Publishers
Jefferson, North Carolina

LIBRARY OF CONGRESS CATALOGUING-IN-PUBLICATION DATA

Names: Ballard, James Buchanan, 1951– author.
Title: William Edmondson "Grumble" Jones : the life of a cantankerous Confederate / James Buchanan Ballard.
Description: Jefferson, North Carolina : McFarland & Company, Inc., Publishers, 2017. | Includes bibliographical references and index.
Identifiers: LCCN 2017038747 | ISBN 9781476670768 (softcover : acid free paper) ∞
Subjects: LCSH: Jones, William E., 1824–1864. | Generals—Confederate States of America—Biography. | United States—History—Civil War, 1861–1865—Biography. | United States—History—Civil War, 1861–1865—Cavalry operations. | Confederate States of America. Army—Biography. | Glade Spring (Va.)—Biography.
Classification: LCC E467.1.J794 B35 2017 | DDC 355.0092 [B] —dc23
LC record available at https://lccn.loc.gov/2017038747

BRITISH LIBRARY CATALOGUING DATA ARE AVAILABLE

ISBN (print) 978-1-4766-7076-8
ISBN (ebook) 978-1-4766-2970-4

© 2017 James Buchanan Ballard. All rights reserved

No part of this book may be reproduced or transmitted in any form or by any means, electronic or mechanical, including photocopying or recording, or by any information storage and retrieval system, without permission in writing from the publisher.

Front cover image of William Edmondson Jones, 1861; *background* Confederate battle flag © 2017 Lalocracio/iStock

Printed in the United States of America

McFarland & Company, Inc., Publishers
Box 611, Jefferson, North Carolina 28640
www.mcfarlandpub.com

To the memory
of Dr. Howard Jones

Acknowledgments

I extend special gratitude to the following individuals for their invaluable assistance in making this work possible. I am indebted to all of them.

Art and Arlene Wills, Raleigh, NC
Carolyn Ryburn, Glade Spring, VA
Diana Powell, Morgan Hill, CA
Karin D. Schulte (deceased), Houston, TX
L.C. Angles (deceased), Blacksburg, VA
Dr. Howard Jones (deceased), Cedar Falls, IW
Gene Matthis (deceased), Abingdon, VA
William Nichols (deceased), Houston, TX
Ron Tallman, Glade Spring, VA
Joella Barbour, Abingdon, VA
Mike Shaffer, Kennesaw, GA
Roger Judd, Fairbury, NE
Steve Johnston, Chilhowie, VA
Robert Vejnar, Archivist, Emory & Henry College, Emory, VA
Lorraine N. Abraham, Director, Emory & Henry College Library, Emory, VA
Eugene C. Tidball, Boulder, CO
Thomas P. Lowry, Woodbridge, VA
Charlie Barnett, Bristol, VA
Patrick Schulte, Houston, TX

Table of Contents

Preface   1

1. Ancestry and Origin   5
2. Emory and Henry College   10
3. West Point   15
4. Manifest Destiny   32
5. Migration, Furlough and Marriage   41
6. Tragedy on the High Seas   44
7. Texas—Into the Desert   53
8. The Civilian Years   67
9. A Call to Arms   80
10. First Virginia Cavalry   91
11. Seventh Virginia Cavalry   101
12. Command of the Shenandoah Valley District   113
13. West Virginia Raid   128
14. Brandy Station   147
15. Gettysburg   156
16. Court-Martial   171
17. Southwest Virginia and East Tennessee   179
18. The Shenandoah Valley—May 1864   205
19. Return to the Valley   211

20. The Battle of Piedmont—June 5, 1864   223
21. Piedmont Aftermath   230

Epilogue   239
Chapter Notes   251
Bibliography   272
Index   279

Preface

On Friday, June 10, 1864, the *Abingdon Virginian*, a Washington County, Virginia, weekly newspaper publication under the joint directorship of Charles B. Coale and George R. Barr printed the following front-page headline and article:

The commentary assumes that a biography of Brigadier General William E. Jones would ultimately "be given." Although brief and partially accurate sketches summarizing the man's life received nominal attention in periodicals and other sources, more than 150 years passed without a complete biography ever being published. Even then, it took years of research, advances in technology, invaluable help from individuals, and luck to accomplish it.

Exactly how he earned the moniker of "Grumble" remains a mystery. Some suggest he received it while attending West Point, where such labels were standard. There are theories that a single event permanently altered his personality, that being the tragic drowning of his wife, an event he had to witness as a helpless bystander only weeks after their marriage.

He was known to have a short temper and an extremely cantankerous personality rivaled only by Jubal Early. Going back to his Old Army service, he was often at odds with his superiors. He openly criticized his subordinates not only for failure but also in situations where success lacked perfection. Jones had a long-standing personal grudge with the legendary James Ewell Brown "Jeb" Stuart. There seems to have been a personality conflict brought on in part by their nine-year difference

> **A Gallant Officer Fallen.**
>
> It is with more than ordinary pain we announce the death of Brig. Gen. Wm. E. Jones, of this county, who fell in the engagement near Staunton on Sunday last. He was a graduate of West Point, and for several years a Lieutenant in the U. S. Army. Just before the breaking out of the war he was elected Captain of the volunteer company known as the Washington Mounted Rifles, and led them to the field among the first that rallied under the Stars and Bars. From that day to the day of his death, he was rarely absent from his post, and participated in some of the hardest fought battles of this great struggle.
>
> As his biography will doubtless be given, we will not pretend to give more at present than the melancholy fact of his death.

This is an image of a news article in the *Abingdon Virginian* published on June 10, 1864 (Emory and Henry College Archives and *Chronicling America*, sponsored jointly by the National Endowment for the Humanities and the Library of Congress).

in age, with Jones being the elder and of subordinate rank. If Stuart had too much vanity Jones had too much pride, and the traits sometimes worked against the better interest of both officers.

William Edmondson "Grumble" Jones is one of the most overlooked personalities of the American Civil War. Within a relatively short lifespan, he was a remarkable overachiever of his generation. His childhood was mostly fatherless and marred by personal tragedy. He was born and raised in the isolated Appalachian Mountain region of Southwest Virginia at a time when the average man was barely literate and rarely ventured more than twenty miles from his home county. Grumble overcame these challenges to earn two college degrees, one of them being from one of the most distinguished institutions in the world. His travels took him across the continental United States, Latin America, and Europe.

Jones's career in the U.S. Army was inglorious but eventful. He participated in the March to Oregon and in the occupation of the Oregon Territory. After losing his wife to drowning in a shipwreck, he served at various outposts on the Texas frontier for almost five years in a life dominated by loneliness and isolation. During that time, he patented a horse saddle improvement and made an acquaintance with a fellow inventor, Major Henry Hopkins Sibley of the U.S. Dragoons. Disillusioned with life in the Old Army following eight years of service, Jones resigned his commission and entered civilian life.

Biographical sketches have portrayed an anecdote that, upon resigning from the Old Army, Jones retired to his Washington County family estate to live out his life as a recluse and terminated his self-imposed exile only upon the outbreak of the Civil War. That could not be further from the truth. In reality, Jones was a private contractor engaged in commerce with the U.S. War Department, and he toured Europe to market his products. According to some of his detractors, his business scruples came into question. But by however means, he reached a certain level of economic success.

During his few civilian years, Jones was also one of the antagonists promoting what would later be deemed the Lost Cause. His viewpoints on slavery and his animosity towards the abolitionist movement were not without controversy. The John Brown raid at Harpers Ferry brought Jones a revised sense of purpose, prompting the formation of a prewar militia company. Following the election of Abraham Lincoln, he joined the extremists who welcomed advent of the Civil War.

During his service to the Confederacy, Jones achieved conflicting outcomes including distinction, administrative setbacks, and obscurity. His surly personality probably cost him his commission early in the Civil War when members of his regiment voted him out of office. Later, following his reinstatement and promotion, local politicians dissatisfied with his progress in the Shenandoah Valley demanded his removal as commander of the Shenandoah Valley District. Upon the conclusion of the Gettysburg Campaign he submitted a written reproach to Jeb Stuart. This impulsive action earned him an arrest, a court-martial conviction, and banishment from the Army of Northern Virginia.

In most of his combat operations, Jones was victorious. When a triumph was not achieved he usually salvaged a stalemate. His prompt actions saved the day at Brandy Station, and he was highly instrumental in the successful withdrawal of the Army of Northern Virginia from Gettysburg. In the latter he held his own against an overwhelming force commanded by the legendary George Armstrong Custer. His successful campaigns in East Tennessee and Southwest Virginia were Southern anomalies for the region. In the only combat engagement he decisively lost, Jones sacrificed his life to turn the tide. He died a classic hero's death but received little recognition.

Jones had his faults and his detractors. However, he was revered by the common soldiers in the ranks under his command. He was known to have declined the special privilege of his rank by sharing their hardships and deprivations. He showed compassion to enemy prisoners of war, particularly the wounded, and was also respected by his war enemies on the Union side. Ironically, most of his adversaries were his administrative superiors and professed the same allegiance to the South as he did.

As a cavalry commander on the regimental and brigade levels, Jones's military tactics combined conventional and partisan warfare. Going back to the days of his prewar militia company, Jones was the first war mentor to the legendary John Singleton Mosby. Unlike partisan rangers in general, Jones was a stern disciplinarian guided by the conventional rules of war.

The intent of this biography is to provide readers with an objective glimpse of one of the most overlooked characters of the American Civil War. In regard to his generation and time in history, many biographies have been written about men of lesser distinction. This one is more than 150 years overdue.

1

Ancestry and Origin

William Edmondson (Edmiston) "Grumble" Jones was descended from a long family line of Presbyterian Scots who emigrated from the lowlands to the Ulster Province of Ireland in the 1600s. Over the next century, generations joined in the mass migration to America. The term "Scots-Irish" was the common designation used to refer to the ethnic group that earned a reputation as being rugged and courageous individualists who were loyal to their clans and contemptuous of authority. Taking risks in exchange for opportunity, they made their distinction as the frontiersmen who built the American nation.

The names Edmondson and Edmiston are often interchangeable and refer to the same family in most situations. Edmiston is a phonetic spelling of the name Edmondson adopted in the eighteenth century.[1] In many instances, the spelling changed back and forth from one generation to the next. For uniformity, this biography will use only the name Edmondson. With the predominance of Edmondsons in Washington County, Virginia, William E. Jones probably identified more with his mother's side of the family. His parents followed the southern Scots-Irish tradition by naming him, as their second son, after his maternal grandfather, Colonel William Edmondson.

Colonel William Edmondson was a hero of the American Revolution and in particular the Battle of Kings Mountain. The dissimilarities between the grandson and grandfather are noteworthy. Grumble Jones married only once, and briefly at that, without fathering any known children in a forty-year lifespan. Colonel William Edmondson married at least twice and was known to have fathered fifteen children in eighty-nine years.[2] Although diverse in personal life experience, the grandfather and grandson apparently came from the same genetic pool. "Grumble" inherited his maternal grandfather's genetic traits including character, courage, and critical components. Among those latter features were quick tempers and lasting grudges.

William Edmondson was born in 1734 as the eldest son of John Edmondson, who had settled briefly in the region of Chester County, Pennsylvania, or Cecil County, Maryland.[3] In the 1740s the family migrated to the Borden Tract of Augusta County (currently part of Rockbridge County), Virginia.[4] William Edmondson's introduction to a soldier's life occurred during the French and Indian War (1754–1763). In 1760 he and his brother, Samuel Edmondson, enlisted in Colonel William Byrd's expedition against the Cherokees. Just as would occur to his grandson a century later, William Edmondson was court-martialed for demonstrating disrespect to a superior officer.[5] He was convicted of "the high crime of addressing an officer without taking off his hat." Outraged by the reprimand and the threat of greater punishment, he vowed to shoot the officer who had "so grossly insulted him." With difficulty, his brother, Samuel, dissuaded him from committing mutiny and murder.[6]

The incident drew the attention of a higher-ranking officer who saw potential in the spirited member of his corps. The officer corresponded with Virginia governor Francis Fauquier suggesting that unless Edmondson received a commission he was only more likely to get into more trouble.[7] Acting accordingly, Governor Fauquier commissioned Edmondson with the rank of ensign for the remainder of the expedition. In 1763 the governor appointed him a commission in the Virginia militia. For his French and Indian War service, Edmondson received, and settled on, two thousand acres in what is now Washington County, Virginia. In 1774 he served in the Fincastle County Militia. A year later hostilities emerged in what would turn out to be the beginning of the American Revolution.

In 1776 Washington County, Virginia, was formed out of Fincastle County as the first geographic entity named after George Washington, commander of the Continental Army and ultimately the nation's father. Captain Edmondson served the Washington County Militia in frontier expeditions against the Cherokees in Kentucky, Georgia, and Tennessee. In 1778 he commanded his militia in an expedition against the Loyalists along the New River. On October 7, 1880, he fought at Kings Mountain in South Carolina.[8]

At Kings Mountain Major William Edmondson served in the Virginia militia as second in command to the highly revered Colonel William Campbell. The Kings Mountain Campaign was an overwhelming victory for the patriot cause, turning the overall tide of the conflict in the South. The Battle of Kings Mountain Patriot Roster contains ten men bearing the last name Edmondson or Edmiston. Five were officers, three died, and one was wounded. William Edmondson was not among the casualties.

By 1783, he had risen to the rank of colonel and assumed the title permanently. Edmondson married and survived Margaret Montgomery and Eliza Kennedy, fathering fifteen children between the two spouses. Contemporaries described him as "bold, manly, open-hearted, and generous." As would also be the case with his grandson, "his attachments were strong and his hatreds bitter."[9]

Following the American Revolution, Edmondson served as county sheriff and judge. In 1795, at age sixty-one, he fathered Grumble's mother, Catherine Moffett Edmondson, born to his second wife, Eliza Kennedy Edmondson. Living until his eighty-ninth year, Edmondson died in 1822, less than two years before William Edmondson Jones was born.[10]

The paternal side of Grumble's ancestry is vague and less distinct. His paternal grandparents were Henry and Martha Jones. If Grumble inherited his character traits through his maternal grandfather, it could be said that he received his economic and social status from his paternal grandfather. In 1820 Henry Jones purchased a 360-acre tract of farmland from John Steel.[11] The land was situated on both sides of the Middle Fork of the Holston River in Washington County, in the vicinity of current-day Lodi, four miles south of Glade Spring Depot, which was established later. Geographic and topographical features allowed for a productive farm in raising cattle and producing crops. An abundance of river frontage allowed for the operation of a sawmill and a grist mill. Grumble Jones would ultimately acquire the property as its sole owner. The southern boundary of the original Henry Jones family land was approximately four miles south of Old Glade Spring. The plot included acreage on both sides of what is now Virginia

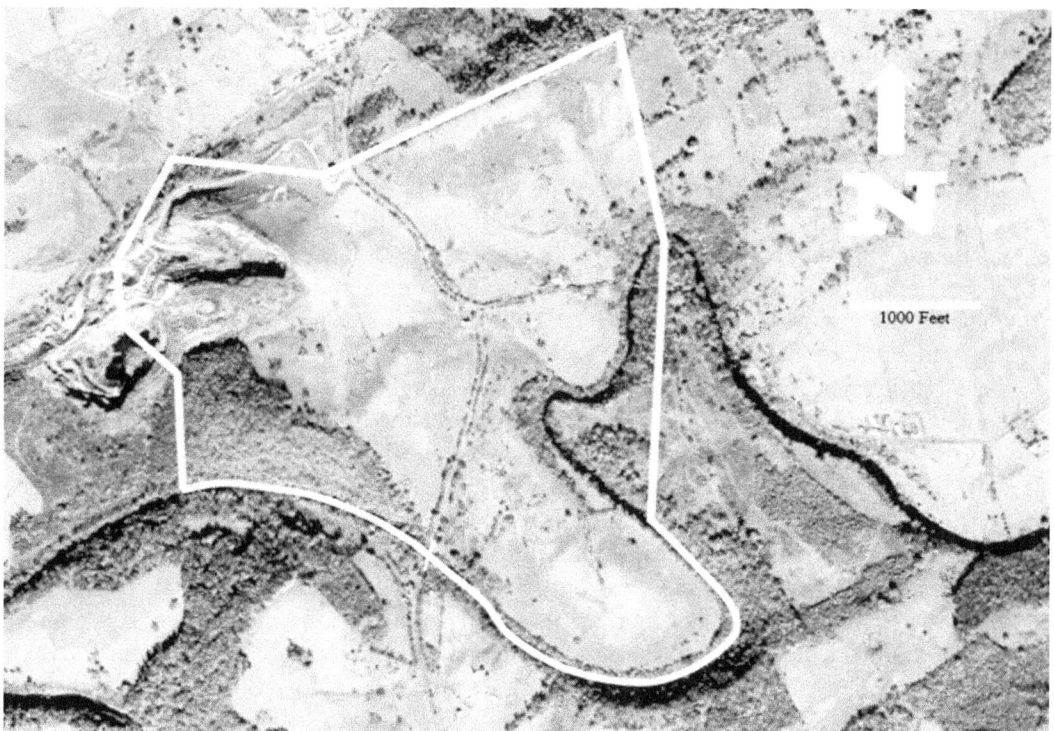

Aerial image of the Jones family farm south of Glade Spring, Virginia, taken October 16, 2011 (courtesy Terra Server Imagery of Raleigh, North Carolina).

Highway 91 and the Middle Fork of the Holston River, which served as the natural southern and southeastern boundaries.

On February 1, 1821, Henry Jones's son, Robert Jones (born March 15, 1798), and William Edmondson's daughter, Catherine "Kate" Moffett Edmondson (born March 12, 1795), were married by the Reverend Alex McCown.[12] The couple resided in a two-story log home situated on the crest of the land overlooking the 360-acre river frontage farm acquired by Robert's father in 1820. In the course of their twelve-year marriage, Robert and Catherine Jones had the following issue:

1. Henry S. Jones, born July 4, 1822;
2. William Edmondson Jones, born May 9, 1824;
3. David R. Jones, born March 21, 1826, died May 16, 1826;
4. Jonathan S. Jones, born September 28, 1827, died October 15, 1838;
5. Robert Campbell Jones, born December 27, 1829;
6. Sarah Eliza Jane Jones, born January 12, 1832;
7. James W. Jones, born February 17, 1834.[13]

Reared in an upper-middle–class family, William Edmondson Jones benefited from a heritage that, although not considered aristocratic, rendered him moderately above most of his peers in regard to social status and prestige. The vast majority of inhabitants of the combined regions of Southwest Virginia and adjacent East Tennessee were of modest means. While most heads of agrarian households at the time were tenant farmers, Robert Jones owned his land outright. As part of the settled rural society, the Robert

Jones family relied upon an economic base of agriculture, a way of life that was assuming a permanent form by 1830.[14] Members of the Robert Jones family were Presbyterians, who were the first of the denominations to settle in the region.

While the typical agricultural tenant farmer class families resided in single-story log cabins, many without windows and chinked with clay mortar, the Jones family occupied a two-story log structure equipped with limestone chimneys, fireplaces, and a foundation. Although a step below the elite class that resided in brick mansions of sound craftsmanship, the Joneses enjoyed an above-average standard of living.[15]

The Robert Jones family was part of a group of inhabitants in Southwest Virginia, the area situated west of the New River, south of the Kanawha River, and extending to the state borders with North Carolina, Kentucky, and Tennessee. The region has always held a close association with East Tennessee, marked as the area between the Great Smoky Mountains and the Cumberland Mountains within the boundaries separating it from North Carolina and Virginia.

In spite of their higher economic and social class, however, the Jones family was part of a society for which life was challenging and primitive. Daily life in the sparsely populated agrarian regions of Washington County varied only slightly from that of the frontier days. Those possessing tangible assets and intellectual graces usually carried a burden to conceal evidence of their achievements and wealth by a very modest appearance.[16] Like its frontiersmen predecessors, the family's immediate concern was survival through wringing a livelihood from the land, a process that forced an abeyance of the cultural aspects.[17] The pressures of immediate need shaped the "rude society" into one that was personally indifferent to the standards of more civilized communities.[18] Upper-middle–class families found relief from the daily routines necessary to survive in primitive distractions of drinking, cockfighting, shooting, horse racing, and other types of dissipation.[19] Fist fighting, often engaged in between friends and without the intent to do permanent harm, was a typical competitive sport. An important social event involved muster drills in the local militia, a factor that may have influenced Grumble's desire to become a career soldier. The leisure pastime of horse racing probably influenced him to select the mounted service.

The legacy of the Robert and Catherine Jones family is steeped in tragedy. David R. Jones, the son who followed William, died less than two months after his birth. By age nine William and his siblings were rendered fatherless when Robert Jones died at age thirty-five, leaving five surviving children and a widowed wife pregnant with their seventh child.[20] A second brother, Jonathan S. Jones, died at age eleven in 1838. Through all of the adversity, the family managed to keep the farm productive.

Robert Jones prepared his last will only ten days before his death, leading to speculation that he knew his demise was near. He appointed his wife's first cousin, Robert Buchanan Edmondson, as executor and granted him the authority to either sell or retain the slaves at his discretion. A bond set at $5,000 in 1834 was indicative of an estate valued well above average.[21] Catherine Moffett Edmondson Jones, age thirty-eight at the time of her husband's death, ran the family farm with eight slaves as noted in the 1840 Washington County census. Within ten years, the estate of Robert Jones expanded to include 150 acres of cultivated land and 250 acres of unimproved land. The property held special meaning to William, who would ultimately acquire sole ownership.

Robert Buchanan Edmondson was a significant influence in the life of William Edmondson Jones. Correspondence suggests that the kinsman assumed the role as surrogate father. Referred to as "the Colonel," Robert Buchanan Edmondson led a local militia group and served on the newly established Emory and Henry College Board of Trustees, a factor that may have contributed to William's admission and enrollment.

William Edmondson Jones's good fortune was that he grew to adolescence at the time of enlightenment in the region of Southwest Virginia and East Tennessee. How he acquired his preliminary education is unknown, but in rural communities such as those where he lived, individuals often established schools to educate their children and opened the opportunity to others in the community.

During the 1830s, rural society in Southwest Virginia and East Tennessee began to look beyond basic survival and toward the cultural development of its next generation. An 1858 publication titled *The Pioneer Preacher; or, Rifle, Axe, and Saddle-Bags and Other Lectures,* authored by William H. Milburn, attributed the intellectual advancement of the western frontier to the church and its ministers.[22] According to Milburn, the rifle, axe, and saddlebags symbolized the successive phases of frontier development. The "rifle" represented the original explorers who secured the area. The "axe" denoted the era when permanent settlers cleared the land for development and cultivation. The "saddlebags" epitomized the church ministers who utilized the devices to carry books and other instruments of learning to the isolated settlers for their "cultural and moral development."[23]

In 1824, the year of Grumble's birth, the Holston Conference separated from the Tennessee Conference of the Methodist Church. By 1830 the Methodists, Baptists, Presbyterians, and other sects turned to establishing their distinct institutions, and the church college movement was in full swing.[24] That new movement in religious and cultural development was coming to full fruition by 1836. For William Edmondson Jones, a life dominated by tragedy, adversity, and a primitive lifestyle was about to realize opportunity with the founding of a liberal arts college less than ten miles from his home.

2

Emory and Henry College

In 1836 Creed Fulton, a Methodist minister, Tobias Smyth, a Methodist farmer, Alexander Findlay, a Methodist merchant, and Colonel William Byars, a Presbyterian philanthropist, directed the founding of a liberal arts college in Washington County, Virginia. The new institution evolved into a community enterprise under the sponsorship of the Holston Conference of the Methodist Church.[1] Development began with the acquisition of 554½ acres of land from the heirs of the Reverend Edward Crawford. Following a formal dedication ceremony, construction of buildings and improvements commenced on September 30, 1836.[2]

Initially, the institution was referred to as the Holston Conference Manual Labor School, a title of accurate description in regard to purpose but lacking "style or grace."[3] The name was changed to honor the recently deceased John Emory, bishop of the Methodist Episcopal Church, and Patrick Henry, former Virginia governor and renowned patriot of the American Revolution. Construction was completed on April 2, 1838, at which time the college accepted students for the first time.[4] Sixty students, almost all from the area of Southwest Virginia and East Tennessee, enrolled in the preparatory department.[5]

The center of the campus was a four-story brick structure, later named Wiley Hall, that accommodated classrooms, dormitory facilities for 150 students, and apartments for faculty members with families. The William Byars House, a three-story structure of about half the size of Wiley Hall, housed the rooms where the first classes were taught.[6] Since the Virginia-Tennessee Railroad was not chartered until 1849, horse or stagecoach provided the only transportation access.[7]

The northeastern United States provided the new college with its academic origins. Charles Collins, a twenty-four-year-old graduate, ranked first in his class of 1837 at Wesleyan University in Middleton, Connecticut. He served as principal of Augusta High School in Maine and was appointed the first president and instructor of Emory and Henry. The first full academic year began in August of 1838, with the enrollment increased to one hundred.

Emory and Henry College was, and remains, an outgrowth of local concern and was a result of the efforts of people who lived in the immediate vicinity of the school.[8] It is the oldest institution of learning in Southwest Virginia. It is also one of the few schools in the entire Appalachian region that opened as a college, continued under its original name, still occupies its original site, and is supported by the founding organization.[9]

The extended family of Robert Jones, deceased, and Catherine Moffett Edmondson-

2. Emory and Henry College

Emory and Henry College, Wiley Hall, circa 1870 (Emory and Henry College Archives).

Jones assumed a role in the early development of the college. Catherine Jones's cousin, Robert Buchanan Edmondson, served on the board of trustees.[10] William's older brother Henry S. Jones enrolled as a member of the student body for the first full academic year of 1838–1839.[11] At the age of fifteen, William Edmondson Jones was among the second wave of students enrolled the following academic year of 1839–1840.[12] Henry did not attend beyond a second academic year; Grumble Jones was a student for five years

The Jones brothers' connection to the trustee member was only one factor regarding their admission and enrollment at Emory and Henry College. The campus was geographically convenient, and the regimen of the "manual labor" program carried a significant element of familiarity, a program that had its origins in Switzerland.[13] In 1833 the Society for the Promotion of Liberal and Common Education Under the Patronage of the Methodist Episcopal Church endorsed the system "so that the body and mind could be disciplined together."[14] Denominational colleges such as Maine Wesleyan Seminary, Allegheny College, Davidson College, and Mercer Institute (later Mercer University) also adopted the system.

The cost of higher education at existing institutions, which limited access to the privileged few, was a factor for those advocating reform.[15] From this sentiment grew the concept that a manual labor program would be more democratic by providing area middle-class agrarian families accustomed to farm work with the means to send their sons to college.[16] The idea also appealed to the surrounding agricultural community and induced many to support the institution financially. All students boarding at the college were required to participate in the labor program during their first three years. On a typical day, time set aside for classes and recitations was from 5:00 a.m. to 1:00 p.m. From 2:00 p.m. to 5:00 p.m. was devoted to labor. The time from 7:00 p.m. to 9:00 p.m. was dedicated to study.

In the manual labor program, a steward sounded a horn signaling the beginning of a three-hour work period on the nearly 600-acre farm connected to the campus. Organized into groups of eight to ten depending on age, strength, and skill, students performed manual tasks under the supervision of a student prefect.[17] Duties included clearing the land, constructing farm-related improvements, and cultivation. Compensation ranged from three to five cents per hour depending on the difficulty. A minimum of eighteen hours per month was required of all students. If they so desired, students were permitted to work up to five hours per day. No student, however, was allowed to earn more than his cost of board and tuition. Tuition charges, depending upon the studies pursued, ranged from $10 to $15 per session. Board was $1.50 per week, with $10.00 paid in advance.[18]

Candidates for admission to the pending freshmen class had to be well acquainted with arithmetic, English grammar, geography, ancient and modern history, and have a broad sphere in the study of classical languages.[19] Taking into consideration William's prior background in a rude society, how he qualified for admission is a mystery. However, he would demonstrate academic proficiency, as evidenced by his academic class advancement each year.

The faculty consisted of the Reverend Charles Collins, president, as well as professor of natural sciences, the Reverend Ephraim E. Wiley, professor of ancient languages and literature, and the Reverend William T. Harlow, professor of mathematics and instructor of modern languages. John G. Winford served as the tutor. The fall semester for the academic year began on the fourth Wednesday in August and lasted until the second Wednesday in January. The spring session commenced on the first Wednesday in March and continued until the second Wednesday in August. In 1842, the long vacation schedule was changed to the summer months by moving the beginning of the spring semester back to the first of February. Each semester was twenty-one weeks in length.[20]

Emory and Henry College offered only a preparatory curriculum until the fall semester of 1840, when freshman and sophomore classes were organized. Eligible students could gain status by taking an examination. By the fall of 1842 students enrolled in one of the following: the four-year curriculum, the preparatory department, or a select course of study for those who did not contemplate taking a degree.[21]

In his second academic year, beginning in August of 1840, William E. Jones enrolled as part of a 147-member student body in the preparatory department. In his third academic year beginning in 1841, students pursuing the four-year collegiate course were supposed to be arranged in freshman, sophomore, junior, and senior classes. All students could place at any grade level by showing proficiency in examinations. However, the 143 members of the student body remained undivided into the four levels of classes.[22]

For the academic year beginning in August 1842 the student body was finally divided, based on examination results, into six seniors, eight juniors, sixteen sophomores, nine freshmen, thirty-five "on a select course" and fifty-two in the preparatory department, for a collective student body of 126.[23] Enrolled in his fourth year, Jones was placed on examination results into the sophomore class, which studied Latin, Greek, mathematics, and English. The course in Latin involved the writings of Horace and Cicero. Greek included the "Memorabilia" of Socrates, Plato, Polyaenus, and Thucydides. Mathematics required geometry, application of algebra to geometry, plane and spherical trigonometry, and surveying and navigation. English covered the subjects of rhetoric, composition, and elocution.[24]

Approaching the end of the fall semester on December 24, 1842, Congressman George Washington Hopkins nominated Jones for a position as a cadet at the United States Military Academy at West Point.[25] Hopkins, from adjacent Russell County, Virginia, was a Jacksonian Democrat who served in the U.S. House of Representatives from 1835 to 1847. A recent law had been passed allowing each representative in Congress to recommend one resident within his congressional district or territory for admission. Although recommended for West Point, Jones had not been officially accepted and therefore continued his studies at Emory and Henry. In August of 1843, following a placement examination, Jones enrolled as one of seven seniors.[26] Fourteen juniors, eleven sophomores, fourteen freshmen, forty-five "irregulars," and thirty-two in the preparatory department formed the collective student body of 123.

During Jones's senior academic year, he studied mathematics, natural science, and English. The math involved mechanical philosophy, astronomy, and optics. Natural science covered the areas of hydrostatics, pneumatics, acoustics, electricity, chemistry, mineralogy, and philosophy of natural history. English involved moral philosophy, Paley's Evidence, Paley's Natural Theology, Bayard's Constitution of the United States, Public Declamation of Original Compositions, and Written Forensic Discussions.[27]

Jones also factored into the creation of what ultimately evolved into the current-day literary and social societies. The Lyceum, organized during the institution's first academic year, changed in name two years later to the Calliopean Literary Society, an offshoot of a literary and debating organization by the same name founded at Yale in 1819. The group was named after Calliope, the first and wisest of the muses in Greek mythology and a daughter of Zeus. Tradition credits President Charles Collins with changing the name from the Lyceum.[28]

In 1841 following an internal dispute, several members separated from the Calliopean Literary Society and organized the Hermesian Literary Society, named after the mythical Greek god Hermes, son of Zeus.[29] The severance marked an intense rivalry between the two societies and divided the student body into bitter factions. Rivalries between fraternities at the relatively small and isolated institution persisted for more than 150 years. According to Dr. George J. Stevenson, who authored a history of the college, friendships rarely crossed societal barriers, and the enmity extended beyond college life.[30] William E. Jones joined the Hermesian Literary Society during the fall semester of 1842.[31]

In 1848 James Ewell Brown "Jeb" Stuart enrolled in the institution as an "irregular" student, satisfied the academic requirements, and advanced to the sophomore level within two years. During his academic tenure, Stuart also joined the Hermesian Literary Society and served as an active member.[32] In 1850 he departed Emory and Henry College to enroll at West Point, where he graduated in 1854. The paths of Jones and Stuart never crossed at Emory and Henry or West Point as they would in the antebellum U.S. Army and the cavalry division of the Confederate Army of Northern Virginia. Having a connection to Emory and Henry College and membership in the same literary society apparently fell short of bonding the two future Confederate generals, who were historically known to despise each other. Even the spirit of fraternal brotherhood had its limitations.

Jones was looking to graduate in the summer of 1844 when, during the spring semester, he received an official acceptance to the United States Military Academy at West Point. Orientation would begin on or about June 1. The timing conflicted with the last six weeks of classes, the final examinations, and the graduation ceremonies scheduled for July 3. Having to allow ten days for travel, Jones withdrew from Emory and Henry College with an incomplete academic status. On May 21, 1844, he departed from Washington County, Virginia, and embarked on his 600-mile journey to West Point.[33] He took an academic risk with this measure, as he had invested five years at Emory and Henry. Two years later, however, he would take advantage of a one-time two-month furlough from West Point and return to Emory and Henry College in the summer of 1846 to complete his final examinations and to receive the twenty-fifth bachelor of arts degree in the history of the institution.[34]

The author of this biography has no knowledge of any specific anecdotes regarding William E. Jones's tenure at Emory and Henry College. It is apparent that the academic curriculum and the physical demands of the manual labor program adequately prepared Jones for the regimen that awaited him at West Point.

3

West Point

The Robert Jones family Bible states the following:

William E. Jones left friends and relationships in Washington County, Virginia for West Point May 21, 1844, and landed at the place of destination on the 30th of May, 1844.[1]

The United States Military Academy at West Point was a relatively young institution growing rich in tradition. Created in 1802 during the Thomas Jefferson presidency, it gained significance in 1817 under the direction of Superintendent Sylvanus Thayer, who modeled the engineering curriculum after that of the École Polytechnique engineering school near Paris, France.[2] With its four-year curriculum, the West Point cadet body was divided by academic class. Seniors were first classmen. Juniors and sophomores made up the second class and third class respectively. First-year cadets, or fourth classmen, commonly known as "plebes," formed the bottom classification of the institutional pecking order.

Initial Rite of Passage

In keeping with tradition, the environment at West Point was psychologically, mentally, and physically intimidating to all new arrivals. First-year cadets, the plebes, were the target of hazing from all upperclassmen. Reflecting on his plebe year, Jones wrote, "The diploma of this noble institution with the privileges flowing there from was worthy of the ambition of all and the hope of its attainment placed a curb on the unruly spirits sufficient to keep them within bounds. Each entering class in succession has to endure the ingenious pranks and smothered indignation handed down by tradition through generations of cadets." He added, "The change in life is disagreeable."[3] Further elaborating, he recalled, "At no school in America is the probationary struggle of the novitiate so trying."[4]

Each newly and conditionally appointed cadet bore the unofficial and nondescript title of "thing" and had to earn the title of "plebe" through an initial month-long rite of passage.[5] Jones was among ninety *things* arriving over a ten-day period to undergo rigorous preliminary admissions testing to screen out applicants deemed incapable of withstanding the regimen that awaited them. Through his experience with the academic and manual labor regimen at Emory and Henry College, Jones had a slight advantage over most of his classmates intellectually, physically, and emotionally. At age twenty he was one of the older cadets in his class. Some were as young as sixteen.[6]

The initiation process commenced immediately with roll call followed by an introduction to military drill with the proper standing formation and the goose step, an exaggerated and torturous stride of standing on one foot while flinging the alternate one forward in sequence. Parade drill was performed several times daily. Tattoo marked the end of the day's activities. Taps signaled the command for lights out. Reveille the next morning was the call to begin the process all over again.

Jones's classmate John C. Tidball, from Ohio, recalled how the indoctrination commenced upon his arrival. Not being deemed worthy of the uniform, "things" donned their civilian garments. Together they formed a "motley gang" of geographical and cultural diversity representing "every degree of provincialism" in their manner of dress, ranging in extremes from rustic homemade clothes to "foppish in city fashion."[7] As they marched, most losing step with vexatious shuffling, their appearance was most outrageously ludicrous and awkward.

The traditional harassment of "things" commenced immediately. Tidball considered hazing at the time to be "rather beneficial than otherwise, a weaning as it were, of new cadets from boyhood to manhood."[8] The most abusive culprits were third classmen, who had endured the same tribulations the previous academic year. New cadets arrived at different times, setting each one up for a separate planned indignity.

Jones vividly recalled the first ordeal of an eighteen-year-old fellow cadet classmate, Thomas Frelinghuysen McKinney McLean, from Randolph County, Missouri.[9] McLean was said to have been the nephew of the late John McLean, a senator from Illinois.[10] Thomas McLean was five feet, ten inches in height and had a square heavyset build, long light-colored hair, a downy-bearded face, and a protruding and firmly set jaw. He wore homespun clothing of "uncouth cut" and arrived carrying all of his possessions in a pair of saddlebags slung over his shoulders.[11] His unique physical appearance drew the attention of the waiting third classmen, who anxiously sought particularly amusing and accessible targets to harass.

West Point cadets had a remarkable aptitude for labeling their classmates with unique and uncomplimentary nicknames, "and fortunate indeed" was "he who escaped without one."[12] These nicknames originated from an accidental set of circumstances or a peculiarity. In addition to his appearance, McLean suffered the misfortune of the unusual pronunciation of his first middle name, "Frelinghuysen," which he revealed during his first roll call. Noting what the last two syllables rhymed with, the antagonists labeled him with the sobriquet of "Bison."[13] Together, McLean's new moniker and outward appearance magnified his perceived fittingness for ridicule.

Unfortunately for McLean, the initial round of hazing went beyond verbal abuse and taunting. Bison "had scarcely landed [at the academy] when meddlesome Third Classmen had him in tow to the barber shop."[14] With Ambrose E. Burnside officiating as master of ceremonies, they shaved half of Bison's face and half of his scalp, leaving him with an outrageous appearance. Moments after he was released back into the ranks, the drumbeat sounded for McLean's very first parade drill and "all had to run, the victim with the rest."[15] In his state of temporary deformity, McLean made his first appearance before the entire association of cadets.

But the third classmen could not break Old Bison, who had a determined spirit. McLean absorbed the humiliation with a demonstration of dignity by assuming his position in the parade drill as if oblivious or indifferent to what had just occurred: "McLean bore the joke so well that he earned the sympathy of all."[16] With his stoic response, he won the admiration of many members of his class, all three levels of upperclassmen, the graduating class, and the administration. The incident made him an instant legend in his own time at West Point.

In his memoirs, Tidball mentioned his personal harassment episodes not because he saw merit to the practical jokes but to "illustrate the absolute power" held over the new cadets due to the newness of their surroundings and the unfamiliarity with their situation.[17] On Tidball's first reveille, most of the sixty new arrivals awoke to find that their clothing was missing. All of them had to run to the parade ground in only the shirts they had slept in minus trousers, drawers, hats or shoes: "The parade was as picturesque as it was ridiculous, but everyone was in attendance. They found their clothing in a pile on the pavement of the sally port of the building."[18]

That evening, Tidball's section received a visit from a cadet team identifying itself as a committee assigned to evaluate the new arrivals for academic proficiency. The group directed the new cadets to illustrate on the blackboard the mathematical problem of "the equator and straw hat." Upon observing an administrative officer approaching the barracks, members of the group hastily darted out the windows.[19] Following lights-out, Tidball's group received another visit from an upperclassman who represented himself as the "officer of the day" and directed them to proceed to the North Barracks for their physical examinations. Unaware that this was another hazing episode, they accepted the situation as "simply one of the curious ways of the place."[20] Faux physicians performing mock physicals deemed the most "foppish" member of Tidball's group as unclean and ordered him to wash in the Hudson. The officer was escorting the individual across the parade ground when he suddenly claimed he had forgotten his lantern, needed to retrieve it, and ordered the new cadet to wait for his return. At reveille, the cadet body found him still waiting.[21]

On the same morning, noted delinquencies from the previous day's parade were posted with the names of each new cadet listed in alphabetical order, followed by his reported transgression. Not realizing that they were experiencing another episode of hazing, all received some type of report. The most common offenses were "late at reveille" and "not being properly dressed."[22] Jones and his roommates were reported for "room out of order at inspection."[23] Others offenses included "inattention to drill" or "losing step in the march." Getting further down the alphabetical listing, some of the charges approached a level of absurdity such as "winking at the chaplain's wife." When the hoaxers exhausted ideas, the general infraction of "highly unmilitary conduct sufficed."[24] Some new cadets offered explanations in futile attempts to have their demerits removed. None realized that at this probationary stage of their enrollment that demerits did not count in the official *Merit in Conduct*.

Arriving at different times, a collective ninety new applicants formed the preliminary fourth class. Their admission at this stage was, however, still conditional.

Official admittance required passing the physical and academic entrance examinations scheduled for June 20. The first three weeks of June were dedicated to educational instruction, intense studies, and recitation in preparation for the tests. This procedure minimized rejections of cadets who would eventually become scholars of distinction.[25] Jones commented that the legendary Thomas Jonathan Jackson might have been rejected had this method not been implemented.[26]

Surgeons performed physical examinations similar to those rendered to army recruits. The medical board rejected one candidate, reducing the new applicant body to eighty-nine.[27]

The academic portion occurred at the library before the superintendent, commandant, faculty, and staff. Applicants demonstrated proficiency at solving mathematic problems on the blackboard and answering any pointed questions. Ordinary recitations verified literacy skills. Fourteen candidates failed in the academic screening, reducing the new plebe class number to seventy-five.[28]

Passing the entrance examinations modestly elevated the new cadets from things to plebes, the term describing the fourth classmen. Jones and seventy-four classmates were officially admitted to West Point on July 1, 1844.[29] As an official cadet plebe, Jones joined an elite and small group of young men who would form the core of officers in what would later be known as the "Old Army," the term for the antebellum U.S. Army before the Civil War. However, they remained plebes and were subject to a year of tribulations.

Reflecting on the difficult life of a plebe, Jones wrote, "Vengeance on the persecutors is out of the question, so the afflicted are left to the comfort misery draws from company."[30] Regarding the futility of appealing to the upper channels of administration for relief, Jones commented, "Officers [school officials and administrators] probably tolerate the mischief as the harmless and efficacious means of subduing the recklessly wild and bringing the over-confidence of spoilt favorites within military control. Doubtless, they [the officials] often turn a deaf ear to complaints, and enjoin in others the troubles of their own early days."[31]

Fourth Class (Plebe) Year

Graduation ceremonies for the class of 1844 had occurred the evening before the things completed their final admission examinations.[32] Honoring another tradition, the graduates threw their hats into the air and then kicked them over the parade ground, a metaphorical ritual that symbolized "kicking" each class up one notch.[33] The graduates recovered their hats by piercing them with a sword or bayonet. Diplomas were distributed while a band played "Auld Lang Sine," "The Girl I Left Behind Me," and other appropriate airs.[34] Relieved of duty at West Point, the graduates changed from their gray cadet uniforms into the regulation blue ones issued by the army. Notable members of the West Point Class of 1844 included Winfield S. Hancock and Alfred Pleasanton. The new plebes embarked on a new phase by marching to the tailors to be fitted for uniforms. They then marched to adjoining Camp Clinton, where they pitched tents before returning to the main campus. At 10:00 a.m., the entire cadet body (except for the newly elevated second class, who were on furlough) marched into the camp with "colors flying and band playing." Plebes brought up the rear.[35] Camp Clinton would be their quarters for the next two months.

No academic classes transpired during the summer months of July and August, a time dedicated to military tactics. Between drills, the plebes performed menial tasks such as fetching pails of water and maintaining the grounds. The labor was not physically difficult, but it was "petty, disagreeable," and took "all conceit" out of them. In looking back on the experience, Jones and Tidball viewed it as "the worst form of hazing—a base kind of servitude."[36] Plebes also took turns bearing sleep deprivation with twenty-four-hour guard duties. All cadets received smoothbore flintlock pattern muskets that required constant polishing and burnishing.[37] Reiterating on his first summer drills, Jones wrote:

All the duties of the solder were imposed upon the cadet and the more menial such as scavenger of the camp and the like fell to the lot of the novitiate—the poor plebe. The third classman, just released from such disagreeable work was the overseer, and took great pleasure in verifying the old saying,- "a new broom sweeps clean." The diversity of employment and of study, as well as the traditional sport and the grades of military authority administered by the various classes, established between them a clannish feeling of the intensest character, and usually the classes nearest together disliked each other the most. To rise above prejudices so universal, and to maintain cast while running counter to them, requires an independence of character and a manifest purity of motive such as mark only the extraordinary man.[38]

As difficult as life was for the plebes during their summer encampment, there was one occasion in which the entire cadet body endured an aggravation that would embarrass the superintendent. The technology for the recently developed Samuel Morse improvement to the single-wire telegraph system was in its infant stages. Long-distance communications received from the War Department in Washington, D.C., depended on the conventional methods of delivery. A rumor circulated that the secretary of the navy would make an unannounced visit to the Point on the following day. Official visits were uncommon, but whenever speculation of their potential occurrence surfaced the authorities desired to mark the occasion properly. During the period of summer encampment no interruption of academic classes was necessary to welcome the honored guest, John Young Mason.

The day was one of sweltering heat and humidity. The entire cadet battalion, including the musical band, marched to the wharf and waited hours in the broiling sun before the steamboat arrived. Tidball wrote, "When the boat at last arrived, a few passengers landed, among whom was a respectable looking well-poised gentleman, whom the Superintendent took to be the Secretary [of the Navy], and addressing him as Mr. Mason, gave his arm, conducting him between the two lines to a carriage in waiting. As they passed along, we presented arms, the colors dipping, and the band playing 'Hail to the Chief.'"[39] The procession marched along escorting the carriage "up the hot and dusty road to the crest of the Plain," where a field artillery unit "thundered forth a salute."

All went according to plan until the carriage suddenly stopped in front of the hotel. The honored guest exited the carriage, "unceremoniously walked away," and disappeared from view upon entering the building. The band ceased playing before the entire battalion detail marched silently back to Camp Clinton. Tidball recalled, "We gave credit to the Superintendent for his kind consideration in not detaining us longer in the sweltering heat." It eventually leaked out that the celebrated guest was not the secretary of the navy but, by sheer coincidence, someone with the same last name. The gentleman was doubtless surprised by the reception and had no idea what was going on. He probably went along with the detail assuming it was "a matter of course—one of the strange ways of West Point." It was said "the incident was always a tender point with the worthy Superintendent, and one not to be alluded to lightly."[40]

On August 28, the recently promoted cadets of the new second class returned from their summer furlough to assume their new standing. A notable member of that group was Thomas Jonathan Jackson. Jones developed a special fondness for Jackson, whom he described as "warm and confiding."[41] Tidball compared "Old Jackson" to the biblical Ephraim, "like a cake unturned" and a "diamond in the rough."[42] He understood that Jackson was an orphaned backwoodsman raised by relatives in the mountains of what later became West Virginia, had received "only a country school education," but had the "grit of manhood in him to surmount every difficulty."[43] Although Tidball carried a prejudice toward southerners in general, he greatly admired Jackson.

The end of August also marked the of the cadet body to the campus barracks for the resumption of academic studies. By this time a sense of fellowship and camaraderie had replaced much of the hazing of plebes, a practice that continued but at a leveled-off pace. For their first academic year, the plebes studied mathematics and French.[44] As the fall semester progressed, class sections were divided according to proficiency. Jones placed in the more proficient first section. The last section contained "those hanging on the edge of deficiency." They were deemed the "Immortals," a metaphor for academic survival, as any cadet ranked below that level was ruled deficient and expelled.[45] Ironically, many Immortals who had avoided expulsion managed to graduate from antebellum West Point and served with distinction. Military drill dominated daily life and always followed class. The period of constant drilling became tedious and discouraging; it seemed endless. Tidball remarked that performing the routine "was like attempting to dip a river dry with a sieve."[46]

Financial consideration also pressed on the new cadets, who received a pay of twenty-eight dollars every two months.[47] They never pocketed any of the money, as board, clothing, and books were charged against it. Thus, by the time of the entrance examinations, a new cadet was already indebted to the United States. Rejection at the academy meant immediate debt, something the cadet "considered his bounden duty to prevent at all hazards."[48]

Although there were exceptions, friendships commonly had a geographical base.[49] Cadets from the same regions of the country tended to drift toward each other and were apt to be prejudiced toward those of other sections. John C. Tidball, a midwesterner from Ohio, regarded those from the Northeast and the South as the "two extremes" that were unfamiliar and peculiar.[50] Prevailing attitudes held that the northeastern Yankee was a conniving individual, "ever on the alert to invent something, or to outwit his neighbor in a bargain." Out of that group, the New Englanders, in particular, regarded themselves as intellectually superior "and what they knew, they had a great facility in telling."[51] They "had a natural aptitude for inquisitiveness which made them familiar with their surroundings."[52]

Tidball judgmentally regarded the southerner as "a saturnine person armed with whip and Bowie-knife, equally ready to thrash his slave or disembowel an abolitionist."[53] In retraction, he wrote, "Among my associates, I recognized no such picture."[54] Further commenting, he felt the southerners "presumed a dignified contentment with what they already knew of the ordinary things about them. In other words, they did not boast of their intellectual prowess."[55] Westerners were typecast by the two extremes. The Yankees regarded the West as "some vast, wild region, of wonderful promise to speculators and enterprising school teachers," and southerners saw it as "a place of refuge for runaway slaves."[56] Dialect, "peculiarities of pronunciation," and sectional expressions also played into the stereotypes placed on all the cadets.

In retrospect, Tidball regarded the prejudices as unjustified and unfounded. He wrote, "Differences there were, it is true, and very marked, but chiefly in the manner of doing the same thing in a different way."[57] He further commented: "In point of general manners and bearing, I could perceive but little difference among us all. With occasional exceptions, we averaged up about the same."[58] The subject of politics was a dividing point of contention. Eighteen forty-four was a presidential election year and the Democrat nominee, James K. Polk, ran on a platform of Manifest Destiny, calling for the territorial expansion of the United States. The proposed annexation of Texas would add another slave state. Ultimately, Polk's foreign policies would also instigate an unpopular war.

The only known close friend William E. Jones bonded with at West Point was Thomas J. Jackson, who was two class years ahead of him. They shared the same age, a Presbyterian Scots-Irish heritage, and the same social class, and both were from the rural western part of Virginia. Their friendship continued after their time at the academy and endured for the rest of their lives. As mentioned, Tidball, who did not form a particular friendship with Jones, highly revered Jackson.

An unauthorized refuge was reached by slipping off campus to frequent Benny Havens Tavern in nearby Buttermilk Falls. Benjamin J. Havens was known as a fifth-generation Irish-American employed by a West Point sutler shortly after the academy was founded.[59] He served in the War of 1812 and after returning to civilian life opened a tavern that rapidly became popular with cadets at the same time it was viewed as a nuisance by the authorities. In 1825 the War Department purchased the property from Havens' landlord and terminated his lease. Undeterred, Benny opened another establishment nearby. Thus began his legend.[60] Although officially off limits to cadets, many of them frequented the establishment, resulting in the phrase "running it."[61]

Christmas and New Year were the only holidays breaking up the routine of that first year. Christmas was celebrated with a banquet and New Year was followed by the January examinations, which involved recitations before the academic board covering all of the studies from the previous fall. About a dozen classmates failed and were dismissed.[62] Passing the mid-academic year examinations completed another rite of passage. Until that time, the plebes' level of admission remained probationary.[63] After the examination results had been tallied, they marched to the chapel to sign a contract and swear an oath to serve in the United States Army for eight years following graduation.

These measures submitted the plebes to a higher standard by order of conduct. From that point, all infractions counted as demerits under an evaluation system detached from the standard academic scale. This system, labeled as *Roll of Cadets, Arranged According to Merit in Conduct*, implemented a scale rating the entire cadet student body altogether. Each, regardless of his class year, was rated by the number of demerits accumulated for the year compared to the whole cadet body.[64] Under this structure, "each delinquency had a numerical value attached to it ranging from one to ten, depending upon the gravity of the offense."[65] Demerits would accumulate over the remaining three and a half years and could count negatively toward the general class standing. The system could in part negate high academic achievement and therefore carried significance in a graduate's future. It frequently determined what arms of service the graduate might be assigned to and his order of seniority in that particular branch.[66]

Under the *Merit in Conduct* numerical scale, minor offenses resulting in one demerit included being late for roll call or losing step while marching. A more serious offense, like failure to salute an officer, might earn eight demerits.[67] Accumulating more than 200 demerits within a single academic year usually resulted in dismissal, regardless of academic achievement. For the academic year ending in June of 1845, Thomas J. Jackson had no demerits, thus ranking first in that category over the 204-member cadet body. In contrast, one of the famous "Immortals" of the second class that year, George Pickett, ranked 189th under the *Merit in Conduct* scale, with 158 demerits.[68]

The plebes resumed their courses in mathematics and French for the second half of the academic year. The June examinations and the Class of 1845 graduation ceremonies concluded the plebe year. Attrition reduced the fourth class cadet body from seventy-five to fifty-seven. Jones ranked tenth in his class based on his overall academic performance, placing eleventh in mathematics and thirteenth in French.[69] On the *Merit in Conduct*, Jones ranked eighty-first out of the entire cadet body of 204, with forty-six demerits.[70]

Jones praised his classmate, Thomas F.M. McLean, for his noticeable overachievement during their first summer drills and the academic segment of their plebe year. Even after enduring the barbershop episode, Bison had to confront challenges from members of his plebe class. According to Jones:

> McLean was quartered with a couple of vain, conceited Pennsylvanians and had been made responsible for compliance by the whole party with the regulations for their room. Among other things all lights were to be out when taps sounded. His companions, having witnessed how he bore the ridiculous pranks played on him, treated lightly his authority. When the drum sounded their beds were not spread. McLean commanded, "Put out that light." Both replied angrily, "It should not be done." McLean said. "It is my duty, and I will put it out." One replied tauntingly, "You will step over the body of William L. Mechling first." Nothing daunted old Bison [who] boxed the ears of both his equals in size and kicked them howling out of the room, and then coolly put out the lights. Henceforth his manly courage not only left him unmolested by the boys, but his fame reached and made him a favorite of the authorities.[71]

Further evaluating McLean as a consummate cadet, Jones added, "He passed through his first encampment with few demerits and commenced his Academic career with high hope and ambition. By dint of hard study and a little favoring on the part of the teachers, he took a place in his class higher than the caliber of his mind would justify. He made extraordinary exertions to maintain his standing. His old saddle bags were ingeniously converted into a dark lantern to avoid the inspectors and study while others slept."[72] McLean's academic and conduct records by the summer of 1845 reflected his achievement. Academically, he finished eighth out of a class of fifty-seven remaining in good standing.[73] On the *Merit in Conduct*, he accumulated only twenty-four demerits to rank forty-fifth out of a cadet body of 204.[74] McLean's record was so flawless by the conclusion of his plebe year that Jones placed him on a parallel with the exemplary Thomas Jonathan Jackson of the second class.

Third Class (Second) Year

In late June of 1845, the fourth class completed their examinations and attended the ceremonies of the graduating first class. Marking the occasion, the seniors "kicked their hats" in the symbolic gesture that metaphorically elevated each class up one notch.[75] The graduates were relieved of their duties as cadets at West Point and transformed to commissioned brevet second lieutenants in the U.S. Army. For Jones, the ceremony marked the beginning of the second summer season for military drills.

Cadets of the second class during the recently concluded academic year moved up to fill the slots of the first class recently vacated by the graduates. Notable members of the new first class included Thomas Jonathan Jackson, George B. McClellan, George Stoneman, Cadmus M. Wilcox, and George E. Pickett.

Cadets of the prior third class received promotions to the recently vacated second class and enjoyed the unique privilege of a two-month furlough, the only extended leave of absence granted to cadets during their entire four-year stay at the academy. They quickly donned their civilian clothes and "were off by the first boat" down the Hudson River.[76]

Jones and his classmates, who received promotions from their former life as plebes, enjoyed the most exhilarating sense of accomplishment. The elevation from the fourth class to the third class was one that caused them elation, with perhaps a greater feeling of satisfaction than those enjoyed by the other classes, including the graduates. The third class would assume the role of noncommissioned officers in their second round of summer drills at Camp Clinton. Tidball described the euphoric transition of rising from a plebe to third classman: "No longer did we stand back, like poor boys at a country frolic, but thrust ourselves forward with all the assurance of our newly acquired positions. Never does a cadet feel more self-important than when a third classman in camp."[77] Jones agreed. Reflecting upon his elevation to the third class, he wrote, "After a year of endurance, the plebe becomes a third classman and changes from the persecuted to the persecutor. It is probably the proudest moment of his whole life. He enters on his new career with the zest of dis-imprisoned youth, and the skill of a doctor just out of the disease. The enjoyment is exquisite and in proportion to the perplexities inflicted."[78]

During the summer drills of 1845, third classman Jones further cemented his friendship with first classman Thomas Jonathan Jackson. Jones reflected, "Jackson chose his companions wherever he found them most congenial, and his sensitive modesty turned him rather to classes below him than above his own. His friendship was warm and confiding, yet his own history and family affairs he seldom ever made mention. He was rather punctilious in the discharge of social and friendly offices, but by no means exacting of others. He enjoyed conviviality and relished but never practiced a joke."[79]

Entering his second season of summer drills, Thomas F.M. McLean had earned a place as "a favorite with the authorities."[80] McLean seemed to duplicate Jackson in perseverance and stamina, but there the similarities ceased. Jones and many West Point associates widely accepted a false rumor regarding an alleged confrontation between Old Bison and Thomas Jackson over an alleged petty theft. Coincidentally, the incident involved two third classmen of near duplicate names, Thomas K. Jackson of Ohio and Nathaniel H. McLean of Ohio.[81] In Jones's mind, the incident revealed a malicious design on the part of Old Bison and marked the beginning of his decline.[82] Whether or not the unjustified stigma was a factor, McLean's other character deficiencies would surface over the next three academic years.

Tragedy struck the third class on July 17, 1845. During an evening break, a squad went swimming in the Hudson at a place commonly referred to as Gus's Point. Cadet David T. Deshler, from Tuscumbia, Alabama, was swept away by the swift currents and drowned. His body was recovered on the following day and buried at the West Point Cemetery with military honors.[83] Deshler was the oldest of three siblings born to a family of wealth and prestige. Described as a most promising youth "prepossessing in appearance and manners," he was a favorite among the cadets and faculty.[84]

There were also occasions of social interaction. Although not compulsory and not part of the curriculum, dance instruction was available to the cadet student body. On Saturday evenings, there was a "cadet hop." All cadets not on guard duty or confined for disciplinary reasons were invited to attend. Plebes, although invited, had to take the metaphoric "back seat" to the whims of the upperclassmen.[85] The events were so popular that the region around West Point developed into a fashionable summer resort patronized by "blushing young misses, flirtatious married women, and prancing widows" who engaged in the festivities in a spirit of competition among themselves.[86] A grand gala event held on August 28 commemorated the end of summer camp. Jones shared some of the pleasure in a letter to his younger brother, Robert Campbell Jones on August 30, 1845:

> On the evening of the 28th, we had one of the most magnificent balls I ever saw or heard of. The decorations of the room were splendid, a result that might have been expected when the best of taste had been backed by labors of the whole corps of cadets for 2 or 3 preceding weeks. The supper was neatly arranged & cost between $700 and $800 so you may guess what kind of an appearance it made. To cap the climax, all the beauties of the North came in to make the last but by all means the most important touch of the whole arrangement. But I will here say if the S.W. Va. girls had made the final polish, nothing earthly could possibly have near equaled (the) West Point ball on that night. The Yankees, however, played their part well as could be expected & made the whole as I have said a magnificent ball. We danced until 4 o'clock in the morning and finished this part with what we call a stag dance.[87]

Coinciding with the conclusion of the summer military drills, members of the new second class returned from their two-month furlough marking the resumption of academic classes. For Jones and the third class, the second-year course of study included mathematics, advanced French, English, grammar, and drawing.[88] Mathematics embraced analytical and descriptive geometry, calculus, and surveying. It was a primary course by order of importance, as it paved the way to the advanced course in engineering.[89] Jones completed his second year ranked eleventh out of fifty-two in his class on this subject.[90]

Advanced French was a continuation of what was studied the first year, but with a different instructor and at a higher standard. Jones finished ninth in this course. Based on what he would accomplish in his travels to Europe a decade later as a civilian, one might conclude that he was proficient in speaking and comprehending the language.

English and grammar involved a course in rhetoric using a textbook by Hugh Blair.[91] In this subject, literature was subordinate to the exact sciences; being neither tangible nor demonstrable, it was slighted.[92] There was no attempt to teach the classics and the library offered "but [a] limited facility for reading."[93] Jones would finish this course of study ranked seventh.[94] A first-year course in drawing was also part of the third-class curriculum. Specifically, the first exposure to this topic involved topographical drawing and landscape penciling. Jones struggled in this particular course and finished forty-fifth.[95]

As the third-class year progressed, Old Bison McLean's shortcomings came to light. He declined academically from eighth to thirteenth in a class size that had already shrunk numerically by standard attrition. His character dropped likewise, as he fell into a habit of telling "less than the whole truth to put off his demerits."[96] In spite of his modest regression, Old Bison maintained his status as a favorite among the officials and many of the cadets. According to Tidball, McLean constructed his legacy, distinguishing himself as one of the great traditions of the academy, which placed him on the level of a "mythological being,–a sort of Jack the Giant Killer."[97]

In regard to the *Merit in Conduct*, McLean finished this second year ranked seventy-fifth out of a cadet body of 213, with twenty-nine demerits. Like his academic standing, McLean's status on conduct had modestly declined from the level of the previous year. One violation near the end of the academic year could have been grounds for expulsion.

Tidball described McLean as being of "uniform amiability" with a "child like mildness" that tempted some to "essay practical jokes at his expense." However, "when aroused to anger, he was a veritable tiger, then his eyes flashed, his teeth gritted, and his flesh before so flabby, gathered into muscular knots, as though ready for a sprout." Toward those who tormented him in any way, McLean had the remarkable capacity to bide his time and get his revenge. Allegedly following the barbershop incident in the summer of 1844, McLean confronted each participant privately to warn them never to "open his mouth" about the incident again under the "penalty of having his flesh pounded to jelly and his bones crushed within his hide. And his manners indicated that he meant it."[98] Further elaborating on McLean's legacy, Tidball described his "ambition of high standing; he was attentive to his studies, and nothing annoyed him more than demerits. This was during the first two years during which he was very good indeed; but afterwards, when he became bad, he was horrid. This change was brought about by a series of accidents, but which no doubt were well conceived by Satan himself."[99]

One of McLean's natural disabilities was his physical awkwardness, which prompted some upperclassmen to place him on report for minor offenses, and the accumulation of demerits raised his anxieties. Tidball felt that some of the infractions charged against McLean were like those issued to plebes during their first semester as a mild form of hazing that would not count toward the offender's permanent record.[100] For a third classman, they would count, and in Tidball's opinion some of the reports on McLean seemed trivial. In June of 1846, with the end of the academic year approaching, first classman Captain David R. Jones placed third classman Thomas F.M. McLean on report for "losing step on the march to the mess hall." The incident was too much for McLean to stand; it was "the straw that broke the camel's back."[101]

Knowing that David R. Jones and two associates habitually strolled the Plain following the conclusion of daily classes, McLean bided his time, awaiting an opportunity.[102] When it came, he approached and assailed Captain Jones with "overflowing wrath." Captain Jones's two companions tried to intervene, but Bison threw them against trees and fences like "a terrier thrashing rats in a pit."[103]

McLean was arrested for assault and court-martialed. Injuries to Captain Jones were apparently minor, as he graduated with his class on schedule. McLean's offense, however, was grounds for dismissal. The court ruled that "in consideration of his previous good character, excellent standing as a student, and strict attention to his duties" the punishment rendered would be reduced to a deprivation of his two-month summer furlough. Tidball remarked, "And this is where Satan stepped in and chalk-marked Bison as his own."[104] Agreeing with Tidball's sentiments, Jones confirmed the facts.[105]

Two months before the conclusion of the 1845–1846 academic year, the United States declared war on Mexico after a protracted border dispute over the recent annexation of Texas.[106] Sentiments were divided geographically. Favoring the doctrine of Manifest Destiny, southerners supported waging war and acquiring new territory.[107] Northerners questioned the morality factor. Ultimately, a sense of patriotism favored the war's prosecution to a glorious end. Tidball commented that his generation had "not yet tasted of blood, and it thirsted like young Indian braves to show its valor." Thirty years of peace had coiled a fighting spirit and inflamed the nation's passions. American society, in his opinion, was following a "law of nature, that every generation must have its war."[108] The preceding West Point classes would fight two armed conflicts.

Of the fifty-seven members who had entered the third class the previous year, fifty-two remained in good standing to form the new second class. Completion of the June 1846 examinations placed Jones at a rank of eleventh in his class, compared to a ranking of tenth the previous year. On the *Merit in Conduct*, he enjoyed his best year, ranking thirty-eighth with only ten demerits out of a collective cadet body of 213.[109]

Graduation ceremonies for the Class of 1846 marked the elevation of the third class to the second class. Although the feeling of accomplishment paled when compared to that of rising from plebe to third classman, members still looked forward to the only extended furlough during their time at the academy. Thomas J. Jackson graduated seventeenth out of sixty.[110] Twenty class members would serve as generals between the two sides in the Civil War.[111] Legend has it that Jackson had improved so significantly with each passing academic year that if the course of study had lasted another year, he would have graduated first in his class.[112] Jackson anticipated combat with enthusiasm.

Given the Mexican War, the graduation service commenced without the traditional ceremony of kicking the hats or the extended furlough previously conveyed upon the newly commissioned brevet second lieutenants departing the academy. In contrast to the graduating class going off to war, the newly elevated second class cadets enjoyed their furlough.

Furlough, Summer of 1846

Fifty-one members of the new second class received their one-time summer furlough. Jones visited his Washington County, Virginia, home and returned to nearby Emory and Henry College to complete his Annual Public Examination concluding the spring session. The Emory and Henry College board of trustees then conferred a bachelor of arts degree upon him.[113] Jones and Joseph H. Price, also of Washington County, composed the entire Emory and Henry College graduating class of 1846 as the twenty-fifth and twenty-sixth students to receive a diploma from the young liberal arts institution.[114]

Back at West Point, the unusual set of circumstances accelerated Bison McLean's decline. With his classmates away on summer furlough, he was without familiar companions. As Jones later recalled, McLean formed disreputable associations.[115] Tidball elaborated that Bison was befriended by a "blasé" youth from New York who, although a scion of respectable lineage, was "accomplished in all the wickedness of the town."[116] Identified as William Hopkins Morris, the "at large" appointee would graduate with the West Point Class of 1851.[117] Through his association with Morris, Bison perfected the art of "running it" to nearby Buttermilk Falls.[118] The object of their escapades was not to consume liquor at Benny Havens Tavern but to consort with the town women.[119]

Second Class (Third) Year

The return of the second class members from their summer furlough marked the resumption of studies for the academic year of 1846–1847. In their third academic year the second class cadets studied philosophy, chemistry, and drawing. The modern-day study of philosophy deals with the realm of ethics, argumentation, debate, reasoning, religion, jurisprudence, and politics. At antebellum West Point, however, "philosophy" was an abbreviation for "material and experimental philosophy." As part of the engineering curriculum, the course included "mechanics, optics, astronomy, electricity and some other cognate branches" entirely devoted to the applied mathematics of the highest order.[120] Jones finished tenth in this course out of forty-three classmates.[121] Chemistry included instruction in geology and mineralogy. Jones ranked tenth in his class on this course as well.[122] The study course of drawing was different from that of topographical drawing taught the previous year. In a marked improvement over the first year in this subject Jones ranked twentieth in the second-year course of drawing.[123]

As part of military drills, the second class cadets received instructions in the basics of horse riding. The instruction was limited to mounting, dismounting, holding the reins, sitting in the saddle, cutting heads, and taking the ring and charge. Cavalry tactics were not taught, and riding did not share the significance of infantry tactics.[124]

Reunited with his classmates, but having been denied the privilege of the summer furlough, Bison McLean was not content to stay confined to the campus. With his companion, William H. Morris from the plebe class, McLean continued to run it to Buttermilk Falls, "where he made [female] acquaintances that aroused in him the passions of a Satyr."[125] Jones noted that Bison's character had deviated from that of a highly conscientious plebe to a third classman who would "tell less than the whole truth to put off his demerits." By the time he reached the second class, he was growing "generally reckless in his deportment."[126]

The June examinations and graduation exercises for the Class of 1847 concluded Jones's second class year. With the Mexican War still in progress, the past ritual of "kicking the hats" was terminated permanently. Upon conclusion of the ceremony, the graduates walked away with the enthusiastic anticipation of participating in the war and leaving the members of the second class to take their places at the top of the ladder.[127]

Jones was among forty-three cadets completing their second class year to earn promotions to the new first class.[128] Overall, he ranked eleventh, the same class standing he held at the conclusion of the previous year.[129] On the *Merit in Conduct*, Jones declined to a ranking of seventy-fifth out of the entire cadet body of 218, with thirty-four demerits. Although he tripled the number of infractions incurred the previous year, he still ranked near the upper third.

Bison McLean completed his third year ranked twentieth academically. Although still in the upper half, he dropped from a level of thirteenth his second year, a decline from a ranking of eighth in his first year.[130] Much more noticeable was his decline in the *Merit in Conduct*. McLean incurred ninety-three demerits with a ranking of 142nd out of a cadet body of 218 during his third year, a noticeable drop from his second year.[131] Bison's conduct record was about to get even worse.

First Class (Fourth and Final) Year

Following the Class of 1847 graduation exercises, Jones and the new first class led the cadet battalion march to Camp Clinton for their third and final round of summer drills. Half of the new senior class assumed the role of commissioned officer. In their new position, Tidball commented, "we were now the big boys of the camp, and it had at last come our turn to have plebes scrub our trimmings and do other accommodating turns for us."[132]

Elevated to the first class, Bison McLean did not have to answer to as many authorities. "Scarcely a night passed in which he was not out from tattoo until reveille."[133] Frequently missing from his tent after lights out during the summer encampment, he always anticipated the discovery and came up with a means of accounting for his absence. Initially, his alibis usually succeeded, and he was able to evade demerits. On occasions when he received demerits, he found ways to manipulate the system.

Under the *Merit in Conduct* method of evaluation, cadet violators could reduce their demerits by performing additional turns at guard duty, a task deemed "walking it off." McLean abused the system by deceiving the medical staff. He performed guard duty and then repaired to the hospital. His common malady was "sore feet," which the beguiled surgeons attributed to the physical strains of guard duty "but which in reality, he got by *running it*."[134] Admitted to the sick rolls, he received credit for the guard duty not performed. He also took quarters in the hospital, which lacked the disciplinary controls of the conventional barracks. The phrase "running it" had described the act of sneaking off campus to frequent Benny Havens Tavern. McLean gave the term a new definition. He did not run it to the tavern and, in fact, did "not know the taste of liquor."[135] During his summer of confinement to campus, he perfected the art of going absent without leave with the "propensity of a tom-cat night prowling."

Classmates Jones, Tidball, and others could see through Bison, but the administrators held him in high esteem based on his past performance. Turning a blind eye, they hoped that the resumption and demands of academic classes would reduce his antics. By that time, however, it was already growing obvious to all, at least privately, that Bison's reputation was on a downward spiral and would not stop until he "reached the bottom."[136]

Academic classes resumed at the end of August 1847. The first class studied engineering (civil and military), ethics, artillery, infantry tactics and a science course with the combined subjects of mineralogy and geology.[137] Tidball commented that engineering was the principle study and "in some form or other it occupied the forenoons of the entire academic year."[138] The instructor was Dennis Hart Mahan, who had graduated first in the West Point Class of 1824 before the War Department sent him to study abroad.[139] He returned with the reputation as an engineer of the highest ability and was appointed to professor of the course at West Point. Endowed with a superior scholarly manner, he chastised any cadet daring to disagree with him on any subject. Even the first classmen were highly intimidated by his "biting sarcasm," which was compared to the "sting of a wasp."[140] Aside from Mahan's vanity and peculiarities, Tidball considered him to be a most thorough and grand instructor. He had a speech impediment in his delivery that made him sound like he had a perpetual head cold. He refuted students for their momentary deficiencies by telling them to "use a little *cobbon sense*," earning himself the irreverent nickname "Old Cobbon Sense." Jones, who finished his academic first class year ranked seventh in engineering, probably received praise from Professor Mahan.[141]

The course of ethics included moral science, logic, international and constitutional law, and the matter of courts-martial. The Reverend W.J. Sprole, a former chaplain to the House of Representatives and acting chaplain of the academy, taught the course as a pulpit orator, with an "easy flow of talk upon the passions and emotions of mankind."[142] The ordained Presbyterian minister often quoted Shakespeare and was endowed with a "twinkling ironical sense of humor—as when he called upon Bison McLean to describe the conditions of mind of a thoroughly depraved man."[143] Jones finished the academic year ranked seventh in this course.[144]

The realm of military procedures was divided into two separate courses: artillery and infantry tactics. The primary emphasis was on infantry tactics based on sound reasoning and experience from previous conflicts.[145] Jones finished the year ranked eleventh in artillery and eighteenth in infantry tactics.[146] The subjects of mineralogy and geology were combined into one course taught by Jacob Bailey, who was also the professor of chemistry. Tidball credited Bailey as being one of the long-term instructors who raised the academic standards at West Point, thus creating a "system commanding the admiration of the world."[147] Jones completed that course ranked eighth.[148]

Also taught in the senior year was fencing, a course that in Tidball's mind was "the least of all to be mentioned," as it required "no mental exertion" and bore no numerical value in class standing.[149] Some class members took an intense interest in the instruction and became skillful, but the majority were so indifferent that they generally "made a farce of" the course and tended to shirk it as much as possible.[150] Since the course had no bearing on class standing, it is unknown how William E. Jones performed in this area. However, while serving the Confederate States of America he would see significant value in the use of the sword.

On the war front, the Treaty of Guadalupe Hidalgo signed on February 2, 1848, concluded the Mexican War and resulted in the acquisition of vast new territories for the triumphant United States. The unpopular conflict lasted just over one year and nine months. Although there was a general feeling of satisfaction with the victorious outcome, there were divisions regarding the cause and consequences.

Bison McLean grew more reckless and oblivious to demerits and their consequences. Continuing his night prowling ways into Buttermilk Falls, he "became a terror to all the maids and matrons round about."[151] Local law enforcement and West Point authorities cooperated in attempts to entrap him, but he always managed to avoid apprehension. His already notorious reputation emerged as "a sort of tantra bogus or bugaboo" in the village. It was said that "mothers subdued their unruly urchins [by] threatening to give them to *the Bison*."[152]

As his anemic alibis failed to explain his absences at reveille, tattoo, or other daily ceremonies, McLean's demerits accumulated. Remarkably, he maintained an academic standing well into the upper half of his class. Bison finished his first class year ranked eleventh in engineering and sixteenth in ethics, the two most academically challenging courses of the year.[153] Bison's sexual indiscretions drew the most attention. Jones recalled that McLean committed his most damaging act of depravity when he seduced a young woman with a "fake marriage."[154] Others familiar with the circumstances elaborated that the girl's name was Effie Conklin, whom Bison allegedly promised to marry in exchange for sexual favors. Going by the nineteenth-century mores of the Victorian era, he "ruined her."[155]

During Jones's tenure, West Point came under public scrutiny requiring supporters to come to its defense. The newly appointed board of visitors proclaimed that the most efficient and cheapest preparation for war was through the "possession of a corps of scientific and skillful officers"[156] This logic contended that during peacetime there was no need for a large standing army and citizens could engage in civilian occupations. In a time of war, patriotism would drive those citizens to supply sufficiently sized armies. Those citizens turned to soldiers would need competent officers to lead them. This line of reasoning assumed that future emergencies would involve threats from foreign powers. The ironic reality was that the antebellum West Point trained officers of the United States for a future struggle among themselves.

A tailor's visit to fit the first classmen into regulation army uniforms marked another ritual of the approaching graduation. A trunk maker from New York built footlockers. There was a festive mood among the first classmen, who viewed their pending graduation with a sense of ritual celebration. Following the final academic examinations, the first class cadets performed a series of military exercises "for the edification of the Board of Visitors and the entertainment of onlookers."[157] The exhibitions included "endless infantry maneuvers" and a demonstration of their acquired horsemanship with mock cavalry charges on the Plain. The battery unit pounded the rocky face of the "Crows Nest" with artillery.[158] That evening, they lit up the sky with a display of fireworks that they had prepared during the previous summer encampment

That celebratory mood on the eve of graduation was dampened when three members of the class were found to be academically deficient and were dismissed. Tidball understood that it was the first time in the history of the academy that anyone had reached his senior year and failed to graduate. James W. "Buck" D'Lyon of Georgia, Hugh B. "Monk" Ewing of Ohio, and Charles W. "Geographic" Greene of Rhode Island were all popular with their classmates, who looked at the academic board "with sullen indignation."[159]

The dismissals for the three deemed academically deficient did not brand them with a permanent stigma of failure. Tidball pointed out that Charles W. Greene served as an infantry captain for the Union in the Civil War.[160] Hugh B. Ewing practiced law with his foster brother, William T. Sherman, in Fort Leavenworth, Kansas, and distinguished himself, rising to the rank of brevet major general in the Civil War. After the conflict, Greene served as minister to Holland and returned to law practice.[161] James W. "Buck" D'Lyon was from a prominent family in Savannah, where he returned to serve as the city surveyor. He died of a sudden illness in 1854.[162]

Bison McLean was the fourth dismissal, his deficiency for conduct.[163] In the month of May, he was charged multiple times with being absent without leave, prompting the officials to detain him to his barracks. While confined, he escaped, returned to his mistresses, and was apprehended again. Academically, he maintained his upper-half class standing. However, the revelation of his sexual scandal in nearby Buttermilk Falls and the accumulation of 258 demerits (200 was the standard threshold) were too much for his past revered reputation to overcome. McLean was finally brought up on multiple charges. This time, the authorities lost patience and dismissed him "on the eve of graduating."[164] Relieved of duty, Thomas F.M. "Bison" McLean departed West Point in disgrace. However, "his myth was just beginning."[165]

Tried along with McLean was his notorious companion, cadet third classman William H. Morris. The court-martial treated Morris with leniency by suspending him for a year. He would graduate in 1851, a year behind the class with which he entered the institution. In contrast to his infamous companion, Morris's career with the U.S. Army and his contribution to the Union in the Civil War would be marked with distinction.[166]

Four years earlier, a class of ninety members had been conditionally admitted to the academy. With the four dismissals on the final day, thirty-eight graduated. According to Tidball, this rate of attrition was standard.[167]

William E. Jones completed his first class year with an overall class ranking of tenth, meriting him the title of topographical engineer.[168] In regard to the role of conduct by the demerit system, Jones completed his last year at West Point with a notable decline. Compared to his previous year, when he ranked seventy-fifth out of a cadet body of 218, he finished his first class year ranked 133rd out of the entire student cadet body of 230, with seventy-eight infractions.[169]

The academic staff held the final decision regarding the branch of service the graduating cadets would serve. Supposedly, each cadet was assigned to the branch for which he was "best fitted." There was, however, an "established scale" in a descending order of prestige.[170] The top five rankings received the title of (civil) engineers. Jones was in the group of the next five rankings that merited the title of topographical engineers.[171] The next level branch was ordnance. The final corps classification was combat arms, which had its descending order starting with artillery followed by infantry and then the dragoons. The last place in the order of assignments was that of the mounted rifles.[172]

Jones's class standing and title of topographical engineer awarded him the choice regarding which branch of service he desired to serve. For reasons entirely up to speculation, he chose the mounted rifles. Cadet John C. Tidball, who finished eleventh, may have referred to Jones with a derogatory comment about his selection. Tidball found it peculiar that anyone awarded the opportunity of choice would select the "mounted service in preference to others" and referred to the branch as "where a good square seat of the saddle was deemed more importance than brains."[173] He further mocked that "through some romantic notion" such graduates saw themselves as entering the life of "a bold dragoon" and "Texas Jack adventures—a kind of Wild West Show in which the officer is a Buffalo Bill."[174] Exempt from the standard regulation to be clean-shaven, members of the mounted service were allowed mustaches. Tidball indicated that the Old Army regarded members of the mounted regiment as "unclean things fit only for dragoons or others addicted to horses."[175]

A final act at the academy was the auditing of the graduates' financial records. After deductions for the charges against their accounts, graduates averaged about $2 per month for the previous forty-eight months and a net cash allowance of $96.[176] In their final parade, each graduate received an order relieving him of duty at West Point. Tidball commented, "While each of us looked on it as the most interesting event of his life, there was no ceremony, not even hat-kicking to lend éclat to the occasion." Graduates returned to their barracks to change from the gray cadet uniform into the regulation blue one worn by the regular army. Tidball added, "A few hasty good-byes to those we were leaving behind and a dash to the first boat to New York closed behind us our West Point Careers."[177] Their diplomas, "crumpled and soiled," followed them by mail.[178] Each graduate received a commission of brevet second lieutenant and a ninety-day furlough in preparation for his first assignment in what historians would years later term the "Old Army." Tidball wrote that when they departed "most of us [were] never to meet again on the planet. And thus terminated a fellowship of four years—a fellowship of fond recollection to me."[179]

Jones visited his home in Washington County, where for the time being his immediate family continued to reside on the family estate. From Glade Spring, on August 21, he corresponded to the adjutant general to accept the appointment of brevet second lieutenant in the Regiment of Mounted Rifles.[180] On the following day he signed before a notary an oath of allegiance.[181] By this stage of his life he had a commission in the army and two college degrees, one of them from a most distinguished institution. Jones was entering a peacetime army burdened with budget restraints while confronting demands brought on by the doctrine of Manifest Destiny.

4

Manifest Destiny

During the four years William E. Jones attended West Point the United States passed through a period of enormous growth and transition. Foreign policy challenges emerged on two fronts engaging two other nations. Diplomacy resolved the one matter, and war settled the other one. The collective results produced a new set of challenges for the Old Army. Although the nation would reap the rewards of its own outward expansion, it would also suffer severe growth consequences.

Oregon Boundary Dispute

The year 1844, when Jones enrolled at West Point, was a presidential election year. Politically capitalizing on a growing expansionist mood, the Democratic Party embraced the phrase "Manifest Destiny," an intensely nationalistic and emotional call justified by divine decree for the U.S. acquisition of all territories to the Pacific Coast. Nominating James K. Polk, the party called for annexation with exclusive rights to the jointly occupied (with the British) Pacific Northwest region from northern California (then part of Mexico) to the southern border of Russian Alaska at the latitude of fifty-four degrees and forty minutes. The platform threatened to wage war with Great Britain as a means. The party simplified its message by adopting a catchall phrase full of alliteration: "Fifty-four forty or fight."

Exploiting patriotic sentiments, Polk was narrowly elected as the eleventh president. Inaugurated in March of 1845, his presidency further promoted mass westward migrations out of a sense of patriotism, economic opportunity, and the fulfillment of divine prophesy. In contrast to its campaign slogan, the Polk administration never intended to wage war with Great Britain. The U.S. acquired the Pacific Northwest territories entirely through diplomacy. Equally willing to negotiate, the British had no interest in colonizing the area where the fur trade was on the verge of collapse following the recent economic depressions. Secretary of State James Buchanan negotiated a compromise establishing the United States' northwestern border at the 49th parallel of latitude. Signed during the Mexican War, the 1846 Oregon Treaty is officially known as the "Treaty with Great Britain in Regard to Limits Westward of the Rocky Mountains" and also as the "Washington Treaty." Through this treaty, half of the doctrine of Manifest Destiny was executed, with relatively little cost.

Mexican Cession

The Polk administration had every intention of annexing the Mexican territories to the southwest and concentrated its military resources to that region. While the United States compromised with Great Britain regarding the Pacific Northwest, it waged war against Mexico to complete the second half of the doctrine of Manifest Destiny.

Anti-Mexican sentiment was aroused in the United States, particularly in the South, going back to the time American settlers in Texas rebelled against Mexico in 1836, leading to the massacres at Goliad and the Alamo. The Texas War for Independence concluded when Army of the Republic of Texas general Sam Houston defeated the Mexican army and captured General Antonio Lopez de Santa Anna at the Battle of San Jacinto. To regain his freedom, Santa Anna signed a treaty recognizing the Republic of Texas. During his absence from Mexico City, however, a new central Mexican government deposed him, denounced the agreement, claimed Texas as its own, and threatened war over the matter.

Under the Polk administration's direction, and despite northern opposition to admitting another slave state, the United States annexed Texas in December of 1845. A diplomatic attempt to purchase what is now New Mexico and California failed. Tensions led to a Texas border dispute. Mexico declared its northern border with Texas to be the Nueces River, while the United States affirmed that border to be further south at the Rio Grande.

In April 1846 a company of seventy U.S. soldiers entered the disputed region between the two rivers and encountered a larger Mexican force. An armed confrontation resulted in sixteen American deaths and the remainder being captured. Under President Polk's urging, Congress declared war against Mexico on May 13. The events prompted the American colonists to capitalize and revolt in California. Early adversities prompted the new central Mexican government to seek the services of Santa Anna from his sanctuary in Cuba. Taking advantage of the opportunity, the former dictator returned from exile, offered his military services, and then seized absolute power once again.

In September 1846 the Americans captured Monterey. In February 1847 General Zachary Taylor defeated Santa Anna at Buena Vista. In March 1847 General Winfield Scott successfully conducted the first large-scale amphibious assault on Veracruz. By the following September the Americans were victorious at Chapultepec, gaining access to Mexico City. From the outset, the unpopular war was a overwhelming triumph for the United States.

On February 2, 1848, the Treaty of Guadalupe Hidalgo ended the conflict. Terms extended beyond clarification of the Texas border at the Rio Grande. Mexico ceded 500,000 square miles, equal to half of its territory, to the United States, leading to the eventual formation of seven states. On the Pacific Coast, the Mexican cession extended to the 42nd parallel, the southern boundary of the Oregon Territory. The terms also called for the United States to pay $15 million and forgive $3.25 million in debt in exchange for the confiscated territories.

The Mexican War was mostly unpopular on moral grounds. Congressman Abraham Lincoln, among fourteen Whigs, voted against the war over President Polk's arguments. In his *Personal Memoirs* published in 1885, Ulysses S. Grant would state, "The Southern rebellion was largely the outgrowth of the Mexican War. Nations, like individuals, are punished for their transgressions. We got our punishment in the most sanguinary and expensive war of modern times." The conflict brought recognition and combat experience to the likes of Robert E. Lee, Jefferson Davis, George Pickett, Ulysses S. Grant, George Meade, George B. McClellan, Ambrose Burnside, Thomas J. Jackson, James Longstreet, and other comrades-in-arms.

With the Treaty of Guadalupe Hidalgo and the Oregon Treaty, the United States claimed exclusive rights to all of the lands on the Pacific Coast from northern Mexico to southern British Columbia. The acquisitions brought new resources and new burdens. In 1848 the discovery of gold at Sutter's Mill in California spread worldwide within a year. Up to 300,000 gold seekers, known as "Forty-Niners," joined the mass westward migration by any means possible. The nation's burden of confronting the new challenges of transition and security fell upon the Regiment of Mounted Rifles.

The U.S. Mounted Rifles

In 1845 the Twenty-Ninth U.S. Congress reestablished the Regiment of Mounted Rifles to construct, maintain, and defend new outposts for the protection of settlers migrating to the western frontier. On detached duty, the unit distinguished itself in the Mexican War in 1846. Over time, the Regiment of Mounted Riflemen name was abbreviated to the Regiment of Mounted Rifles and eventually was more commonly known as the U.S. Mounted Rifles. As the name implies, it was not a cavalry unit but a regiment of "mounted infantry" in which the soldiers maneuvered to their destination on horseback but fought on foot using muskets (or preferably breech-loading rifles). Lieutenant Colonel William Wing Loring commanded the regiment.

Born in 1818 in North Carolina, William Wing Loring migrated with his family to Florida. After serving in the 1835 Seminole War, he received an education in Alexandria, Virginia, and at nearby Georgetown University. He practiced law and served in the Florida state legislature until accepting a commission and enrolling in the Regiment of Mounted Rifles for the Mexican War. Loring distinguished himself in combat actions, losing his left arm at Chapultepec and receiving two brevets for "gallant and meritorious conduct."[1] Declining a discharge option at the end of the conflict, Loring remained in the Regular Army to reorganize the regiment for the pending expedition to the Oregon Territory.

Under the doctrine of Manifest Destiny, the U.S. Congress authorized the establishment of a series of military outposts stationed along a path from Independence, Missouri, through the Kansas and Nebraska territories, and into Oregon country. The action called for the deployment of the Regiment of Mounted Rifles to provide security in those regions. These government measures further prompted masses of civilians to utilize the path connecting the military garrisons. The informally named Oregon Trail served as a major highway for the masses of migrating settlers, who were encroaching upon regions the Native Americans had inhabited for generations.

The Oregon Trail

It would probably be more accurate to call this the "Oregon, California, Colorado, Nevada, Montana, and Other Points West Trail."[2] For settlers traveling to the western extreme, the Oregon Trail was a 2,000-mile journey beginning at the Missouri River and terminating at destinations in either Oregon or California. For others, such as the Mormon Settlement of Salt Lake City or gold seekers destined for Colorado, Idaho, or Montana, the distance was relatively shorter. Contrary to the Hollywood screenwriter's traditional portrayal of emigrants warding off savage attacks with a "circle the wagons" line of defense, Native American tribes rarely took hostile actions during the 1840s. They exhibited a harmless curiosity toward the white settlers passing through and overlooked the damage that the mass migration was causing to their livelihood.

A rare exception to the Indians' benign demeanor received notable attention. Near present-day Walla Walla, Washington, in 1847, Dr. Marcus Whitman's mission confronted a measles epidemic that originated with its European-American settlers before spreading rapidly to the native Cayuse tribes. Exposed to a new disease for which they lacked a sufficient immune system, the Cayuse children suffered a high mortality rate, while the American children survived. The native tribes grew suspicious that Dr. Whitman was intentionally causing the deaths to their children while curing the white children in his colony. On November 29 a band of panic-stricken Cayuse attacked the mission, burned it, and murdered the entire Whitman family along with several followers.

News of the "Whitman Massacre" caused the project to secure the Oregon Trail to be resumed with a greater urgency. Alarmed over possible Indian hostilities, Congress appropriated funds to reinforce the outposts between the Missouri and Columbia rivers. Those fortresses would be connected by the establishment of a military highway used by the masses of emigrants as well as soldiers over partially unexplored territories. No significant government-funded overland expeditions had occurred since the Lewis and Clark expedition more than forty years earlier.[3]

Ironically, the congressional action brought conflicting objectives. With the conclusion of the Mexican War, Congress liberalized conditions for veterans to receive discharges in order to reduce the size and expense of the military. With the adoption of the Oregon Treaty, Congress appropriated funds to restaff the military for the Oregon expedition. As a fiscal compromise, the deployment of the Regiment of Mounted Riflemen was deemed the most economical solution.[4]

Within a month following Jones's graduation from West Point, Congress officially organized and named the region of the Oregon Territory, which included the later-established states of Oregon, Washington, and Idaho, along with portions of Montana and Wyoming west of the Continental Divide. When originally established, the Oregon Territory had a population of about 10,000, a number that was growing at a rapid pace. Joseph Lane received the appointment territorial governor. Eventually more than a quarter of a million people would embark on the Oregon Trail.[5]

Jefferson Barracks, Missouri

After the Mexican War the headquarters of the Regiment of Mounted Riflemen transferred to the Jefferson Barracks, Missouri, Military Post, situated on the Mississippi River just south of St. Louis. The U.S. War Department had established the military installation in 1826 and named it after the former president, who died that same year.

Lieutenant William E. Jones reported to Lieutenant Colonel Loring at the Jefferson Barracks in the summer of 1848. Within a short time he requested a seven-day leave of absence to make arrangements for his mother, who was preparing to migrate from

Virginia to the region around Memphis, Tennessee, situated approximately three hundred miles to the south along the Mississippi. Taking the position that Jones had just recently completed an extended furlough, Loring denied his request with a reply that his "valuable service could not be dispensed with."[6] Jones contended that other junior officers returning from extended furloughs received preferential assignments to recruiting duty in places near their acquaintances. More than three years would pass before Jones received another leave of absence, a sensitive issue regarding his relations with superiors in the Old Army.

Camp Sumner

By the beginning of 1849 the Regiment of Mounted Rifles was preparing for a pending westward expedition. Jones dedicated his activities to recruiting, conditioning, and training mounted troops. Requisitions included over half a million pounds of supplies, more than 400 wagons, and almost 2,000 transport animals. The troops vacated the Jefferson Barracks, boarded steamboats, and sailed upriver to reassemble at Camp Sumner, five miles west of Fort Leavenworth, Kansas.[7]

The officers anticipated that they would encounter desertions and other disciplinary issues within the ranks. On March 27, 1849, Jones submitted a requisition for "nine balls & chains and three sets of double irons."[8]

Discipline troubles sprouted early. Jones rode eighteen miles out on a routine mission to retrieve stray horses when he received word of an armed deserter twenty to thirty miles ahead of him. Since Jones himself was unarmed, he returned to Camp Sumner to report the fact. Loring chastised Jones for his failure to pursue, apprehend, and return the deserter.[9] Jones would neither forget the humiliation nor forgive Loring for issuing the reprimand.

March to Oregon

On May 10, 1849, the regiment assembled their mounts, equipment, and supplies at Camp Sumner for what would be a five-month, 2,017-mile march.[10] In a token ceremony, Brevet-Major General David E. Twiggs gave the official order to launch the expedition.[11]

The mission began under dire circumstances. With the outset of warm weather, the area was stricken with a severe cholera epidemic. Nearby St. Louis, a relatively new city in the West, with an inadequate clean water supply and a congested transient population brought in by the gold rush, lost about one-tenth of its population to the disease.[12] Cholera in nineteenth-century America has been compared to the fourteenth century Great Plague of Europe. With dramatic symptoms of diarrhea, acute spasmodic vomiting, painful cramps, consequent dehydration, skin discoloration, and other horrific indicators, cholera could bring about death within a day and sometimes hours. Approximately half of its victims died. Substandard sanitation practices and contaminated water sources were the primary means of transmission.[13] The farther travelers advanced beyond the populated areas, the more the threat of cholera tended to diminish. However, among the masses of emigrants were disease carriers who contaminated the few water sources along the way and thereby passed the ailment on to the group that followed.

Another nuisance was monotony. In less than two weeks, the expedition advanced beyond the Missouri Valley and on to the Great Plains, which Major Osborne Cross described as "an endless prairie, which strikes one as being very beautiful at first sight, but becomes tiresome beyond any description after the novelty has worn off."[14] Cross added, "It could hardly be expected to be otherwise when you see nothing from day to day but the broad heaven above, and the greensward below."[15] A lack of trees also meant a lack of firewood. Following the same path of so many before them, the troopers confronted forage shortages of feed and sustenance. Wild game was in short supply. Grasses needed to feed the regiment's livestock were depleted.

Treaties were made with potentially hostile Indian tribes that were "ever warlike, well mounted, and well armed." The mass migration was causing a "rapid disappearance of their accustomed means of subsistence," compelling them to "fight, steal, or starve."[16] Providing them with alternative hunting grounds appeased them during the march. Although Native American tribes rarely posed a threat, the troopers of the Mounted Rifles had to maintain a constant state of alert.

By May 31 the Mounted Rifles had advanced 300 miles to reach Fort Kearny, situated at the head of Grand Island on the Platte River in the Nebraska Territory. From an elevated distance Major Cross observed the discouraging sight of an estimated 20,000 civilian emigrants and 50,000 animals traveling along the Platte River ahead of them.[17] Skeletons and rotten carcasses of transport animals driven by preceding emigrants would litter the trail along with abandoned furniture and broken-down equipment. After pausing three days to rest and graze the animals, the regiment resumed the march toward the next outpost, Fort Laramie.

Desertions accelerated after departing Fort Kearny. Four men ran off with a supply-filled wagon. One teamster escaped with a government mule, and another threatened to shoot an officer. The culprit was arrested, confined, and transported under guard. It was unclear whether the desertions were out of fear of cholera or if the recruits had enlisted "for getting comfortably transported to California at the expense of the government."[18]

Small cemeteries of hastily dug shallow graves marked the Oregon Trail. Typically, makeshift wood or rock monuments bore the inscription of the deceased's name followed by the inscription "Cholera."[19] While progress remained far from the western destination, fear of cholera was a primary reason for desertions.[20] Worse than the sight of graves or corpses, the troopers often witnessed diseased victims agonizing in a delirious state of mind; death often followed.

"Wood became so scarce that a tree might be looked upon as a curiosity."[21] Grazing pastures were limited to the high bluffs far from the water supply. It may have been just as well; the Platte River water was thought to have been contaminated by cholera, evidenced by the fact that the regiment lost more personnel to the disease. Indians were benign but curious. A friendly Sioux war party traded food for supplies and guided the troops in their first crossing of the Platte River at Kearney Ford.[22]

By June 22 the Mounted Rifles had marched 327 miles from Fort Kearny to reach Fort Laramie, Wyoming, which provided an abundance of grasses and an opportunity to resupply. However, scouts from Salt Lake warned that mass migration had depleted the grazing pastures beyond. The march resumed on the following day. On July 1 a loyal teamster developed symptoms of cholera and died within a few hours. It was, however, the last known case.[23]

The expedition reached the Black Hills, where the scarcity of grasses and a stampede resulted in the loss of more transport animals. More desertions followed with the loss of more mule teams and mounts. While negotiating the final crossing of the Platte River, two troopers drowned in the rapid current. After crossing the Platte River for the last time, the expedition entered the desert environment of the Red Hills, where the soil was sterile, rendering grazing grasses even more scarce and contaminating the water supply with alkaline.[24] The regiment pushed on through the night and arrived at a good water supply at Willow Spring in Sweet Water Valley on July 7.

The regiment reached the vicinity of Independence Rock, an unusual 120-foot-high granite formation and unique natural landmark on the Oregon Trail. It was a well-known point of rendezvous for many travelers and received its name from folklore that emigrants needed to arrive at it by July 4 in order to reach their western destinations before the mountain snowfalls. At Independence Rock forty men deserted, prompting Lieutenant Colonel Loring to offer a $200 bounty for their capture.[25] Mountain trappers apprehended five and turned them over at Fort Bridger (Wyoming), but the remaining thirty-five escaped.[26] By this stage, most contemplating desertion had used the Mounted Rifles as a means of support until they could join emigrating parties. However, the civilian emigrants regarded the deserters as burdensome freeloaders and were usually willing to assist in their apprehension.

By August 5 the march had advanced through the Bear River Valley to arrive at Fort Hall (Idaho). Major Cross commented that they had completed two-thirds of their march "over probably the most uninteresting route which can be found on the northern continent."[27] Fort Hall was the last resting place before they began the most challenging leg, a 700-mile trek to The Dalles, Oregon.[28] In a reorganization the regiment discharged soldiers lacking dedication and terminated teamsters of questionable character.

The regiment reached American Falls (Idaho), which Cross described as a "magnificent scene."[29] Although the scenery was improved, they encountered more physical barriers, with gullies carved by runoffs fed by melting snows. It was an ironic situation in which water was scarce, the river was in view, but the steepness of the banks denied access. Completing a slow and arduous descent to the river basin did not ease the struggles. In crossing the Snake River, one man drowned, and the fording operation was aborted. The regiment then marched along the river basin only to come upon more gorges, necessitating a deviation from the river and the water supply. For three days and about sixty miles they marched over a country mostly destitute of grass and water. Many more transport animals died. With the depletion of mounts, the main body of the regiment continued marching on the high banks along the Snake River while a detachment used the river was a highway. Lieutenant W.E. Jones navigated an India rubber boat for a portion of the way, arousing the curiosity of local Indians on August 27.[30]

Two days later, they reached Fort Boise on the banks of the Snake River before proceeding 130 miles to the base of the Blue Mountains. A strenuous march across the Cascade Range took them to The Dalles, where the headwaters of the Columbia River formed a set of rapids. There, six men drowned when their raft capsized.[31] Beyond The Dalles, the navigable Columbia River took them ninety miles to Fort Vancouver (Washington). The Mounted Rifles arrived at Oregon City on October 13, concluding an expedition that began on May 10 and covered 2,017 miles.[32]

Some considered the march of the U.S. Mounted Rifles from Missouri to the Oregon Territory to be "the greatest military feat on record." One must take into account that the expedition encountered no combat actions against hostile forces, foreign or Indian. Aside from the forces of nature, their greatest enemy consisted of deserters and plunderers from the regiment's ranks. Taking into account that the four-month journey exceeded 2,000 miles, it was a remarkable accomplishment. However, considering the nation's history at the time, even as young as it was, to call it the "greatest feat" may have been an exercise in hyperbole. Lieutenant William E. Jones did not agree with those who glorified the mission and would speak of it in tones of mockery over praise.

Oregon Territory

Reaching their destination at the mouth of the Columbia River added new problems. The citizen settlers of the Oregon Territory were unenthusiastic about the arrival of the mounted regiment and resented the soldiers' presence.[33] Instead of satisfying any needs for security, the mounted troopers earned a notorious reputation for drunkenness and disorderly conduct.[34] The lure of finding gold spawned more desertions, burdening officers with the task of their pursuit and apprehension.

In March of 1850 Jones was part of a detachment of thirteen officers and eighty enlisted men dispatched by Loring to track more than a hundred troopers who had deserted to seek gold along the Pogue and Klamath rivers.[35] With the assistance of civilian volunteers organized by territorial governor Joseph Lane they captured seventy-three, but the remainder escaped in canoes.[36]

To clamp the hemorrhage, Lieutenant Colonel Loring relocated the Eleventh Military District headquarters from Oregon City to Fort Vancouver. Sending a message, the citizens of Oregon City burned down the recently vacated local barracks to discourage the government from stationing any more troops there again.[37] Within a short time, Oregonians urged their delegates to the U.S. Congress to declare that they would fight their Indian wars, and the government could withdraw its rifle regiment whenever it wished.[38]

Jones received modest recognition while in the region. In an apparent attempt at administrative reconciliation, Loring appointed him as his quartermaster at Fort Vancouver.[39] On November 30, 1850, Jones received a promotion from brevet second lieutenant to the full rank of second lieutenant.[40]

Return Voyage

On May 10, 1851, the two-year anniversary of the launching of the expedition, "eight skeleton companies" of the U.S. Mounted Rifles departed Astoria on the Oregon coast by a Pacific sea voyage and arrived at Benicia, California, three days later.[41] A detachment transferred to the First Dragoons to remain on the West Coast. The rest, including Jones, reboarded ship to continue the sea voyage. They received a ten-day respite in San Francisco while their ship underwent repairs.[42] There Jones enjoyed a reunion with some of his West Point associates for the first time since his graduation. In the course of their many conversations, Jones received follow-up word regarding his notorious classmate, Thomas F.M. "Old Bison" McLean.

Within the three years since their final day at West Point, rumors, legends, and anecdotes about Bison had already surfaced. One report indicated that once turned adrift, McLean had joined an expedition to Cuba and the Central American states.[43] There were details that he had journeyed to Texas, where he had engaged in various occupations.

Recent reports indicated that Bison resorted to the life of an outlaw before taking up the savage life with one or more Indian tribes in New Mexico and Arizona. Jones recalled what he had learned of McLean:

> In Texas, he commenced the study of law but quit this for the newly discovered gold fields in California. He was discovered as the passenger who had not paid his fare on one of the steamers. Refusing to work his way, he was ironed and thrown into the coal hole and put ashore at Mazatlan. From there, he found his way to California where he and others murdered and robbed a ferryman. For this, he had to take refuge among the Tuscan Indians, a low and degraded tribe. His courage and skill in their wars raised him to the dignity of a petty chief and to the enjoyment of some half a dozen wives. When last heard of, he had just been restrained by his fellow citizens from murdering a poor peddler for a handful of his wares.[44]

Those were the last words Jones would ever hear of his West Point acquaintance. None of the rumors was either confirmed or refuted, but McLean's myth would endure beyond the era of the Civil War.

From San Francisco, the regiment sailed more than 3,000 miles, arriving at Panama on June 26.[45] Twenty officers, fifty-nine noncommissioned officers, and an unspecified number of enlisted men conducted a three-day overland march across the isthmus to board the Atlantic steamer *Falcon,* which transported them to Havana, Cuba. On July 2 they transferred to the USS *Massachusetts,* which transported them to New Orleans, and from there river transportation carried them up the Mississippi. The regiment arrived at the Jefferson Barracks in July 1851 as a skeleton of its original self.[46]

Territory politicians later questioned the wisdom of pressuring the War Department to remove the regiment. Unfortunately, it was too late to reverse the order for troop withdrawals. Politically and militarily it was an easy decision to dispatch the Mounted Rifles to the Texas frontier. The regiment would not return to the Oregon Territory. Jones's career in the Old Army was about to go in a new direction.

5

Migration, Furlough and Marriage

At the Jefferson Barracks, assistant quartermaster and Second Lieutenant Jones completed accounting and administrative duties. In November of 1851 he received his long-awaited furlough that, with extensions, would last five months.

The period of Grumble Jones's expedition to and occupation of the Pacific Northwest was one of transition for the family of Robert Jones (deceased) and Catherine "Kate" Moffett Edmondson-Jones in Washington County, Virginia. During that time the immediate family split up and migrated westward. In 1849 William's older brother, Henry S. Jones, departed Washington County at age twenty-seven and headed west. According to legend, he enlisted in a regiment raised in St. Louis for the Mexican War. That anecdote is inaccurate, as the Mexican War had ended the previous year. It seems likely that he joined the masses participating in the California Gold Rush. He was said to have taken sick and died in a New Orleans hospital that same year.[1] The time and geography lead one to speculate that he was one of many cholera victims.

Grumble's widowed mother, Catherine "Kate" Moffett Edmondson-Jones, and his three remaining siblings continued to reside in Washington County until sometime after the taking of the 1850 Census. Catherine, along with her remaining children, Robert Campbell Jones, Sarah Eliza Jane Jones, and James W. Jones, then embarked on a westward migration. The exact time of the movement can be narrowed down to a period between the census and the summer of 1851. The family traveled through the entire state of Tennessee before ultimately settling in Crittenden County, Arkansas, directly across the Mississippi River from Memphis. Family members held joint residency in both Crittenden County, Arkansas and Shelby County, Tennessee.

The reasons for the westward migration are unknown. The family farm in Washington County was productive, and the terms of Robert Jones's last will prohibited its sale. Speculating on the motives, we may surmise that Washington County would have been a reminder of sadness and despair. Two members of the family died as children, and the patriarch had died as a young man. Grumble's mother, Catherine, may have desired to join a community already well-established by her extended family. Her older brother, Andrew "Jolly Andy" Edmondson, had previously settled in that region to the west of Memphis, and the name carried prominence. The unincorporated town of Edmondson, Arkansas, was established in Crittenden County. The progress of the migration was recorded by the marriage of William's sister, Sarah Eliza Jane Jones, to Jefferson Greer of Lincoln County, Tennessee. The wedding ceremony occurred on July 3, 1851, in Shelby County, and the couple resided in Memphis.[2] The migration to the region of east Arkansas and west Tennessee was permanent. Catherine Jones, Sarah Eliza Jane Jones Greer, and James

W. Jones never returned to Virginia. Robert Campbell Jones would visit Washington County in the years following the conclusion of the Civil War to settle Grumble's estate.

Upon receipt of his furlough, Second Lieutenant William E. Jones took river transportation southward to Memphis to visit his immediate family. During his month-long stay there he secured a power of attorney from his mother and Robert Campbell Jones, transferring administrative authority of his father's estate from Colonel Robert Buchanan Edmondson to himself.[3] At the time of his father's death Grumble was nine years old. By now, however, he was twenty-seven, the oldest of the surviving issue, and possessed of proven credentials qualifying his fiduciary position.

Jones then traveled to Washington, D.C., to conduct administrative matters with the War Department and request a furlough extension. Ultimately, his leave of absence would last until April 10. He then traveled to visit his Washington County, Virginia home for the first time in three years to address matters regarding his father's estate and pursue personal objectives. During his stay in Washington County, Jones married Eliza Margaret "Pink" Dunn, the daughter of Dr. Samuel Dunn and Jane Beattie Ryburn Edmondson-Dunn of Glade Spring. Grumble and Eliza Dunn were distant half cousins. Grumble was the grandson of Colonel William Edmondson by his second wife, Eliza Kennedy. Eliza Dunn was the great-granddaughter of Colonel William Edmondson, but by his first wife, Margaret Montgomery. The marriage of Pink and Grumble was apparently spontaneous. How well Jones knew his bride is another mystery. She was seventeen years old at the time of their wedding, and Jones's most recent prior visit to the county, three years earlier, had been a brief one.

The Washington County *Register of Marriage Licenses* states that William E. Jones and Eliza M. Dunn obtained their marriage license on January 13, 1852, and married two days later.[4] There is an absence of details regarding the ceremony location, the presiding official, or any of the other pertinent information customarily recorded on such an occasion. It was probably a very private ceremony. Having already left Washington County, Grumble's immediate family did not attend. There is no mention of the marriage in the Robert Jones or the Sarah Eliza Jane Jones family Bibles.

Born in 1834, Eliza Margaret "Pink" Dunn was the third of nine children of Dr. Samuel Logan Dunn and Jane Beattie Ryburn Dunn. Dr. Dunn had been a practicing physician for about twenty-five years. Eliza's mother, Jane Beattie Ryburn Edmondson Dunn, had inherited the log house where she and the doctor lived, just north of Glade Spring. The ten-year age disparity between William E. Jones and Eliza would have fit the norm had she completed the voyage to Texas. In the antebellum U.S. Army, officers' wives ranged from seventeen to twenty-seven years of age and were an average of ten years younger than their husbands.[5]

On February 9, 1852, Lieutenant W.E. Jones filed a petition with the county clerk declaring that his cousin, Robert Buchanan Edmonson, willingly relinquished to W.E. Jones his title as administrator of the estate of Robert Jones. From that point on, Grumble Jones would serve that fiduciary position in the interest of his mother and siblings. In the same document, William E. Jones assumed the legal guardianship of his youngest brother, James W. Jones, who was a minor.[6] Interestingly, even with this highly unusual and distant custodial arrangement, James W. Jones had migrated westward with his mother to Arkansas.

Before embarking on his journey to his new assignment in Texas, Jones corresponded with the War Department:

5. Migration, Furlough and Marriage

Glade Spring, Virginia, Feb. the 10th, 1852
To: Brevet Major General R. Jones
Adjutant General U.S. Army
Washington City, DC.

Sir

I have the honor to apply for an extension of my leave until the 15th of next month. My time up to the present has been consumed in settling my father's estate. I start today for Memphis, Tenn. where my mother now resides. I fear I will not be able to reach my company by the expiration of my leave if I make any stay with her. If the good of the service will admit it, I would be glad if she could see me & my newly married wife a few days before we go to the Far West. If my application is successful, please telegraph me at Memphis as soon as convenient. Very Respectfully your Obedient Servant, W.E. Jones, 2nd Lt., RMR.[7]

Lieutenant Jones, Eliza Dunn-Jones, their cousin Thomas Benjamin Estill Edmondson (son of Colonel Robert Buchanan Edmondson), and four servants departed Washington County and headed for the Texas frontier via Memphis and New Orleans. During the stop in Memphis, Jones and his wife met up with his immediate family members, who for the time being had settled in Shelby County, Tennessee.

On March 8, 1852, Jones prepared a document confirming the partial distribution of the estate of his father, Robert Jones. Executed in Shelby County (Memphis), Tennessee, the document stated:

We hereby acknowledge that we have made a division of the slaves & houses & the proceeds of the sale of property belonging to the estate of Robt. Jones, Dec'd & that we each of us have received what is due us on these accounts & that there more remains only the real estate in Virginia to be divided between us.[8]

Signers of the document were W.E. Jones, his mother, Catherine Moffett Edmondson-Jones, his brother-in-law, Jefferson Greer, his brother James W. Jones, and his brother Robert Campbell Jones. Witnessing the document were Jones's cousin from Washington County, Virginia, Thomas Benjamin Estill Edmondson, and another cousin, Thomas Tate Edmondson from Crittenden County, Arkansas.

From Memphis, the couple and their entourage took river transportation southward to New Orleans. Within a short time, Grumble would find that the personal tragedy he experienced as a child would follow him on to this stage of his life as well.

6

Tragedy on the High Seas

The final phase of the journey to Jones's new assignment on the Texas frontier required steamship travel on the Gulf of Mexico from New Orleans, Louisiana, to the port city of Indianola, Texas. It would end tragically and be the emotional nadir in Grumble's life.

The 1850s was the decade of expansion and prosperity for the Texas Gulf Coast and particularly the Morgan Steamship Line. The Mexican Cession had further opened up the southwestern United States to the Americans. The discovery of gold in California in 1848 added to the drawing influence of the West. The combination of these factors drew prospectors and immigrants in masses. The port cities along the Gulf coastlines of Alabama, Mississippi, Louisiana, and Texas grew in prominence with increased patronage. With its vast hinterland of numerous natural harbors and navigable rivers, Texas in particular impressed merchants and settlers.

In 1837, Charles Morgan, a transportation magnate operating out of New York, opened a steamship line from New Orleans to Galveston. Within a decade, the service extended westward to Indianola, Texas. Situated approximately fifteen miles inland from the entrance to the bay from the Gulf of Mexico, Indianola provided a haven for ships drawing deeper drafts. Soon after its founding in 1844, the town grew in significance surpassed only by the ports of Galveston and New Orleans. There was, however, one major drawback. For any seagoing vessel to dock at Indianola, it had to negotiate Pass Caballo, the only entrance into Matagorda Bay from the Gulf of Mexico.

Pass Caballo is a narrow strait dividing Matagorda Island from Matagorda Peninsula. It earned the reputation as being hazardous for Gulf shipping going back to 1685 with the abortive attempt of René-Robert Cavelier, Sieur de La Salle, to establish a French colony. Two of La Salle's ships wrecked at the pass after striking sandbars.[1] Maritime shippers came to realize that no vessels could negotiate the pass without risk. Although almost two miles wide, waters of the pass with sufficient depth to support large ships bearing a draft spanned only about two thousand feet.[2] Flows of water in and out of the bay with each changing tide resulted in a continuous shifting and repositioning of sandbars. With no consistency about the channel position, there never was a straight shot through the pass. Seagoing vessels had to proceed with extreme caution, taking advantage of high tides and favorable wind directions.[3]

In January of 1851, the steamship *Palmetto* of the Morgan Line ran aground on an unsuspected sandbar after a long history of successful entries and exits.[4] Efforts to dislodge the ship grew futile when the weather turned adverse, creating a dangerous situation. Ultimately, all passengers and crew were successfully evacuated in lifeboats.

However, the ship, cargo, and passenger baggage were a total loss.[5] This incident was a foreshadowing of things to come.

Aware of the potential hazards, Morgan Steamship Line authorities stationed qualified coastal pilots at the pass. The task of the pilots was to remain familiar with the constant hydrographic and topographic changes and thus serve as competent guides to maneuver the ships between the sandbars.

In spite of the obstacle presented by Pass Caballo, Indianola grew rapidly as the Calhoun County seat, drawing such nicknames as "First Gateway of Texas" and the "Dream City of the Gulf."[6] The antebellum U.S. Army utilized the town as a supply depot for the Texas Frontier.

Steamship Independence

Lieutenant William E. Jones and his entourage arrived in New Orleans, Louisiana, and boarded a Gulf steamship bound for Indianola. The steamship *Independence* was a new ship constructed at the Westervelt & Mackay Shipyard in Hoboken, New Jersey.[7] A standard side-wheeler, it was the type of ship that was very common on the Gulf Coast. The ship was embarking upon its maiden voyage with passengers. Combined passengers and crew numbered 167.[8] The schedule called for a three-day voyage to Galveston, where the ship would dock for two days followed by a one-day continuation trip to Indianola.

William and Eliza Jones were among the first-class passengers. Considering the rough life on the Texas frontier that awaited them, this voyage was to be their last indulgence in luxury for an extended period. Journeying on one of the Morgan Line sidewheelers was reported to be a pleasurable experience, with inclement weather causing the only exceptions.

On board, Lieutenant and Eliza Dunn Jones developed acquaintances with several other passengers. One group consisted of Mt. Carmel, Illinois resident Charles W. Eldridge, his wife, Hannah Mitchell Avery Eldridge, of Groton, Connecticut, and Hannah's mother, Lucy Mitchell.[9] Eldridge was a professional artist by trade who frequented Indianola to visit family members. Another group of passengers making social contact with the Jones entourage was Stephen Minot, his wife, Louisa Papley "Lucy" Minot, their two daughters, and a governess. Stephen Minot was an Englishman migrating from Kingston, Jamaica, to Gonzales, Texas.[10] Representing Charles Morgan's interest on board was Captain Lauchlan McKay, the younger brother of Donald McKay, a prominent shipbuilder and designer, particularly of clipper ships. Lauchlan McKay had published *The Practical Ship Builder* in 1839. McKay attended the maiden voyage as an investor and celebrated designer of the new ship. He bore the title of captain along with John Ayers and Charles Stoddard.[11]

The ship departed New Orleans in the early morning hours of Saturday, March 20. Following three days at sea, it arrived at Galveston late in the evening on Monday, March 22, where it remained docked for two days. On Tuesday evening of the 23rd, "the owners of the ship gave a magnificent dinner on board, at which the principle citizens of Galveston sat down, and the toasts drank and speeches made, betoken their interest in, and in the flattering prospects for success in the new line, of which this splendid ship was a pioneer."[12] On Wednesday morning, March 24, the ship departed the Twenty-First Street docks at Galveston and headed west-southwest in the Gulf of Mexico, toward its ultimate western destination, a journey of approximately one hundred nautical miles.

By late Wednesday evening, the *Independence* had arrived within sight of the entrance to Matagorda Bay at Pass Caballo. Conventional wisdom directed that no attempt should be made to negotiate the pass at nighttime. The *Independence*, therefore, remained out in the Gulf of Mexico to await daylight before making entry.

Wreck of the Independence

Early Thursday morning, the 25th, Charles Eldridge received an invitation to join other passengers to watch the ship going through the pass. After hastily dressing and leaving his stateroom, he felt the progression of the ship come to a sudden halt. He ventured to the outside deck and saw a sea "white with foam" and the ship "stranded in the midst of fearful breakers."[13] He learned that Captain Charles Stoddard had received word that earlier that morning the U.S. Mail steamer *Louisiana,* a ship bearing a draft one foot deeper than the *Independence,* had completed a successful entry through the pass without incident.[14] Deluded by that knowledge and misinterpreting the messages from signal flags on shore, he committed the "censurable" act of attempting to negotiate the pass without the guidance of a coastal pilot.[15] Consequently, the ship struck and became stranded on a sandbar. Initially the ordeal appeared to be a minor inconvenience.

For the duration of the day, excess cargo and baggage were cast overboard to lighten the ship, but the measures were futile. With the approach of nightfall, calm weather provided a false sense of security. By the following morning, Friday, the 26th, a cold front, perhaps what Texans commonly call a "blue norther," swept into the region. Gusting north winds caused towering waves with a force resisting any means to reach land. As a seasoned steamship line traveler, Eldridge knew their circumstances closely paralleled those of the steamship *Palmetto* a year earlier. The *Palmetto,* however, ran aground much closer to land, and all passengers survived unharmed even though the ship was destroyed. With weather conditions deteriorating, the state affairs on the *Independence* would only get more precarious with the approach of nightfall. The crew fired the distress cannon and lowered their flags to half-mast. The calls drew the attention of other vessels. A sailing schooner approached, but with unfavorable winds and conditions it could not draw close enough to render any assistance.

Coastal pilot Captain William Nichols was the first operative respondent. Nichols and his assistant, George Morgan, and a third seaman approached in a pilot schooner that anchored inside of the breakers approximately a half-mile distant.[16] Nichols and Morgan set out in a skiff and rowed toward the stranded *Independence.* The sight of their small vessel mounting the crest of the towering waves, descending and then rising again, brought mixed feelings of hope and anxiety to the passengers. Nichols and Morgan reached and boarded the stern of the *Independence.* Captain Nichols assumed command of the ship to direct an orderly evacuation of passengers and crew.

Four volunteer passengers boarded the pilot skiff. While Nichols remained on the *Independence,* Morgan rowed the evacuees to the pilot schooner, where the third member of the pilot team weighed anchor and transported them on to Indianola. Upon their arrival, they issued a general declaration regarding the fate of the *Independence.* The steamship *Louisiana* and other vessels departed to answer the distress call. Pilot George

Morgan attempted to return to the *Independence* as the sole occupant of the skiff. Although the previous successful evacuation measure had been somewhat reassuring, deteriorating weather conditions were going to render all future evacuations more hazardous.

The *Independence* possessed only four lifeboats, and evacuation required a series of launches. The raging storm further fueled passenger reluctance. Although the *Independence* was a doomed ship, it maintained its structural integrity for the time being and appeared to offer a safer haven than any lifeboat. As Eldridge later wrote, "the sight of the breakers was too terrifying" for most people to risk confronting them in a small lifeboat.[17] During attempts to deploy the lifeboats, a series of events reinforced passengers' anxieties.

Captain Nichols directed the crew to make preparations to launch the first lifeboat, which descended, void of occupants, with the idea of then boarding evacuees with lines. The raging sea waves swamped the vessel, severed it from its lines, and washed it out to sea. Simultaneously, while Pilot Morgan was attempting to return to the *Independence* from the pilot schooner, the waves swamped his skiff, resulting in the loss of his oars. The current carried him in his disabled skiff farther out into the Gulf of Mexico. The second empty lifeboat was lowered into position when an unexpected turn of the side-mounted paddle wheel swamped it with water. The lines remained attached, but passengers were reluctant to board.

Captain Nichols had intended to man the second lifeboat and row the next group of passengers to safety. However, upon realizing that his assistant, George Morgan, was in immediate danger, he abruptly changed his plan. He directed the crew to hoist the second lifeboat back on deck and clear it of water in preparation for another launch. He then launched the third lifeboat with an appointed crew and embarked out into the Gulf to rescue Morgan. Once Nichols had departed, the *Independence* chief mate, Hubble Hovey, selected two crewmen to clear the water from the rehoisted second lifeboat and prepare it for the next evacuation. This time, the occupants would board the suspended craft at the deck level and seat themselves in preparation for a descent into the water. Hovey and two crewmen would man the lifeboat to transport the occupants.

On the second-level deck, Charles Eldridge assisted Eliza Dunn-Jones, the Minot daughters, his wife, and his mother-in-law in boarding the second suspended lifeboat.[18] Donning her wedding gown, Eliza sat with Hannah Eldridge, Lucy Mitchell, Louisa Papley Minot, the two Minot daughters, and the Minot governess (name unknown) in preparation for the descent. Lieutenant Jones, Stephen Minot, and Charles Eldridge waited on the second-level deck for their turn in a later evacuation.

Just before the lowering mechanism was about to be engaged, an unexpected rotation of the side-mounted paddle wheel doused all the occupants with water. Moments later, a wave from the raging Gulf assaulted the side of the ship, further swamping the suspended lifeboat. Unnerved, Hannah Eldridge and Lucy Mitchell withdrew from the craft while the other occupants remained seated. With the sudden vacancy, a passenger known only as Mr. Horrell from St. Louis took their place. Mr. Horrell was among the first-class group of passengers and was the nephew of the famed General Alexander Somervell.[19] The crew proceeded to bail out the water and resume the launch as planned. Having elected to remain seated, Eliza Dunn-Jones and the Minot family women trusted Chief Mate Hovey to transport them to safety. The lifeboat descended into the water, and once the lines were disengaged, Hovey and the two crewmen proceeded to row.

Charles Eldridge, Stephen Minot, and Lieutenant W.E. Jones observed the events unfolding from the second-level deck. At the moment, Eldridge was unaware that his spouse and mother-in-law had vacated the lifeboat. He soon experienced the conflicting emotions of horror and relief as he watched what took place. The rough seas swamped the lifeboat and caused it to capsize. In his written account, Eldridge elaborated:

> I hastened up to the deck—and oh! Fearful to relate, the Boat was filled with water. I immediately returned to between the decks, where I had left Hannah & Mother and oh! My God what gratitude filled my heart that they were there—I told them my fears—aided them upon deck—when oh— horrors of horrors— the worst was realized—the Boat was swamped—and before our eyes—beyond our reach—all were struggling in the water—the young and beautiful bride of Lieut. Jones—the excellent Mrs. Minot & her three most lovely children [Eldridge assumed the Minot Governess was a third daughter]—Mr. Horrell & Crew—and oh the cries of anguish, the groans—the lamentations—shrieks & prayers of those on board—no tongue can describe them—no imagination can picture the terrible scene—on the bottom and clinging to the capsized Boat we could see some—the two little girls were noticed—embraced in each others arms—before they sank for ever—Mrs. Jones caught Mr. Hovey around the neck from which he could not disengage himself—they drowned together—She had her bridal hat, plume, and dress "decked for the Bridal, decked for the grave" she was seen after he had disappeared—supposed supported by him—.[20]

A moment of hope surfaced when Captain Nichols returned in the third lifeboat after successfully rescuing Morgan. Nichols arrived in time to save the two crewmen and Mr. Horrell from "a drowning state."[21] However, it was too late to save any of the women or Chief Mate Hovey. The three male survivors were hoisted back on board the *Independence* and Horrell was revived. The six women had been pulled under by the weight of their gowns. According to legend, Mrs. Minot and her daughters carried the family's gold coins in satchels in their lace dresses, further inhibiting their chances to stay afloat.[22]

Charles Eldridge expressed empathy for Lieutenant Jones and Stephen Minot, who had witnessed the tragedy as helpless bystanders. Stephen Minot had "at one fell swoop, been robbed of all."[23] In contrast, Eldridge recalled that the "calmness of Lieut. Jones was almost fearful."[24] The only distraction from the sudden bereavement was that all on board remained in danger of suffering the same fate. As nightfall approached, the weather conditions remained adverse. Water was gaining on the ship, which was now down to two lifeboats. With the onset of darkness, all further evacuation attempts were suspended.

The bad situation got worse when a portion of the crew consumed the ship's abundant liquor supply even though most of the excess cargo and baggage had been discarded. Charles Eldridge described the group as being not only "unsafe but dangerous from the maddening influence of liquor—with which alas—the ship hold contained too much and which it was impossible to prevent their using—bottles of brandy and wines of all kinds— were more abundant than water."[25]

By Saturday morning, the 27th, the weather remained unabated. That afternoon, the outlook brightened when the propeller-driven steamship *Rayburn* anchored about three-quarters of a mile distant, inside of the surf. Passengers took further measures to lighten the ship by shoveling about 100 tons of fuel coal overboard. There was a forlorn hope that the combined factors of reducing the tonnage along with a high tide might dislodge the ship. Eldridge wrote:

> The wind was howling a tempest, and fearful waves came dashing against the sides of the ship, with a violence that seemed nothing could withstand—and while at work it would make breaches through the gangways—and washed us all from our posts—I told the men when washed away—we must go

back—that we were working for our lives—this was our last hope—that I was slight—but would stand there as long as the stoutest or sink at my post.[26]

Captain R. Hulton Kerr and a crew of the *Rayburn* rowed a skiff to the *Independence* and attached a line with the idea of towing the ship off the sandbar. Although damaged, the *Independence* remained intact and capable of landing its passengers if it could be dislodged. Otherwise, it would ultimately fragment against the sandbar. Captain Kerr offered to transport another group of passengers, including Hannah Eldridge and her mother, in the process. Charles Eldridge tried to convince his spouse and mother-in-law to go "but the recent disaster had unnerved every soul."[27] Kerr and his crew returned to the *Rayburn* without any *Independence* passengers. The attempt to tow the *Independence* off the bar failed, and any hope of saving the ship expired.

After reboarding the *Independence,* Captain Nichols offered to transport Hannah Eldridge and her mother to safety in the third lifeboat, and this time they consented to go. Eldridge described a miraculous scene in which the sea waves seemed to depart, leaving an open passage through which the oarsmen rowed. Eventually they passed the last breaker and reached the calmer waters of Matagorda Bay. Nichols transferred the group to the *Rayburn* and returned to the *Independence* to transport one more group in the same manner. The fourth and final lifeboat successfully evacuated another party of passengers. With the lifeboat supply exhausted, all souls remaining on board were on their own. Passengers ripped wooden planks from the decks to construct makeshift rafts. Others seized chests, boxes, and any object that might provide flotation.

The steamship *Louisiana* arrived on to the scene and anchored just north of Pass Caballo in Matagorda Bay, approximately three miles away. Three lifeboats set out on a rescue mission, but the first craft to reach the breakers capsized. The crews of the other two boats diverted their attention to saving their comrades on the overturned vessel. With darkness approaching, the *Rayburn* weighed anchor and sailed to safer moorings in Matagorda Bay. Aborting their mission to reach the *Independence,* the lifeboat crews returned to the anchored *Louisiana.*

Back on the *Independence,* the passengers confronted a new threat in addition to the weather. A faction of the intoxicated crew was committing mutiny. Those ship-hands became a drunken, piratical mob that Eldridge described as "demons in human shape."[28] Armed with axes, knives, and pistols, they invaded individual cabins, burst open trunks, and plundered. After gathering their spoils, they congregated on the second-level deck and seized the best passenger-constructed makeshift raft. Charles Eldridge observed the movements of the mutineers, who had tied their spoils to the seized raft and revealed their intention to abandon the ship at daylight. During the night, however, the effects of the alcohol would take further effect.

Captain Laughlin McKay organized a selected group of passengers and loyal crewmen to squelch the mutiny with a surprise assault against the marauders as they slept. Concluding the onslaught, Captain McKay held a pistol against the head of the leader, who immediately acquiesced. Intimidated by the turn of events, the other gang members capitulated and surrendered the seized raft. An understanding prevailed that the mob would not leave the ship until every passenger had evacuated ahead of them. Although a sense of justice prevailed, most concluded that they would not survive.

The passengers devised a plan whereby each person would take whatever might provide flotation and attempt to swim ashore. Each able-bodied man would take a child with him and commence at daylight with a favorable tide. Success appeared to be a long

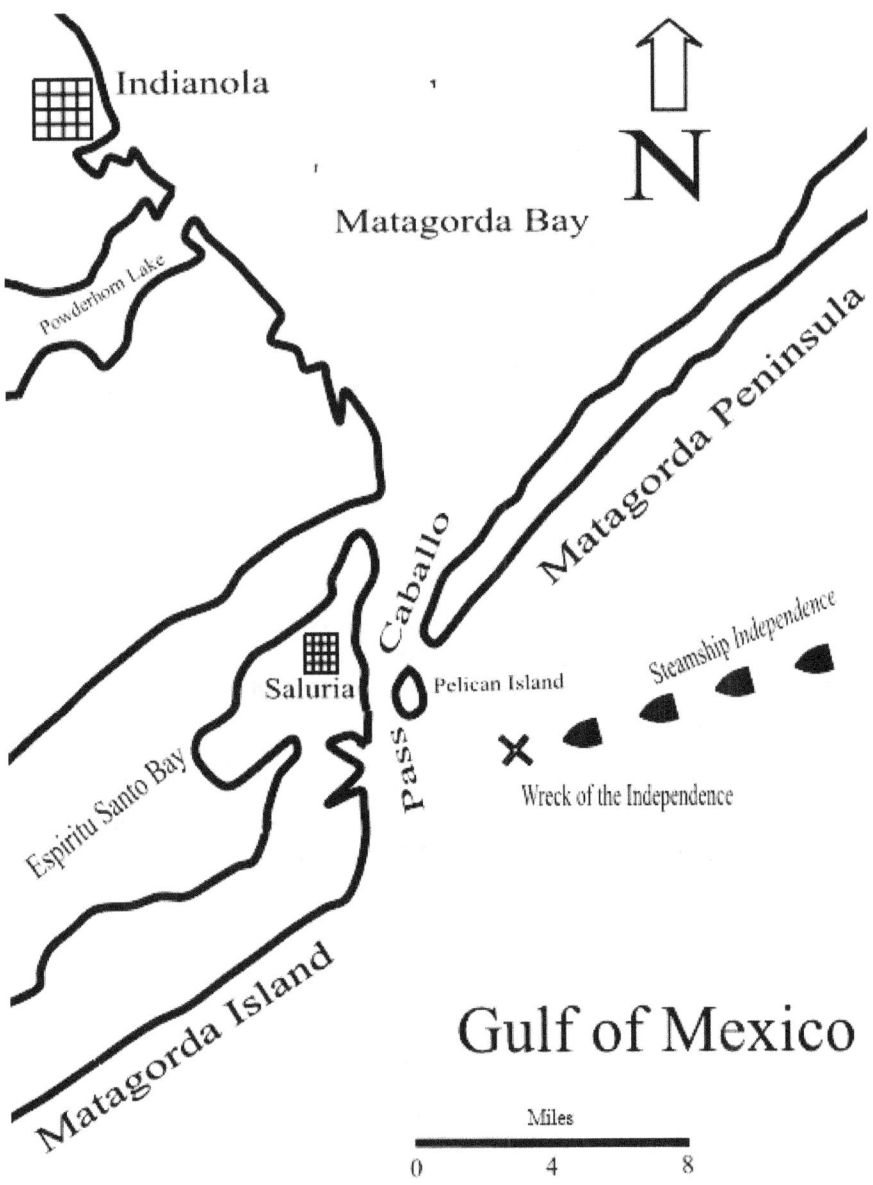

Pass Caballo (sketched by the author, 2017).

shot, as they were up to two miles from the nearest land, Pelican Island. Charles Eldridge wrote what he thought would be his final words on a sheet of paper, placed the document into an empty corked bottle, and cast it overboard.[29]

The approach of dawn on Sunday brought a hopeful development. The worst of the storm had passed. The *Rayburn* returned to the breakers and anchored within a mile. Three lifeboats from the *Louisiana* reappeared. From the south came the *Diamond*, a smaller ship bearing a shallow draft that maneuvered alongside the *Independence*. Restricted in capacity, the *Diamond* received all of the women and children passengers from the *Independence* and transported them to the *Rayburn*. The three lifeboats from the *Louisiana* reached the *Independence* and, in a series of launches, transferred all the remaining passengers to the *Rayburn*. The *Rayburn* then crossed over into Matagorda Bay, pulled alongside the larger *Louisiana*, and transferred all passengers to it, which transported them to Indianola.[30] The abandoned *Independence* ultimately fragmented.

Many ships responded to offer assistance. However, some crews took advantage of the situation to gather floating plunder, ignoring entreaties to help in the rescue.[31] On board the steamship *Louisiana* en route to Indianola, the rescued passengers from the *Independence* passed and observed the New York cotton schooner *Clinton*. Its decks were covered with previously discarded furniture, baggage and other merchandise that had been cast overboard from the *Independence*.[32]

Aftermath

While on board the *Rayburn*, Lieutenant Jones, and his cousin Thomas Benjamin Estill Edmondson joined twenty-five other passengers in signing a petition praising their rescuers. Charles Eldridge took up a monetary collection to honor them with medals. A year later, the group awarded coastal pilot, Captain William Nichols a commemorative silver cup that bears the inscription: "To Captain William Nichols from the Passengers of the Steamship *Independence*, 1853." Several others probably received similar tokens of appreciation.

Eliza Dunn-Jones, Louisa Papley Minot, the two Minot daughters, the Minot governess, and Chief Mate Hubble Hovey, all occupants of the ill-fated lifeboat, were the only six fatalities. Five of the bodies were recovered. Only the Minot governess remained missing.[33] Stephen Minot completed a solitary migration to Gonzales, Texas. According to legend, his hair turned white when he witnessed his entire family drown.[34] On New Year's Day 1853, he remarried and went on to father a new family.[35]

Eliza Dunn Jones's decomposed body was among the five washed up on the beach on Matagorda Island. According to legend, Lieutenant Jones was able to identify Eliza by the brooch she was wearing on her gown. Her remains were buried in a Matagorda Island cemetery near the town of Saluria. Three years later Jones would arrange to have her remains exhumed and reinterred where they currently rest at Old Glade Presbyterian Church Cemetery in Washington County.

It was said that life was never the same again for Lieutenant William E. Jones: "Whatever there was of gentleness in his heart seemed to have been destroyed."[36] Jones witnessed humanity in its extremes. On the one hand, he saw seamen risk their lives to save others. On the other, he saw some act in self-interest. He wrote an account of the tragedy to his sister-in-law, Florence Virginia Dunn. If he elaborated on his particular involvement in the ordeal, the information has been lost. Jones sent Florence a map of the Texas coast upon which he noted the locations of the wreck, where Pink's body was recovered, and her place of burial. According to legend, Lieutenant Jones would have suffered the same fate as his wife had it not been for the heroic efforts of his cousin Thomas Benjamin Estill Edmondson.[37] Unfortunately, those details remain a mystery.

Jones would travel on to his post on the Texas frontier. His cousin Thomas accompanied him and resided in Texas as a civilian for a period. Thomas later received a letter from his father, Colonel Robert Buchanan Edmondson, relaying what he had learned about the maritime accident. Jones was distraught and embarrassed by the fact that his relations in Washington County had received notice from other sources before his correspondence arrived. In a letter replying to Jane Edmondson Dunn on June 1, 1852, Jones stated:

> I see from the Col's letter to Tom dated April the 18th that you had received the fatal news through the papers & persons little acquainted with the accident. I am sorry that my letters did not reach you first. I hope you have before now the full account I sent you. I hope you will get either a copy of it I sent you by Memphis. Surely you have one & I may safely spare myself going again through all of the particulars of that sad affair the slightest thought of which makes my heart bleed.[38]

These images of Eliza Dunn Jones and Lieutenant William E. Jones were taken as a daguerreotypes in New Orleans in 1852 while they were en route to the Texas frontier (courtesy Carolyn Ryburn and Art Wills collections).

Word of Eliza's death reached Washington County through the Texas regional newspaper accounts before Jones's version arrived. The report published in the *Indianola Bulletin* was vague and failed to elaborate on many details. Although passenger Charles Eldridge was a source for the article, the *Indianola Bulletin* provided only a summary of his eyewitness account. His more detailed account was not published and never reached Washington County.

The lack of details gave rise to further speculation tarnishing Grumble's legacy: "Back in Virginia, there was open and cruel talk by some about her death not being an accident."[39] J.E.B. Stuart biographer John W. Thomason, Jr., wrote, "There is some legend about the death of his young wife, soon after he married."[40] Mosby biographer, Virgil Carrington Jones commented "there was considerable talk back home [Washington County] about the mysteriousness of her death. Folks recalled Jones's reputation as a hard, cruel fighter, but there the matter dropped."[41] In a biographical sketch of Grumble Jones published in *Confederate Veteran* in 1903, Thomas W. Colley wrote that Eliza "was swept away from the arms of her husband by the angry waves and drowned."[42] Colley probably intended to use his words as a metaphor, but some took them literally to surmise that Jones had some measure of physical control.

Following his brief stay in Calhoun County to make burial arrangements for his wife, Jones embarked on a hundred-mile overland journey westward and reported for duty at the U.S. Mounted Rifles outpost at Fort Merrill.

7

Texas—Into the Desert

Jones would satisfy the balance of his eight-year commitment to the U.S. Army on the Texas frontier. His fifty-five-month tour of duty would be protracted, inglorious and unfulfilling. Already in a state of melancholy, he was commencing a life full of monotony, social isolation, disillusionment, and more personal tragedy. These factors may have altered the young officer's personality and may have contributed to his earning the moniker "Grumble."[1]

Jones served in a drastically downsized peacetime army inhibited by budget restraints and overburdened with an enormous number of duties maintaining the peace over a vast region. Millard Fillmore assumed the U.S. presidency after serving as vice president to Zachary Taylor, who had died in office unexpectedly. Although the initial objectives of Manifest Destiny had been achieved, maintaining the terms of the doctrine was another challenge. Any national euphoria for the Mexican War triumph had subsided. Congress demanded that the War Department implement cost-saving measures by having the army make sacrifices. The soldiers in the field would be understaffed and ill-equipped while patrolling a vast desert wilderness of rough terrain in extreme climate conditions.

The previous expedition to, and occupation of, the Oregon Territory added to the financial strain of the national budget and further enhanced the antimilitary sentiment. Congress compelled the War Department to reduce the 40,000-man army to a small and homogeneous unit of fewer than 10,000.[2] The army divided the already reduced-in-size U.S. Mounted Rifles into small detachments and dispersed them at garrisons throughout the largest-area state in the union. In 1852 only 3,016 U.S. troops served in all of Texas.[3]

Initially Jones served at two outposts, Fort Merrill and Fort Ewell, both situated along the banks of the Nueces River. As strategic conditions changed due to shifting civilian migration patterns, the army permanently abandoned those installations and constructed new garrisons in regions farther westward and more remote. Jones concluded his service on the Texas frontier at a series of outposts along the Rio Grande.

Migrating to Texas in large numbers, American settlers were intruding on the Apache, Comanche, Kiowa, Lipan and other tribes who had inhabited the region for centuries. The new settlements forced the Indians to either starve or take up armed resistance. The Treaty of Guadalupe Hidalgo burdened the United States with the responsibility of preventing Indian raids from Texas into Mexico. International boundaries meant nothing to the Indian tribes, which had resisted the Spaniards and Mexicans for generations. Mexico itself was in a constant state of political turmoil. Not only was it impossible to prevent Indian raids into Mexico, but also those targeting the Texas side of the border used Mexico as sanctuary.

Fort Merrill

Lieutenant William E. Jones arrived at Fort Merrill, Texas, on April 10.[4] Situated in current Live Oak County, on the south banks of the Nueces River, the garrison was approximately one hundred miles south-southeast of San Antonio and sixty miles northwest of Corpus Christi.[5] It was probably named after Captain Moses Merrill, who had been killed in the Mexican War. Second Lieutenant W.E. Jones served as the executive officer in Company G, consisting of fifty-nine men and commanded by Captain (Brevet Major) John Smith Simonson, a veteran of the War of 1812, the Seminole War, and the Mexican War.[6] The garrison stood on high ground providing a panoramic view of the surrounding region and protecting it from occasional flooding. Aside from times of extreme drought, the river was not fordable, limiting access to the site by ferriage. Typical of the south Texas climate, summer temperatures frequently exceeded 100 degrees Fahrenheit.

Within a matter of months, shifting civilian migrating patterns and the inadequate living conditions rendered Fort Merrill obsolete. By August of 1852 Jones and his company transferred to Fort Ewell, situated approximately seventy miles to the southwest and up to the headwaters of the Nueces. Intermittently, Jones and his company would reoccupy Fort Merrill on an interim basis depending upon the strategic circumstances.

Fort Ewell

Fort Ewell was established on May 18, 1852, under the direction of U.S. Mounted Rifles commander, Lieutenant Colonel William Wing Loring.[7] Situated on the south bank of the Nueces River in current La Salle County, the garrison was named after the late Lieutenant Thomas Ewell, who had served in the regiment and had also died in the Mexican War. Aside from being a larger garrison, living conditions at Fort Ewell were no better than those at Fort Merrill.

The terrain surrounding Fort Ewell prohibited self-sustainability. The river averaged just over four feet deep and a seventy-five-foot width during normal weather conditions.[8] A sudden onset of heavy rains could flood the region and expand the river width up to a mile, drowning horses and livestock. The vicinity lacked timber or stone for construction and had neither adequate grazing pastures nor proper soil for cultivating vegetation. Summer daytime temperatures also frequently exceeded 100 degrees Fahrenheit. In his June 11–12, 1853, inspection report, Colonel W.G. Freeman remarked, "Indeed, a less inviting spot for occupation by troops cannot be conceived." He recommended abandoning the outpost.[9]

With the transfer to Fort Ewell, Brevet Major John Smith Simonton commanded the collective Companies E, G, and I, forming a division within the Regiment of Mounted Rifles.[10] Second Lieutenant W.E. Jones commanded Company G.[11]

Reflections on the Tragedy

Jones dwelled on his sadness for more than two months after his arrival in Texas. He wrote to his relations:

7. Texas—Into the Desert

I may consider myself abandoned by man and sorely punished by God. My transgressions with the latter have been numerous, and many offenses have I committed of a grievous and aggravated nature, but surely my punishment has been commensurate with a whole life of the vilest sin. I bear the decrees of heaven with all the fortitude I am master of—complain as little as the disposition nature has endowed me with, will allow. My lot is hard yet would I make it a thousand times worse here & hereafter, if my so doing, could be beneficial to her I loved, love, and ever will to the end of my being. Often I have lamented that my life and earthly happiness were not wrecked together. But God's will be done & all Earth approve![12]

To man, I have been a friend. Few can lay complaints to my charge. Sorely would it grieve me to fall under the displeasure of those I love best. Surely some of you have written to me & have extended such sympathy as would be a cordial to my poor bruised heart. I have written several letters but have been waiting some weeks to receive a reply. I can wait no longer. If time does not bring relief, death is to be the best friend I am ever to meet in this world. I try to forget what cannot be remedied. God in his goodness may have in store some happiness for me yet in this world. May I be useful to those whom my misfortunes have brought sorrow. That my own heart should become desolate is bad enough but how much worse the others should be involved in sorrow. If ill luck is to be my companion through life, how much better would it have been for me to have confined my misfortunes to myself. Let me ask of you what I strive to do myself—forget what cannot be remedied.[13]

Jones maintained his unique relationship with his distant cousins and immediate in-laws, the Dr. Samuel Dunn family. Demonstrating generosity, he assisted his deceased wife's younger sister, Emily J. Dunn, with a promise to send her $50 each month for her education. In 1853 Emily enrolled at the Odd Fellows Female Collegiate Institute at Rogersville, Tennessee.[14] His commitment to his sister-in-law exceeded a third of his salary.

Jones detailed his account of the tragedy in correspondence to his West Point friend professor Thomas Jonathan Jackson at Virginia Military Institute. Jackson, in turn, responded, "A man cannot realize an affliction as a general rule to its fullest extent until he is called to pass through its dark waters. Sad were the tidings brought by your letter after she who you had above all others selected, to journey through life with you, to be the object of your affection, and the earthly source of your joys had passed from this Earth of cares and sorrows."[15] Jones coped with his sadness and seclusion by delving into literature. He wrote,

In my loneliness, I have been driven to the study of ancient history. Much of it is well suited to the present temper of my feelings. At one time lost in admiration of the heroic patriotism of the Spartan mother, at another of the profound wisdom and foresight of the primitive law-givers of Greece, & irresistible courage of her more mature philosophic virtue, my time glides insensibly away. Morn, noon, & night are on each other heels; gone ere they were looked for. In a month or two that I am to be here by myself, I will get my head so full of this ancient wisdom & my tongue wound up so tight for want of someone to talk to that the first comer will be confounded with the extent of my learning & multitude of my words. I will be worse than Old Johnna Smith on temperance.[16]

He found himself in a dilemma regarding his wife's burial site in Saluria, Texas. Five months into his tour of duty, he wrote, "I have paid about $500 of debts I owed when I got to Texas. I am nearly even with the world & hope in a short time to have enough money to erect a handsome tomb over poor Pink. If this is in accordance with your wishes, let me know."[17]

Grumble's mother-in-law, Jane Edmondson Dunn, asked him to transport her daughter's remains back to Washington County, a task he would ultimately complete. The delay was due to the ambiguity on the part of Dr. Samuel Dunn. By the end of the year, Jones wrote, "You express a wish that I would have my poor wife's remains removed to Va. This I will make arrangements as soon as practicable to effect if you have concluded to live & die in that county yourself. The Doctor speaks of moving to Texas. If this is still his intention, had we not better wait to see where you locate & move her there rather than to Va? Write me soon on this subject, for if she is not soon removed, I must have a tomb stone placed on her grave & a suitable enclosure made around it. Her grave is enclosed but not as I would like to have it."[18]

A Venting of Rage

On August 4, 1852, Jones drafted a letter written in a stream of consciousness mode intended for his commanding officer, William Wing Loring, stationed at the same Fort Ewell garrison. There is no particular order or organization to the writing that revealed his utter contempt for his commanding officer. Jones jumped from one topic to the next within the same paragraphs and between sentences before bringing up the same subjects all over again.

He launched his emotional dissertation of his grievances by recalling Loring's rejection of his application for a leave of absence in 1848. Jones had requested a seven-day pass to visit Memphis and make arrangements for his mother, who was preparing to migrate to the region. According to Jones, Loring responded by presenting a smile "with all the brilliancy of the rainbow played on the countenance of the old & be frayed out" and a verbal reply of "your valuable service cannot be dispensed with." Jones challenged Loring's position by citing that other officers had just recently returned from special recruiting duty, which bore the characteristics of a leave of absence. From that point, the document reflects an incoherent and emotional exposition of multiple allegations and innuendos. In the midst of it all, Jones would write, "I have other scores to settle." Not only did he refute his regimental commander's leadership capabilities and integrity, but he also suggested allegations regarding Loring's sexual indiscretions with implications of bisexual preferences.

Addressing the rejection of his requested leave of absence, Jones commented that he had to "relieve an officer who was kept in St. Louis nominally on recruiting service but shrewdly suspected by some to assist the one armed tie in his matrimonial affairs." Jones went on to comment, "I hope you had a good time of it. I have seen no wife. Your stomach may have been satisfied with one of those one night fellows." Jones was not only suggesting the possibility of a male-to-male sexual encounter, but he also was slurring Loring's physical condition of having only one arm, the result of heroic combat action in the Mexican War. At some point he even commented, "Pity it was not a head."

Later in the correspondence, Jones remarked, "If you remember, you had a love scrape about this time with one of your captains." Elaborating, Jones sarcastically added, "True love never runs smooth. You & this captain quarreled. You wanted me to take your part being on your staff & to swear for you. I preferred to stand mute in the quarrel & to tell the truth. I have incurred your everlasting hatred by so doing." Continuing, Jones added, "After we crossed the Isthmus [of Panama], you again wanted me to take sides against your sweetheart." These comments suggest that, at least according to Jones, Loring was sexually involved with one or more of his junior officers.

Jones's accusations extended to heterosexual indiscretions as well. He wrote, "I have seen a dark complexion boy said to be yours." Near the end of his writing, he added, "I see you are taking better care of your little son. The hot weather tans him badly & his hair begins to nap a little. If you will make friends, I will recommend a powder that will give him a skin much whiter than your soul ever will be."

Jones challenged Loring's highly revered reputation as the leader and commander of the March to Oregon. On at least three occasions, he referred to the recognition of the expedition as the "greatest military feat on record" with a tone of mockery and contempt. The march had sustained a heavy burden of desertions by personnel, the deaths of personnel (by drowning), and devastating loss of transport animals. Conventional wisdom attributed the character of the enlisted men to the desertions and environmental conditions for the demise of the mounts. Jones, on the other hand, blamed the attrition on Loring's "stupidity." Supporting that contention, he wrote, "I have no doubt you would rival Jonathan Wild if you had half the sense of Peter Simple."[19]

Finally, Jones accused Loring of taking bribes from one or more of his junior officers in exchange for preferential duties. His final remarks are up for too much speculation to be accurately interpreted: "These facts answer & that to your shame. Bribery! Bribery! Corruption! The American Flag trails in the dust. Lt. _____ [intentionally left blank], look for the Rifle Regt. Now you may squat."

To say the letter was disrespectful would be a gross understatement. The document is unsigned, and it is highly unlikely that Jones ever submitted it or even a modified version. In any event, he never discarded the letter but kept it among his personal articles. Colonel Loring would eventually transfer to the U.S. Mounted Rifles headquarters in Santa Fe, New Mexico, allowing distance to mitigate some of the tensions.

Life on the Texas Frontier

Conditions at the military bases on the Texas frontier were primitive. The U.S. War Department guidelines for establishing outposts under Fillmore's administration were more general than specific. Garrisons were to be constructed on sites that could be "easily supplied, protect the citizens, and fulfill the treaty obligations with Mexico."[20] Ideally, they would be self-sustaining, with access to a water supply, grasses for grazing, timber or stone for building, a level parade ground for drills, and arable soil for planting. Realistically, the extreme climate and the harsh desert terrain prohibited most of those conditions.

Although commonly called forts, the garrisons had nothing in common with the bastion style Spanish missions (e.g., the Alamo) that preceded them by a hundred years or the barricaded stockades commonly portrayed in Western movies. Withstanding a siege was not a priority. The layouts were usually nothing more than a collection of utility structures to provide mounted companies with habitation in proximity to the areas they canvassed. Structures formed a perimeter encircling a parade ground. Barriers were nothing more than a picket fence to corral the horses and other livestock.

Access to clean water was a constant challenge, with heavy demands causing overconsumption. When wells dried or became contaminated the army transported water over in tanks hauled by mule teams.[21] The burden on transport animals was so problematic that the War Department experimented with camels.[22] Boiling water was rarely an option because firewood was at as much of a premium as the water itself.[23] Food spoilage was rampant. Droughts and parasites drastically limited local crop production. Jones commented on this matter: "Crops are very uncertain [to grow] and when raised [are] soon destroyed by the weevil."[24] A balanced diet was rare among the troops and health problems were a consequence.

Understandably, diseases were common. Malaria, dysentery, and scurvy resulted in more casualties than those from combat.[25] On average, the soldier stationed in Texas between 1849 and 1859 was ill more than three times a year, with a mortality rate at about 3.5 percent.[26] Fortunately, cholera was limited to major cities like San Antonio and did not spread to the outposts. Jones was not immune to diseases but fared better than most. From Fort Ewell he once wrote, "I have escaped my chill & the Doctor says he thinks me safe for the season."[27]

A shortage of qualified doctors enticed Jones's father-in-law, Dr. Samuel Dunn of Washington County, Virginia, to contemplate a Texas migration. When Jones received word of this, he discouraged Dr. Dunn from making the move. He wrote to Jane Ryburn Dunn: "This part of the country would not suit him." Jones went on to say, "Stay in Va all who are able. Educate your children & make yourself comfortable & you will act wisely."[28]

The antimilitary sentiment in Texas paralleled the situation in Oregon. Politically, the Texas American attitude prevailed that a large national army threatened hard-earned liberties.[29] Many Texas Americans held the notion that they could provide their protection from outside threats with civilian militia groups such as the Texas Rangers.

Ironically, a symbiotic relationship existed between the military outposts and the civilian communities that emerged around them. Once well established, a garrison evolved into an active center of commerce that attracted private enterprises.[30] Conversely, the closing of a military outpost meant an imminent demise to the local economy. The antebellum U.S. Army stimulated the early economic growth of Texas more than any other entity.

Jones began and intermittently served his tour of duty in Texas as assistant quartermaster and director of subsistence at the different garrisons. Admitting that the position lacked adventure, he wrote to his mother-in-law: "I might as well acknowledge it, for my language shows I have charge of baking of bread. I am the commissary of subsistence of this post, a kind of head keeper of a provision store."[31] Jones was in charge of uniforms, equipment, weapons, provisions, and just about every kind of tangible property necessary for the continued sustaining of the garrisons. This service would provide him with background credentials he utilized later in a brief civilian career. The office also granted Jones the privilege of a special assignment in 1855 that necessitated his travel to the East.

The status earned him a level of commendation. Colonel W.G. Freeman reported, "Lieut. Jones's accounts were regularly kept and appeared to be correct. He is a young officer of good judgment and attention to his duties."[32] Service in the administrative role placed Jones in a unique position. He received additional pay of $14 over his base salary of $104 per month and thus was part of the economically elite class, enabling him to later acquire sole ownership of the family estate in Washington County.

In spite of the praise, the job had its difficulties. Jones had to perform a balancing act between the convenience and security of the soldier on the field while working within the confines of budget restraints. He was responsible for the purchase and care of horses that were not acclimated to the Texas desert. Overexertion, lack of water, grass shortages, and disease caused the demise of many of them.[33] While on patrols and scouting missions, troopers frequently dismounted and led their horses on foot to conserve their strength.[34] Mounts were a favorite target of theft by Indians. Unlike slow-moving cattle, horses could be stolen rapidly. Feeding horses required purchasing grain that could not be adequately stored because facilities lacked sufficient shelter. The extreme environmental conditions caused considerable wear to the riding equipment in the way of saddles, bridles, and blankets. Supply attrition was a constant problem. The burden of justifying the replacement of such supplies fell upon Lieutenant Jones as commissary.

Beef was the primary means of sustenance for the soldiers manning the outpost. As purchaser, Jones carried the burden of dealing with local ranchers and businessmen. Many contractors were unreliable in a system tainted with bribery and mismanagement.[35] Seeking an alternative that would benefit him and the army, Jones invested in cattle and considered acquiring ranch lands at the headwaters of the Nueces. He wrote to his mother-in-law: "Money invested in cattle increases at the rate of 33⅓ percent per annum."[36] He attained eleven dairy cows and predicted that in two years he could own as many as 500 head of beef cattle. Cattle were better acclimated to the Texas environment than horses were and moved too slowly for Indians to herd away in their raids.[37] By the end of the year, however, Jones gave up on the idea.

In reality, cattle fared only slightly better than horses, and the War Department relied upon civilian contractors to supply food for the outposts with budget restraints in mind. Even the sole-proprietor sutlers tended to charge outrageous prices for inferior quality goods. In later years with the Confederate service Jones would reveal his past animosities against merchants who profited at the soldiers' expense.

During a typical fiscal year, the antebellum War Department spent $73,000 for the construction and maintenance of nineteen outposts in Texas. It then cost an additional $390,000 to transport supplies to the occupying troops.[38] Jones frequently found himself under managerial pressure to justify the maintenance costs to the authorities in Washington. He often had to justify the replacement of supplies that did not endure the standard rate of attrition. Supplies coming to Gulf port cities had to be shipped overland great distances, taking a toll on the wagons and horses and adding enormous transportation costs. Conditions on the Rio Grande and Nueces rarely ever allowed navigation. When delivered to the garrisons, supplies were exposed to the weather, parasites, and theft.

Arming the Regiment of Mounted Rifles was problematic. The rifle was inaccurate, unreliable, and hazardous to carry while on horseback. Mounted troops transported it unloaded and holstered it in their boots, which caused a riding imbalance.[39] The pistol, a Colt six-shot revolver, was in short supply due to budget restraints. During Jones's service at Fort Ewell in 1853 forty handguns were issued to his company of fifty-nine troops.[40]

Personnel

The quality of the enlisted men on the Texas frontier was no better than that during the expedition to and occupation of the Pacific Northwest Territory. More than 60 percent of the enlisted men stationed in Texas listed foreign places of birth.[41] Many enlisted under false names and with misinformation regarding their backgrounds. "Gold fever" had diminished, and the army drew recruits by offering a level of economic security. Qualifications were minimal, resulting in a "motley collection of bounty jumpers, criminals, and ne'er-do-wells."[42] Dubious motivations for enlisting included a desire to escape prosecution for past crimes or to gain a government-sponsored migration to the West. Officers like Jones also endured the burden of court-martial duty, a procedure that required travel to different outposts to convene them. The most common offenses were desertion, theft, and alcohol abuse.[43] About one-third of the enlisted men who joined the army after the Mexican War deserted.[44]

Officers bore the task of policing the troops as well. Thefts of the quartermaster's storage and local sutler's stores were rampant. Deserters often crossed over into Mexico with their army-issued horses, arms, and other equipment. As assistant quartermaster, Jones had to explain the losses to the hierarchy. He often confronted area civilians who wore army uniforms or footwear and asked how they acquired the items. Some responded that they found them discarded. Others admitted that they had purchased them from soldiers. As quartermaster, Jones bore the burden of accounting for all missing supplies. He, therefore, took particular exception to violators. Commonly stolen items included firearms, tobacco, whiskey, flour, building materials, and other dry goods.

In September of 1852 Lieutenant Jones investigated the burglary of a Fort Merrill sutler's store resulting in the theft of firearms, tobacco, and other goods. The suspects, Privates John Wilson and William Cook of the Mounted Rifles, arranged to sell their plunder to a private citizen across the Nueces. Jones and the store clerk conducted surveillance to observe the privates returning from their contact's home with a different set of commodities from what had been stolen. Rather than confront the suspects, Jones interrogated the contact, who confessed his arrangement to purchase the stolen articles. Instead, however, the suspects brought cash to purchase other items. Jones concluded that the suspects sold the stolen goods to another party for cash and used the proceeds to buy different ones. He arrested and charged both privates with burglary and selling of stolen property.[45] Jones testified against the suspects during a court-martial hearing in Galveston the following January. He conveyed that "the general conduct of" the named suspects "was such as to create suspicion." They possessed more money than could be reasonably expected. In his report he described the two accused as "drunkards & worthless soldiers."[46]

Jones engaged a female informant known as "Big Ann," who identified the parties who traded with her. On one occasion, she aided in the recovery of four barrels of flour stolen from the quartermaster's department. Inside the barrels were several pairs of army-issued shoes.[47] Building materials in a region that lacked timber or stone were also a desired commodity.

Social interaction between enlisted men and officers was rare. While the common enlisted men had questionable character or intellect, the corps of officers was an elite group. West Point alumni made up more than two-thirds of the commissioned staff.[48] On many occasions, officers convened for court-martial duty as either a witness or on the panel of inquiry, which necessitated travel between garrisons. Although there was a sense of camaraderie, there were some occasions of discontent between officers. Even the higher pay could not provide a decent standard of living in such a harsh environment. Another strain was the limited opportunities for promotion in the down-sized peacetime army.

Ringgold Barracks, Escort Duty and a Saddle Patent

Following the closing of Fort Ewell in 1853, Jones received an interim assignment to the Ringgold Barracks, where he was temporarily relieved of quartermaster duties and assigned to escort the commanding general of the Department of Texas.[49] Fort Ringgold was the southernmost of the western tier of forts constructed at the end of the Mexican War and stood guard over the Rio Grande and Rio Grande City in Starr County.

On June 13, 1854, Lieutenant Jones received U.S. Patent No. 11,068 for his invention of an adjustable steel frame improvement to the riding saddle.[50] It was a slight modification to the Grimsley, the regulation saddle in use at the time. A spring attached to the two side panels allowed for an adjustment so the saddle could fit different sizes of horses. Jones's invention came about at a time when other officers, mostly professional engineers with a West Point education, were creating designs for potential adoption by the War Department. President Franklin Pierce's secretary of war, Jefferson Davis, and Quartermaster-General Thomas Sidney Jesup both saw the potential conflict of interest issues with army officers engaging in business with the military. Jones would wait and pursue the matter with more diligence after he left the army in early 1857.

Return to Quartermaster Duty

In late 1854 Jones returned to quartermaster duty, a position that awarded him a special assignment the following year. For much of early 1855 he enjoyed the privilege of being away from the Texas outposts, conducting official business for the purpose of "purchasing horses."[51] He traveled to the Northeast to visit the War Department in Washington, D.C., and to Baltimore. Although on an official business trip, he could attend to his personal affairs, including a visit to his home in Washington County.

While in Baltimore, Jones purchased the engraved headstone that marks Eliza Dunn-Jones's grave.[52] He also arranged to have her remains exhumed from Matagorda Island and transported back to Glade Spring via Lynchburg.[53] Details of the arrangement are not known, but logical speculation has it that Eliza's remains were transported by Gulf and Atlantic sea transportation to Hampton Roads in eastern Virginia. From there, a river barge carried her remains by the James River and Kanawha Canal to Lynchburg, a western hub of the system.

Lieutenant William E. Jones was more than likely the author of the poetic words inscribed on Eliza's tombstone at Old Glade Presbyterian Church Cemetery, which read:

> Sacred
> To the memory of
> Mrs. Eliza M.
> The Wife of
> Lieut. W.E. Jones
> U.S. Mounted Rifles
> She was born on the
> 3rd of May 1833 in
> Washington County
> Virginia, was married
> on the 15th of Jan. 1852,
> and was drowned on the
> 26th of March of the
> same year when attem
> pting to land from the
> wreck of the Steam Ship
> Independence at Pass

Eliza Dunn Jones's grave marker (photograph by the author, November 1986).

*Caballo, Texas. She was
personally beautiful had
a sweet disposition and
an intellect uncommonly
brilliant. The early death
of so hopeful a sister
child and wife left
friends, parents, and her
husband in unspeakable sorrow*

While in Glade Spring, on February 2, Jones received a promotion to the rank of first lieutenant at a time when advancements were rare.[54] Returning to Texas, he stopped in Memphis, Tennessee, to visit his mother and siblings in eastern Arkansas and western Tennessee to purchase their interest in the Washington County family property.[55] The combined transactions settled the estate of Grumble's father, Robert Jones, whose will required the estate to remain open until his youngest child reached age twenty-one.[56] With James W. Jones having just reached that age during the visit, Grumble was legally able to settle with all beneficiaries. By the conclusion of this trip, he was the sole and absentee owner of the family land on the Middle Fork of the Holston River. First Lieutenant Jones also visited his sister, Sarah Eliza Jane Jones Greer, in Shelby County, Tennessee. He took particular pleasure in seeing his two nieces for the first time—and what would also be the last time.

While on his outing, Jones received a letter from the Quartermaster's Department in Washington, D.C., relieving him of assistant quartermaster duty and directing him to report to the adjutant general for reassignment.[57] He took river transportation to New Orleans and a Gulf steamer to one of the western Texas port cities. An overland journey took him to a new outpost assignment at Fort Duncan, Texas, situated near Eagle Pass along the Rio Grande. Arriving with the satisfaction of having completed a very successful excursion, Jones received word of more personal tragedy. While he was in transit, his one-year-old niece by Sarah Eliza Jane Jones Greer had died. Two weeks later, the child's father, his brother-in-law, Jefferson Greer, died at the age of twenty-eight.[58]

Fort Duncan and Fort Bliss

In addition to the news of the recent tragedy, the environment at Fort Duncan brought on more melancholy for Jones. Situated about a hundred miles upriver from Rio Grande City and well beyond the terminus for steamship navigation, the garrison was even more remote and more isolated. Although strategically important, the Eagle Pass area was an unproductive, barren country that caused men and livestock to suffer from exposure. As with the two outposts on the Nueces River, Fort Duncan was not self-sustaining, and all supplies had to be transported overland.

In January of 1856, Jones suffered the loss of his mother, Catherine Moffett Edmondson Jones, who died at age sixty in Crittenden County. Toward the end of 1856, he was reassigned to Company K at Fort Bliss on the upper Rio Grande, near El Paso del Norte. Fort Bliss was the only Texas frontier outpost that Jones served in that has survived into the present day as a military installation. There, he engaged in expeditions and mounted patrols into the New Mexico Territory.

Social isolation, depression, and a lack of advancement opportunities dominated a soldier's life in antebellum Texas and commonly terminated the careers of many qualified officers like Jones. Describing an officer's discouraging life in 1855, Lieutenant Colonel Robert E. Lee corresponded with his wife with words of advice regarding his son's preparation for adulthood: "Let him never touch a novel. They paint beauty more charming than nature, & describe happiness that never exists."[59] A year later, Lieutenant Colonel Lee advised his nephew, Fitzhugh Lee, "My experience has taught me to recommend no young man enter the service."[60]

Most officers in the antebellum U.S. Army in Texas persevered to make the best of a difficult situation. Service on the Texas frontier provided Jones with a reinforced spirit of independence. The familiarity he gained as quartermaster provided him with skills he would utilize in a brief civilian career. Having graduated from West Point in the upper quarter of his class, he had managed to achieve only the rank of first lieutenant in eight years, adding to his disillusionment with army life. His Texas frontier duty began with the loss of his wife; the loss of his mother, a niece, and a brother-in-law followed. Having performed his duties faithfully, he received only modest recognition. Midway through the year, he satisfied his pledge to serve the U.S. Army for eight years. The idea of civilian life was becoming more appealing.

On September 4, 1856, while stationed at Camp Crawford, New Mexico, Jones corresponded with the adjutant general, Department of New Mexico, requesting a two-month leave of absence "with permission to ask for an extension." Without elaborating on details, Jones added that "urgent personal business makes it almost absolutely necessary that I should give it my attention even at the sacrifice of my official position."[61] Through the proper channels, Jones's application arrived at the office of Lieutenant Colonel William Wing Loring.

In forwarding the request up the administrative ladder, Loring commented that granting Jones a furlough would result in a shortage of officers to command the companies in the field. Loring also contended that Jones had recently received a similar benefit with his official business trip to the East. Although acknowledging that Jones's recent absence was part of a special assignment fulfilling his official duties as quartermaster, Loring also took the position that in that capacity Jones furthered "his own interest."[62] With all things considered, Loring recommended that the department reject Jones's application.

Six weeks later, the assistant adjutant general (AAG), Major W.A. Nichols, wrote to Jones stating that due to the limited number of officers in the Rifle Regiment, the department commander could not accede. Nichols further advised Jones that his best recourse would be to appeal to the next level up the chain of command.[63] Taking the assistant adjutant's advice, Jones wrote directly to Secretary of War Jefferson Davis in Washington, D.C. Jones stated, "It is my intention to resign my commission at the termination of the leave & I ask it that I may be able to defray my expenses home & have some time to settle myself in a new profession."[64] Four days later he followed up by corresponding with Assistant Adjutant General Major W.A. Nichols, requesting a two-month furlough to attend to his private affairs that demanded his immediate personal presence. He specified that if his request could not be granted, to consider and accept the communication as his letter of resignation.[65]

AWOL and Resignation

Jones did not wait for an answer. In receipt of a seven-day pass, he departed knowing that he would not be able to return to his post within the allotted time frame. Before leaving, he wrote the following communication to the assistant adjutant general:

> The passing of a Government train presents and opportunity of reaching San Antonio without the great expense that must otherwise be incurred. I have heard that several of the Rifle officers whose absence caused the refusal of my application of the 4th of last September had returned to this Department. Again, my application of the 14th inst contains a conditional tender of my resignation at the direction of the regimental commander. These things together with a great necessity of attending

Antebellum Texas (sketched by the author, 2016).

to my private business will I presume in some degree excuse me for having taken the unauthorized step of quitting the department on a seven days leave. In this, nothing is farther from my intention than exhibit a contempt for authority. On the contrary, a pressure of private business propels me to run the risk of displeasure of the Dept. commander. Please present my conduct to him in this light & ask him, if any application of the 14th inst has not been acted on, to deal with me as leniently as he may deem compatible with his public duty & also ask him to give this his earliest convenient attention.[66]

Not present by the termination of his seven-day pass, Jones was absent without leave, and his company was without a commanding officer. On November 27, a day following the expiration of Jones's pass, Lieutenant Colonel Loring reported, "Lieutenant

Jones, in temporary and highly responsible command of Company K, has left the Department of New Mexico without authority."[67]

Jones's actions were grounds for a court-martial, with charges ranging from dereliction of duty to outright desertion. The matter was referred to Lieutenant Colonel Robert E. Lee in Brownsville, Texas, for a recommendation of appropriate measures. Lee felt that the actions seemed out of character for Jones, whose conduct up until that time had been considered exemplary. Taking Grumble's record into consideration, Lee recommended to the lieutenant general commanding all U.S. Army forces that the mildest action to be taken should be the acceptance of Jones's resignation.[68]

On the supply train Jones made his way to San Antonio, Texas. By the time Lee had submitted his recommendation, Jones was visiting the home of S.B. Williams, who would assist him in his new career by referring him to his brother-in-law, S.C. Greenhow, the treasurer of Richmond, Virginia. On December 24, 1856, Williams wrote:

> Dear Brother in Law,
>
> Allow me to introduce to you my friend, Lt. W.E. Jones. He is going on Friday to Richmond and may perhaps locate himself there. Any kindness or favor you can extend to him will be highly appreciated. Mr. Jones is an old friend and acquaintance of mine.[69]

Jones departed San Antonio on the day after Christmas and traveled to the Northeast, reaching Washington, D.C., by mid–January. The War Department had not officially accepted Grumble's resignation, as the language in his most recent correspondence was conditional. On January 15, 1857, Jones formally submitted his resignation and personally delivered it to the War Department. Following an auditing of his accounts, on January 27, Secretary of War Jefferson Davis officially accepted Grumble's resignation from the U.S. Army.[70]

Secretary Davis was serving in the cabinet of the outgoing President Franklin Pierce, who had failed to acquire the Democratic Party's renomination for the 1856 presidential election for James Buchanan. Buchanan, in turn, won the election over the first Republican candidate, John Fremont.

Jones's decision to resign from the army was not impulsive. He had carefully planned a course of action once he left the army. Ultimately, he received an honorable discharge from Secretary of War Jefferson Davis. The circumstances under which Jones left the Old Army, however, draw scrutiny and do not leave an entirely unblemished record. In any event, Jones was on his way to a civilian life about which only glimpses of information are known.

8

The Civilian Years

Biographical sketches allege that after resigning from the Old Army William E. "Grumble" Jones toured Europe before retiring to his family estate in Washington County, Virginia, to live out his life as a recluse—until the outbreak of the Civil War terminated his self-imposed isolation. It is factual that Jones toured Europe and that he was the sole owner of the productive family farm, which had doubled in value since his father's death. However, for most of that time Jones was an absentee owner and not in Washington County. Contrary to local perceptions that he was a hermit, Jones pursued an active life as an entrepreneur operating out of Richmond, Baltimore, Washington, Philadelphia, Newark, and New York. Partially explaining the misconception, Jones was part of a culture that desired to conceal evidence of achievement and wealth.

Through his previous quartermaster service, Jones was familiar with the Old Army standards regarding cost efficiency and serviceability. He was equally aware of the congressional pressure on the War Department to supply and sustain the military with budget restraints in mind. He possessed the intellectual and administrative knowledge to fulfill the needs of the military as a private contractor.

Jones's entrance into civilian life coincided with the change in presidential administrations. Elected in November of 1856 President James Buchanan took office on March 4, 1857. A fellow Washington County resident and former Virginia governor, John Buchanan Floyd joined Buchanan's cabinet as secretary of war. By their common residency in Washington County, Jones and Floyd were already acquainted. Floyd was going to promote significant changes in the military establishment and thus allow for the creation of new opportunities. The War Department had a longstanding history of deficiencies regarding its accountability, competence, and morale. One of the more measurable failures was in the realm of commissary and supply.[1] Floyd intended to bring about radical change to improve the efficiency of the military establishment. As the new secretary of war, John Buchanan Floyd would confront challenges from a politically divided Congress and the press. Both entities scrutinized his administrative dealings. Floyd possessed a fighting spirit that placed him at odds with an anti-administration-dominated Congress that desired a continuation of the post–Mexican War cost-saving measures.

Floyd had the overall support of the military establishment dominated by southern officers. To revamp the military, he advocated removing the authority regarding supply purchases from the quartermaster general,[2] but his measures drew partisan congressional investigations concerning his alleged improprieties in administering government contracts. In a professional relationship with the secretary that was more subtle, Jones was not implicated in any of the major scandals that marred Floyd's career in the

Buchanan administration. He did, however, benefit from his association with the secretary.

Jones Saddle

Jones sought to capitalize on U.S. Patent No. 11,068, issued in 1854, for his invention of an adjustable steel frame improvement to the riding saddle.[3] Theoretically, one size of the manufactured saddle could be adjusted to fit any size mount.[4] Jones promoted his invention as a significant cost-saving measure.

Looking to the international scene, he visited the British consulate in Baltimore on July 8, 1857, and applied for a patent with the British Office of Patents in the twenty-first year of the reign of Her Most Excellent Majesty, Queen Victoria.[5] He later visited London to complete the patent transaction and received British Patent No. 1892 on January 8, 1857.[6] The invention merited an entry into the London-published *Mechanics Magazine* no. 1795 on January 2, 1858.

Jones deemed his invention "an improvement in trees of riding saddles."[7] In his written declaration, he elaborated, "My invention consists in the introduction of a hinge at the apex of the pommel and cantle, in combination with adjusting screws controlling the movements of said hinge, whereby the saddle may be enlarged or contracted at pleasure to suit the size of the horse to which it is to be applied; and in the combination with hinged & adjustable pommel and cantle just described of self-adjusting side pieces, which are attached to the lower extremities of the pommel and cantle by pivots or bolds, about which they are capable of movement, so that said side pieces present the same surface to the back of the horse however much the saddle may be contracted or expanded."[8]

Jones entered an arrangement with Lacey & Phillips, Saddlers, situated at 30 and 32 South 7th Street, Philadelphia.[9] The U.S. Army Quartermaster Department approved the purchase of three hundred Jones Saddles in 1857 and 1858.[10] Unfortunately, the effectiveness of the adjustment mechanism depended on a hardware device in the way of a spring that, with the limited technology of the times, could not withstand the constant pressure from hard use in the field. The War Department tested the Jones adjustable tree saddle against the McClellan, Hope, Grimsley, and Campbell saddles. All of the competition outperformed the Jones saddle, which proved unsatisfactory for general adoption.[11] In 1859 the War Department selected the McClellan saddle as its standard, with cost and durability as the deciding factors. The inventor of the chosen saddle was the future commander of the Army of the Potomac and 1864 Peace Democrat candidate, George B. McClellan.

Grumble enjoyed more success as a civilian contractor when he entered into a business arrangement with Major Henry Hopkins Sibley of the U.S. Dragoons. In regard to his saddle improvement invention, there was too much competition. In the new venture with Sibley, the potential appeared wide open.

Sibley Tent

The army did not just need saddles. The emerging tent manufacturing industry is one of the most overlooked segments of the nineteenth-century military-economic land-

Jones Saddle Patent, 1857 (British Office of Patents).

scape. By the conclusion of the Civil War, the U.S. Army would spend as much money on tents as it did on footwear.[12] Tent suppliers and manufacturers would conduct twice as much business as gun foundries and rank among the nation's leading military contractors.[13]

Major Henry Hopkins Sibley of the U.S. Dragoons was eight years older than Jones, but the two officers had much in common. Both were southerners and West Point graduates and had served with mounted regiments on the Western frontier. Although West Point graduates might never serve at the same garrisons, they found that they operated in a small world, particularly through court-martial duty.

Major Sibley came up with the idea of a portable shelter after studying the Indian lodge more commonly known as the tipi. He designed the "Sibley Tent," a conical or bell-shaped portable structure that was easily pitched and erected on a tripod holding a single pole. The layout included an eighteen-foot diameter on the ground level, a twelve-foot height, and an eighteen-inch diameter opening at the top to provide ventilation. A single pole mounted onto three bars of iron forming a tripod of four-and-a-half feet in height above the ground provided the structural support. On the ground level within the perimeter confines of the tripod, a campfire could burn beneath a kettle suspended by a chain mounted to the tripod. With the capacity to burn a campfire inside, the tent design features provided warmth and allowed for cooking.

The tent design brought advantages in fuel efficiency in situations when firewood was scarce and could also conceal the campfires from a distant enemy. Structurally, the tent was more resistant to high winds than conventional units. In mild weather, it provided better ventilation. An examining board conducted at Fort Belknap, Texas, concluded that the tent was more economical in that it could shelter up to twenty-five men and their equipment. Theoretically, four tents would accommodate an entire company.

While serving on court-martial duty at Fort Riley, Kansas, a panel of officers including Colonels Joseph E. Johnston and Robert E. Lee inspected the tent and expressed favorable impressions.[14] The tent won the praises of Kansas Territorial governor John White Geary, medical officers, and several field officers leading expeditions. Many officers called for the official army adoption of the tent. which some purchased at their own expense. The tent also had its limitations. It weighed more and cost more than the conventional tents currently in use. The only measurable economic advantage was that it could theoretically be purchased and transported in fewer numbers.

In June of 1855, Sibley entered into a partnership agreement with First Lieutenant William Wallace Burns of the Fifth Infantry. In April of the following year Sibley, with the help of Burns, received U.S. Patent No. 14,740.[15] They agreed to conduct business and share the interest equally.[16] Burns proposed that they outline their agreement in writing, but Sibley replied that "none [was] necessary between such friends"[17] It was an oral arrangement that Burns would regret.

Notwithstanding the extensive praise for the tent, opposition rested with the high command. Quartermaster General Thomas Sidney Jesup, who held his office for more than forty years, questioned the tent's features. Secretary of War Jefferson Davis supported Jesup's contentions for the same reasons. Both General Jesup and Secretary Davis had reservations about an army officer engaging in private enterprise with the War Department.[18]

The timing of Grumble's resignation from the army coincided with a period of turmoil for the U.S. Army career of Sibley. By the end of 1856 Sibley's wife and children were residing in New York, and the major was growing weary of the difficult life on the western frontier. Financially, Sibley was not in a position to leave the army, and he was unable to negotiate directly with the War Department on his invention. He needed the intervention of a third party acting on his behalf. On March 9, 1857, five days after Buchanan's inauguration, Sibley hired Jones to serve as his agent to promote the Sibley tent in exchange for 25 percent of the profits.[19] Captain H.P. Brewster witnessed the transaction. Noticeably absent from the written contract was the signature of Sibley's partner, First Lieutenant William Wallace Burns.

Jones acknowledged that the former secretary of war (Jefferson Davis) and the current quartermaster general (Thomas Sidney Jesup) viewed a matter of impropriety with army officers engaged in contracting for military supplies. To alleviate this concern, Jones proposed that he, acting as Sibley's agent, would furnish the tents, and this action should thereby remove the objection of the War Department to conducting business directly with an officer in the army. Jones's Washington County acquaintance John Buchanan Floyd replaced Secretary Davis with the change in presidential administrations. However, General Jesup continued to hold his office and still saw a conflict, even with the Jones representation.

Jones launched a vigorous campaign to persuade the War Department to adopt the Sibley tent as the standard portable shelter for the U.S. Army. On March 26 he wrote to Secretary John Buchanan Floyd and reiterated the evaluations of the Sibley tent beginning with the proceedings by the board of officers at Fort Belknap. He outlined the success of the tent when it had been used on a march from Texas to Kansas. Nine field officers of the panel at Fort Riley had signed a declaration recommending its adoption. Thirty-one officers signed a document with similar findings at Lecompton, Kansas.

Jones entered into an arrangement with a Solomon Parrett and George Patten to manufacture the tents out of Baltimore, on an as-needed basis. Jones did not limit potential customers to the government. By May of 1857 his group had sold thirteen tents to James B. Leach, superintendent of the El Paso & Fort Yuma Wagon Road.[20] Leach intended to construct a new stagecoach route to the West with Memphis as its eastern terminal. The tents, however, had only limited appeal to the civilian populace. Although westward migrations remained part of the American culture, the enthusiasm had waned with the diminishment of gold fever. Lucrative sales of the tents depended on their official adoption by the U.S. War Department for the army.

Although the Sibley tent was a new invention, mass production would not require new materials or new manufacturing technologies but could rely on the already well-established maritime industries of sailcloth production and sailmaking.[21] Cotton canvas, also called "duck," used to produce sails was flexible but dense enough to repel water and contain heat. Although ships harnessing the wind for propulsion still vastly outnumbered the steamships, sail manufacturing on its present scale was on its way to eventual obsolescence. The sail-producing sector welcomed the potential opportunity of converting their seamstress operations and textile mills into tent production. Along this line, Jones entered into a business relationship with Dr. John H. Landell, a sailmaker and ship chandler of Newark, New Jersey. Landell's company would manufacture the tents according to specifications and ship them to destinations based on demand. Jones and Landell developed an association in other ventures as well.

In his marketing efforts to persuade the War Department to adopt the Sibley tent, Jones elaborated on the cost-saving benefits addition to the health and comfort of the troops. He pointed out that the regulation tent "now in use" sheltered eight men and cost $18.61. Based on that premise, Jones calculated that the conventional tents cost $46.52½ to accommodate twenty men. One Sibley tent, on the other hand, cost $36.00 and could shelter twenty. Summarizing the cost saving measures, Jones argued that full adoption of the Sibley tent would save the government $10.52½ for every twenty soldiers in the

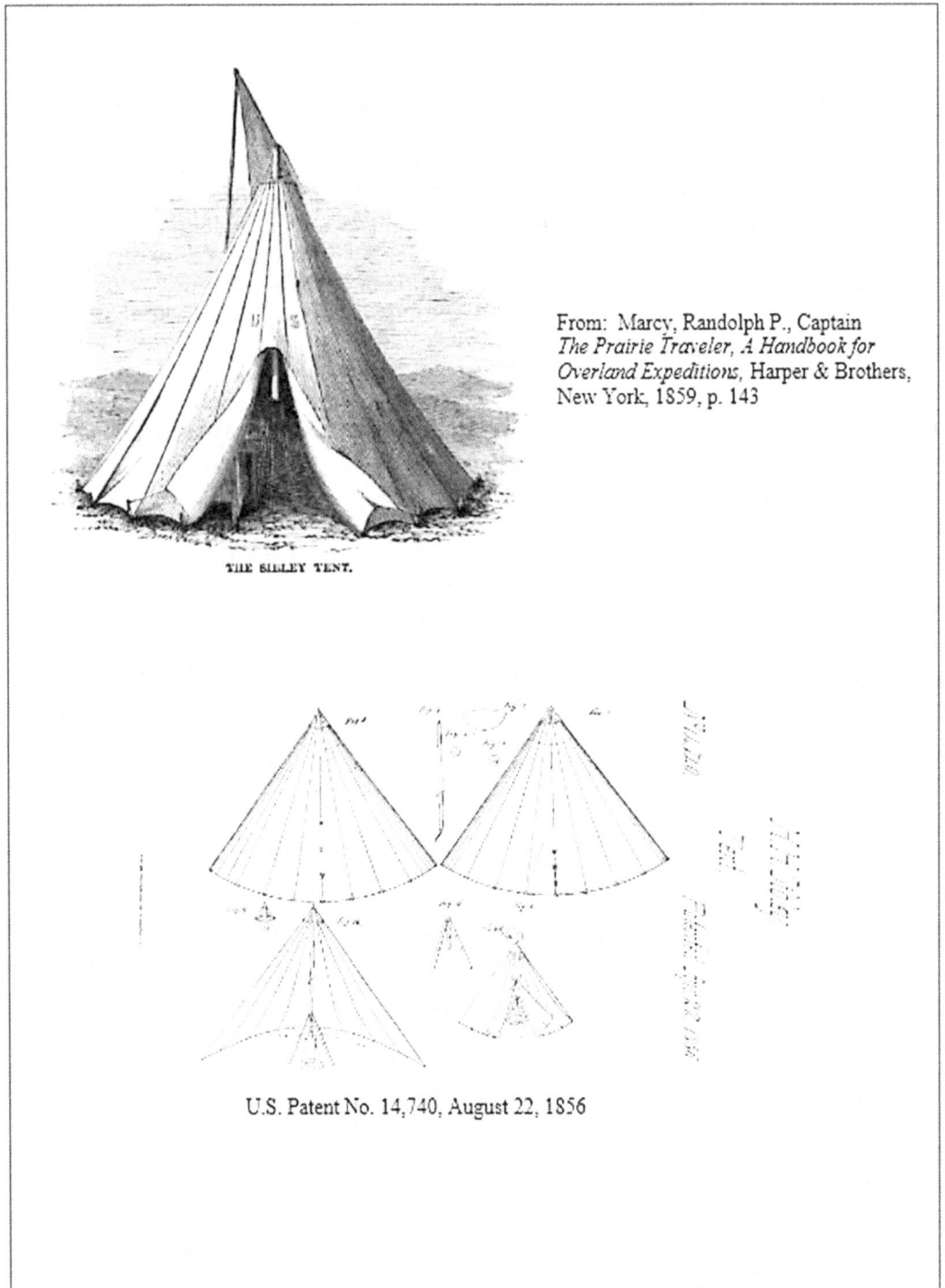

Sibley tent sketch and diagram of the Sibley tent (*The Prairie Traveler: A Handbook for Overland Expedition*, Captain Randolph P. Marcy, Harper & Brothers, New York, 1859).

field while providing for their greater comfort and health.[22] But for the immediate time being the War Department took no decisive action.

Utah War

Following his inauguration in March of 1857 President James Buchanan enraged the Latter-day Saints settlers in the Utah Territory by replacing Mormon leader and territorial governor Brigham Young with a new staff of officials. Young and his followers refused to recognize the new government and took up armed resistance. Already undersized and overextended with Indian wars and Bleeding Kansas,[23] the U.S. Army suddenly found itself burdened with an uprising in Utah. The Buchanan administration dispatched troops from Fort Leavenworth to the Utah Territory, with the expedition launched in mid–September. The advent of the Utah War provided the Sibley-Burns partnership represented by Grumble Jones with a lucrative opportunity. Jones capitalized on his past acquaintance with Secretary of War John Buchanan Floyd. Begrudgingly bowing to political pressure from above, the Quartermaster Department's General Jesup agreed to a partial adoption of the Sibley tent. On a trial basis, the War Department purchased 250 of the tents for deployment in the expedition into Utah. Shipping problems complicated matters. A significant number of tents failed to make it beyond Fort Laramie, Wyoming. Of those that arrived, not all met specifications. Some lacked the necessary parts for complete assembly. Out of the 250 tents ordered, only 150 made it to the field in an acceptable condition.

In Utah, the winter weather was as early as it was severe. Although a relatively bloodless campaign in regard to combat, casualties resulted from exposure to the elements with minus 23-degree temperatures by mid–October.[24] A November blizzard kept temperatures at minus double digits and produced deep snowdrifts. More than 130 transport animals froze to death in a thirty-six-hour period.[25] Many soldiers suffered from frostbite, and some perished. The expedition into Utah was the first large-scale test of the Sibley tent qualifications; those that arrived in the field performed admirably and miraculously. With the capacity to contain a campfire inside, the tents provided sufficient warmth to the soldiers they housed.

Quartermaster General Jesup conceded that in regard to the comfort and health of the soldiers in the field, the Sibley tent was "preferable to the one [currently] in use."[26] However, the weather event in Utah for that part of the year had been an anomaly. Jesup had complaints regarding the shipping and manufacturing flaws. Primarily, he questioned the tent's alleged weight and cost advantages. Also, even though Jones acted as Sibley's agent, Jesup continued to see conflict issues with military officers profiting indirectly through an enterprise with the army.

Europe

It is not exactly known when Jones went to Europe. He had his reasons for not wanting acquaintances and clients to know his activities. Transatlantic steamship passenger lists bear the names of hundreds of individuals with the name of "William Jones" traveling to and from England in the late 1850s. By October of 1857, Jones was receiving pressure from a business associate, George Patten, to go to Europe and make sales calls to the British and French governments. Jones had hoped to sell the patents for his saddle and the Sibley tent to the British and French. Recently, the alliance of England and France had concluded their costly engagement in the Crimean War. Neither nation was very interested in the mass purchase of any new military hardware. Jones's travel to Europe apparently did not turn out to be as lucrative as he had hoped. As a consolation, he was introduced to the wine industry while touring France. He would also cite his European travel on his resume in the coming years.

Return to America

After returning to the United States, Jones resumed his marketing campaign for the adoption of the Sibley tent by the U.S. Army Quartermaster Department. Demand for the tents depended on other variables. A negotiated settlement concluded the Utah War, and the U.S. Army restricted its activities to subjugating the Indians on the western frontier and with Bleeding Kansas. Those conflicts were limited engagements involving small expeditions, keeping demand for the tents nominal. On January 20, 1858, Jones pressured Quartermaster General Jesup for an answer on adoption. He wrote, "If you wish me to make the tents, I presume the officers of your corps stationed here and myself can arrange the particulars and conclude a bargain equitable to the Government and myself. If you wish them made at the arsenal, I will advise the superintendent in regard to their improvements contemplated and will allow the Government to make so many as may be required if I am paid ten dollars per tent for the use of the patent. I would prefer this arrangement and in the meantime, I would try to make arrangements for the sale of the patent to the Government."[27]

Grumble did not receive an immediate reply and went over the quartermaster general's head and corresponded directly with Secretary Floyd. Jones stated, "Not having heard of steps yet being taken for the adoption of the Sibley Tent from the Q.M. of the Army, I write this to urge upon your attention the necessity of speedy action in the matter, and to state my readiness to make arrangements equitable to the Government and my principal either for the manufacture of the tents or for a transfer of the patent right. I would also beg leave to avail myself of the present opportunity to reply to objections raised by the Quartermaster General to the tent."[28] Jones did not spare the hyperbole. He contended that the tent not only protected the soldiers from "the bitter cold of winter" and "the burning heat of summer" but also "against the drenching rains and sweeping tornadoes of [the] western prairies."[29] He further argued the tent's cost saving advantages through its accommodating more men per unit. The same benefit applied to the weight. Jones explained that the Sibley Tent, at 92 pounds, housed twenty soldiers compared to the current tent, which weighed 68½ pounds and sheltering only eight. Jones suggested that Secretary Floyd do the math before he arrived at any conclusions derived by General Jesup.[30] To make his point, Jones declared, "I have been a strong believer in eyesight versus theory since a Virginia farmer *proved* to me the grass I saw growing in Texas was not grass because it was south of the parallel of latitude 36 degrees."[31]

Jesup was annoyed that Jones had gone over his head by contacting the secretary of war. In spite of the tent's success in Utah and broad support from officers in the field, Jesup remained unsold on the tent's qualities to the point of adoption. Situations such as what had occurred in Utah were uncommon, and the army already had an inventory stockpile of conventional tents. Jesup provided statistical data challenging Jones's assertion that the tents sheltered as many as twenty soldiers. If those contentions were valid, 150 tents would have housed 3,000 soldiers. Reports from the assistant quartermaster on the Utah Expedition indicated that 150 tents sheltered about 2,000 troops. Doing the math, Jesup concluded that the actual capacity of the tents was thirteen to fourteen men, a third less than what Jones alleged.[32] In spite of its advantages in adding to the comfort and health of the men in the field, the tent offered no measurable economic or efficiency advantage, which was Jesup's priority.

The Sibley tent, however, continued to win additional praises from the Medical Corps. One surgeon declared that the tent had kept the sickness rolls "remarkably small" considering the elements to which the soldiers were exposed.[33] General Albert Sidney Johnston called the tent "the only tent suitable for a soldier's lodging."[34] Western mountain trapper, scout, and folk hero Jim Bridger described the tent "as comfortable as an Indian lodge."[35]

The spring of 1858 saw interest in the Sibley tent spread beyond the army. Tent and ship sail manufacturer John H. Landell wrote to Jones advising of a mass of gold prospectors congregating at Fort Leavenworth and Atchison, Kansas, insinuating that there was the possibility of a second gold rush. Landell suggested that Jones purchase advertising in Pratt and Hunt's *A Guide to the Gold Mines of Kansas*.[36] By the end of March in 1859 Jones had established an office in St. Louis to oversee the shipment of tents from Newark to destinations in the West. More U.S. Army officers purchased Sibley tents manufactured by the John H. Landell Company for their personal use. In expanding production to accommodate civilians, Landell modified the tents to a reduced size for smaller groups and individuals for use in sporting expeditions or other purposes. A salmon fishery in Canada also showed interest.[37] To further promote the product, Landell sent smaller-sized tents to the mayors of Boston and St. Paul.[38] The Sibley tent, however, attracted only modest appeal from civilians. The second gold rush in Kansas did not materialize. Unless officially adopted by the U.S. Army, the Sibley tent did not appear it would be as lucrative as had been hoped.

Ultimately, Colonel Charles Thomas, assistant quartermaster general, who also served as director of the Office of the Army Clothing and Equipage, made a commitment to Jones to acquire fifty more of the tents for the army. Thomas further proposed that in exchange for "use of the patent," the Quartermaster Department would produce fifty tents at its arsenal in Schuylkill County, Pennsylvania, and pay a royalty of $10 per manufactured tent. The War Department would then pay a royalty of $5 per tent for the next hundred. From that point on, the War Department would pay a royalty of $5 per tent and would produce a minimum of 200 per year.[39] Thomas reiterated that such an arrangement would benefit the patentee financially while relieving him of any responsibilities associated with production and shipping. Secretary of War John B. Floyd was the major influencing factor in this arrangement.

On Slavery

The 1860 Washington County census indicates Jones owned one slave. His personal finances did not seem dependent upon the preservation of the institution. Historians have suggested that revered Southern legends such as Robert E. Lee were at least partially opposed to slavery. Born at a time when the institution was a component of everyday life, William E. Jones was not among that group. His father's will called for the selling of designated slaves and the conditional retention of others. Jones took the extremist position, ardently defending the institution. He appears to have been a benevolent master who bore some emotional attachment to his slaves. From a prioritized economic standpoint, however, he assumed a highly objective position. While serving in the Old Army on the Texas frontier, Jones hired out his slaves to perform labor duties for other masters. In a letter to his mother-in-law Jones illustrated his attitude toward his servants: "Old Andy and Ellen are both down with diarrhea & I have some fears of being obliged to send them out of the county. They have the best of attendance & as good attention as the county will admit of. They have been useful in a pecuniary as well as in a comfortable way. I believe them to be perfectly honest & faithful & feel strongly attached to them. I shall be sorry to see them leave but will readily yield to necessity. I hope they may get well and be able to remain."[40]

While in London, Jones observed the European debate on the issue at a time when Bleeding Kansas and the Dred Scott decision had intensified emotions. Published in 1852, Harriet Beecher Stowe's *Uncle Tom's Cabin* was a best seller in England and further enflamed passions. The Anti-Slavery Society frequently convened at Exeter Hall, an auditorium-style building on the north side of the Strand in London. Grumble revealed his extremist views on slavery with a letter he drafted to the editor of a London newspaper. The letter is not dated and it remains a mystery as to when he wrote it. Although the opinionated article to which Jones responded is not known, one can derive its content from his remarks. The editorial apparently supported an antislavery platform and predicted that the abolitionist North would prevail in any potential armed conflict against the pro-slavery South. Jones suggested that the editor's remarks were so flagrant and so outrageous the reading audience might misinterpret the content as satire. He wrote the following: "Your logic is too much that of a fifteen c[s]hilling lawyer to allow us for a moment to suppose you're sincere, yet the English are a matter of fact people and would hardly expect an editor of a leading paper to indulge in pointless fiction."[41]

A series of treaties between the United States and Great Britain called for the suppression of the transatlantic slave trade by maintaining a fleet of gunships off the African coastlines. Both nations regarded slave smuggling as an act of piracy subject to the death penalty. The London newspaper had criticized the United States for its alleged relaxation of the international cooperative efforts. Jones protested that "America's relaxation of the guard of the African coast was not a commencement of bad faith in the treaty." He added: "You do not understand [the] prevalent Southern sentiment in regard to the slave trade. The introduction of African slaves would be in the highest degree detrimental to the pecuniary interest of present owners."[42] Southerners like Jones strongly supported the ban not for humanitarian or altruistic reasons but for economic ones. Slaves sold on the pirated market for between $150 and $200 in the "culture of cotton" competing with "legal" slaves valued at $1,200 to $1,500 could result in an "80 percent loss of their value."[43] The prohibition protected the value of slaveholding assets, a factor that drew criticism from the Fire Eaters.[44]

Jones decried the hypocrisy of private British and northern shipowners engaged in the profitable smuggling industry. Responding to the allegations of relaxed enforcement against the piracy, he wrote, "America felt no longer bound to a yearly sacrifice of money and life for the mere purpose of securing a monopoly in a detestable traffic." Jones suggested that England as a whole covertly benefitted economically from the slave piracy and that British politicians who criticized American policy were merely trying to divert attention from themselves. Jones saw the British attitude as the ends justifies the means, of which the primary object was money, "and if Exeter Hall gets its good share, piety will be as subservient as in the days of James II."[45] Expounding upon the folly of British policymakers, Jones used alliteration to make his point by claiming that for centuries the British yielded to "the importunities of fanatical fools miscalling themselves philanthropists."[46]

Jones asserted that the basic principles of economics required slaveholders to provide for the health and well-being of their servants. He wrote, "They have an abundance of good wholesome food and good clothing. If sick, the same physician who prescribes for the master also attends the slave. And in old age, they are well cared for."[47] Jones further commented: "No people under the sun have increased [advanced] so rapidly as slaves of the United States nor have anywhere so many been converted from Paganism to Christianity. On the contrary, in the Northern states the Africans have constantly decreased [receded] since their emancipation both there and in the West Indies [where] they are rapidly approaching the moral condition of the Hottentot. Those who treat them best are shamefully abused; those who treat them worst are lauded to the skies."[48]

Jones declared that slaves in the United States fared far better than the individuals in the English apprenticeship system and downtrodden Chinese laborers in the West Indies.[49] Comparing the plight of the American slaves to other downcast groups, he wrote, "How different among the poor white women of Europe! Even in Louisiana, ditching and the unwholesome work falls to the Irish."[50] Further arguing his point, Jones lashed out at the London editor: "If your readers are truly fond of the horrible, give them a few pages of Cobden's White Slaves of England."[51] It was a reference to John C. Cobden's *The White Slaves of England* (published in Auburn, New York, by Derby & Miller in 1853). The publication, compiled from official documents, described the British sectors of mining, manufacturing, sweatshops, high-seas kidnapping and impressments into the navy, Irish slavery, and coolie slavery. It expounded upon the harsh conditions afflicted on minorities, seamstresses, child laborers and other victims of the economic times.

Jones viewed the potential armed conflict between the abolitionist North and the slave-holding South as a resumption of the 1642–1651 English Civil War between the Parliamentarians under Oliver Cromwell and the Royalists favoring the monarchy of King Charles I. In contrasting the regions, Jones wrote, "New England was settled by ambitious canting Round Heads; the South by English gentlemen and French Huguenots, and both sections retain the characteristics of their ancestry." He signed his letter to the London paper as "American South." In a postscript, he added, "If a fight begins, we will not stop till we have captured the scalps of our ancestors in the Tower."[52]

Establishment of a Vineyard

In early 1859 Jones received an order of grapevines and fruit trees from the Vilmorin Andrieux & Company in Paris. That company had established ground-breaking research for the modern seed breeding industry and existed for more than two hundred years.[53] The items were shipped from Paris to Liverpool and then sent by the steamship *Asra* to

New York, where the Sibley tent manufacturer and business associate, John H. Landell of Newark, New Jersey, arranged to complete the shipment to Glade Spring.[54] With the assistance of local French and German immigrants, Jones established a vineyard on his Washington County estate.[55]

Sibley Tent Royalties

The U.S. War Department partially adopted the Sibley tent. Following the conclusion of the Civil War, a congressional inquiry determined that between March of 1858 and August of 1861 the Quartermaster's Department manufactured a total of 3,583 Sibley tents and paid a royalty to the patent owners of $5 each for 3,377 of them.[56] Under the terms of his written agreement with Major Sibley, Jones would have received more than $4,000 in commissions. The bulk of the proceeds, exceeding $14,000, should have been divided between Sibley and Burns. It is unclear as to whether Sibley and Burns received their due portions.

In December of 1859 Major Sibley discharged Jones as his agent and assumed direct control of the Sibley tent matters regarding the arrangement with the War Department.[57] With terms already established that the government would manufacture the tents on an as-needed basis and pay the Sibley-Burns partnership $5 per unit, no agent was necessary. On the sale of tents outside of government control to civilians, Sibley established his business relationship with John H. Landell.[58]

At the urging of Secretary Floyd, Sibley reemployed Jones less than a month after dismissing him. Captain William Wallace Burns protested the rehiring of Jones, whom he did not believe to be "honest or capable."[59] Further commenting, Burns wrote, "But Sibley's known carelessness about business matters will readily account for Jones having such control as the Sec. of War had the power to decide upon claims coming for payment in his department and as Maj. Sibley and myself and officer in the army, his decision would have the might of law between us."[60] Burns alleged that he had not received any royalties after Jones assumed the agency role. At the same time, Jones was authorized to draw funds. Having received only $400, tendered the past December, Burns felt entitled to "several thousand due."[61] By June of 1860 Burns had yet to receive additional royalties and implied he would consider legal action.

Sibley, who had the greater role in inventing the Sibley tent and thus had more say in the matter, did not seem as concerned about the royalties as did his partner, Burns. Sibley apparently prioritized his position as an army officer over that of an inventor. While Burns agonized over the nondistribution of royalties, Sibley was engaged in Indian campaigns in New Mexico.

Major Sibley's wife, Charlotte, on the other hand, did not share her husband's leniency toward Jones's handling of the matter. From her New York residence on October 27, 1860, she sent Jones correspondence as follows:

> New York
> October 27th, 1860
>
> Dear Sir
>
> I am this morning in receipt of yours of the 24th last containing a draft for $150 for the same please accept my thanks though I assure you I find it a very small sum just at this time particularly as Helen's school bill alone amounts to $441 from the fact of it not having been paid up last year—of

course, it keeps accumulating. I don't understand at all, why you do not hear from the major on this subject for in all his letters to me he seems to be confident that I shall be supplied by you with the necessary funds to carry me through the winter & encourages me accordingly—her bill for boarding will be due at the last of this month too, so under all these embarrassing circumstances please for your judgment what I had best do? I suppose it will be impossible for you to get a letter now from Major Sibley or at all events for any time, as I got a letter very recently from him stating he was then in the Wasatchie country and expected to attack the Indians two days after and did not know when I could hear from him as he was so remote from any opportunity to send a letter. This is truly the most embarrassing position I have ever experienced. My only fear is that I shall be obliged to remove my children from school if things do not change very soon for the better & this I know the Major will disapprove of decidedly. Well, for the present I must wait the results of affairs I suppose hoping at the same time things will wear a brighter aspect before long. Please accept my thanks, sir, for your kindness & believe me.

Yours respectfully,
C. Sibley

P.S. I enclose you the signed receipt in this.
C.S.[62]

The content of Charlotte Sibley's letter suggests that the Sibley end of the partnership was not receiving its entire anticipated share of the royalties either. By this time, however, events of far greater consequence were occurring. As feared by the southern extremists, Lincoln won the November election to the presidency. Southern states would react by proceeding toward secession. Southern officers would submit their resignations from the U.S. Army.

Jones continued in his role as a private contractor conducting business with the War Department. On the national scene, the debate over slavery versus abolition was gaining more momentum. The primary catalyst had taken place a year before, in October of 1859, resulting in political turmoil and providing Jones with a revised sense of purpose.

9

A Call to Arms

Tensions between abolitionists and the supporters of the institution of slavery had been escalating since the original settlement of the English colonies. Territorial acquisitions inflamed passions regarding the expansion of the institution versus its prohibition into those newly acquired regions. Legislative compromises and Supreme Court rulings only temporarily quelled the emotions on both sides. For the state of Virginia, matters reached a critical point on October 18, 1859, when abolitionist John Brown instigated his ill-fated raid on the federal arsenal at Harpers Ferry.

Although it failed, John Brown's insurrection left a profound political and emotional impact on Virginia. Violence associated with Bleeding Kansas had contaminated Virginia's sovereignty. Sectional patriotism and inflamed animosity toward the North replaced any faded sense of nationalism associated with Manifest Destiny. Suspicions and allegations arose that Brown had received financial and other support from factions within the new and rising Republican Party. Rumors floated that more of Brown's followers lurked in the nearby mountains ready to attack again.

While southerners regarded John Brown as an outlaw and a terrorist, they took note of the northern abolitionists who praised him as a folk hero and a martyr. Grumble was not an active participant in the events surrounding Harpers Ferry, but they marked a significant turning point in his life. For the time being, he remained engaged as a marketing agent for Major Henry Hopkins Sibley, overseeing the production and distribution of the Sibley tent. Privately, however, Jones and many southerners sharing his sentiments regarded John Brown's measure as the first effective shots of the American Civil War. The bombardment of Fort Sumter would not occur for another eighteen months. From Jones's perspective, Brown's insurrection was an unprovoked measure of northern aggression.

Desiring to assume a neutral position, the Buchanan administration was about to enter its final year. Congress was already at odds with the executive branch. The Republican Party, with its abolitionist platform, was gaining political momentum. On a similar scale, southern mistrust of the federal government in Washington was escalating.

Secretary of War John Buchanan Floyd was particularly alarmed by the events surrounding Harpers Ferry. His father had served as governor of Virginia during Nat Turner's Rebellion of 1831 in Southampton County, which resulted in the deaths of hundreds. In a political climate full of regional tensions, Floyd was a moderate. John Brown's raid, however, placed him at odds between his official duties to the nation and what he considered a moral obligation to look out for the security of his home state. Working with Colonel Robert E. Lee and Lieutenant James Ewell Brown Stuart, Floyd mapped out a successful strategy to end Brown's occupation of the arsenal within forty-eight hours.[1] He then supported the speedy trial and execution of John Brown in a futile attempt to mitigate the emotional effects.

Floyd's states' rights and pro-slavery sentiments marked his legacy at the War Department. Although opposed to secession, he took the position that to avoid disunion and conflict the federal government must guarantee the protection of slavery in its present form.[2] His outspoken sentiments and his actions drew suspicions and allegations that he authorized the stockpiling of southern arsenals with munitions and supplies in anticipation of their future capture by southern forces.[3] There is evidence to suggest that Grumble Jones worked with Secretary Floyd in some covert capacity to achieve part of that outcome.[4] Specific details regarding Jones's involvement, however, are not known.

During a speedy trial John Brown was convicted and sentenced to die by hanging on December 2 at Charles Town, Virginia (later West Virginia). Tensions were high, as the ordeal gained national attention and generated the fear of subsequent uprisings. Militia groups from Virginia marched to provide security and to bear witness. Supporters of the abolitionist movement also converged. Between Brown's conviction and execution, Floyd tendered the following correspondence to Virginia Governor Henry A. Wise:

> Washington, D.C.
> 26th Nov., 1859
>
> His Excellency, Gov. Wise
>
> Dear Sir
>
> This will be handed to you by Mr. Jones of the county of Washington who proposes to furnish the state with troops (and) equipage if her need requires it. The tent has been termed by the U.S. Army as the best here to fore constructed.
>
> Mr. Jones is a graduate of the West Point Academy & is in every way a gentleman of the highest character and intelligence and is entitled to the fullest confidence.
>
> I am Sir Very Respectfully
> Your Obedient Servant,
> John B. Floyd[5]

Although Secretary Floyd may have been promoting Jones's product, the Sibley tent, his communication to Governor Wise had other, underlying motives subject to interpretation. Floyd may have been taking measures to arm and supply Virginia in preparation for eventual secession and armed conflict against the federal government he was currently serving. From another perspective, he may have been suggesting that Virginia take measures to facilitate law and order in dealing with the immediate crisis. The pending execution of John Brown was attracting national attention, fueling fear and speculation of a rescue plot. Grumble Jones drafted an essay responding to the events at Harpers Ferry. He called upon Virginians to respond to the event by preparing for war implementing short and long-term objectives:

> The recent occurrences at Harpers Ferry render painfully evident Virginia's need of a thorough and permanent military defense. A decent respect from the opinions of mankind make ashamed of having been successfully resisted more than twenty-four hours by a mere handful of desperate men who were at last taken by Federal troops. Had the least disaffection existed in our midst, immense mischief might have resulted from that wicked and foolhardy enterprise. While shame for the past mantles our cheek, let us in prudence prepare for the threatening of a most ominous future. It is as much our duty to prepare for the coming changes as to defend our assailed rights and none but the obstinate blind can fail to see dangers great and most horrible in our future. Timid economists may urge

procrastination but it is sincerely hoped that Virginia will only hesitate as to the most feasible plan and when that is clearly ascertained that she will act promptly and with all her might.[6]

Jones called for a ten-to-fifteen-year plan of establishing an army for the defense of the state and the training of officers at the "Military Institute at Lexington."[7] Either he anticipated that armed conflict would be delayed or if it commenced it might progress at a moderate pace to last indefinitely. His recommendations drew only modest attention. However, there was a consensus that the state needed to prepare for potential armed conflict by forming citizen soldier organizations. Thus, one of the most significant results of Brown's insurrection was the escalation in the establishment of civilian militia companies in Virginia and the southern states. The immediate concern was the possibility that guerrilla-style warfare between Free Soilers and pro-slavery factions might escalate. Passions called for the formation of local volunteer militia units for the purpose of preventing or confronting future insurrections. It was a time for recruiting, training and arming on the contingency that war might come if and when the political climate deteriorated.

The newly formed militia companies assumed names identifying the geographic location of their home bases or the individual founders. Most were infantry units. Officers were elected. At their early stages, the groups appeared neither impressive nor intimidating. The recruits, having no prior military experience, donned civilian clothes and drilled with either outdated or simulated weapons. The ordeal provided participants with a mild sense of adventure, socialization, and the concept of performing their duty. The movement toward militarization appeased the moderates by rationalizing its objective to prevent or confront future uprisings similar to the John Brown insurrection. War was not necessarily inevitable. Conversely, there was a contention that by being well prepared a conflict might be avoided.

Washington Mounted Rifles

The Washington Mounted Rifles surfaced as one of the newly formed local militia companies. William E. Jones assumed the rank of captain and command. Second in command was Abingdon resident First Lieutenant William W. Blackford, a University of Virginia graduate and a civil engineer engaged with his father-in-law, former Virginia governor Wyndham Robertson, in a local plaster mining company.[8] Historical logic assumes that Jones organized and named the unit after his home county and his former Old Army regiment. Lieutenant Blackford contended otherwise.

Blackford alleged that he was the one who had "conceived the idea of raising a cavalry company" and that he contacted William E. Jones as a logical choice to lead the unit.[9] Blackford further wrote, "[Jones] agreed to it provided I would take all the trouble of getting it up. At that time I knew nothing of cavalry tactics and thought his instruction was absolutely necessary, though as it turned out, he took little interest in either raising or drilling the company, and the whole burden fell upon me. I canvassed for it and then called a meeting in Abingdon. Jones did not attend, but we elected him captain."[10] Regarding Jones's demeanor after the regimental organization Blackford wrote, "Most of the time our Captain was in Richmond trying to get higher rank, but failing in this he returned and took command of the company."[11] Blackford did concede, "After taking command, however, he made a very efficient officer."[12]

Blackford's allegations regarding Jones's role (or lack thereof) in the formation of the Washington Mounted Rifles can neither be confirmed nor refuted. Blackford survived the war, and Jones did not. In his postwar writings, Blackford frequently demonstrated contempt for Jones and prejudice against West Point graduates in general. He conveniently overlooked the fact that his idols, Robert E. Lee and J.E.B. Stuart, were products of that same institution.[13] Blackford established a recruiting station at the county courthouse in Abingdon. In contrast to infantry units, the cavalry had a distinct appeal to athletic young men seeking adventure.

Jones seemed willing to delegate administrative tasks to his executive officer when war was not imminent, and the enrollment numbers were nominal. During the early stages of the company's development, Jones diverted his attention elsewhere, engaged as a private contractor. By early 1861, Jones was campaigning as a lobbyist for the secessionist cause at the Virginia Convention. Until Virginia seceded from the Union, making war inevitable, Jones regarded the Washington Mounted Rifles as a secondary priority.

Reluctant Warrior

In the summer of 1860 William W. Blackford was manning the Washington Mounted Rifles recruiting station at the Washington County Courthouse when he recognized a former University of Virginia acquaintance, John Singleton Mosby. Residing in nearby Bristol, Virginia, Mosby had practiced law in the area since 1855 and was conducting a trial. Blackford solicited Mosby's enrollment in the militia cavalry company. Mosby declined out of mixed feelings toward secession and indifference toward the military in general.[14] Reinforcing his reluctance was the fact that he was the married father of two young children.

Mosby had grown up in Nelson County, Virginia, and attended the University of Virginia before being expelled in 1853 for shooting and wounding a fellow student in a boardinghouse brawl. An Albemarle County jury convicted him of a lesser charge of "unlawful shooting," and sentenced him to a year in jail.[15] While serving his sentence he was befriended by the prosecuting commonwealth's attorney, William J. Robertson, who introduced him to the study of law and loaned him the resources for it. After receiving the governor's pardon, Mosby continued his education at Robertson's law office until he received admission to the bar. While practicing law in the area, he married Pauline Clarke of Franklin, Kentucky. To be closer to her parents, he opened a law office in Bristol and conducted business at the courthouse in Abingdon.

1860 Presidential Election

On May 16 the new Republican Party nominated Abraham Lincoln in Chicago. Although the party's platform did not openly call for the outright abolition of slavery, it pursued its prohibition into newly acquired territories. Southern moderates supported Senator Stephen A. Douglas and his platform of popular sovereignty. Regarding the Republican Party as a hostile organization, southern extremists walked out on two Democratic conventions, reconvened with their own, and nominated John C. Breckinridge. Their self-destructive action divided the opposition against Lincoln, who won the 1860 presidential election without even being on the ballot in most southern states. South Carolina seceded on December 20, prompting more southern states to follow suit during the first month of the new year. Jones joined the radicals, adamantly calling for secession and preparation for armed conflict. Following the election he drafted a letter he intended to submit to the editor of a newspaper. Responding to the recent election of Lincoln and John Brown's insurrection at Harpers Ferry the previous year, Jones's essay was full of emotional expressions and metaphors:

> To longer persuade ourselves that anything human can avert the pending revolution is to shut our eyes to reason. The triumphant North is defiant in its threatened wrongs and persistent in refusal for any amends for past injury. Slanders, taunts, and insults have done their last work. The chains are forged for the South and the scoffing infidels in the Federal City boast of their readiness to close the external rivet. The iron is in the fire, and the brand of inferiority awaits us at once unless we evince the spirit of our ancestry. In tones of thunder a voice is heard throughout our land (that) the South is ready for her fate, but it is death rather than dishonor. Unity of action alone can save us from ruin. Can we as one man raise the defense of our liberties? Are we ready for a sacrifice of all prejudice and envy of persons of property and personal ease to follow and implicitly obey ability and merit? Our ancestors were skillful in the use of arms for they gained their daily subsistence thereby and a constant acquaintance with danger made them all brave. They followed the heroic and experienced Campbell and were more than a match for the best troops under the sun. But peace and safety presided at the birth of the present generation and have attended all its growth. If the deeds of the primitive days of our country are to be reenacted, it is time we should be making thorough preparation. With the old and the young drills and rifle practice should be the order of the day for we may have to meet the enemy abroad and at home. Yes, the very women should know the use of fire arms for the fiends of the North might deliver them up to more than a thousand deaths. Organize companies to scout combined action and practice with arms to make it effective. Let the rich give their means and all their time, and in a few months the devil in the shape of an abolitionist might well be defied.[16]

In addition to passionately expressing his rage against the North and the abolitionists, Jones's essay reflected pride in his ancestor who had fought under Colonel William Campbell against the Loyalists in the Battle of Kings Mountain during the American Revolution. Like many of the southerners, he compared the northern abolitionists to the British.

Following the presidential election, the enrollments in the Washington Mounted Rifles and other militia units expanded. More Virginians were gradually yielding to calls for states rights, security of the homeland, and preservation of the southern way. Moderates like Mosby, however, remained ambivalent. Yielding to regional sentiment to consider the matter, Mosby relented and attended a drill meeting of the Washington Mounted Rifles in January of 1861. He inquired of other recruits as to the identity of the "rugged individual dressed in blue jeans, a hickory shirt and an old homespun coat with soldier straps unevenly attached to the sleeves."[17] It was his first introduction to the militia commander. Although impressed, Mosby remained noncommittal and did not officially enroll.

By February 1, 1861, South Carolina, Mississippi, Florida, Alabama, Georgia, Louisiana, and Texas had seceded from the union. Their representatives convened at Montgomery, Alabama, formed the Confederate States of America, and selected Jefferson Davis as their president. For the time being Virginia remained with the union and sent representatives to the Washington Peace Conference of 1861. Ambivalent Virginians maintained a unionist position. Colonel Robert E. Lee was among the moderates facing the dilemma of having to choose allegiance between their state and their nation. Honoring the terms of his commission with the U.S. Army, Lee hoped that Virginia would remain with the union. Grumble Jones, on the other hand, was with the extremists who had already made up their minds. Jones's extremist advocacy toward secession reached the point that he pledged to renounce his allegiance to his home state if Virginia did not secede when he submitted the following correspondence:

> Richmond, VA
> Feb. the 16th, 1861
>
> Hon. Jeff. Davis
> President of the Confederacy
>
> Dear Sir: About four years ago, you accepted my resignation from the Mtd. Rifles and since that time, my home has been that of my nativity—Virginia. If she adheres to the North, I must change my nationality and therein I expect to be accompanied by a great preponderance of wealth and enterprise of the State. Such being my determination, when you are assailed if Virginia does not come to your assistance, my home must be in the South and my services in any capacity you choose will be at your command. My address is Glade Spring, VA.
>
> Very Respectfully
> Your Obt. Svt.
> W.E. Jones[18]

Near the time of Jones's commitment to the new Confederacy, the Virginia General Assembly called for an election of delegates to a secession convention. With sentiments divided among secessionists, unionists, and moderates, the delegates convened in Richmond to enter into a two-month-long debate. Within that time frame, the Washington Peace Conference would adjourn in failure leaving the state's ultimate fate up to the Virginia Conference in Richmond.

1861 Virginia Convention

Jones lobbied on behalf of the secessionists at the Virginia and Washington conventions. He drafted an essay blaming the actions of the federal government for inciting the secessionist cause. Warning the secessionists of the challenges that stood before them, he wrote:

> To my mind, it is clear that our present military organization is inadequate to the demand soon to be made and unless the greatest activity is displayed in differentiating military instruction and in collecting all the material of war, disaster awaits us when the conflict ensures. For the enemy at the North will at once adopt the organization of the United States Army, defective it is true in many respects, but nevertheless in vigorous hands capable of great exertion and competent to lead if well sustained to grand results. Against odds in numbers and an organization securing unity of action and secrecy of design we can oppose only the patriotism of our people acting in detail, but fighting for their homes. And just here we encounter one great trouble. Those most capable of directing feel most keenly our wrongs and are in the front ranks of our volunteers. The first fight Virginia would be like Sampson shorn of his hair, unless we take measures to change speedily our means of defense.[19]

Continuing his essay counseling for the preparation of war, Jones added:

> If our Legislature was serious (to consider it a joke is out of the question) when it proclaimed to the world that coercion of seceding states by the Federal Government would be an act of war on Virginia, no time should be lost in making ready for the worst. While our love of peace flatters the hope that the Border State Conventions now in Washington may succeed in adjusting our differences, yet should we act as if the war is certainly approaching until the contrary is perfectly certain.[20]

Demonstrating his contempt for the North, Jones added:

We have dared an ambitious people whose courage has never faltered when chances were fair for an accumulation of wealth. Though high honor actuates him not, yet a kind of material religion devotes him sincerely to his pursuits. To establish his dogma or obtain his end, he is unscrupulous. For the one, he has discarded the Bible and for the other the fundamental principles of honor. While we may hope God will punish the monster, let us recollect that in the battles of man in this world God usually rewards skill and courage or in other words, God takes care of those who take care of themselves.[21]

Jones returned to Washington County to assume a more active role as commander of the Washington Mounted Rifles. Uncertainty remained as to what course Virginia would take. Without committing to enrollment, Mosby attended and participated in a drill training session in early April of 1861 and encountered Captain William E. Jones for the second time. Mosby described Grumble as "a peculiar man, only a week or two short of his thirty-seventh birthday, eccentric, stubborn, irascible. He was warm-hearted but profane. Curse words gushing too fast to come from memory, rolled off his tongue like corn from a sheller. He cracked them harshly in the ears of his listeners, and picked neither time nor place to loose the flow."[22] Although impressed with Jones, Mosby remained uncommitted. Aligned with the unionists and moderates, Mosby supported candidate Stephen A. Douglas and the platform of popular sovereignty regarding slavery in new territories. He debated Fire Eater, William L. Yancey, and informed the *Bristol Courier* pro-secessionist editor, J. Austin Sperry, that he would support the union in the event of an armed conflict.[23]

Secession and War

In South Carolina the bombardment of Fort Sumter, concluded on April 14, formalized a declaration of war between the Union and the new Confederacy. Lincoln's administration dispatched an appeal for Virginia to provide 75,000 volunteers to squelch the uprising. The inevitability of war required Virginia to choose sides. On April 17, delegates at the Virginia Convention passed the Ordinance of Secession. They then appropriated $100,000 for the defense of the state, suspended federal authority, and authorized Governor John Letcher to communicate Virginia's desire to join the Confederate States of America.[24] The action was pending ratification by a popular vote that would overwhelmingly approve the matter a month later. The capital of the Confederacy would relocate from Montgomery, Alabama, to Richmond, Virginia.

As Blackford alleged, Jones traveled to Richmond to volunteer his services in the new military of the new government. Jones possessed excessive pride and ambition; two traits would conflict with one another. On April 28, while visiting the state capital, Jones corresponded with President Jefferson Davis. Following up on his previous pledge of allegiance to the new Confederacy, Jones wrote:

Richmond, VA

April 28, 1861

His Excellency, Jeff. Davis
President of the Confederate States

Sir

As early as the 16th of Feb. last, in a letter addressed to you, my services were pledged to the South in case Virginia adhered to the Union. Having escaped the misfortune on which my offer hinged, it may not be amiss to call your attention to the fact that I am ready and willing to enter the military service of our country for the present war. I graduated from West Point in 1848 and served in the Regt. of Mtd. Rifles until 1856. If in your opinion I can be useful, have instructions sent to me at Glade Spring, VA.

>Very Respectfully,
>Your Obt. Svt.
>W. E. Jones[25]

On the following day, Jones wrote to Virginia Governor John Letcher:

>Richmond, VA
>April 29, 1861
>
>His Excellency, Jno. Letcher
>Governor of Virginia
> Sir,
>
>If a regiment is to be formed in South Western Virginia, I claim that I am in some degree entitled to the command. I graduated at West Point in 1848 and served actively on the frontier eight years in the Rifle Regiment. If any reproach attaches to any part of my service, it is beyond my knowledge. Since retiring from service the opportunities afforded me in a business tour of Europe connected with [the] military have not I hope passed unimproved. When you were a candidate for the office you now hold my friends aided me in your work and those now seeking your favor in that section opposed you to the utmost. But if my qualifications do not entitle me to the office as a matter of course, I cannot expect it, and ought not to have it. My address is Glade Spring, Va.
>
>Very Respectfully
>Your Obedient Servant
>W.E. Jones[26]

Having requested the command of a full regiment, he anticipated a commission with the rank of colonel. After recommending his own appointment, Jones returned to Washington County to await a reply and assume full-time duties as commander of the Washington Mounted Rifles. The answer Jones received fell short of his expectations. On May 9, Major-General Robert E. Lee, commanding the Virginia Volunteers, dispatched the following:

>Headquarters, Virginia Forces,
>Richmond, Va., May 9, 1861
>
>Maj. William E. Jones, Virginia Volunteers, Abingdon, Va:
>
>Major: I have the honor to inform you that you have been appointed major in the Virginia volunteers. Under the authority of the governor, by his proclamation of the 3d instant, you are directed to call out and muster into the service of the State volunteer companies from the counties of Washington, Russell, Scott, and Lee, to rendezvous in Abingdon. The whole number of companies so called into service must not exceed two mounted companies and eight companies of infantry and riflemen. You will proceed to organize them into a regiment, and make arrangements for their instruction, subsistence, etc. You will report, as soon as possible, their number, condition of arms, etc., and hold them in readiness for prompt movement. To aid in their armament five hundred of the best arms for issue will be sent to you, which you will distribute at your discretion, taking the proper receipt, etc., from each captain for the security of the state.
>
>R.E. Lee, Major General, Commanding[27]

Lee had previously enhanced his reputation as a heroic southern figure by leading the Marine detachment that squelched John Brown's raid in 1859. At the time, however, his legacy was relatively nominal. He had incorrectly addressed Jones with the title of "major" of the local militia group and offered him that rank in an official capacity of the Virginia Volunteers. Contrary to Jones's expectations, command of the overall regiment was awarded to the Honorable Samuel Vance Fulkerson, judge of the Thirteenth Judicial District. Fulkerson was a thirty-eight-year-old veteran of the Mexican War who had served on the Virginia Military Institute Board of Visitors to earn the confidence of Thomas J. Jackson.[28] Had Jones accepted Lee's offer, he would have been second in command to Fulkerson. Comparing Fulkerson's qualifications to his own, Jones regarded his appointment to serve as Fulkerson's executive officer as an insult. Bypassing Lee, he wrote directly to Governor Jonathan Letcher:

> Abingdon, VA
>
> May the 11th, 1861
>
> His Excellency
> Jno. Letcher
> Gov. of Virginia
>
> Sir
>
> I am compelled to decline the commission of Major in the Virginia Volunteers for the following reasons. The company now commanded by me is composed of my best friends whom I cannot leave except to command them as colonel. The gentleman you selected from this county for a colonel is my inferior in military education and experience. To accept a post subordinate to him after having called your attention to these facts previous to his appointment would be acquiescence on my parting your decision of my unfitness for a high position. You could scarcely expect me to place such a seal on myself. From the time of Brown's raid I have commanded a volunteer company the success of which has been discouraged by the men you have honored. My services in Richmond last winter towards arming the state for present emergencies can be seen in the bill printed by the House of Delegates for that purpose. The Ordnance Bill was mainly my work. My efforts to secure rifled cannon and munitions generally you are aware of. Still, you want me a major to a briefless lawyer as colonel. In all due deference to your position, I beg leave to prefer the office I hold to the one you offer.
>
> Very Respectfully
> Your Obt. Servt.
> W. E. Jones[29]

Grumble chose to decline the rank of major, settle for that of captain, and to resume the subordinate position as commander of the Washington Mounted Rifles. Revealing his personal pride, he may have been impulsive in his evaluation of Fulkerson, who would ultimately command the local infantry companies mustered into the Confederate service as the Thirty-Seventh Virginia Infantry Regiment. The "briefless lawyer" Jones referred to would serve with distinction in Jackson's Shenandoah Valley Campaign before being killed in action at the Battle of Gaines Mill on June 27, 1862.

In early May of 1861, Virginia Governor John Letcher issued an official proclamation declaring Virginia in a state of war and stating that it was "a solemn duty of every citizen of this state to prepare for the impending conflict."[30] The appeal created an atmosphere of emotional patriotic excitement. Assuming that the actual fighting would be of a short duration, enthusiastic recruits signed up for three-month enlistments.[31] Even the moderate John Singleton Mosby joined in the fury. After making his final court appearance in Blountville, Tennessee, he closed his law practice and joined the unit commanded by William E. Jones.[32]

Grumble's return to Washington County from Richmond brought drastic changes to the training conditions within the Washington Mounted Rifles. Recruits who regarded the preparation for war with a sense of glory and adventure received a dose of reality from their company commander. On the morning after Mosby joined, Grumble drilled the Washington Mounted Rifles and another company from Marion with hard lessons on the life of a soldier. Mosby recalled, "Captain Jones had strict ideas of discipline, which he enforced, but he took good care of his horses as well as his men. There was a horse inspection every morning, and the man who was not well groomed got a scolding mixed with some cursing by Captain Jones."[33]

Drill sessions under Jones were long, strenuous, and tedious. Raw recruits had to learn the standing position of a soldier while grasping the reins of their mounts. The simple exercise of mounting could last an entire day. Demanding perfection, Grumble Jones was the master of the Trooper's Manual.[34] Private Mosby, who had no prior military training and a 125-pound frail body, drew the wrath of Jones for his shortcomings. In spite of the hazing, Mosby revered the captain. During the evenings, Mosby visited Jones in his quarters to hear accounts of his experiences at West Point and the Old Army. The future partisan leader later attributed much of his success to the knowledge he gained from his conversations with Captain Jones.[35]

Several of Grumble's Washington County acquaintances joined the mounted company. His cousin and fellow Texas traveler Thomas Benjamin Estill Edmondson enrolled as a sergeant and instructed Private Mosby on his first picket duty.[36] Also among the enlistees was Dr. William Logan Dunn, the brother of Grumble's deceased wife.[37] Without regard to his profession as a physician, Dunn enrolled as a private in the company with the full intention of serving as a soldier. Like Mosby, he intended to forgo the privileges of his professional background, a status that would change during the war.

The Washington Mounted Rifles enlistment rolls expanded, rendering the courthouse grounds at Abingdon an inadequate facility as a military training post. Captain Jones saw an opportunity to utilize the dormitory facilities at his nearby first alma mater, Emory and Henry College. With a mass exodus of applicants, students, and faculty to recruiting stations, the institution faced a financial predicament and political pressure to contribute to the new cause. Jones approached the board of trustees and requested the conversion of the campus into a training base. His cousin Robert Buchanan Edmondson, serving on the board, was the only member who voted to approve. All other members voted to reject it.[38] (The college campus would ultimately be converted into a Confederate convalescent hospital.)[39] With access to Emory and Henry College denied, the Washington Mounted Rifles and other cavalry companies established a new training camp on the grounds of Martha Washington College in Abingdon.

Soon after Virginia seceded, Governor Letcher ordered all military organizations to converge on Richmond to join with units from other Southern states in the formation of the new Provisional Army of the Confederacy. Colonel Fulkerson's infantry would take rail transportation to Richmond. With other units coming from far more distant places throughout the South, ample time was allowed to travel at a more leisurely pace. Jones and his cavalry company would conduct a mounted march to the capital in a journey that would take up to three weeks. On May 30, Captain Jones and his 102 troops forming the Washington Mounted Rifles embarked on a mounted expedition to Richmond. Donning civilian clothes and carrying personal side arms, members of the company departed Abingdon in a parade-like atmosphere. After advancing ten miles the company divided into squads that encamped in and around Glade Spring, and on the following morning they rendezvoused at Old Glade Presbyterian Church. There is a sense of irony that Grumble's first place of pause on his way to join the war effort would be his final resting place as a result of it. The march resumed and lasted eighteen days before the company arrived at the south banks of the James River in Richmond.

Volunteer forces representing all states of the new Confederacy converged by rail, horse, and on foot, with a constant flow upon the Richmond Fairgrounds. Preparations for the arrival of President Jefferson Davis made for a highly festive atmosphere.

Jones marched his mounted troops on the cobblestone streets toward the capital to the ovation of civilian bystanders and infantry soldiers along the sidewalks. In spite of their filthy appearance after a 300-mile march in dilapidated civilian dress, the orderly and disciplined troopers managed their horses and conducted themselves like well-seasoned veterans. Compared and contrasted with other units outfitted with stylish uniforms obtained through wealthy connections, Jones's troops were the best-looking company arriving in Richmond. It was a credit to their commander and tactical instructor, Captain William E. Jones.[40]

Their brief time in Richmond allowed individual soldiers to reconnect with acquaintances serving in other units. Mosby met up with a political orator, Tom Rives, who, familiar with Mosby's educational and legal background, suggested that he qualified as an officer and encouraged him to appeal to Governor Letcher for a commission. Mosby declined for the reason he had no prior military experience and would serve better "under such an able commander as Jones."[41]

The Washington Mounted Rifles marched eighteen miles north to a new training camp at Ashland in Hanover County, where the intense training resumed. Jones made requisitions for uniforms and weapons. Breech-loading Sharp's carbines partially filed the order of rifles. All troops received uniforms, but the delivery "almost caused a mutiny."[42] Made of fabric spun on the looms of the state penitentiary in Richmond by convicts, the uniforms were "ugly, ill-fit, dingy, coarse, and drab-colored." All but Mosby and his close companion, Fountain Beattie, scornfully rejected the "penitentiary cloth" garments and piled them up in front of Captain Jones's tent. They then proceeded to a Richmond retailer to purchase "neater" but "less durable outfits."[43]

Other developments were in progress. General Beauregard, the hero of Fort Sumter, commanded a 20,000-man Confederate force in Prince William County. General Joseph Eggleston Johnston commanded an additional 11,000 Confederate soldiers at Harpers Ferry. Union general Irvin McDowell devised a strategy to engage Beauregard at Manassas Junction. Simultaneously, Union general Robert Patterson would lead an attack on Johnston at Harpers Ferry.

At Harpers Ferry, several companies of Virginia mounted militia were forming a cavalry regiment under the command of Lieutenant Colonel J.E.B. Stuart. Stuart was second in command to Colonel Thomas Jonathan Jackson, who had arrived with a group of his cadets from the Virginia Military Institute.[44] Johnston withdrew to Winchester to defend the Manassas Gap Railroad between Manassas Junction and Strasburg. Leading the cavalry units, Stuart established a base nine miles north of Winchester at Bunker Hill in Berkeley County.[45]

Captain William E. Jones marched his company to Winchester and joined Johnston's forces, which when reinforced by the collective units coming from Richmond swelled to about 65,000 men. Johnston detached Jones's Washington Mounted Rifles and dispatched the company nine miles to join eleven other prewar cavalry militia units under Stuart. The first major battle in the Eastern Theater was about to commence.

10

First Virginia Cavalry

A reorganization divided the prewar militia company formerly known as the Washington Mounted Rifles and assembled the troops into two separate companies. Jones, Mosby, and about half of the members were mustered in as Second Company D. The others, William Logan Dunn among them, formed Company L. Both new companies and others from different regions throughout the state merged into the First Virginia Cavalry under the command of Colonel James Ewell Brown "Jeb" Stuart.

Colonel J.E.B. Stuart was an 1854 graduate of West Point. His service with the U.S. Mounted Rifles and in the First U.S. Cavalry included Texas, the Kansas Border Disturbances, and the Utah Expedition. His tenure in the Old Army overlapped the final eighteen months served by Grumble Jones. Although never assigned to the same garrisons, the two Virginians served at outposts situated along the Rio Grande within a hundred miles from each other.[1] Thus, going back to their days in the Old Army, the two officers were acquainted and shared some degree of familiarity.

Like Jones, Stuart was born to an agrarian upper-middle-class family in rural western Virginia. The Patrick County native held academic ties to Emory and Henry College. Also like Jones, Start had graduated from West Point ranked in the upper quarter of his class and chose the U.S. Mounted Rifles, regarded as the least desirable branch by their peers.[2] Notwithstanding their similarities, their nine-year divergence in age, Stuart being the younger, and personalities placed them at odds. Stuart was a charismatic and clairvoyant extrovert who basked in the attention he frequently brought upon himself. Jones, the antithesis of Stuart personality-wise, was known to be cantankerous and withdrawn.

Contrasting life experiences partially explain the personality differences between the two men. Jones's career in the Old Army had been an unfulfilling tenure marked by despair, isolation, and personal tragedy. Stuart's career in the antebellum U.S.Army entailed glory, adventure, and even romance. Stuart engaged in an amorous relationship with the daughter of his commanding officer, Colonel Phillip St. George Cooke. Their blissful marriage would persist in spite of family divisions regarding allegiance during the Civil War (his father-in-law served as a Union general).

Stuart's Old Army record justified his glorified reputation. He had demonstrated courage under fire in the Kansas Territory when he led a charge into three hundred Cheyenne warriors in a line of battle. In the fight, he saved the life of a comrade and received a close-range gunshot wound to the chest that miraculously glanced off a bone without causing serious injury.[3] While on a leave of absence, he volunteered and served as adjutant to Lieutenant Colonel Robert E. Lee in leading the squad of U.S. Marines against John Brown's insurrection at Harpers Ferry. Stuart's notable performance in the identification and capture of John Brown further enhanced his recognition as a hero for the Southern cause. Endowed with the charming charisma of a dashing cavalier, Stuart drew the admiration and reverence of most of the men under his command, including many serving under Jones. Lieutenant William W. Blackford met Stuart at Bunker Hill for the first time and they became lifelong friends.[4] Likewise, Stuart's aura greatly impressed Private John Singleton Mosby.

Jones's new commission with the rank of captain and command of Second Company D of the First Virginia Cavalry provided him with a lateral move only. From the original formation of the Washington Mounted Rifles up to that moment, he had enjoyed independent command, during which time he proficiently led his company from raw recruits to the level of a crack outfit (except for experience under fire).[5] Jones also felt that he had a proven record based on his class standing at West Point and his eight years of service in the Old Army. With the reorganization, he would have to answer to the younger Stuart, who held the higher rank. Jones took an instant dislike to Stuart and vowed that he "would take no orders from that young whippersnapper."[6] Stuart equally disliked Jones.

First Bull Run (AKA First Manassas)

In the First Battle of Bull Run, or First Manassas, which concluded on July 21, 1861, Jones experienced major combat operations for the first time and showed striking characteristics of a hardened veteran. The ten months that followed would try his patience. The engagement revealed a conspicuous lack of preparation on the part of the Union side. Like their Southern counterparts, the Federal forces stationed in and around Washington, D.C., were a collection of various Northern state volunteer militia units whose members anticipated a short conflict. By mid–July, masses of three-month enrollments were about to expire, forcing a political urgency to take action.[7] General Irvin McDowell, leading the main Federal force, intended to drive Beauregard's troops from the vital railroad junction at Manassas while General Robert Patterson and his collective Pennsylvania militias would obstruct potential Confederate reinforcements from the Shenandoah Valley.

Although Stuart's First Virginia Cavalry was modestly engaged, its contribution may have won the battle.[8] Deploying a strategy of nighttime maneuvers and deception to harass the Union outposts, Stuart disguised his nominally sized regiment to appear as an entire army, and Patterson declined to engage.[9] Stuart successfully screened CSA General Joseph E. Johnston's eastward movement to reinforce Beauregard.

At dawn on July 17 Captain Jones and his Second Company D were positioned in a field and holding the bridles to their horses waiting for further orders. A distant Union battery fired an artillery shell that landed and burst near Jones. Responding calmly and stoically, he slowly ordered his men to mount up and led them out of range. He acted as if "in no hurry than if he had been bossing a gang of field hands."[10] His composed demeanor under fire was reassuring to his recruits who were experiencing hostile fire for the first time. Amazingly, it was Jones's first exposure to hostile artillery fire as well.[11]

Dividing his command, Stuart dispatched part of his regiment to join Beauregard at Manassas Junction and held the other to keep Patterson at bay. Stuart issued Jones six Colt revolvers to distribute to selected men, who included Private Mosby, for a reconnaissance mission. Jones explained to those who did not receive the handguns that the six selected would be doing the most dangerous work.[12] By this early stage of the war, Jones realized Private Mosby's potential.

The mission proved to be uneventful. After returning, Jones and his squad joined the command of Major Robert Swan, a Marylander and distinguished veteran of the Mexican War who sided with the Confederacy even though his home state remained with the Union.[13] The battle turned into a Southern rout of the Federals, who fled toward Washington, D.C. Jones pleaded for authority to join in the pursuit, but Major Swan's orders were not to engage. Jones protested: "Major Swan, you can't be too bold in pursuing a flying enemy." Swan directed Jones's company to remain in reserve and eventually to go back to the rear. An enraged Jones responded with a flow of profanity that justified, "if never before, the sobriquet of Grumble."[14] Jones later dispatched Mosby, as his interim adjutant, to the upper command with a recommendation for Swan's arrest.[15] Years after the war, Mosby would comment, "Swan did not get a man or a horse scratched. He did life insurance business that day. Instead of Swan supporting the battery, the battery supported Swan."[16]

The shocked and humiliated Union forces retreated across the Potomac to Washington, D.C., to regroup. Stuart's First Virginia Cavalry established an outpost at Centerville south of the Potomac in Fairfax County alongside Jackson's infantry brigade. "Not the least conspicuous of its figures was Captain Grumble Jones. He was delighted to be in the open, surrounded only by men, where he could swear until the trees rocked with his rhythm. His blasphemous flow was noticeably unstinted these days."[17] Only partially satisfied with the victory, Jones was frustrated by his company's lack of participation. Many from the ranks questioned the failure to pursue their defeated enemy. Private George Cary Eggleston would write decades later about the "presidential stupidity that feared *aggression* might anger a people with whom we were at war."[18] Rumors spread that as victors they would launch a counteroffensive, but the orders never arrived. The euphoria of victory gradually faded into a protracted period of inactivity and boredom.

The Southerners had won the battle due to superior leadership. The reputations of Joseph Eggleston Johnston, P.G.T. Beauregard, Thomas Jackson, and Jeb Stuart were just starting to emerge. Out of those recognized heroes of the First Battle of Bull Run, Thomas Jonathan Jackson was the one whose fame would reach the highest level, he earning the moniker "Stonewall."

Jones and Jackson rekindled their friendship once again. An ardent and devout Scots-Irish Presbyterian, Jackson abstained from alcohol and tobacco and "never touched a card."[19] His warrior life was a paradox in that he chose not to fight on Sundays. As the antithesis of Grumble, he refrained from the use of profanity. There was an anecdote that during the lull in the fighting following First Bull Run, Jackson was "terribly provoked" by the apparent shortcomings of a soldier in the ranks but at a loss for words to address the matter. Grumble intervened and suggested, "General, let me cuss him for you."[20]

Mosby frequently visited Grumble's quarters to hear his assessment of the situation. Jones spoke freely of how the victory was less than overwhelming and an opportunity had been squandered. Influenced by Jones's sentiments, Mosby would later write, "It is paradoxical but true that the Confederate cause was lost at [First] Bull Run."[21]

The First Virginia Cavalry occupied Centerville until the spring of 1862. Although within Virginia, Fairfax County was more a buffer zone than one of uncontested occupancy. Federal scouts and patrols established outposts within the same region. Troops in the First Virginia Cavalry took turns and served as mounted pickets on patrols in groups of three. Jones experienced a close encounter while leading Private Mosby and Private Benjamin J. Haden on a three-man night patrol near Annandale. The trio rode into a Federal ambush and received a volley of fire that killed Grumble's horse.[22] Mosby wrote to his wife about it: "We were perfectly helpless, as it was dark and they were concealed in the bushes." He continued, "The best of it was that the Yankees shot three of their own men—thought they were ours."[23]

Private Hadden recalled Jones's measures to salvage his patented saddle: "His saddle was one he prized very highly, being supplied with a screw, by which it could be adjusted to fit any horse, and not wishing to leave it, he hallowed out at the top of his voice 'Forward on the right,' and left their skirmishers. And although he hadn't a man, they left, and he came in with his saddle on his back."[24] Although the U.S. Army did not officially adopt the Jones saddle, Grumble valued it over the competition.

In late August of 1861, Jones assigned Mosby to a three-man scouting party manning an outpost near Lewinsville. Jones informed the reconnoiter force that no friendly forces were beyond their outposts and to fire at anything coming from the enemy's direction. After completing his turn at watch duty, Mosby slept, only to be alerted by the current watchman that a mounted squad was approaching. Mosby fired his carbine while mounted on his horse. Although this horse had faced nominal combat conditions, it had not experienced fire from its rider. The startled mount galloped uncontrollably through the thickets before it tumbled and rolled, knocking Mosby unconscious. Mosby woke up in the bed of a private home to the sounds of Jones shouting profanity at members of his cavalry company. Contrary to his orders, they had been patrolling east of the outpost and were the missed targets of Mosby's friendly fire.[25]

On September 11 Stuart led Jones's Second Company D, another company from the First Virginia, and 305 members of the Thirteenth Virginia Infantry on a night patrol advance from Falls Church. In a small skirmish Stuart's combined force won an overwhelming victory at the cost of no casualties. The incident at Lewinsville capped off a series of successes by Stuart going back to the Bull Run Campaign.

Three days after Lewinsville, General Joseph E. Johnston made an official recommendation to President Davis through the Confederate War Department to establish the cavalry as a separate division and to promote Colonel Stuart to brigadier general as its commander.[26] Supporting his proposal, Johnston communicated, "Our numbers in cavalry are by no means in due proportion to our infantry and artillery, yet without cavalry in proper proportion, victory is comparatively barren of results; [with cavalry,] defeat is less prejudicial; retreat is usually safe."[27]

Command of the First Virginia Cavalry

Promoting Stuart created a vacancy in the command of the First Virginia Cavalry. In his same report, Johnston wrote, "I, therefore, recommend that Capt. William E. Jones, who now commands the strongest troop in the regiment, and one which is not surpassed in discipline or spirit by any in the army, be made colonel. He is a graduate of West Point, served for several years in the Mounted Rifles, and is skillful, brave, and zealous in a very high degree. It is enough to say that he is worthy to succeed J.E.B. Stuart."[28] On September 28 Jones received his official appointment to the rank of colonel and command of the First Virginia Cavalry.[29]

The promotion did little to mitigate Jones's animosity toward Stuart. Stuart biographer Major Henry B. McClellan would write, "In the fall of 1861, soon after Jones had been promoted and assigned to the command of the cavalry regiment of which Stuart had been colonel, there was an unfortunate interruption of their personal relations, after which kind cooperation between two such positive natures was hardly possible. On several occasions General Stuart recorded his high estimate of Jones's abilities and with equal clearness, [so was] his protest against the assignment of promotion of Jones under *his* command."[30]

Without directly acknowledging it, Johnston recognized Jones's call for the arrest of Major Robert Swan, who had refused to authorize pursuit of the retreating enemy at First Bull Run. Taking a diplomatic approach, Johnston called for Swan's reassignment to a Maryland regiment.[31]

Soon after receiving his appointment, Jones made an immediate impression on at least one member of the rank and file. Decades after the Civil War, former Private George Cary Eggleston turned author and published *Southern Soldier Stories*, reflecting on his service with the First Virginia Cavalry. In his 1898 publication, Eggleston recalled an anecdote regarding his regiment's new commander:

> It is a fixed principle of military law that no person is allowed to sell supplies within the lines of a camp without permission of the commandant.
>
> It is also a fixed principle of military law that he must sell only at the prices approved by the commandant.
>
> I shall never forget how I first learned of these military rules. We were at Camp Onward, and old Jones had just become our colonel.
>
> One day, a farmer came to camp with a heavily laden wagon. It was in the summer of 1861 when food in Northern Virginia was abundant, and when our money was as good as anybodys.
>
> Our farmer had among his supplies dressed turkeys, suckling pigs, lamb, mutton, watermelons, cantaloupes, string beans, lima beans, green peas, and in brief, almost all those things that we read about on the bill of fare of a swagger hotel kept on the "American Plan."
>
> He had butter also, and lard. He had eggplants and pumpkins, and a great many other things.
>
> We were a rather hungry lot, and more strongly inclined to buy from him.
>
> But this farmer had evidently made up his mind to get comfortably rich off that single wagon load of provisions. Two years later, we should not have been surprised at his prices, but at that time, we were appalled. Nevertheless, some of us were buying with recklessness of men who do not know at what hour a bullet may draw a red line below all accounts.
>
> Just then old Jones came out with his yellow coat and his pot hat, looking more like a farmer than the wagon man did. Speaking through his nose, and with that extraordinary deliberation which always made his conversation a caricature of human speech, he asked: "What are you chargin for butter?" And soon on through the list, receiving a reply to each query, and carefully noting in his thoroughly organized mind.
>
> Then he turned to one of the men and said: "Send the regimental commissary to me."
>
> When the commissary came, he said to him: "Take these supplies and distribute them equitably among the different messes according to their numbers."
>
> By this time, the farmer had become alarmed. He said: "Who's going to pay for all this?"
>
> "I am," said old Jones. "In my own way."
>
> "Well, hold on," said the farmer.
>
> "No, I reckon we won't hold on," said old Jones.
>
> "But I'll send for the colonel of the regiment," said the farmer.
>
> Then old Jones replied with a relish: "I am the colonel of this regiment. And I have ordered these food supplies distributed to the men in the messes. The regimental commissary will obey my order. And as soon as your wagon is emptied, you will get out of this camp in a considerable of hurry"—perhaps he used a shorter word than "considerable"—"or I'll hang you in front of headquarters.

There's no court of appeals in this camp. Now, git!" as the last of the supplies were taken out of the wagon by the regimental commissary.

We were quite a little bit sorry that the poor farmer should lose his entire load. And we sympathized with old Jones's remark as he walked away.

"I'll teach these thieves that they can't loot a camp that I'm a runnin."[32]

With his strong agricultural background, Jones knew the value of farm commodities. While serving in the quartermaster department of the Old Army on the Texas frontier, he had grown contemptuous of private contractors who took financial advantage of soldiers.

During the lull following First Bull Run, Fairfax County was a contested region with neither side claiming its exclusive occupation. Most of the confrontations were small skirmishes between patrols on probing missions. The South anticipated a major Union invasion from the District of the Potomac base around Washington, D.C. The cavalry's mission was to observe the Federal maneuvers and determine whether they were full advances, probing actions, or diversions.

In his *Southern Soldier Stories* published in 1898, Eggleston reflected on another incident in the fall of 1861. From a distant observation post near Centerville, General Stuart spied a Union column of mounted troops, infantry, and artillery, the combination bearing the characteristics of a major offensive. Stuart communicated to Grumble, "Colonel, I wish you'd take a dozen or twenty men, get into the rear of that force, and find out how much it means." Jones selected a detail with Captain Charles Irving of Company G as his executive officer. Under the cover of brush, they rode to the rear of the column and noted the absence of a wagon supply train. The observation confirmed that the Union force was serving as a mere diversion and not a full-fledged advance.

Jones turned to Captain Irving and remarked, "The whole thing's an egg-shell, isn't it?" Captain Irving responded, "Yes, an egg-shell easily crushed." After pausing for a few moments, Jones said in his nasal drawl, "I wish I could communicate with Stuart. I'd break through that line and save the trouble of a ride around." Irving responded, "Why not break through anyhow, Colonel? Don't you think Stuart would understand? I've never found him slow in getting to windward of things." Jones replied, "Well, if you say so, Captain, I guess we'll do it. It'll save the horses anyhow." Jones then ordered the remaining squad to draw sabers and charge.

From the opposite side of the column Stuart observed Jones's action and ordered the main body of cavalry to charge as well. The Union column converged "like a telescope" into a defensive position, allowing the Jones squad to pass through unmolested. The encounter was bloodless; there were no casualties on either side. Psychologically, Jones's maneuvers demonstrated Southern superiority in cavalry tactics.

In his memoirs Mosby wrote, "Jones was always kind to me."[33] Their relationship was demonstrated in January of 1862 when Colonel Jones endorsed Private Mosby's request for a six-day furlough to visit his sick family in Nelson County. Jones wrote, "Private Mosby left home a lawyer in good practice as a private in the ranks and has always been ready in the most active and dangerous duty, rendering brilliant service. If any is entitled to consideration, surely he is. His application is most cordially and urgently recommended."[34] Upon Mosby's return, Jones summoned the private to his quarters to announce his promotion unceremoniously to first lieutenant. Jones also offered Mosby the position as his full-time adjutant, which he accepted.[35]

State of the Confederacy

February of 1862 marked the first anniversary of the Confederacy. Government and political authorities in Richmond commemorated the event with formal receptions and military review drills. The festivities conveniently masked the fact that there was far more cause for despair and alarm than for celebration.

Notwithstanding the military successes in northern Virginia, the strategic situation in the overall Confederacy had deteriorated. In Tennessee, Forts Henry and Donelson had fallen to a previously unknown Union general named Ulysses S. Grant. In his first campaign of the Civil War, General Robert E. Lee failed at Cheat Mountain in the region that would later become West Virginia.[36] In North Carolina, Union forces under General Ambrose P. Burnside captured Roanoke Island and New Bern to seal off the southern Atlantic coastline. The economic front was also a calamity. Runaway inflation was destroying the Confederate monetary system, and its paper currency was becoming worthless.

In the Eastern Theater, the previous Southern victories at First Bull Run and Lewinsville had diminished in significance. It was overwhelmingly apparent that the Confederacy was facing an enemy with superior numbers and resources. It was also imminent that General McClellan was reorganizing the armies at Washington and preparing for a major offensive on Richmond. The uncertainty was when it would take place and from which direction it would come.

Recognizing the futility of occupying Fairfax County, and even the lines of Manassas in Prince William County, General Johnston ordered his forces to evacuate those regions and consolidate closer toward Richmond. In March of 1862, the infantry regiments withdrew, leaving the cavalry to screen their movement and to burn the storage facilities containing vast stockpiles of supplies they could not take with them. Implementing the scorched-earth policy to deprive the Federals of their supplies was demoralizing to the Southern troops, who questioned the wisdom of such an order. Captain William W. Blackford wrote "Here, right within our lines and close to the camps, quantities of grain were stored on the farms and we, all the winter, were drawing from Richmond and the interior; and it all to be burned to keep it out of the hands of the enemy. This may have been West Point science, but to ordinary mortals, it looked not wise. At Manassas there were huge piles of bacon burned, as high as a house. The flames did have a curious look, a sort of yellow and blue mixed, and the smell of fried bacon was wafted for twenty miles."[37]

Bringing up the rear guard was Colonel William E. Jones's First Virginia Cavalry, whose scouts observed a pursuing Federal column. Jones reported the matter to Stuart, who wired General Johnston in Richmond. Johnston then directed Stuart to determine whether the Federal column was McClellan's full invasion force or a feint. Volunteering to serve as a scout and investigate, Mosby rode out and returned the following day to report his observations. Mosby's findings revealed that the pursuing Federal column in Northern Virginia was a mere diversion. More important, the primary force of McClellan's Division of the Potomac was boarding transport ships at Washington and heading for Fortress Monroe in southeastern Virginia to conduct an amphibious landing and march up the Virginia Peninsula toward Richmond. After relaying Mosby's discovery to Johnston in Richmond, Stuart dispatched Jones's First Virginia Cavalry to disperse the Federal column at Warrenton Junction. Johnston sent General John Bankhead Magruder's brigade to Yorktown to form a front line of defense and obstruct McClellan's anticipated advance.

Stuart was elated with Mosby for his successful intelligence-gathering mission. It was the first official recognition of Mosby's scouting abilities and launched his career as a legendary partisan ranger.[38] Although Mosby was Grumble's adjutant, Stuart was becoming more aware of his talents.

Bringing up the rear in the evacuation, Jones and his First Virginia Cavalry were bivouacked under the cover of a pine forest when they encountered a severe March sleet storm. They were over-stocked with the provisions they had salvaged after having destroyed massive quantities of them. Captain William W. Blackford described high spirits among the troops, who prepared for an evening of feasting in spite of the severe conditions. The night of indulgence turned into a mild calamity. Blackford elaborated: "But a disaster was hanging over us, literally. When the heat rose through the heavy masses of sleet suspended in the treetops, its icy bonds were loosed and all of a sudden down it came like an avalanche, upsetting the coffee pots and frying pans and extinguishing every spark of fire in camp. Again and again, they were rekindled until absolutely worn out; we had to eat our food as it was, half cooked, and get what sleep we could stretched out on the cold snow."[39] On the following morning, the cavalry rear guard resumed its march.

Tensions with Stuart

Jones earned praise from Jeb Stuart for maintaining "utmost vigilance" in his reconnaissance and observations of Federal movements in Fauquier County.[40] Grumble, however, was in a state of discontent regarding his situation, particularly with serving under Stuart's command. While camped at Bealeton approximately eleven miles south of Warrenton Junction, he submitted correspondence to the CSA secretary of war, George W. Randolph, as follows:

Bealeton, VA   March 24, 1862

Hon. Geo. W. Randolph
Secretary of War Confederate States
Richmond, VA

Dear Sir,

I am sorry to trouble your difficult position with my private claims but Gov. Letcher for reasons not known to me has placed me the junior of my Old Army companions. I have worked hard in this war and before you are aware, I urged on a measure that would greatly have bettered our condition. If you can judge me worthy of promotion and can assign me duty in S.W.V. I shall feel very grateful.

Very Respectful Your Obt. Svt.,
W.E. Jones[41]

Grumble referred to Stuart as the "junior" of his "Old Army companions" and clarified three objectives. He desired separation from Stuart, transfer to Southwest Virginia ("S.W.V."), and promotion to brigadier general. Secretary Randolph took no action on the matter. In the course of the war, however, Jones would acquire all three objectives, though not necessarily in the order or under the circumstances he desired.

Back in Richmond, Johnston's infantry units arrived from northern Virginia followed by Stuart's cavalry. Although appearing highly unpolished by donning worn and dirty uniforms, Stuart's mounted division was greeted in a parade-like atmosphere by citizens who lined Franklin and Broad streets. This ragged army had won a significant victory the year before at Bull Run and had held the enemy at bay for the duration.

Jones and his First Virginia Cavalry formed the last group of defenders to arrive in Richmond, on April 16. In anticipation thereof, the *Richmond Dispatch* reported, "This regiment will pass through this city this morning en route to another field of action. The First Virginia has been in the war for the last twelve months and has seen very hard service."[42]

Implementing Johnston's strategy, the Confederate infantry and cavalry units marched eastward to establish defensive positions around Yorktown. It seemed imminent that McClellan's forces of as many as 100,000 were going to invade and that a significant engagement for the sake of their capital would ensue. For the first time in the war, Richmond was at risk.

Grumble's First Political Setback

In spite of the dire circumstances, the Confederate government had already enacted "one of the most stupid laws ever passed by a legislative body."[43] Earlier in the year the Confederate congress passed legislation granting the soldiers in the field the right to cast ballots to determine which officers would serve as their commanders. The intent was to "introduce an element of democracy into the army."[44] Addressing the matter, Stuart wrote to his wife, Flora: "Congress has thoroughly disgraced itself by the passage of the most outrageous abortion of a bill ever heard of for the reorganization of our forces."[45]

William Blackford described the reorganization of the army as one of near anarchy: "All discipline was suspended, and every company became the theatre of the arts of the demagogue. I remember passing a company in camp one morning when the roll was being called; not a man turned out but answered their names from their beds, the orderly-sergeant walking up and down the tents to awake those still sleeping. One telling point in favor of a candidate was that he would not *expose his men,* as they called it; namely, would not make them fight."[46]

Aside from acknowledging that Grumble was an efficient officer, Blackford held contempt for Jones. Blackford contended that "the ugly and surly Colonel Jones" negatively contrasted with the "handsome, dashing Lieutenant Colonel [Fitzhugh] Lee," his election opponent.[47] Blackford alleged that Jones, who realized through his unpopularity that he "would stand no chance of election," promised to take the men out of harm's way and back to Southwest Virginia in exchange for their vote.[48]

Blackford and other critics were correct in that officers won elections based on popularity rather than their military abilities. It was therefore of little surprise that the stern disciplinarian Colonel William E. "Grumble" Jones was voted out of command in favor of Fitzhugh Lee. Embittered and suspicious of improprieties regarding the election, Jones drafted a letter of resignation that he neither signed nor submitted, nor did he discard it. The content was as follows:

April the 28th, 1862

Hon. G.W. Randolph, Sec. of War

Sir,

On the 22nd inst., Brig. Gen'l J.E.B. Stuart held an election for the company officers in six companies of the 1st VA Cavalry in four of which companies were less than half of the minimum numbers prescribed by law. After this, he held an election for field officers by the company officers of these six companies and those of the remaining company officers of the regiment. This election at war with equity and in violation of law denies me of my command, but could I feel the proceeding free of malice, I would willingly abide by the result. However, being fully aware of my inability to refrain the mischief by the stupidity and wickedness of my superior officer, I hereby relieve the Department of all embarrassment by tendering my resignation to take effect on the 30th inst. I am fully satisfied that the officers of but two companies out of ten had any right to vote in this latter election and that in law and equity, my office is not yet vacated. However, my presence in the regiment could not now repair the mischief already done, and I tender my resignation of the 1st VA Cavalry to offer my services when and where in your opinion they can be useful.[49]

Jones reconsidered the idea of going on record accusing his commanding officer, Stuart, of "wickedness" or "stupidity." He also refrained from public accusations that ineligible voters participated. However, he harbored suspicions that Stuart had covertly campaigned for his ouster for Fitz Lee. Unable to alter the outcome, Jones tendered his official resignation with a more objective tone.

In a twist of irony, Blackford, who supported the ouster of Jones, lost his election as the captain of Second Company D. Blackford, however, received the benefit of Stuart's intervention, which resulted in his receipt of another commission, as captain in the Department of Engineers.

Lieutenant John Singleton Mosby was particularly distressed by the election results that replaced Colonel Jones with the appointment of Fitzhugh Lee to command the First Virginia Cavalry. Mosby's dislike for Fitzhugh Lee festered for the duration of the war and may have originated with Lee's lack of a sense of humor.[50] Having practiced law in Washington County, Mosby had developed the knack to emulate the drawl of his local clients, legal adversaries, and court officials. On the day following the reorganization, Mosby approached Fitzhugh Lee and announced with an exaggerated Southwest Virginia dialect, "Colonel, the horn has blowed for dress parade." An enraged Fitzhugh Lee retorted, "Sir, if I ever again hear you call that bugle a horn, I will put you under arrest!"[51]

Mosby resigned his commission the day after Colonel Jones tendered his, and Colonel Fitz Lee accepted it. Mosby justified his resignation to his wife in a letter to her: "The president has commissioned me for the war, but I would not be adjutant of a colonel against his wishes or if I were not his first choice."[52] Cognizant of Mosby's scouting mission revealing McClellan's plan, General Stuart intervened on Mosby's behalf. Stuart reassigned Mosby, sans commission for the moment, to his staff as a scout, marking another step advancing Mosby's career as a legendary partisan ranger.[53]

The administrative change terminated the professional relationship between Jones and Mosby, who was so influenced by the contrasting and clashing personalities of Jones and Stuart. From this point on, Stuart would assume the new role as Mosby's mentor. In his postwar writings, Mosby would contribute to Stuart's legacy. Although he would acknowledge Jones favorably, Mosby had only observed a glimpse of his former commander in their time together.

Stuart took no measures to salvage the career of Grumble Jones, who suddenly stood without a commission. Jones returned to Richmond to await a new opportunity. It was a time for reflecting and brooding.

11

Seventh Virginia Cavalry

Between April 22 and July 20 of 1862, Colonel William Edmondson Jones stood without a commission. Although the Confederate high command deemed the CSA congressional action a major debacle, the damage had already been done and, for the time being, could not be reversed. Jones and other highly qualified Confederate officers would have to stand idly by while the war progressed.

As a West Point graduate himself, President Jefferson Davis was not about to let an asset like Jones go to waste. Jones patiently remained in Richmond to await a new assignment. In June of 1862 that prospect surfaced with the death of the legendary Turner Ashby. The unique timing of this major setback resulted in the need for the Confederate War Department to fill two positions. The first was the command of the recently formed Ashby Cavalry Brigade. The second was the command of Ashby's famed Seventh Virginia Cavalry Regiment within the Ashby Cavalry Brigade.

Following a Legend

The Confederate high command regarded Colonel W.E. Jones as the most logical choice to replace the recently deceased Turner Ashby and lead the Seventh Virginia Cavalry. Grumble's challenge was to convince the men serving in the regiment that he was worthy of their allegiance. He found himself in the uncomfortable position of having to follow a highly revered legend. To fully understand the task at hand, one must look at the prodigy Jones replaced.

Turner Ashby was a self-trained warrior with a fighting reputation on the mythological level. His distant ancestors had fled to Virginia during the Cromwellian period of the English Civil War and the execution of Charles I. Later generations settled in Fauquier County, discovered the natural pass through the Blue Ridge Mountains into the Shenandoah Valley, and named it Ashby Gap. A line of paternal predecessors served in the French and Indian War, the American Revolution, and the War of 1812. Born in 1828 to a family of wealth and prestige, Turner grew up in a privileged environment at Rose Bank, a large plantation in Fauquier County. Fatherless at age six, he received his education from his widowed mother and private tutors. By the time he reached adulthood, the family fortune was exhausted. Ashby regained that affluence by engaging in a successful mercantile enterprise and then acquired another Fauquier County estate that he named Wolf's Craig. He enjoyed the social standing of his aristocratic heritage and the merit of self-acquired wealth, factors that designated him a Virginia elitist. In the luxury of his economically secure lifestyle, he developed his athleticism and horsemanship while following a personal code of honor. Physically, Turner Ashby fit with the romantic stereotype of the dashing and cavalier cavalry commander. D.S. Freeman wrote, "To romantic Southerners, he looked as if he stepped out of a Waverley novel."[1]

Ashby's military experience commenced in 1859 when he organized a local mounted militia company named the Fauquier County Rangers. As captain and commander, he marched his unit to Harpers Ferry to serve in a reserve capacity during the aftermath of John Brown's insurrection, staying on to provide security during Brown's trial and execution.

As a slaveholder allegedly opposed to disunion, Ashby reversed his sentiments with John Brown's uprising.[2] Immediately following the Virginia Ordinance of Secession, he departed Wolfe's Craig, never to return.[3] He marched his cavalry company to Harpers Ferry to join a unit of VMI cadets absorbed into a brigade under the command of Thomas Jonathan Jackson.

On June 17, 1861, the Seventh Virginia Cavalry was organized with the appointment of Turner Ashby to lieutenant colonel and second in command under Colonel Angus W. McDonald, Sr. The Fauquier Mounted Rangers were mustered into the regiment as a company led by Turner's younger brother, Captain Richard Ashby. Sixty-two-year-old Colonel McDonald delegated most of his authority to Ashby, and for all practical purposes Ashby commanded the Seventh Virginia Cavalry, which was unofficially known as "Ashby's Cavalry."

Turner Ashby's warrior career reached an emotional turning point ten days after his regiment was formed. He ordered his younger brother, Captain Ashby, to lead a small detachment and apprehend a Northern sympathizer at Kelley's Island on the Potomac River. Responding to the sound of gunfire, Turner then led a squad to investigate and found Richard suffering from multiple gunshot and bayonet stab wounds. They transported the wounded captain to a field hospital, where he languished and died seven days later. The regiment buried him with honors at Indian Mound Cemetery near Romney.[4] Turner vowed vengeance and inspired the members of the Seventh Virginia Cavalry to follow.[5] The incident achieved mystical appeal and generated a universal desire among recruits to join the Seventh Virginia Cavalry.

In July of 1861 Ashby's Seventh Virginia Cavalry joined with Colonel J.E.B. Stuart to screen the movements of Joseph E. Johnston's and P.G.T. Beauregard's forces before the Battle of First Bull Run. Serving as a deception, their actions determined the outcome for the South. To their disappointment, however, they saw no combat in the actual battle.

Following a minor engagement at Bolivar Heights, Ashby recognized the need, and applied to the War Department, for the authority to establish a company of mounted artillery. As a result, Preston Chew, an eighteen-year-old VMI graduate, organized what was to be later known as "Chew's Battery," that would serve with distinction throughout the war.[6] Future brigade commanders Grumble Jones and Tom Rosser would both benefit from Ashby's insight to acquire this unit.

Ashby's participation in Jackson's Shenandoah Valley Campaign, considered to be "one of the most brilliant operations in military history," further enhanced his legacy and elevated his fighting reputation.[7] In the spring of 1862 the Division of the Potomac commander, George B. McClellan, devised a three-pronged invasion plan to capture Richmond. Leading the largest force, McClellan would conduct an amphibious landing and march toward Richmond on the Virginia Peninsula. The Army of the Rappahannock commander, Irvin McDowell, would advance on Richmond from the north at Fredericksburg. The Department of the Shenandoah commander, Nathaniel P. Banks, would proceed toward Richmond from the northwest by way of Winchester. Stonewall Jackson countered with a brilliant strategy to disrupt McClellan's plan with diversions. Although heavily outnumbered, Jackson's and Ashby's maneuvers would ultimately deny McClellan reinforcements from the northwest and doom his offensive to failure.

On March 23 Jackson opened his Valley Campaign with the Battle of Kernstown, just south of Winchester. The inexperienced Ashby committed contrasting blunders and heroics. On a reconnaissance mission, he grossly underestimated the enemy strengths and reported his findings to Jackson, who then ordered an infantry advance. Consequently, Jackson's outnumbered forces were routed. Ashby's cavalry then counterattacked with hit-and-run tactics, allowing the Stonewall Brigade to conduct an orderly withdrawal. Deceived by Ashby's audacity, the Federal forces overestimated the strength of their enemy, remained on the defensive, and refrained from a pursuit. Jackson's forces retreated southward, regrouped, and on May 8 defeated the Union forces at McDowell in Highland County, Virginia. Screened by Ashby's cavalry, Jackson's infantry then marched northward toward Strasburg. On May 23, while Ashby's cavalry feigned an attack, Jackson maneuvered his "foot cavalry" across Massanutten Mountain, merged with Ewell's Corps, and converged on Front Royal with a combined force to rout the undermanned Federals.

Jackson pursued Major General Banks's retreating forces when Ashby's lack of discipline resulted in a setback. The companies of the Seventh Cavalry disintegrated into a plundering mob that looted discarded equipment, supplies, and horses. The pause saved the Union forces from annihilation and allowed them to cross the Potomac. Jackson was enraged by the lost opportunity for an overwhelming victory.[8] However, Union forces had been expelled from the valley, and Jackson further enhanced his reputation. Ashby's contribution resulted in his promotion to brigadier general. He assumed command of the newly organized Ashby Cavalry Brigade consisting of the recently enlarged Seventh Virginia Cavalry, the Second Virginia Cavalry, the Sixth Virginia Cavalry, and Chew's Horse Artillery. The Confederate high command hoped that with his promotion, the resourceful Turner Ashby would be less exposed.[9] Conversely, he would live only another ten days.[10]

Turmoil over Jackson's exploits evolved into an obsession within Lincoln's administration, which failed to recognize they were a diversion.[11] Aborting McClellan's strategy to take Richmond, the U.S. War Department shifted all priorities to trapping Jackson and dispatched three Federal armies, numbering 50,000, into the Shenandoah Valley. On June 2 a Union cavalry force routed the rear guard of the heavily outnumbered Confederates below Woodstock. Ashby rallied the stragglers, hastily organized a defense, and burned a bridge spanning the North Fork of the Shenandoah River, stalling the Federal pursuit for several days. On the morning of June 6 Ashby observed a Federal force threatening Jackson's right flank. Ashby led three infantry regiments on an all-out assault that the Federals repulsed. Rallying his disorganized troops, he led a second charge and met a volley of fire that shot his horse out from under him. Undaunted, Ashby resumed leading his charge on foot and received a musket shot through his heart, which killed him instantly.

Ashby's final rear guard action and ultimate sacrifice allowed Jackson's infantry to regroup. Two days later, Jackson's forces routed the Federals at Cross Keys. A day later, Jackson concluded his Valley Campaign with a decisive victory at Port Republic, expelling all Union armies from the Virginia Shenandoah Valley.

Ashby's body was retrieved from the battlefield and transported to Port Republic to lie in state. As one of many bereaved mourners, Jackson departed to join Lee and the Army of Northern Virginia for the Seven Days' Battles. Ten months later, Jackson reported on his Valley Campaign. In tribute to Ashby, he wrote, "As a partisan officer, I never knew his superior; his daring was proverbial, his powers of endurance almost incredible; his tone of character heroic, and his sagacity almost intuitive in divining the purposes and movements of the enemy."[12]

Ashby's remains were transported by rail to Charlottesville for burial in a cemetery connected to the University of Virginia. Although he had never attended the school, the authorities reasoned that "the students of the institution would have before them the high ideals and standards of duty and patriotism for which Ashby stood."[13] Following the conclusion of the Civil War, the remains of Turner Ashby, his brother, Richard, and hundreds of other Confederate dead were reinterred at Winchester.[14]

Ashby's death placed the Confederate high command in the dilemma of having to fill two vacancies. First and foremost, the hierarchy needed to appoint a replacement brigadier general to command the recently organized and unofficially named "Ashby's Brigade." Second, a new commander needed to be appointed to lead the original ten companies forming Ashby's original Seventh Virginia Cavalry. In Richmond, Colonel William E. Jones, formerly of the First Virginia Cavalry, and Colonel Beverly Robertson, formerly of the Fourth Virginia Cavalry, were on standby. Both officers were West Pointers and Virginians; they had each been assured of a command once an opportunity arose.[15] General Jackson was not consulted and the Army of Northern Virginia commander, Robert E. Lee, was not sold on any of the potential candidates to replace Ashby. Following a brief period of interim replacements, President Jefferson Davis selected Colonel Beverly H. Robertson for promotion to brigadier general and command of the Ashby Brigade of cavalry.

Robertson had graduated 26th in his class of 1849 at West Point and served in the Old Army until the outbreak of the Civil War. Commissioned in the Confederate service, he rose to the rank of colonel, commanding the Fourth Virginia Cavalry. Like Jones, Robertson was a stern disciplinarian and a drillmaster who subjected his troops to arduous training. Also like Jones, he lost his command with a defeat in the April field elections. Robertson bore a non-distinct reputation as a better organizer than a fighter.

Jones, inactive since the April elections and having been promised a position, was the most logical choice to command Ashby's original Seventh Virginia Cavalry within the Ashby Brigade. President Davis appointed Colonel William E. Jones to the command of the regiment on July 20, 1862.[16]

Command of the Seventh Regiment Virginia Cavalry

Assuming command of the Seventh Virginia Cavalry, Jones had to confront geographic prejudices, social barriers and preconceived unfavorable assumptions regarding his leadership. As a Southwest Virginian, he characterized the Scots-Irish agrarian labor class, in stark contrast to the aristocratic gentleman farmer status held by the late Turner Ashby. Southwest Virginia was not represented in the regiment of companies mostly organized in the northern valley counties of Fauquier, Rockingham, Shenandoah, Warren, and Loudon. In physical appearance, Jones was the antithesis of their late commander, who had been described as dashing, flamboyant, and charismatic. Conversely, Grumble Jones possessed a character of modesty that "almost amounted to bashfulness."[17] Neither his horsemanship nor his martial presence made a significant impression. He wore a faded featherless slouch hat that concealed a receding hairline.[18] His modest appearance often deceived others into mistaking him for a tramp, a farmer, or a private in the ranks.

The men of the Seventh Virginia Cavalry labeled both their new brigade and regimental commanders with the stigma of conventionalism. Robertson and Jones were "West Pointers" who held reputations as stern disciplinarians. Robertson, in particular, was rumored to be far more interested in subjecting his men to repetitive, tedious, and arduous drilling than to fighting itself, an assumption unjustifiably also attached to Jones. Under Ashby, the members of the Seventh Virginia Cavalry had grown accustomed to a less disciplined, more adventurous, and more romanticized version of warfare. Most of their experience up to this time had involved fighting in limited engagements deploying guerrilla warfare tactics in regions close to their homes. Unfamiliar with Jones's background and their conception reinforced by stereotyped prejudices, many assumed he had previously commanded an infantry unit. It was not surprising that Grumble's appointment almost caused a mutiny.[19] With sentiments that their new regimental commander should come from within their ranks, members held an unofficial election. The Confederate War Department completely disregarded their actions.

In his first order of business, Grumble requisitioned the delivery of grindstones into camp and ordered the men to sharpen the blades on their sabers. Feeling that swords were weapons of ancient times and obsolete against firearms, the men questioned the purpose of the ordeal. Jones answered, "If you want to cut, have something you can cut with; if you want to bruise, better get a club."[20] Reacting to their new commander's remarks, some of the men complained, "We will not have much need for either saber or club. We'll never get close enough to the Yankees to use either while commanded by this old *infantry* colonel."[21] Within a short time the men would find out to the contrary. Future engagements would involve close-in, hand-to-hand combat.

Jones assumed command of the Seventh Virginia Cavalry following the conclusions of Jackson's Shenandoah Valley Campaign and Lee's Seven Days' Battles, which collectively defeated McClellan's Peninsular Campaign. The Lincoln administration relieved McClellan and appointed General John Pope commander of the newly organized U.S. Army of Virginia. Pope issued a proclamation declaring a strategic change from a defensive to an offensive posture. After repositioning the Federal armies, he ordered a series of maneuvers targeting the Virginia Central Railroad that served as Richmond's western lifeline.

Anticipating Pope's strategy, Lee ordered Jackson's forces to secure the Gordonsville Loop of the Virginia-Tennessee Railroad and A.P. Hill's Corps to occupy the region. Pending the arrival of Hill's infantry corps, Jackson directed General Beverly Robertson to proceed toward the area and hold off any Union advances. The Ashby Brigade of regiments, including Jones's Seventh Virginia Cavalry, established an outpost in Orange County at Gordonsville.

Orange Courthouse

In his service to the Army of Northern Virginia, Grumble Jones would distinguish himself in the well-known Battle of Brandy Station and the Gettysburg Campaign. With that said, the comparatively smaller and by far lesser-known cavalry action at Orange Courthouse on August 2, 1862, may have been the most important combat engagement of his career. On that day, Colonel William E. Jones led a 200-man mounted detachment from his Seventh Virginia Cavalry on a reconnaissance mission toward the picket outpost along the Rapidan River. The mission appeared routine, with no combat anticipated. Lieutenant John Blue of the Sixth Virginia Cavalry volunteered to join the mission to get away from the boredom of camp and to "take a look at the country."[22] Blue further commented that he "didn't expect to see any Yankees and was not looking for a job."[23] Many members of the detachment, however, were growing restless.

By chance, 1,200 to 1,500 U.S. Cavalry troops consisting of companies from the Fifth New York, the First Vermont, the First Maryland and a Michigan regiment had forded the Rapidan River and occupied the town of Orange Courthouse. Unaware of the development, Colonel Jones's detachment marched to an elevation approximately a mile southwest of the town. Riding at the head of the column, Jones, from a distance, observed a mounted Union soldier ride behind the railroad depot. Jones halted his column and announced, "Boys, that Yankee is not alone; there may be a troop down there."[24] He could only speculate as to the strength of the enemy force and had to weigh his options. He could ascertain a better estimate of the enemy numbers while sending for reinforcements. On the other hand, he could engage his detachment against an enemy of unknown strength in a possible suicide mission but one that would exploit the element of surprise.

The troops accompanying Jones could not view the streets of Orange Courthouse proper and assumed their new commander was being overly cautious. One of the men ridiculed in low tones, "He is getting ready to run from one Yankee. We will not get a chance to dull our sabers today."[25] The critics had no idea as to the extent in which they had underestimated Jones. Contrary to the mocking prediction, Jones announced, "We will go down and see what is there." A moment later, he shouted for the command to ride forward. The column marched toward Orange Courthouse in an "oblique direction" with Jones ostensibly leading the way.[26] As the column passed the south end of the Orange & Alexandria Railroad Depot, Jones shouted in a clear and distinct voice to draw sabers and charge.[27] All 200 mounted troopers drew sabers and joined their commander in a forward gallop, shouting the famed "Rebel yell."[28]

A full-blown cavalry engagement ensued in the center of the town. Building structures restricted the fighting to extremely close contact between the mounted enemy forces. Members of the Seventh Virginia Cavalry realized the value of their sabers, particularly after their six-shot revolvers spent all of their rounds. Well trained in the use and sharpening of sabers, Jones's forces held a distinct advantage and fought with superiority.[29] As in many of his future combat engagements, Jones was in the midst of the fight.

Major Thomas A. Marshall led a squadron toward the railroad depot, where they were encircled by a Federal flanking party. Most managed to escape, but Marshall found himself alone and out of ammunition. Engaged in a saber duel, he received a blow to the head from a mounted Union trooper and fell disoriented from his horse. The Union trooper was about to finish off Marshall when Jones galloped in and shot the Union trooper with his revolver, killing him. More Federal troops were rapidly closing in, and Marshal was too disabled to be rescued. Jones had to leave him behind. Marshall survived his wounds but was captured.[30]

Fighting opposition to their right and rear, Jones's heavily outnumbered scouting party was forced to give ground.[31] Building structures obstructed their potential escape routes to a single alley limiting passage to one horse and rider at a time. Most managed to escape, with Jones bringing up the rear. Lieutenant John Blue wrote, "Col. Jones was at one time separated from his men and entirely surrounded by Yankees, but being an expert swordsman, he carved his way back to his men and escaped with a slight cut across his hand."[32]

Jones and his troops regrouped on a forested knoll about two hundred yards southwest of the town. Anticipating a Federal counterattack, he dispatched a courier nine miles to the Gordonsville outpost to request reinforcements. The Sixth Virginia Cavalry under Colonel Thomas Flournoy arrived, and the combined forces resumed the offensive. By that time, however, the Union forces were voluntarily withdrawing and falling back toward the Rapidan River. Jones and Flournoy pursued, but upon observing the Federals cross the river at Raccoon Ford they gave up the chase.

Jones estimated the enemy losses at eleven killed, thirty wounded, and twelve missing. He reported his losses at ten wounded and forty missing for a total of fifty casualties.[33] From a tactical standpoint, Jones could declare victory. In spite of being grossly outnumbered, he had taken the offensive. Although repulsed, he resumed the assault with the help of the Sixth Virginia and expelled the enemy from Orange Courthouse. However, with fifty casualties out of 200 engaged against similar losses to an enemy of 1,200 to 1,500, most military analysts would evaluate the results an inconclusive draw at best.

For Jones, however, the action was a personal triumph. By his command decisions and actions he had won the respect of the men of the Seventh Virginia Cavalry. He had not merely sent his men into harm's way but also led them by riding at the head of his column. Jones demonstrated that he would not recklessly expose his men to any more danger than he would himself. He was also among the last to leave the fight. Answering his critics, Jones clarified the logical and necessary purpose of subjecting his men to drilling, saber grinding, and other means of battle preparedness. Those who had previously questioned their commander's capabilities now revered him. Lieutenant Blue wrote, "I never heard any one after that day doubt the old *infantry* colonel's fighting qualities. He was soon liked by his regiment and was afterwards the idol of the brigade, which he commanded."[34]

Jones had taken on a major gamble by launching the offensive. On August 7 he clarified his decisions: "No time could be afforded for inquiries—to fight or run were the only alternatives; I chose the former and as it turned out, against immense odds."[35] He concluded his report with this profound remark: "There is more danger in running than in fighting bravely."[36] He had to justify committing his detachment to battle without full knowledge regarding the enemy strength. To have withdrawn from the prospect of battle or to have delayed action pending the arrival of reinforcements would have resulted in a crisis of leadership.

Jones earned the support of his West Point friend and commanding officer, Stonewall Jackson. Jackson blamed the Ashby Cavalry Brigade Commander, General Beverly H. Robertson, for failing to support Jones promptly and for the setback. Jackson's report praised Jones, who "received intelligence before he reached Orange Courthouse that the enemy was in possession of the town" and he "boldly" charged into the Federal column.[37]

Jackson followed up by writing to General Lee with a recommendation to relieve General Beverly Robertson from command of the Ashby Brigade and to promote Jones to brigadier general to replace him.[38] Unconvinced, Lee perceived that his famed corps commander was a brilliant strategist but one who made impulsive administrative judgments. Evidence of Jackson's flaw was supported by the court-martial proceedings against Brigadier General Richard Garnett, who was vehemently contesting the charges regarding his conduct at Kernstown.[39]

On the concept of replacing Robertson with Jones, Lee replied to Jackson: "As regards for General Robertson, I will today see the Secretary of War. That subject is not so easily arranged, and without knowing any of the circumstances attending it except as related by you, I fear the judgment passed upon him may be hasty. Neither am I sufficiently informed of the qualifications of Col. W.E. Jones, though having for him a high esteem, to say whether he is better qualified."[40]

Cedar Mountain

On August 9 Jones and his Seventh Cavalry conducted a night reconnaissance and engaged in a minor cavalry skirmish during the Battle of Cedar Mountain, capturing eleven enlisted men, three officers, and an officer's servant.[41] Jackson praised Jones as the exception to Robertson's overall cavalry, which in his opinion contributed little.[42] Jackson won an overwhelming victory at Cedar Mountain and wanted to pursue the retreating Federals to Culpeper. Riding out to meet Jackson in person, Jones reported that the Union general Franz Sigel was reinforcing Banks. Upon the advice and intelligence that Jones provided, Jackson halted his pursuit to consolidate his forces.[43]

On August 11 Jackson wrote to Adjutant General Samuel Cooper formally requesting a "good Brig. Gen." to command his cavalry and if none was available that "Col. W.E. Jones be promoted and ordered to report" to him.[44] It was Jackson's second official endorsement of Jones and his second attempt to have Beverly Robertson removed from command of his cavalry, but no action was taken.

Lee's Army of Northern Virginia and Pope's Army of Virginia each recoiled to positions divided by the Rapidan River. The conclusion of Cedar Mountain evolved into the beginning stages of the Second Bull Run, or Second Manassas, Campaign. In preparation, Robertson's Ashby Brigade transferred from Jackson's to Stuart's command.[45] For the second time, Jones found himself placed under the command of his long-time nemesis, Jeb Stuart. However, with a major campaign pending, the two officers set their differences aside.

Second Bull Run (AKA Second Manassas)

The Second Bull Run Campaign commenced with cavalry operations seeking to locate a vulnerable point in Pope's lines. In a probing mission on August 20 Colonel Jones and his Seventh Virginia Cavalry forded the Rapidan River and routed the enemy cavalry in hand-to-hand fighting. Brigade commander Beverly Robertson reported, "My thanks are especially due to Colonel Jones for the admirable disposition made of his skirmishers and regiment during the engagement with the First Maine on picket duty."[46] Jones also received praise from his division commander and antagonist, Jeb Stuart, who reported, "Colonel Jones, whose regiment so long bore the brunt of the fight, behaved with marked courage and determination."[47] Stuart added, "The enemy, occupying woods and hedge roads with dismounted men, armed with long range carbines, was repeatedly dislodged by his [Jones] bold onslaughts."[48]

Lee exploited Pope's mediocre generalship with deception and diversionary maneuvers. On August 28 an inconclusive engagement at Groveton in Prince William County resulted in heavy losses on both sides. In a surprise attack, Jackson's and Longstreet's collective corps routed the Federals on August 29 and 30. The campaign concluded with the Battle of Chantilly on September 1 when Jackson struck a final blow and drove Pope's army back to Washington, D.C.

Second Bull Run concluded a three-month-long series of engagements that started with the Peninsular Campaign. With fewer numbers and resources, the South's military leadership demonstrated obvious superiority at this stage of the war in the Eastern Theater. The war front that previously approached Richmond had now shifted to the outskirts of Washington, D.C.[49] With momentum on his side Lee prepared to launch his first invasion of the north.

On September 5, in a reorganization of the cavalry, General Beverly Robertson was transferred out of Stuart's command to organize a brigade in North Carolina.[50] Colonel Thomas Taylor Munford replaced Robertson as temporary commander of Ashby's Cavalry Brigade.

Antietam

Lee marched the infantry units of the Army of Northern Virginia across the Potomac into Maryland. Concluded on September 18, 1862, Antietam was the bloodiest conflict in the war up to that point. North and South losses were comparable, with collective casualties exceeding 25,000. The cavalry saw only limited action and covered the withdrawal back across the Potomac.

Although he had been reinstated as commander of the Army of the Potomac, McClellan failed to obstruct Lee's exit from Maryland and denied the North a clear tactical victory. The campaign did, however, mark a reversal of fortunes to the North for the first time in the Eastern Theater. Although disappointed, Lincoln declared a victory and announced the long-awaited Emancipation Proclamation.

From the Southern perspective, Antietam was an inconclusive draw, and morale remained high. The two opposing armies recoiled to positions on the opposite sides of the upper Potomac River. Anticipating that McClellan would launch a new offensive, Lee placed the main elements of his Army of Northern Virginia in a twenty-mile line of defense between Winchester and Martinsburg. Stuart's cavalry division assumed reconnaissance duties farther to the east along the banks of the Potomac River between Williamsport, Maryland, and Harpers Ferry.

At the invitation of the Dandridge family, Major General Jeb Stuart established his cavalry division headquarters on the grounds of a large plantation called the "The Bower" situated between Martinsburg and Charles Town. The family had occupied the antebellum-style mansion for generations. Approximately one hundred members of Stuart's staff including officers, servants, and couriers camped within the vicinity of the immediate premises. Family members marveled at the spectacle. Stuart accepted the Dandridges' hospitality and returned the favor by hiring musicians and other entertainers to perform gala events. Jones and his Seventh Virginia Cavalry did not partake in the luxuries of The Bower. His Seventh Virginia Cavalry, along with the other regiments of the Ashby Cavalry Brigade, took positions approximately five miles to the northwest at the village of Darkesville in Berkeley County (WV).

Festivities at The Bower were interrupted on the evening of October 1 by a report that a Union cavalry force had crossed the Potomac and raided an outpost deep within the Confederate lines near Martinsburg. Stuart dashed to intervene but could only engage with a rear guard; the main body of the Federal column had already recrossed the Potomac. Stuart's group returned to The Bower, and the gaiety resumed. Although the raid resulted in only modest damages, it was an ominous sign of future attacks. For the sake of morale and security, there were calls for retaliation.

Stuart's Chambersburg Raid

Authorized by Lee, Stuart summoned his brigade and regimental commanders to select 1,800 of his most reliable and best-mounted troopers to embark on his second ride around McClellan's army, a mission later deemed Stuart's Chambersburg Raid (AKA Stuart's Second Ride Around McClellan). With interim commander of the Ashby Cavalry Brigade, Colonel Thomas Taylor Munford, on detached duty Colonel W.E. Jones assumed temporary command. In the right place at the right time, Jones was among an exclusive group of senior officers including Brigadier General Wade Hampton and Colonel William Henry Fitzhugh "Rooney" Lee. The stated objective was to observe McClellan's movements, to requisition replacement horses, and to inflict as much damage on the enemy as possible. The mission also called for the abduction of hostages to be used in exchange for selected Marylanders imprisoned for their loyalty to the Confederacy.[51]

Stuart performed four solos with his banjo in a "farewell concert to the ladies" at The Bower, a performance that lasted past one o'clock on the morning of October 9.[52] At noon on the same day, the selected group convened at Jones's headquarters at Darkesville and from there the mission commenced. By the following day, the expedition reached Pennsylvania. The raiders encountered little resistance en route to Chambersburg, where the town officials unconditionally surrendered. Stuart appointed Wade Hampton as "military governor," and Hampton's brigade encamped in the streets.[53] They captured and paroled 275 sick and wounded Union soldiers at a nearby infirmary. The raiders seized a supply depot stocked with Union army overcoats, undergarments, and a cache of 5,000 small arms. They gathered what they could take and burned an estimated $1,000,000 in military supplies left behind. Hostages reported that the Confederates demonstrated courtesy and acted with admirable discipline.[54] Grumble Jones led a detachment in a nocturnal undertaking to destroy the iron bridge spanning the Conochocheague Creek. However, with the bridge structure's resistance to torches and axes, that portion of the mission failed.[55] Although it was a marked disappointment, Jones learned from the setback and would succeed on a similar future expedition.

Rather than return predictably by the same route, Stuart maneuvered eastward toward Gettysburg as a diversion. McClellan's cavalry tried to obstruct Stuart's exit at various crossings of the Potomac. Lee's artillery batteries intervened to drive off the Federal cavalry units at White's Ford, allowing Stuart's raiders to cross back into Virginia unmolested on the morning of October 12.[56] The raid covered 126 miles, the last 80 conducted without a halt.[57] Stuart praised Jones and the other brigade commanders in "lasting gratitude for their coolness in danger and cheerful obedience to orders."[58]

In addition to the property damage inflicted on the enemy, Stuart's men confiscated 1,200 horses, up to forty military prisoners and the same number of civilian hostages. With a casualty rate of none killed, only a few wounded and only two presumed captured, the mission incurred a minimal loss. It boosted Southern morale and significantly embarrassed McClellan. The raid also highlighted Stuart's vanity. He declared "the hand of God was clearly manifested in the signal deliverance from danger and the crowning success attending it."[59]

The Chambersburg Raid drew criticism and inflamed old animosities between Stuart and some of his subordinates.[60] Wade Hampton considered the mission to be one of Stuart's many "glorified horse rides of little or no strategic importance."[61] If Grumble Jones was among the disgruntled, he kept his grievances confidential. Still, the raid was a psychological triumph for Stuart and the Confederate cavalry division. For the second time in four months, Stuart had maneuvered around and humiliated McClellan, with the entire mission being performed in enemy territory. Northern newspapers promoted the "dash and nerve of the raiders" while censuring McClellan for his inability to "thwart, confront, or contain their advance into or out of hostile territory."[62]

Promotion to Brigadier

With General Beverly Robertson's reassignment, Lee needed to appoint a permanent commander of the Ashby Cavalry Brigade. On September 24, 1862, General Jackson had submitted a third official recommendation to promote Colonel W.E. Jones as brigadier general in command of the Ashby Cavalry Brigade. Elaborating, Jackson wrote to Adjutant and Inspector General Samuel Cooper reiterating Jones's prompt and efficient discharge of duty and demonstrating gallantry at Orange Courthouse. Jackson concluded, "I am not acquainted with any other field officer of cavalry whom I feel so well qualified for commanding a Brigade."[63] It was Jackson's final tribute to his West Point comrade before the Seventh Virginia Cavalry transferred to Stuart's division. Although Jackson fully backed Jones, Stuart did not.

Stuart endorsed interim Ashby Brigade commander Colonel Thomas Taylor Munford, who had the prior commission to the rank of colonel. Nothing more demonstrated Stuart's contempt for Jones than his correspondence to Lee on October 24, 1862. Stuart's tone was in stark contrast to the praise he had previously expounded upon Jones following the Second Bull Run Campaign and the Chambersburg Raid. From his headquarters at The Bower, Stuart wrote a most scathing non-endorsement of Grumble Jones to General Lee:

> General:
>
> Believing that Brigadier General W.E. Jones (lately Col, 7th Va Cavalry) who received his appointment without my recommendation, to take command at Winchester, may possibly be assigned to the command of the Brigade now commanded by Col. Munford, I have the honor to state that in a paper

concerning the organization of my Division forwarded this day, I have asked that Col. Munford be appointed Brigadier General to command that Brigade. I have the honor to state further that I do not regard Brig. Gen. Jones as deserving this command or as a fit person to command a Brigade of Cavalry. I say this from a thorough acquaintance with him in every grade from Lieutenant up. With Munford in command of that Brigade, I shall expect hearty cooperation, zealous devotion, and indefatigable attention to his duty. With Brig. Genl. Jones, I feel sure of opposition, insubordination, and inefficiency to an extent that would in a short time ruin discipline and subvert authority in that Brigade.

Profoundly impressed with the correctness of my views on this subject based upon intimate acquaintance, I must beg the commanding General to avert such a calamity from any Division, and if there is any who entertain different views in regard to Gen. Jones, let such have the benefit of his services and his talents.

If the matter were to undergo investigation and witnesses would testify who could, his appointment of Brigadier General would not receive the sanction of the Executive, & never could get any recommendation.

            Most Respectfully Your Obedient Servant,
            J.E.B. Stuart, Major General"[64]

Request that Brigadier General Jones be assigned to some other command, not in cavalry.

Lee did not concur; Stuart's efforts at dissuasion were to no avail. On October 31 William E. Jones received the appointment of brigadier general retroactive to be effective September 19, a significant factor in cases involving officers of equal rank, as those with prior commissions held authority.[65] On November 8, Lee issued a general order placing Jones in command of Ashby Cavalry Brigade, which had been previously and tentatively commanded by Colonel T.T. Munford.[66] Two days, later Lee called for a reorganization of the cavalry establishing the Second Brigade, also known as the W.E. Jones Brigade, consisting of the Sixth, Seventh, and Twelfth Virginia Cavalry regiments, the Seventeenth Virginia Cavalry Battalion, and White's Cavalry (AKA Thirty-Fifth Battalion Virginia Cavalry).[67] Captain Preston Chew's Battery of mounted artillery also joined the mix.

Lee concluded that Jones had demonstrated his capabilities as an administrator and a field commander. Jackson's official written recommendations may have been the greatest influence on Lee's decision. While Jones perceived his promotion as well-deserved recognition for his merit, Stuart regarded it as a lack of better judgment on the part of Lee. Lee hoped that Jones and Stuart would overcome their differences. For the time being, he had the luxury to keep the two officers separated. Stuart and the bulk of his cavalry division joined Lee in the defense of Richmond. Jones and his brigade were detached and assigned to the Shenandoah Valley. Notwithstanding the fact that he held independent command once again, the promotion would prove to be the beginning of many difficulties for Jones.[68]

12

Command of the Shenandoah Valley District

Promoted to brigadier general, Jones assumed command of the former Ashby Brigade, which officially became known as the W.E. Jones Brigade of the Army of Northern Virginia. In one of his first administrative measures, Grumble wrote to Secretary of War George Wythe Randolph, requesting that First Lieutenant Warren M. Hopkins of Company D, First Virginia Cavalry, transfer to the Jones Brigade and serve as his aide-de-camp.[1] Born in Powhatan County, Virginia, Hopkins had moved to Washington County and enrolled in the Washington Mounted Rifles. With Jones's request approved, Hopkins received the assignment on November 21.[2]

Jones implemented the same methods he used when he had assumed command of the Seventh Virginia Cavalry. He subjected the men of the Ashby Brigade to interminable drilling, a procedure that was the only break in the monotony of camp life. Saturday was designated as saber-grinding day, another nuisance the men resented.[3] Just like their comrades of the Seventh Virginia Cavalry, the men of the newly named Jones Brigade regarded the sharpening of sword blades as a complete and unnecessary vexation. Eventually, however, they would see value in the ritual.

An anecdote describes another occasion in which Grumble's modest appearance deceived others into thinking he was someone besides a high-ranking officer. Soon after taking command, he was riding between outposts when he observed one of his enlisted men high up in a cherry tree, gathering bounty. Jones ordered him to descend.

"Not yet," replied the soldier. "Haven't got enough, be down presently."

Indignant over the insubordination, Jones shouted, "Come down, I say at once sir! I am General Jones."

Not believing he was conversing with his new brigade commander, the soldier answered, "General, glad to meet you; come up; plenty for both; my name is Jones too."[4]

A Shift in Strategy

The combined measures of Stonewall Jackson's Valley Campaign, Second Bull Run, Antietam, and Stuart's Chambersburg Raid had rendered 1862 an eventful year in the Shenandoah Valley. By the fall, however, coinciding with the time of Jones's promotion, abrupt changes to the strategic situation were taking place. From the perspective of the opposing sides, priorities shifted out of the valley to locations east of the Blue Ridge

Mountains. The Federal high command had reevaluated the strategic importance of the valley. In addition to armed resistance and distance, the topography of the Blue Ridge Mountains rendered the valley an impractical back-door avenue to advance upon Richmond. Logic dictated a more direct route from Washington. Large Federal troop concentrations reverted to Washington, D.C., in preparation for the next offensive. The Federals would maintain a presence in the valley, but it was on a much smaller scale and with the limited objective to defend the vital Baltimore & Ohio Railroad, which crossed the Potomac River at Harpers Ferry.[5]

The Confederate high command noted the recent Federal maneuvers and concluded that the next advance on Richmond would not come from the upper Potomac region but from somewhere along the Rappahannock River. With no imminent threat against the valley's resources, the South had no choice but to shift its priorities east of the Blue Ridge. The new circumstances called for the outnumbered and divided Army of Northern Virginia to consolidate.[6]

Limited in manpower and resources, the Confederate high command lacked the option to deploy a large force to guard the valley. The area would have to be secured by a much smaller but more mobile force of cavalry after being previously defended by Jackson's forces. Jackson's Corps of 38,000 troops, including four divisions of infantry and twenty-three batteries of artillery, withdrew from the region, marched eastward, and joined with Lee in the direct-line defense of Richmond.[7] Recently promoted Brigadier General Jones and his "skeletal" cavalry force of less than 4,000 were detached to maintain the security in the lower Shenandoah Valley "during the absence of Lieutenant General Jackson."[8] The wording of Lee's orders suggests that he considered the arrangement temporary in order to ease public apprehensions about the change.[9]

The Shenandoah Valley is a 200-mile region of the Great Appalachian Valley stretching between the James and Potomac rivers, bound by the Blue Ridge Mountains and the ridge-and-valley Appalachians. Of particular strategic importance was the area along the Shenandoah River, which flows northward as a tributary of the Potomac. The unusual directional flow of the river can render the topography somewhat confusing. The "lower" Shenandoah Valley is the northern region in the cismontane counties of current West Virginia, where the Shenandoah flows into the Potomac. The headwaters of the Shenandoah River form in the central region. The "upper" valley is the southern region in the vicinity of the James River near Lexington.

Jones established his headquarters along Opequon Creek in Frederick County, and from where he was to secure the vast majority of the Shenandoah Valley ranging from the Potomac River to Staunton. Jackson's exit left a tremendous void. Neither the civilians of the valley nor their political representatives would be reconciled to entrusting the unproven brigadier general with a small force to preserve their lives, properties, and livelihoods. From the perspective of the local civilian populace, Jones was following a legend for the second time.

Political Transformations

The appointment of Grumble Jones also coincided with a time of dramatic political changes. Two significant political events were well underway by the fall of 1862. One was Lincoln's Emancipation Proclamation, which would take effect on January 1, 1863. The other (and perhaps having a greater and more immediate impact) was the further progression toward the establishment of the separate state of West Virginia.

Dating back to Colonial times, the Allegheny Mountains had formed a physical, economic, social, and cultural barrier that divided the isolated inhabitants of Virginia's northwestern counties from the southwestern, central, and eastern portion of the state. For generations the rugged individualists of the trans-Alleghenies desired independence from the central government of Virginia, both in Williamsburg and in Richmond. In contrast to the plantation and slave-based economy of the middle and eastern sections, northwestern Virginians' economy was based on small farms, logging, and mining. Wedged between bordering Kentucky, Ohio, Pennsylvania, and Maryland, northwestern Virginians identified more with the inhabitants of those states. Economic and social differences eventually led to political ones.

Internal state strife climaxed in April of 1861, when the Virginia General Assembly passed the Ordinance of Secession and joined the rebellion. Residents of the northwestern counties held a mass meeting in Clarksburg and reconvened at Wheeling. Following a series of conventions, delegates established a new legislature, elected Francis H. Pierpont as its governor, and created a new constitution. Initially, the new government in western Virginia regarded itself as the *legitimate* authority of all Virginia but one in exile. With the support of the Lincoln administration, supplies and manpower for the Unionist factions flowed in from neighboring Ohio, Pennsylvania, and western Maryland.

In June of 1861, Major General George B. McClellan defeated a Confederate contingency at Philippi. In September, Union brigadier general Joseph J. Reynolds handed General Robert E. Lee his first defeat at Cheat Mountain. Other Confederate nominal attempts to recover the region failed in early 1862. Although these campaigns were relatively minor, they solidified pro–Union sentiment.

By the end of 1862, the trans-Allegheny region and six cismontane counties entered into a movement that would eventually lead to secession from Virginia. The reorganized government applied for admission to the Union as a new and separate state. West Virginia would be admitted to the Union on June 20, 1863. Neither the Virginia state government nor the Confederacy recognized the separation. For the interim, the counties of northwestern Virginia and the cismontane counties forming the eastern panhandle served as a sanctuary for Union troops along with secure domain for the Baltimore & Ohio Railroad. With its lines running through pro–Union territory from the Ohio River to the eastern seaboard, the B&O Railroad served as an unchallenged lifeline to Federal forces operating in central Virginia and to their naval forces enforcing the Atlantic blockade.

The preliminary establishment of the new state provided the Federals with a psychological boost as well. Splitting the strongest state in the Confederacy and admitting a new state into the Union was both a political and military victory for the Federal government at a time when it was most challenged by Lee's campaigns.[10]

Robert Huston Milroy

A prominent instigator supporting the Unionist cause in northwestern Virginia was Indiana-born General Robert Huston Milroy. After graduating from the American Literary, Scientific, and Military Academy (now Norwich University) in Vermont at the top of his class, he was denied a commission in the regular army. In 1846, however, he volunteered, received a commission, and served in the Mexican War. Following his discharge, he earned a law degree from the University of Indiana at Bloomington in 1850 and served as a judge. He joined the Republican Party as a staunch supporter of its abolitionist platform. With the outbreak of the Civil War he raised a company of Indiana volunteers and received a commission.

Serving in McClellan's western Virginia campaigns of 1861, Milroy distinguished himself at Grafton, Philippi, Carrick's Ford, and Laurel Hill, earning a promotion to brigadier general and command of the Cheat Mountain District. His forces performed gallantly against Jackson's Shenandoah Valley Campaign. In the summer of 1862 he performed admirably and further enhanced his fighting reputation during the Second Bull Run Campaign. He returned to command of the Cheat Mountain District in northwestern Virginia, establishing dual headquarters at Petersburg and Moorefield in Hardy County.[11]

Motivated by his extreme religious, political and patriotic sentiments, Milroy considered himself anointed with a mission to end slavery and preserve the Union.[12] He demonized himself in the eyes of the secessionists and placed himself at odds with his superiors, particularly with Lincoln's military advisor and general-in-chief, Henry Wagner Halleck. To advance his agenda, Milroy would take the fight to all facets of the enemy, including civilians. He demanded that loyal citizens of the region make sacrifices for the Unionist cause and threatened pro-secession elements with consequences.

Although the prevailing political climate supported the North, northwestern Virginia was a border region that also sent fighters to the Confederate side. During this period of transition, animosities between Unionists and Confederate sympathizers escalated.

John D. Imboden

Confederate colonel John D. Imboden headed a partisan counterinsurgency against Milroy in the contested region. The Augusta County, Virginia, native had attended Washington College (now Washington and Lee University) in Lexington, Virginia, and served at the Virginia School for the Deaf in Staunton. He practiced law and as a member of the Whig party served in the Virginia house of delegates. Widowed in 1857, with five offspring, he remarried in 1859 and fathered three more children.[13] Imboden enrolled in the Virginia Militia in 1858. Following John Brown's Raid on Harpers Ferry he organized the

Robert Huston Milroy, circa 1863 (Library of Congress).

Staunton Artillery in 1859, remained in the realm of politics, and further supported the cause of secession.[14]

When Virginia joined the Confederacy, Captain Imboden's Staunton Artillery served in General Joseph E. Johnston's command and distinguished itself in the First Bull Run Campaign. In March of 1862 the Staunton Artillery joined the defenses at Yorktown to confront the anticipated invasion. A month later the Confederate government enacted congressional legislation empowering the soldiers in the field to elect their officers, the same elections that cost Grumble Jones command of the First Virginia Cavalry. Harboring other ambitions, Captain Imboden declined to run for the office of his rank and resigned his commission.[15]

Imboden was impressed by Turner Ashby's guerrilla warfare tactics deploying small mobile squadrons to confront larger forces with ambushes and raids. Realizing that the South lacked the means to fight solely by conventional methods, partisan warfare

John D. Imboden, circa 1870 (Library of Congress).

was the most logical means of defense. On April 21, 1862, five days after the Confederate congress passed the Conscription Act, the Virginia general assembly passed the Partisan Ranger Act.[16] Imboden requested authority to raise a partisan unit that would concentrate in the familiar Shenandoah Valley. Secretary of War George W. Randolph granted his request. Imboden's First Virginia Partisan Rangers was the first such unit so authorized,[17] and his unit joined Stonewall Jackson's Valley Campaign on June 9 near its termination.

For the remainder of 1862 Colonel Imboden led his First Virginia Partisan Rangers on a series of raids and small engagements against Federal targets in northwestern Virginia. Since his unit was not part of any of the Confederate armies, Imboden, in his unique capacity, answered only to the secretary of war and to President Davis.

Partisan Warfare: Milroy Versus Imboden

In September 1862, during the Antietam Campaign, Imboden's First Partisan Rangers created a diversion with a raid into northwestern Virginia that inflicted only a nominal amount of damage. Following the recruitment of more troops, they conducted a more successful raid in October, temporarily disrupting traffic on the Baltimore & Ohio Railroad and capturing 150 Union troops along with an assortment of supplies.[18]

Imboden's success was negated by Federal raids of retaliation against his base camps. He then altered his strategy by dispatching smaller raiding parties to commit ambushes, raids, and abductions of personnel at Union outposts, and to destroy the properties owned by Union sympathizers. Implementing the unconventional Turner Ashby–style of guerrilla warfare, Imboden earned himself the reputation as a regional folk-villain, and his First Virginia Partisan Rangers were viewed as outlaws.[19]

The marginal success of Imboden's excursions frustrated Union general Milroy, who was unable to neutralize the Confederate partisans with a decisive blow. Milroy resorted to intimidating civilians suspected of being Southern sympathizers. In late November, he directed Captain Horace Kellogg of the One Hundred and Twenty-Third Ohio Regiment to deliver a summons to suspected Confederate sympathizer Job Parsons of Tucker County (West Virginia), ordering him to appear on the following day at the county courthouse at Saint George. Parsons appeared and received a second summons that ordered him to pay a monetary assessment "in consequence of certain robberies which have been perpetrated upon Union citizens of Tucker County, Va. by bands of guerrillas."[20] More infuriating was the segment of the document directed to Captain Kellogg:

> If they fail to pay at the end of the time you have named, their houses will be burned, and themselves shot and their property all seized, and be sure that you carry out this threat and show them that you are not trifling or to be trifled with. You will inform the inhabitants from ten or fifteen miles around your camp on all roads approaching the town upon which the enemy may approach that they must dash in and give you notice and that upon failure of anyone to do so, their houses will be burned and their men shot.
>
> By order of Brig. Gen. R. H. Milroy[21]{/ext}

Job Parsons reacted by seeking out Imboden at his Shenandoah Mountain headquarters and enlisting in his band of partisan rangers. Parsons informed Imboden that Milroy had also levied assessments of $300 and $700 against his father and another relative. Imboden reported his findings to President Davis. Days later, Imboden received information that Milroy had issued an edict containing similar language and a $285-levy against St. George resident Adam Harper, who was eighty-two years old, crippled, and illiterate. Imboden arranged to have the Milroy edict published in *The Crisis,* a Northern newspaper that was critical of the Lincoln administration for its antislavery platform and war policies.[22]

The Unionists and secessionists engaged in psychological warfare, action by one provoking retaliatory measures by the other. Tensions in the mountainous region escalated to the potential for more violence until the onset of a very harsh winter with extreme weather conditions diminished the capacity of either side to make significant progress. A lull in regional fighting temporarily prevailed while a major development well east of the Blue Ridge received most of the strategic attention.

On December 13 Lee's Army of Northern Virginia repulsed Burnside's Army of the Potomac and inflicted significant losses on it at Fredericksburg. In the aftermath, neither side realized the vulnerability of its opponent. The Federals feared that in the luxury of his overwhelming victory Lee might return Jackson's Corps to the Shenandoah Valley and impose an imminent threat to the Baltimore & Ohio Railroad (B&O).[23] The U.S. War Department directed General Benjamin Kelley, commander of the Upper Potomac District, to prioritize security of the B&O from the Ohio River to Harpers Ferry. The Federals had already established garrisons in the pro–Union region at Romney, New

Creek, Harpers Ferry, and Cumberland. However, the B&O remained exposed to a potential attack from Winchester.

From the Southern perspective, the lower Shenandoah Valley was exposed on two fronts. To the north there stood multiple Federal garrisons of the Upper Potomac region. Positioned to the west in Hardy County (WV), Milroy's Cheat Mountain District posed an equal threat. Recognizing the necessity to centralize his force, Jones withdrew from Opequon Creek, fell back approximately fifty miles, and established his new headquarters at New Market in Shenandoah County.

On December 22, the Federal high command directed that Milroy transfer the bulk of his forces to Kelley's Upper Potomac District and occupy Winchester as soon as possible. Kelley dispatched a 200-man mounted reconnaissance unit, which observed Jones's withdrawal from Opequon Creek, leaving Winchester devoid of defenses. Milroy then directed General Gustave Paul Cluseret, a French national serving the Union army, to lead a 2,500-man infantry detachment to march on Winchester and act as an initial occupation force.

Contrary to what the Federal high command had feared, the Army of Northern Virginia could not spare Jackson's Corps to return it to the valley. Lee had recently detached Longstreet's Corps to southeastern Virginia on a foraging expedition. The Army of the Potomac was regrouping and preparing to renew the offensive along the Rappahannock. Jackson's Corps had to stay put. Lee would have to rely upon the cavalry brigade of William E. Jones, supported by Imboden's First Virginia Partisan Rangers and Colonel Henry B. Davidson's regiment at Staunton, to provide security for the entire Shenandoah Valley.

Jones Versus Milroy

From his New Market outpost on December 23, Jones led his brigade on a routine scouting mission and observed Cluseret's Federal detachment marching through Woodstock en route to Winchester. Jones trailed the Cluseret column to Kernstown and engaged in a minor skirmish with the rear guard before withdrawing. In the action, Jones's forces captured a Major Henry H. Withers of the Tenth (West) Virginia Infantry.[24] Major Withers possessed four sets of orders issued by Milroy through his adjutants from his Petersburg and Moorefield garrisons and directed to the citizens of Hardy County and vicinity.

Milroy's first edict, published on December 11 demanded that the residents provide three days of subsistence to his troops stationed in and around the area. Clarifying his intentions, Milroy stipulated the levy as either a "contribution" to the war effort or "punishment" for prior aid rendered to the Confederate partisans.[25] His second edit, issued the following day, ordered the citizens of Moorefield to provide more than two collective tons of beef, pork, flour, and cornmeal to the war effort. He added that "citizens not having the articles named can furnish money or some eatable article."[26]

In his third edict, dated December 20, Milroy declared (prematurely) that the State of West Virginia had been admitted to the Union and called upon all citizens within its boundaries to swear an oath of allegiance. Failure to comply would result in forfeiture of all rights and protection of the Cheat Mountain District.[27]

Most ominous was Milroy's fourth set of orders:

> All citizens of Moorefield and vicinity, in the county of Hardy, State of West Virginia, desiring the protection of the United States for their property and persons, are hereby notified to call at these headquarters and take an oath of allegiance to the Government of the United States and the State of West Virginia.
>
> All persons refusing or neglecting to comply with this order will be called on to furnish supplies of provisions and forage for the use of the U.S. Army. Their property will be used to quarter troops, for Government store-rooms, etc.
>
> While loyal men are obliged to leave their families and homes, endure the hardships, take risks of a soldier's life, and shed their blood in defense of the only truly republican Government in the world, rebel sympathizers, aiders, and abettors, seeking its destruction, must be made to feel the strong arm of the Government, whether found in arms against it or at home with their families.[28]

Knowledge of Cluseret's advance on Winchester and the captured set of orders served as a twofold alarm to the Confederate authorities. By occupying Winchester, Milroy could pose an imminent threat to the lower Shenandoah Valley, a primary source of sustenance to the underfed Army of Northern Virginia. Politically, it was assumed that Milroy would direct the same oppressive policies against civilians in the Virginia Shenandoah Valley. Reporting to General Robert E. Lee, Jones remarked, "Enclosed, I send you copies of his recent orders, which, for harshness and cruel injustice, rival the best efforts of Pope and Butler."[29] Lee forwarded Jones's report and copies of Milroy's orders to Secretary of War James Seddon. In a measure of retaliation, Lee recommended that Major Withers not be paroled but "retained as a hostage."[30]

On Christmas Eve Cluseret's detachment marched into Winchester unopposed, marking another of multiple instances in which possession of the town changed hands between the two sides.[31] Reinforced by the scouting unit, Cluseret's 2,700-man occupational forces almost doubled the town population greatly diminished by the war demands. Cluseret declared martial law, established a curfew and authorized foraging in preparation for winter quarters. Homes were searched for sustenance, firearms, and liquor. Outbuildings and fences were dismantled for firewood.[32]

The main body of Milroy's command arrived in Winchester on New Year's Day 1863. The Frederick County seat saw multiple occupations during the Civil War, but Milroy's five-and-a-half–month tenure would be the most repressive in the opinion of its defiant residents. Milroy immediately set out to enforce the terms of the Emancipation Proclamation, which went into law effective the same day. He issued his own "Freedom to the Slaves" proclamation, which he declared as "the most important event in the history of the world since Christ was born."[33] Liberated slaves boarded freight cars with their few possessions and departed on a journey to the North.

Word of Milroy's crusade into Winchester spread rapidly. Addressing the Virginia general assembly, Governor John Letcher denounced Milroy's Freedom to the Slaves proclamation and vowed to make an example out of any captured Federal officers attempting to enforce it.[34] Combining their resources, the Confederate congress and the Virginia legislature placed a $100,000 bounty on Milroy.[35]

Although alarmed by Milroy's occupation of Winchester, Lee had to deal with an even greater dilemma well east of the Blue Ridge. Following the Battle of Fredericksburg, the Army of the Potomac, under its new commander, Joseph Hooker, did not retreat to Washington but maintained a threatening presence. With Longstreet's Corps detached, Lee had to concentrate his forces in the region and could not spare any to aid Jones in the Shenandoah Valley. With limited options, Lee officially appointed Jones to command the Shenandoah Valley District. He directed Imboden's First Partisan Rangers and Colonel

Henry B. Davidson's regiment at Staunton to consolidate under Jones's overall command. This measure had its limitations, as the Confederate forces in the valley were dispersed and heavily outnumbered. Lee urged Jones to make every effort to expel the Federals from Winchester and suggested either creating diversions or severing Milroy's communications with the Baltimore & Ohio Railroad.[36]

Jones lacked the resources to conduct a successful direct assault on Milroy's Winchester garrison. After weighing his options, he devised a strategy to lure Milroy out of Winchester by launching an offensive against his adversary's base headquarters, the Cheat Mountain District Federal Army of Occupation at Moorefield.

Jones's Moorefield Expedition

On January 2, 1863, Jones conducted a night march on Moorefield with his Sixth, Seventh, and Twelfth Virginia Cavalry regiments, the First Maryland Battalion Cavalry, the First Maryland Battalion Infantry, and Chew's Horse Artillery. Imboden's First Partisan Rangers united with them en route. There was a sense of urgency to reach their destination before enemy reinforcements arrived from nearby Petersburg.[37]

Jones's forces launched an artillery assault. To his disgust, his "six pieces of artillery with their *defective* ammunition, were no match to two of the enemy."[38] Jones complained, "Nearly all of our shots fell far short, while theirs either passed over or struck in our midst."[39] Jones's forces revealed their position and consequently received incoming Federal artillery projectiles in response. Reiterating his criticism of the quality of his ammunition, Jones reported, "Though they reached us with ease, they were out of *our* range."[40] Hoping to thwart the enemy units from uniting, Jones held his position for two hours until his artillery battery "expended the last of its well-husbanded worthless ammunition."[41] He then withdrew his forces up the South Fork of the Potomac to regroup.

Jones then divided his command. Separate detachments captured twenty enemy soldiers near Moorefield and forty-six more at Petersburg, where Jones's men burned a church filled with supplies. Jones renewed his attack on Moorefield three days later, capturing thirty-three men and killing one. His forces also seized forty-six horses and five wagons.[42] He regarded the mission as a "partial success" but lamented what he might have accomplished with effective artillery ammunition.

Jones's report to Lee on January 6 addressed his complaints regarding the quality of the ammunition. Lee forwarded the report to Colonel Josiah Gorgas of the Ordnance Department. Agitated, Colonel Gorgas wrote Lee a scathing reply passed on to Secretary of War James Seddon:

> Officers are always ready to praise when they succeed and to blame when they fail. Colonel [Henry Coalter] Cabell, of the artillery at Fredericksburg, complimented our ammunition yesterday. Every effort is constantly made to overcome the many obstacles we have had to contend with in the production of the laboratory and I am quite as much inclined to blame General Jones's artillerists as he is to blame my ammunition. Without wishing to detract from his skill as an officer, I may be allowed to state that he is known to be very apt to find fault. His depreciation of the ammunition is however taken in good part and will only stimulate the endeavor to improve where there is much room for improvement.[43]

Jones tried to report his overall Moorefield expedition on a positive note. Lee congratulated the brigadier on what he had accomplished. Judging solely by standard battlefield casualty statistics, the mission appeared overwhelmingly successful. At the cost of only one horse and two wounded men, Jones's forces captured ninety-nine enemy troops, including three officers, and killed one. They confiscated fifty-one horses and five wagons and inflicted up to $20,000 in damages. It was, however, a hollow victory, one resulting in absolutely no improvement to the strategic situation. Recognizing Jones's expedition as a diversion, Milroy remained well entrenched at Winchester, with 15,000 Federal troops between there and nearby garrisons.

The mixed results at Moorefield caused discontent within the ranks as well. A disgruntled Private William Lyne Wilson of the Twelfth Virginia Cavalry wrote in his diary: "This fruitless expedition gives rise to a good deal of criticism upon the General's efficiency and fighting propensities."[44]

A Stalemate

Jones's failure to draw the Federals out of Winchester emboldened Milroy, who was anxious to exploit Jackson's exit from the Shenandoah Valley. Unsatisfied with merely guarding the railroads, he conducted small offensive operations in the guise of foraging expeditions. Dispatched from Winchester, raiding parties embarked in a variety of directions to multiple destinations. They struck at Front Royal, Berryville, and Strasburg, where they looted, pillaged, and arrested civilians suspected of being partisan guerrillas or their sympathizers. With most of the able-bodied male residents away serving in the armies, Milroy's marauders met only token resistance. During the first two weeks of January the raids occurred in four counties over a combined area exceeding 1,300 square miles.

Jones was frustrated by the manner in which the winter weather in the mountainous terrain restricted his capacity to respond effectively to Milroy's raids. In mid–January he dispatched Colonel A.W. Harman with an 800-man detachment to confront a reported Federal raiding party at Front Royal. Weather conditions delayed their progress, and by the time they arrived they had missed their target by twenty-four hours. A recent accumulation of snow prohibited a pursuit. Facing a lack of sustenance to feed the exhausted horses, Jones concluded that pushing the mounts to the extreme would render them ineffective even once weather conditions improved.[45]

Milroy's raids drew outrage from the citizens of the lower Shenandoah Valley and their political representatives. On January 10, 1863, the Honorable M.R. Kaufman, a member of the Virginia house of delegates from Frederick County, submitted a letter to Secretary of War Seddon as follows:

> We have no earthly protection from our forces; the enemy are allowed with impunity to make raids through the different counties without fear of molestation. While I do not wish to find fault with our commanding officers, not knowing whether they are acting under orders or not, it is quite strange to me that 1,200 or 1,500 of the enemy should be allowed quietly to march into Strasburg, take peaceable possession, be allowed all sorts of thefts and robberies, retire a few miles down the valley, commit similar atrocities, remain several days, and retire to Winchester, when we have a force in the valley nearly double that amount of men, who upon every move of the enemy continue to fall back father and farther from the enemy. I speak what I know when I say the nearest our pickets are stationed to the Federal lines is about twenty-eight miles, and only on one occasion since the occupation of Winchester has a scouting party been sent out in that direction. My residence is about ten miles south of Winchester. I have on three occasions visited my home with a view to get all the information I could,

and wrote General Jones from Woodstock giving him a statement of facts gained by operations, and promised to act as guide provided he would send a scouting party down. I am sure we could have captured several foraging parties. My entreaties were in vain. Of the late campaign of our forces to Moorefield, you may obtain accurate information by summoning Charles Williams, Esq, delegate from Hardy County who was with them. I saw the Yankee cavalry in Strasburg last Saturday, which is eighteen miles from Winchester. I have since learned that a scouting party entered Woodstock, thirty miles from Winchester. There is still a large amount of wheat in the lower valley, certainly enough to keep an army sufficient to keep the valley clear of the public enemy. Could we have such protection large preparations would be made for a crop of corn, which must be very essential to the support of the army.

I feel a delicacy in writing this communication to you, and only to the protection of our people.

Very respectfully, your obedient servant,

M.R. Kaufman House of Delegates, Frederick County, Va.[46]

Representative Alexander Robinson Boteler, of Virginia's Tenth District with the Provisional Congress of the Confederacy, joined the political frenzy of discontent. Boteler and Kaufman compared the current state of regional security to the strategic situation when Jackson's Corps had previously defended the region.

For Jones, responding to Milroy's raids with conventional warfare was not an option. Restricted in manpower and resources, he deployed guerrilla warfare tactics against Milroy's defenses, supply lines, and the Baltimore & Ohio Railroad. Jones divided his brigade into units that harassed Milroy's troops with partisan-style ambushes. Earning his later moniker of "Old Night Hawk," he concealed his movements with night marches, utilizing darkness and inclement weather as a cover.[47]

On one occasion Jones rested his force following a night-return march from Winchester to Strasburg during a time of freezing weather. He instructed the men of White's Thirty-Fifth Battalion on how to get through the night with the most comfort. He stated, "Lie down by the fire on the opposite side from where the wind blows. The fire keeps the wind from you while the smoke blows over you and keeps off the frost or dew." Unconvinced that such an arrangement would provide satisfactory comfort, a trooper complained, "But the smoke is a little too bitter for me." Jones shouted a response: "Yes, you get some of the bitter; but you get a damned sight of the sweet too!"[48]

Jones held an optimistic but futile hope that controversy over Lincoln's Emancipation Proclamation might lead to mass Federal defections. Some Federals considered the moral high ground to be based on the preservation of the Union without regard to the issue of slavery. Lincoln's Proclamation added emancipation as a war objective, one that would be questioned by some within the Union ranks. It spurred a few to alter their allegiance.

In late January Jones reported that a lieutenant with the One Hundred and Tenth Ohio deserted and came over to the Confederate side due to dissatisfaction with the Emancipation Proclamation. Jones suggested that if such individuals received kind treatment, more defections of similar fashion might follow.[49] Having said that, Grumble regarded one defection with suspicion.

On a rain-filled night in mid–February of 1863, Captain Charles T. O'Ferrall, commander of Company I, Twelfth Virginia Cavalry, was approached by his pickets escorting a "tall man in a Federal uniform with sergeant's chevrons on his sleeves."[50] The man in question, Sergeant James M. Flynn, was a Federal deserter and carried a letter from a Morgan County acquaintance. O'Ferrall had received prior correspondence from the same contact assuring that Flynn's defection would be genuine. O'Ferrall took Sergeant Flynn to the brigade headquarters in Edinburg and informed General Jones of what he knew about him. Jones asked Flynn, "Why did you desert?" Recalling Flynn's reply, O'Ferrall wrote, "Flynn answered that he had been converted to Southern views by Southern women; that he believed the South was right and wanted to fight for her."[51]

It was not the reply Jones anticipated. He then inquired as to the positions and strengths of Federal troops in the lower valley. Flynn answered, "General, I must bear the odium of being a deserter. I must take the chances of being captured and hung. I am willing to bear this odium and take these chances for the sake of my convictions, but I cannot give you information which I obtained only as a Federal soldier."

Looking at Flynn intently, Jones paused and turned to O'Ferrall declaring, "Well, this man is the strangest deserter I ever saw. Have you faith in him?" Vouching for his fellow Irishman and Morgan County resident, O'Ferrall replied, "I have assurances of his sincerity which I cannot disregard. I have the word of as true a Southerner as lives, and I can trust him, and I will trust him if you will allow me. I will put him on the rolls of my own company."[52] Jones answered, "All right." Following a pause, he added with a low tone, "You better watch him."[53]

Some Federal troops philosophically opposed Milroy's policies of emancipation and hostilities toward civilians. The vast majority, however, including those who disagreed with the course of action, obeyed his orders begrudgingly and viewed emancipation as a means to end the war.

Experimenting with diplomacy in hopes of persuading the Federal authorities to restrain Milroy's atrocities against civilians, Lee corresponded across enemy lines with the commander-in-chief, Henry W. Halleck, enclosing copies of the orders that Milroy had issued in West Virginia.[54] Lee commented, "I am unwilling to believe that such threats against unarmed and defenseless civilians as are contained in the extract from what purports to be an order from Brigadier-General Milroy have received the sanction of any soldier, and have the honor to ask whether the extract from the order referred to is literally or substantially correct. Should it, unfortunately, be true, I am instructed to ask whether your government will tolerate the execution of an order so barbarous and so revolting to every principle of justice and humanity."[55] Lee politely indicated that if the Federals did not act to restrain Milroy, the Confederate government would "be compelled to protect its citizens by stern retaliatory measures."[56]

Halleck reacted by writing to the Eighth Army Corps commander, Robert Schenck, in Baltimore that Milroy had no authority to issue such orders, that they were in violation of the laws of war, and that they should be revoked.[57] Schenck, in turn, sent Halleck's communication to General Kelley, commander of the Upper Potomac District at Harpers Ferry, to relay to Milroy.

Milroy saw no reason to change his policies. His controversial orders had been issued in the pro–Union region of what was about to become West Virginia and were intended to discourage Confederate guerrillas from victimizing the Unionists. With his forces occupying enemy territory, Milroy was not making the same demands upon the civilians. He justified his raids as foraging expeditions, a strategic necessity for his army of occupation. Lee's efforts resulted in little more than a strained relationship between Milroy and Halleck. Milroy would ultimately suffer the consequences of that estrangement, but for the time being his raids persisted.

Jones's guerrilla tactics partially succeeded. Apprehensive as to what Jones might do, Milroy had to maintain a constant state of alert. Milroy pleaded with his superiors for the authority to act decisively and eliminate Jones as a threat. In one request, he declared that if he could have two infantry regiments from Romney plus another one of cavalry he "would bag the whole of them."[58] Milroy alleged that he was surrounded by Jones's forces, which were strengthening in preparation for a major offensive against him. He added, "It is cruel to keep me here so helpless."[59]

Conceding that he would not receive the support to launch a full-fledged offensive, Milroy proposed that with nominal reinforcements he could not only hold Winchester but also conduct raids up the valley into Luray and as far south as Staunton. He argued, "The railroad can be much better defended and more securely protected by offensive operations against the enemy that threaten it from 20 to 100 miles away from it than by a greater defensive force scattered along its line"[60]

Generals Benjamin Kelley of the Upper Potomac District and Robert C. Schenck of the Eighth Army Corps answered to General-in-Chief Henry Halleck, whose primary objective was to protect the Baltimore & Ohio Railroad. The Federal high command regarded Jones's guerrilla tactics as a diversion and a mere nuisance. Furthermore, Halleck felt that Milroy's raids on civilian targets only provoked the enemy, which could respond by reinforcing the Shenandoah Valley and pose a greater threat to the railroad.

Refusing to stand complacent, Milroy demanded that the injunction be removed and threatened to resign, "as I would much prefer being a private in an active fighting army to being kept in command of a stationary advance under a brigadier general not very hostile or pugnacious."[61] In the same report, Milroy advised that his scouts had captured an enemy partisan who was a "known bushwhacker, horse thief, and murderer." With a tone of sarcasm, he added, "I'd like to hang him if Jefferson Davis and Halleck did not make too big a fuss about it. He richly deserves it."[62]

Political Fallout

Milroy retaliated against Jones's guerrilla tactics with more raids on civilian targets in the guise of foraging operations. Raiding parties destroyed dwellings and barns after they looted and seized personal property and livestock. Victimized citizens of the valley complained to their political representatives, who carried their grievances to the Confederate War Department. Secretary of War James Seddon protested to Lee over Jones's lack of results in the valley. Defending Jones, Lee wrote to the secretary: "I can only say that General Jones, who has always borne a high character as an officer, was selected last fall by General Jackson to take command of the Valley District. His force was small, but was deemed at the time sufficient for the defense of that district, and proved so during the season when active operations could be successfully in that mountainous country. Now that the season [winter] has advanced, and the climate in the region being so severe, it is almost impracticable to operate with any beneficial results."[63] Lee cited Jones's partial success at Moorefield. Seddon was unimpressed, as strategically the Moorefield expedition accomplished very little.

Congressman Alexander Boteler filed a petition with Secretary Seddon demanding the removal of Jones as commander of the Valley District.[64] Seddon redirected the petitions to Lee and demanded a change. Even Milroy reported that Jones was relieved and superseded by a colonel.[65] A week later, Milroy reported that Fitzhugh Lee would soon replace Jones as commander of the Valley District.[66] Lee forwarded Seddon's communication to Jones and enclosed a copy of Boteler's petition. Lee commented, "I think it is proper to enclose to you a letter of the Hon. A.P. Boteler which has been referred to me by the Sec. of War, not that you require to be informed how easily any animosity becomes dissatisfied when the interests are affected but that you may know of the existence of that feeling where you are concerned and do all in your power to remove it."[67]

Victory at Woodstock

From his latest base outpost below Woodstock, Grumble continued to conduct operations in the same manner, harassing Milroy's defenses with nighttime maneuvers and hit-and-run tactics. On most occasions, the skirmishes had inconclusive or inconsequential results. A guerrilla-style raid on February 26, 1863, was an eventful exception.

Captain Frank A. Bond of the First Maryland (CSA) Cavalry, taking the initiative, led a one-hundred–man cavalry force that slipped behind the enemy lines to strike Milroy's pickets at Winchester, Middletown, and Kernstown. Gunfire was exchanged, resulting in an undetermined number of Federal casualties. Bond's force abducted fourteen Federal soldiers before breaking off the attack and withdrawing back to their base outpost. Enraged by this audacious action, 500 inexperienced members of Milroy's Thirteenth Pennsylvania Cavalry and the First New York Cavalry impulsively gave chase.[68] Unaware that they were setting themselves up, Milroy's pursuers committed what their commander's superiors had specifically ordered him not to do.

Bond had sent a courier to notify Jones of what was taking place. Two miles south of Woodstock, Jones, along with his Seventh, and Eleventh Virginia Cavalry regiments, awaited the pursuing Union cavalry. Upon their arrival, Jones and his two regiments charged into the Federal columns, "bugles blaring, yelling like demons with drawn pistols, carbines, and sabers."[69] Both Federal regiments fled in confusion back toward their Winchester garrison. Jones pursued them twenty miles to Middletown, where hand-to-hand combat culminated the engagement. Jones reported, "[We] cut them up very badly. We have about 200 prisoners and killed and wounded many more."[70] The victory cost the Jones Brigade only a modest number of casualties.

Lieutenant John Blue commented that the captured Union cavalrymen of the Thirteenth Pennsylvania were new troops experiencing combat for the first time. They were also well equipped with new arms, saddles, halters, and uniforms. The men of Jones's Brigade enthusiastically supplied themselves with the new equipment captured in great numbers.[71]

The engagement results were a humiliation for Milroy, who blamed his subordinates. He contended that the Thirteenth Pennsylvania and the First New York regiments delayed their response to the initial attack and violated his orders by giving pursuit.[72] Milroy commented that his two regiments should have prevailed, as their "force was the greater."[73] He described the conduct of his cavalry units as "disgraceful and cowardly."[74] Jones enjoyed his most impressive victory over Milroy since taking command of the Valley District.

Grumble's Second Political Setback

Jones's modest triumph could not save him from the mounting political pressure to remove the Union presence from the valley. On the same day of the engagement, Secretary Seddon outlined his concerns to Lee. Seddon wrote:

> The well-ascertained sentiment of the people in the Valley of Virginia, concurring with the best judgment I can form in relation to the operations of General W.E. Jones in that region, constrains me to request that he may be relieved from his command there, and that General Fitzhugh Lee be substituted in his stead. Whether in effecting this object it may be most judicious merely to exchange these generals, or whether and what change in the distribution of troops shall accompany the substitutions of General F. Lee to the command, are questions which are committed with confidence to your superior knowledge and judgment as to the circumstances of your army and their respective commands; but it is the decided wish of the [War] Department that the exchange of the command in the Valley should be made with as little delay as may be consistent with your conviction of the practicability of such movement of troops as you may deem advisable.[75]

Lee mildly protested the judgment of the secretary of war, who had already made up his mind. Seddon was obviously unaware of Jones's most recent triumph, which Lee later revealed, but it was too late.[76] Without further challenging the secretary's administrative decision, Lee begrudgingly consented to replace Jones with his nephew (Fitz Lee) "as soon as circumstances will permit."[77] Lee added, "I beg to say, in justice to General Jones, that I do not know that under the circumstances, with his force and that opposed to him, any one would have done better." On the impracticality of removing the Jones Brigade, Lee went on to say, "General Jones brigade is that formerly commanded by General Ashby. It has always served in the valley, and I believe, is organized of men principally from that region." In closing his report, Lee stated, "General Milroy is reported to have under his command 15,000 men stationed at Harpers Ferry, Martinsburg, Winchester, Romney, and New Creek. General Jones's force is not more than sufficient to restrain marauding."[78]

In his second major administrative setback, Jones lost his title as commander of the Valley District for political reasons. The adversity, however, came with a silver lining: He maintained command over his brigade of experienced and battle-hardened veterans. Furthermore, the administrative change released Jones from the overwhelming burden to provide security for a vast mountainous area plagued by winter weather conditions, all the while with limited manpower resources. Relieved from the encumbrance, Jones was free to devise an ambitious undertaking.

13

West Virginia Raid

The removal of Jones from command of the Valley District was a symbolic formality to appease Secretary of War James Seddon, who was receiving similar pressure from local civilian politicians. Jones maintained command over his experienced brigade and resumed a state of autonomy while detached from Stuart's cavalry division. With Fitzhugh Lee assuming the responsibility for the security of the lower Shenandoah Valley, Jones relocated his headquarters to Lacey Spring in Rockingham County.

By the spring of 1863 the political movement at Wheeling under Francis H. Pierpont's leadership was officially progressing from a government in exile into one seceding from Virginia and the formation of a separate state aligned with the Union. Neither the Confederacy nor the Virginia leadership in Richmond would recognize the new state, but they had to deal with the strategic reality. The counties of northwestern Virginia and the cismontane counties of the eastern panhandle were providing sanctuary for Union troops and, most important, a safe domain for the Baltimore & Ohio Railroad.

Recently promoted Brigadier General John D. Imboden, who had led a counterinsurgency against the Unionist movement in the region for much of 1862, devised a bold strategy to reclaim the region for the Southern cause. He submitted a report to Lee outlining an ambitious plan for a large-scale, guerrilla-style offensive in the northwestern trans-Allegheny region.[1] Imboden's idea originated with partisan ranger John H. McNeil, who had drawn up a proposal to destroy the Cheat River Bridge at Rowlesburg.

Expanding upon McNeil's initiative, Imboden called for a joint operation in which his and Jones's brigades would commit a simultaneous two-prong offensive into the contested region. Imboden predicted that a successfully executed expedition would facilitate recruiting area men of Southern allegiance, and thus the size and strength of the attacking forces would expand while the operation was in progress. Confident that "four-fifths" of the region's population supported the Confederacy, he forecasted that the central government at Wheeling would collapse.[2]

Jones submitted his separate plan prioritizing the destruction of the Baltimore and Ohio Railroad bridges and trestles between Grafton, (West) Virginia, and Oakland, Maryland. Imboden's force would simultaneously attack Federal outposts in the region. Each offensive would serve as a diversion for the other. Such a measure could render General Benjamin Kelley's fortifications (which included Milroy's garrison at Winchester) in the Upper Potomac region obsolete.

Recalling that his first campaign in the region had been an inglorious failure, Lee doubted all of Imboden's objectives were realistic. However, he approved Jones's plan with two obtainable goals in mind. Anticipating offensive action by the new Army of the Potomac commander, General Joseph Hooker, Lee saw merit in temporarily disrupting traffic on the B&O Railroad and thereby thwarting potential enemy reinforcements from the west. As a diversion, the raid could draw Union reinforcements under General Robert Huston Milroy westward from Winchester, only to be neutralized by the loss of bridge access to advance against the raiding parties. The second and perhaps more important objective was forage. The raid as Jones proposed it could resupply his army with cattle, grain, and other means of sustenance.[3]

As the time neared a launching date, Lee detached Lieutenant William G. Williamson of the First CSA Engineers Regiment, Army of Northern Virginia, to the W.E. Jones Brigade. Williamson had been instrumental in the destruction of the Monocacy Bridge during the Antietam Campaign, and his expertise in demolitions would be most beneficial. Emphasizing the need for secrecy, Lee noted to Jones, "You will have to supply the implements he [Williamson] may require, as he will not know for what purpose he joins you."[4]

Jones organized a "pioneer corps" within his brigade to serve under Lieutenant Williamson.[5] The pioneer corps was an unofficial title given to a small squad of individuals selected from different regiments. They were an elite group of men chosen for their athletic and other capabilities to perform special operations. In preparation for the expedition, Jones submitted a requisition to equip this special outfit with demolition and explosive supplies.[6]

Expeditions Launched

Imboden embarked on his expedition from Staunton on April 20. Coincidentally, it was the same day that President Lincoln signed a proclamation admitting West Virginia into the Union at the end of sixty days, to be effective June 20, 1863. Imboden's Brigade consisted of four cavalry and three infantry regiments with a collective strength of 3,365.[7] On the following day, April 21, Jones launched his expedition from Lacey Spring.[8] Jones's brigade as it initially embarked on the expedition consisted of the following units: the First Maryland Cavalry Battalion commanded by Major Ridgley Brown; the Sixth Virginia Cavalry Regiment commanded by Lieutenant Colonel John Shac Green; the Seventh Virginia Cavalry Regiment commanded by Colonel Richard H. Dulaney; the Eleventh Virginia Cavalry Regiment commanded by Colonel Lunsford Lindsay Lomax; the Twelfth Virginia Cavalry Regiment commanded by Colonel Asher. W. Harman; the Thirty-Fifth Battalion Virginia Cavalry, a former partisan ranger group known as the "Comanches," commanded by Lieutenant Colonel Elijah V. White; the Thirty-Fourth Battalion Virginia Cavalry commanded by Lieutenant Colonel Vincent A. Witcher; a detachment of the First Maryland Infantry, including a battery from the Baltimore Light Artillery; Captain Robert Preston Chew's Battery commanded by Lieutenant Colonel James R. Herbert.

Jones was secretive about the mission. No one below the rank of colonel had knowledge regarding their destination. Each man was to prepare ten days of rations.[9] Records fail to document the actual numerical strength of Jones's force, but estimates suggest it began with about 3,500 men.[10]

Moorefield and Petersburg

Embarking upon his mission, Jones partially retraced the route of his earlier expedition against General Robert Huston Milroy's Moorefield and Petersburg outposts in

Hardy County.[11] Melting snows from the previous winter swelled the rivers and streams, while recent precipitation rendered the roads nearly impassable. It took three days for the Jones Brigade to arrive at Moorefield, where they found the South Branch of the Potomac had risen well "past fording."[12] Jones diverted his column upstream to Petersburg, where fording conditions were not much improved. He described the crossing as "wide, deep, rough, and from the strength of the current, exceedingly dangerous," but crossing at that point was the only option.[13] Pro-Southern citizens offered assistance and served as guides, but fording operations remained hazardous.[14]

A trooper of the Sixth Virginia Cavalry leading the way was swept away to his death along with his horse. The others, who witnessed their comrade's misfortune, proceeded with apprehension. Captain William N. McDonald would write, "Men who would be quick to charge a battery, if ordered, were appalled at the rushing, angry waters."[15] Lieutenant George Baylor recalled, "The Israelites never moved through the Red Sea with more awe and solemnity."[16] A sergeant with the Twelfth Virginia was swept off of his horse but managed to save himself by grasping his steed's tail and recovering with his horse about a quarter of a mile downstream.[17] In all, one man and twenty-seven horses drowned.[18] Only the mounted troops could successfully cross. The supply wagons, infantry, and mounted artillery could not. Jones had to either wait for improved conditions or commit to a very early-stage, high-stakes gamble. He chose the latter.

Anticipating that he would face similar climatic and topographical conditions throughout the expedition, Jones elected to sacrifice supplies, provisions, numerical strength, and firepower for mobility. He directed his infantry, teamsters, supply wagons, and the mounted artillery to return to the Shenandoah Valley.[19] His raiders would have to rely upon their swiftness of movement, the element of surprise, and foraging off the land in a hostile region. His initial force, estimated at 3,500, was suddenly reduced to about 2,200.[20] Jones's expeditionary force diverted back toward Moorefield and camped on the west bank of the South Branch. Morale was extremely low. Without having engaged in combat, Jones had drastically reduced his numerical strength. Also, with the prior deviation to Petersburg, they had spent an entire day to advance only two miles.

On the following morning, Jones's column set out on an anticipated several days' journey to the primary objective, the Cheat River Bridge at Rowlesburg in Preston County. The selected route took them to Greenland Gap, an 820-foot deep natural pass over New Creek Mountain, lined on both sides by towering sandstone cliffs in Hardy County (now Grant County). Jones's raiders followed the North Fork of Patterson Creek and reached the vicinity by late afternoon on April 25 and encountered their first armed resistance.

Greenland Gap

At Greenland Gap, pro–Union citizen scouts had warned Federal authorities of the approaching Southern raiding party. With full knowledge of their enemy's strength, companies from the Twenty-Third Illinois Infantry ("Irish Brigade") and the Fourteenth Regiment of (West) Virginia Volunteers Infantry united to form a combined force of eighty-three, who converted a log church and adjacent schoolhouse into defensive fortifications.[21] Both Federal units, dispatched from General Benjamin Kelley's headquarters at New Creek, were under the command of Captain Martin Wallace and had fought against Jones in his January expedition to Moorefield.[22] Although heavily outnumbered, the

Federals possessed an ideal defensive position that, protected by the surrounding natural barriers of Patterson Creek and the towering cliffs, would serve as a formidable obstacle to any further progression of Jones's expedition. Captain Wallace positioned his men inside the barricaded log walls of the two structures, with adequate views to fire in any direction. Wallace completed his preparations by stationing pickets along the outer perimeter of the area.[23]

The situation presented Jones with a dilemma. Greenland Gap was not a military objective but it had suddenly posed a daunting obstacle to his mission. He had two options. He could either divert his brigade to avoid an armed confrontation or he could take on the enemy by force. Jones determined that any deviation would be costly in time for an operation that had to be expeditious to succeed. Reasoning that he had already conceded the element of surprise for the balance of his undertaking, he ordered a direct frontal assault. The Seventh Virginia Cavalry spearheaded a two-pronged advance led by Lieutenant Colonel Thomas A. Marshall and Colonel Richard H. Dulany. They abducted four pickets and learned the enemy strength was that of only two companies with no artillery support.[24] The regiment then proceeded toward the log fortifications.

The awaiting Union defenders opened fire, forcing the attackers to break off the assault and leave their casualties on the field. Colonel Dulany was wounded in the arm, and his horse was killed. The second wave of attack brought similar results.[25] Repulsed twice, Jones's Seventh Cavalry gained little in exchange for three killed, ten wounded, and the loss fourteen horses. Jones's forces dismounted, took covered positions, and poured a volley of small-arms fire onto the log fortresses but with little effect. Lieutenant George Baylor would write decades later, "We sorely missed our artillery, [as] with one piece of artillery the loss would have been avoided and precious time saved."[26] Jones found his numerically superior forces neutralized in a standoff.

Calling for a cease-fire, Jones sent a courier under a flag of truce to the Union position. The messenger informed Captain Martin Wallace that Jones's raiding party "had a force of thousands."[27] Captain Wallace responded, "Go back with the rag [truce flag]; I don't care if he has a million."[28] The courier departed, and both sides resumed firing. Jones then called for a second cease-fire and sent a different messenger under a flag of truce to the Union position. This time, the messenger was one of the captured Federal pickets abducted during the initial advance. The bearer brought a written ultimatum informing the Federals that Jones had a force sufficient beyond doubt to take their position, and if they refused, he would not be responsible for the consequences. Captain Wallace sent a written rejection and instructed his men to fight on.[29]

Jones's measure of sending a prisoner as a messenger backfired. His forces were spread out beyond his ability to communicate with them, and the onset of darkness further complicated matters. Upon observing the courier in the Federal uniform who carried the truce flag walk away from the fortification, members of the First Maryland Cavalry perceived that their barricaded enemies were surrendering. Under that mistaken assumption, they advanced without caution. Captain Wallace in turn erroneously assumed that the Confederates had used the temporary truce as deception. Wallace called for the Marylanders to halt, but they continued and advanced within range. The Federals opened fire, killing two and wounding a third. The Marylanders retreated to their covered positions under the perception that the Federals had deployed a false truce to lure their targets to within range. Firing from a distance resumed, and the standoff continued.

Jones tried to negotiate a resolution by sending a messenger under a flag of truce for the third time. In a bluff, the messenger relayed a threat to deploy artillery. With full knowledge that Jones's artillery was nonexistent, Captain Wallace responded, "Tell him he has got none; if he has, bring them on. We are Mulligan's men and will fight to the last crust and cartridge."[30] Having anticipated another rejection, Jones directed his messenger to request time to remove their dead and wounded men from the battlefield. Captain Wallace allowed thirty minutes, after which the firing commenced from a distance and the stalemate continued.

By 8:30, Jones engaged his elite squad of pioneers. Equipping one group with axes and bundles of straw, he directed them to cut openings into the building, set fire to the bundles of straw, and cast them inside. Jones outfitted the second group with a keg of powder (originally intended to blow up the Cheat River Bridge) and directed them to place it in the crawl space beneath the church building. The joint undertakings, however, were stalled because the enemy fire remained too intense for either group to make progress.

Jones then called for a fourth truce. Acting as his own messenger, he approached the Federal position on his mount.[31] He communicated that his forces had successfully placed kegs of gunpowder beneath the building and "politely informed" Captain Wallace that he had five minutes to surrender or he would "blow them all to hell."[32] Calling his bluff, Captain Wallace responded "with equal politeness" that Jones "could go there himself."[33] Jones departed, and the standoff resumed.

Next, Jones ordered the storming parties to wade across the waist-deep stream under heavy enemy fire.[34] Colonel Brown's Marylanders took positions to the rear of the building, while White's Battalion took cover in the front. Although they had the fortress surrounded, their situation remained at an impasse. Around midnight, one of the pioneers, Private Thomas E. Tippett of the Thirty-Fifth Battalion, Virginia Cavalry, ascended the log church chimney with a bundle of straw and set the roof on fire.[35] Diverting the enemy's attention, Private William Alexander Buck of the Seventh Virginia Cavalry charged the barricade firing all rounds of his pistol into the crevices and holding his position despite the loss of his mount.[36]

Captain Wallace had to reassess his situation. Uncertain as to whether Jones was bluffing about the powder keg beneath the structure, he realized the futility of fighting inside of a burning fortress that might explode. He surrendered by waving a flag of truce. Before exiting, the defenders left their arms inside the burning church to deny their use to the enemy.[37]

The cessation of hostilities evolved into an emotional confrontation within the Jones Brigade between the Virginia and Maryland units. Having misunderstood what had taken place during the second cease-fire, Captain Frank A. Bond and the First Battalion Maryland Cavalry contended that the Federals had instigated a false truce to lure members of his company within range. Having suffered three casualties, the Marylanders demanded retribution. The Virginians, members of the Thirty-Fifth Battalion, in particular saw the matter from an entirely different perspective. Viewing their enemies as "Virginians" defending their homes from invaders, they expressed admiration for their opponents, who "left no stain upon the honor of Old Virginia in their defense of the pass."[38] A tense situation emerged, with doubts as to whether the Marylanders could restrain their rage. General Jones intervened and announced to the emotional troops, "Boys, these men have thrown down their arms and must be protected and treated as prisoners. It would be cowardly to do otherwise. These men have done their duty as brave men and what I hope you would do. These men must be cared for."[39] Submitting to their commander's orders, the outnumbered Marylanders relented.

Among the captured was a man "by the name of Shreve," referred to by some as a "Swamp Dragon" and others as a "bushwhacker."[40] By either term, he was considered an outlaw associated with a notorious gang demonized by both sides.[41] The captor suggested singling out and executing the prisoner. Jones replied, "You should have never taken him alive; but since you have brought him to me, he shall be treated as a prisoner of war."[42] The prisoners were marched under guard to Moorefield and were ultimately escorted to Staunton and then by rail on to Richmond.

The skirmish at Greenland Gap was an overwhelming victory for Jones, but Federal reports claimed victory likewise. Captain Wallace alleged that his force of eighty-three against 3,100 had inflicted 104 casualties on the raiders.[43] Both figures were highly exaggerated. Jones reported his brigade losses at seven killed and twenty-two wounded.[44] Among the Confederates killed was Private James Flynn, who had defected from the Union side to the Twelfth Virginia Cavalry in mid–February.[45] By accounts on both sides, Union losses were two killed and between six and eight wounded among the eighty captured.[46]

Union General Benjamin Kelley visited the site three days later. Putting a positive face on the matter, Kelley reported, "The affair at this place on Saturday was one of the most gallant since the opening of the war."[47] Exaggerating the enemy casualty statistics, Kelley declared that "the killed and wounded of the rebels outnumbered our force engaged."[48] Kelley recommended that the U.S. secretary of war present each of the Federals with a medal in recognition of their gallantry.[49] For the time being, however, Kelley's heroes were prisoners of war traveling under guard to Richmond.

Jones regarded the entire incident as "an unfortunate detention of four hours" that deprived his mission of valuable time to reach other objectives.[50] News of the fight would spread rapidly and deprive his expedition of any element of surprise as they ventured farther into enemy territory. Between the combined casualties and detachments for prisoner escort duty, Jones's force was further diminished in strength by some accounts to as few as 1,300. He led his expedition on a night march to the northwestern grade of Mount Storm, near the border with western Maryland, and arrived about two hours before daylight.[51] The men would undergo more than thirty-six hours without rest, for which Jones felt they did not have the luxury. Having conceded the element of surprise, he needed to strike his targets before reinforcements could arrive.

Taking another high-stakes gamble, Jones divided his brigade and launched a three-pronged offensive against the Baltimore & Ohio Railroad. Jones and the main body rode toward Rowlesburg in Preston County. Two detached units would simultaneously target the railroad bridges in western Maryland. Colonel A.W. Harman led a detachment consisting of the Twelfth Virginia Cavalry, Brown's Maryland Battalion of Cavalry, and John H. McNeill's partisan rangers to destroy the bridge at Oakland.[52] As the third prong, Captain E.H. McDonald led a detached squadron from the Eleventh Virginia Cavalry to destroy railroad trestles at Altamont before rejoining Harmon's detachment. Ultimately, all three units would rendezvous at Morgantown.

Rowlesburg

Jones led his column westward toward the B&O Railroad Cheat River Viaduct, the primary objective of the entire raid.[53] Destruction of this particular target justified all of the risks in the expedition. Of all the railroad assets in northwestern Virginia, the Cheat River Bridge would have been the hardest and most time consuming to repair. Earlier in the war Lee had written, "The rupture of the railroad at Cheat River would be worth to us an [entire] army."[54] The same conditions that rendered the Cheat River Viaduct difficult to repair also made it a challenging target to destroy. The Federals gave it a high priority and, combined with the surrounding natural defenses, it did not require a large force to protect the structure adequately. Jones and his force arrived in the vicinity and captured a squad of pickets without incident. From the prisoners, Jones learned that as few as 250 men guarded the bridge, but they were well positioned defensively on each end.[55] Jones ordered Lieutenant Colonel John Shac Green of the Sixth Virginia Cavalry and Captain O.T. Weems leading a company of the Eleventh Virginia Cavalry to conduct coordinated advances to take control of the bridge. To his disgust, both frontal assaults failed. Jones chastised his two subordinate officers by reporting, "From the feebleness with which my orders were executed here, the attack failed."[56] In a follow-up, he elaborated: "Colonel Green allowed himself to be stopped by twenty men."[57] Jones chastised Captain Weems, who, with eighty sharpshooters detached from the Eleventh Virginia at his disposal, attacked "feebly with only 28 men, leaving the remainder of his command to guard his rear against an imaginary foe."[58]

By the end of the day, Jones's forces were exhausted and famished following a thirty-six-hour march.[59] To renew the attack without the elements of surprise, infantry or artillery would be futile. Jones withdrew his detachment westward "leaving the railroad bridge and trestle-work unharmed" and the defenders in their rear.[60] His mission to destroy the most prioritized target was an inglorious failure, one that Private John Opie of the Sixth Virginia Cavalry would describe as "feeble and ineffectual."[61]

The affair at Rowlesburg capped a trinity of failures and was the most discouraging moment of the entire expedition. Jones had experienced a difficult crossing of the South Branch of the Potomac, a meaningless yet costly victory at Greenland Gap, and a failure to destroy his primary target at Rowlesburg. Cognizant that the enemy would be sending reinforcements while his provisions neared depletion, Jones withdrew his forces farther westward in hopes of succeeding against secondary targets and ultimately reuniting with his detached units. He was not only frustrated by the recent failure, but his divided forces were also proceeding deeper into hostile territory and were heavily outnumbered. Early in the mission, they had already conceded surprise or secrecy. They would have to parole all prisoners, as they could not assume the burden of transporting them under guard. For the sake of obscurity, they would have to camp many nights without fires in near-freezing temperatures.

The troopers had to be wary of more than just enemy forces. Bands of armed mountain men consistently observed their movements. The mountaineers rarely attacked but were always present to follow, watch and be potential bushwhackers.[62] Jones recognized these mountain men as independent individuals whose allegiance was uncertain. Aware that his expedition would be in peril if they chose confrontation, he took extreme measures to avoid antagonizing them. Their watchful eyes on the brigade provided more benefit than harm by serving as provost guards to prevent stragglers, desertions, and looting throughout the entire mission.[63] Their threat also broke the monotony by requiring the brigade members to stay on alert. Mindful of the "observers," Jones implemented a no-tolerance policy for plundering and enforced it by humiliating the violators. A trooper who looted a hoop skirt was forced to wear it around his neck for an entire day.

Another who took an umbrella was ordered to carry it open before the column for an afternoon.[64]

Jones marched his column to Evansville in Preston County encountering no resistance. After setting up camp, he dispatched scouts to locate his detached forces. With no word on their whereabouts, he proceeded to Independence, where his troops destroyed a two-span railroad bridge.[65] Jones then led his column on another night march northward in the direction of Morgantown, the point of rendezvous.

Oakland, Altamont, Cranberry Summit and the Runaway Train

As part of Jones's three-pronged simultaneous offensive, Colonel Asher W. Harman led the Twelfth Virginia Cavalry, Brown's Maryland battalion, and John H. McNeill's company of partisan rangers to Oakland to torch the Youghiogheny River bridge. Captain Edward H. McDonald commanded the third prong, a detachment from the Eleventh Virginia Cavalry, which ventured to Altamont, Maryland, to destroy smaller bridges. Both units were directed to complete their tasks, march westward through Kingwood, and ultimately rendezvous with Jones's column at Morgantown.

Colonel Harman's band reached Oakland with swiftness and surprise, capturing the unsuspecting Union soldiers on their way to church services. Most confrontational exchanges were limited to verbal barbs, and most of them were with the captured Union soldiers' female companions. A young raider approached a couple, tipped his hat, performed a courtly bow, and informed the Union soldier he was now a prisoner. Recognizing his hopeless situation, the soldier immediately succumbed. His female companion, on the other hand, broke out into a tirade, calling the raider a "bald-headed son of a bitch!" Emotionally shaken, the naïve and pious raider exclaimed to his comrades, "Please God, I never heard a woman talk that way before."[66] Private William Lyne Wilson of the Twelfth Virginia Cavalry Wilson engaged another female accompanying a captured Union soldier. Flirting with the lady, Wilson remarked, "Don't you think the Rebels are better-looking men than the Yankees?" The young woman responded, "You good looking? You look like your mustache had been dyed three weeks in buttermilk." Overhearing her remarks, Wilson's comrades mocked him for his arrogance.[67] The raiders encountered no resistance when they took approximately forty prisoners, cut the telegraph wires and proceeded to burn several small bridges spanning the Potomac River.[68] After destroying the Youghiogheny River bridge, the raiders paused to await the arrival of the Eleventh Virginia Cavalry dispatched to Altamont.

As the third prong, Captain McDonald's squadron from the Eleventh Virginia Cavalry reached Altamont, approximately eight miles east of Oakland, and burned numerous small bridges in the vicinity. From the cover of woods just outside of the town, they observed a westbound locomotive hauling eight to ten cars approach, arrive, and stop at the station. The train operators exited and departed into town. Jones later reported that had it not been for the delay at Greenland Gap, this squadron would have captured Colonel Mulligan's staff of officers, who had previously evacuated the train taking much of the cargo with them.[69] As matters stood, McDonald's squadron captured the unattended and unoccupied train.[70] All of the cars were empty except for two that contained grain. After feeding their steeds and stocking up on what each man could carry, the raiding party proceeded to destroy the tracks behind (east of) the train.

Captain McDonald intended to derail and topple the train by backing it up a short distance over the void where the tracks were removed. Theoretically, backing the engine at full throttle would cause the locomotive to roll down an embankment once it derailed. McDonald asked the men if anyone knew how to operate a locomotive. According to Lieutenant John Blue, Dr. John Dailey answered that he could operate the train and volunteered to do so. Dailey boarded the engine, opened the valves to full throttle, and then jumped off. Daily thought that he had locked the engine into reverse gear. The train was actually in forward gear and proceeded without an engineer or passengers westbound on a level grade. As the train advanced, its speed accelerated to a rate that Lieutenant John Blue recalled, was "never equaled before or since."[71] The runaway train raced westward. Eight miles ahead, at Oakland, Harman's detachment took notice that a train was approaching at full speed and with no whistle. Assuming that the freight cars carried Union troops, they took cover in anticipation of an assault. To their surprise, the train raced past the station in its westerly direction. Ultimately, the locomotive exhausted its fuel supply just as it reached the abutment of the destroyed Youghiogheny River bridge. It came to a stop with its front engine wheels dropped just over the edge.[72]

McDonald's squad rode westbound and united with Harman's detachment at Oakland. Merged into a single unit, they proceeded northwest toward Kingwood. While en route, they captured fifteen members of a home guard and destroyed the railroad tracks at Cranberry Summit (now Terra Alta).[73] Harman's command combed the countryside from Kingwood to the Pennsylvania border to requisition cattle and horses.[74] The detachment then resumed the march and proceeded to Morgantown.

First Occupation of Morgantown

One of the more high-profile raiders during the dual occupations of Morgantown was Private William Lyne Wilson of the Twelfth Virginia Cavalry. The Jefferson County, (West) Virginia, native had graduated from the Columbian College of the District of Columbia (now George Washington University) and was pursuing a masters degree from the University of Virginia when the Civil War broke out. It seems remarkable that with his educational background he remained an enlisted man for the entire duration of the war, but this may have been by his choice.[75] History is filled with irony, and Wilson's case was no exception. Three decades later, he would be appointed as the third president of West Virginia University (founded in 1867), followed by five terms in the U.S. House of Representatives serving the West Virginia Second Congressional District. For the time being, however, he was a mounted member of Grumble Jones's invading force and drew the contempt of the town inhabitants.

Although they were already in territory inhabited by Unionists, Private Wilson described Monongalia County as "the meanest Union hole" they entered.[76] The town citizens already knew about the Confederate raiders' actions at Altamont, Oakland, and Cranberry Summit. With no local Federal forces to protect them, some residents evacuated with their horses to Pennsylvania; others hid their livestock in nearby wooded pastures.[77] Senator Waitman T. Willey was among those who fled.[78] Not all took evasive action. Several hundred civilian citizens banned together to offer armed resistance.

Leading a scouting party, Captain Frank A. Bond of the First Maryland Cavalry rode into Morgantown under a flag of truce about midday on April 27. He approached the band of armed citizens and demanded their unconditional surrender. He cautioned them that resisting would only result in the needless loss of life and the unnecessary destruction of property.[79] Bond assured the group that General Jones had no intention of sacking any towns and would limit his objectives to gathering forage and destroying military targets, particularly the railroads.

Agreeing to Captain Bond's terms, the citizens deposited their firearms at the county courthouse and retired to their homes.[80] Colonel Harmon's main detachment force then marched into Morgantown and declared a state of occupation. The raiders "cut down the Stars and Stripes" and replaced it with the Confederate banner on the courthouse lawn.[81] Complying with General Jones's standing orders, there was no looting. The only significant problems regarding military conduct occurred when two of the raiders had to be restrained from fighting a duel over the potential affections of one of the town's attractive females.[82] The object of their attention apparently wanted nothing to do with either admirer. There was a lame attempt to befriend a group of barmaids who when asked to sing defiantly chanted pro–Union songs.

By five o'clock Harman's collective detachment withdrew from Morgantown and marched toward Independence to unite with Jones. The Morgantown residents immediately dispatched couriers to warn the surrounding region of the Confederate invasion. The Fayette County, Pennsylvania, courthouse bell at Uniontown sounded and an atmosphere of excitement and panic prevailed. Wheeling, in Ohio County, (West) Virginia, received a warning. Factories and mills closed as citizens organized home guards. Sizeable amounts of currency were transported to Pittsburg, whose residents prepared for a pending emergency.[83]

Second Occupation of Morgantown

At 2:00 on the morning of the 28th between Independence and Morgantown, Jones and his column rendezvoused with the detached forces under Colonel Harman. Harman reported their overwhelming successes at Oakland, Altamont, Cranberry Summit, and the first occupation of Morgantown. Up until that moment, all indications had pointed to the potential failure of the overall mission. With reports of the recent accomplishments, the outlook dramatically improved. United for the first time since Greenland Gap, the Jones Brigade conducted a night march. The Morgantown residents were in for an unpleasant surprise. The departure of the invasion force on the previous day was not only temporary but it also would return with even greater numbers. Reconsolidated to full strength, Jones's entire expeditionary force arrived on the following morning, resulting in the second occupation of the Monongalia County seat.

The return march was not without incident. Captain Frank A. Bond's scouting party reached the outskirts of the town and encountered gunfire that killed Captain William I. Rasin's horse. Rasin's troopers dismounted and apprehended three highly respected local citizens who alleged they were on a squirrel hunt.[84] Captain Bond ordered a "short trial" that resulted in a conviction of the three captives as criminal bushwhackers, who were sentenced to death by firing squad. Two of the captives died by execution, but the third feigned death and survived.[85] The raiders encountered no further resistance entering Morgantown for the second time. With General Jones in charge, guards prohibited visitations to the local taverns. There was no looting, but the men purchased goods from the town stores, paying for them with Confederate script.[86]

Forewarned Morgantown inhabitants who hid their livestock before the first pending invasion had returned with their assets, only to lose them to the foraging details with the second one.[87] Private William Lyne Wilson took an active role in the requisitioning of the horses, an accusation that his political opponents would try to exploit three decades later.[88] Foraging details combed the Monongalia County countryside seizing horses and cattle all the way to the Pennsylvania border. Panic and exaggerated accounts of Jones's force multiplied. Hysteria prevailed over logic among the civilians and even spread to elements of the military. At Grafton a telegraph operator was so convinced of a Confederate invasion that he destroyed his instruments and fled.[89] Colonel Nathan Wilkinson of the Sixth Regiment (West) Virginia Volunteer Infantry did Jones's bidding by burning a bridge and destroying the railroad tracks at Bridgeport between Grafton and Clarksburg. Wilkinson justified his action by saying he "thought it better to burn a bridge at Bridgeport to prevent their [the Jones Brigade] from coming this way by rail."[90]

General Robert Schenck, the commander of the Eighth Army Corps, headquartered in Baltimore, telegraphed Lincoln's general-in-chief, Henry Halleck, in Washington with reports of "unnecessary panic at Wheeling, Pittsburg, and Parkersburg."[91] Schenck also telegraphed Colonel Wilkinson a message stating, "You are evidently in a causeless panic, as my last telegram will show you. Your burning of the bridge at Bridgeport is disgraceful."[92] Schenck later communicated to Halleck that Jones was not within forty miles of Wilkinson, against whom he would consider bringing court-martial proceedings.[93] Later, Wilkinson tried to explain his impulsive action by communicating, "I have been going four days and nights without sleeping, and am somewhat wearied."[94]

Generals Halleck and Schenck concluded that Jones's raid was a mere diversion. Both suggested that the commands of General Benjamin S. Roberts at Clarksburg and General Benjamin F. Kelley at New Creek concentrate their efforts on obstructing his exit.[95]

Jones and his reunited expeditionary force withdrew from Morgantown on the evening of April 28 and marched in a southwesterly direction toward their next objective. At dawn on the following day, they arrived at the outskirts of Fairmont in Marion County.

Fairmont

Like Morgantown, Fairmont is situated along the banks of the Monongahela River. Strategically distinguishing it from the former, Fairmont harbored the Wheeling-to-Grafton railroad tracks including the iron superstructure bridge spanning the river. Signifying its tactical importance, the Federals garrisoned about four hundred infantrymen to secure the bridge.[96] Aware that Jones's force had recently departed Morgantown and was marching in their direction; the Union military authorities were not going to be taken by surprise. Jones would have to deploy several acts of deception.

Jones divided his brigade to attack two fronts. In a flanking maneuver, his main column shifted around the guarded Buffalo Creek Bridge and the Union-occupied surrounding hills to arrive from the west. They then charged pell-mell into the streets of Fairmont, driving the panic-stricken troops eastward to regroup at the primary railroad bridge. Colonel A.W. Harman led a detachment force that crossed a suspension bridge south of town before moving up to attack from the east side. After offering only moderate resistance, 260 Union troops surrendered.[97] Upon taking possession of the primary railroad bridge, the raiders were in the process of collecting captured firearms when a new development surfaced.

From about twenty miles to the southeast at Grafton, a train hauling Union artillery and infantry approached, stopped on the east side, and unloaded its arsenal for an offensive against Jones's force. Commanded by Colonel James A. Mulligan, their objective was to retake the railroad bridge. In preparation for an infantry advance, Mulligan's artillery lobbed shells onto Jones's positions on the west side of the river. Jones's forces dismounted and took cover behind a hill, rendering the artillery bombardment harmless. For the time being, the Monongahela River provided a natural barrier to any potential Federal infantry assault. From the east side of the river, Colonel Harman sent word to Jones that with modest reinforcements, his detachment could flank and neutralize the attackers from Grafton. Jones, however, was more interested in destroying the bridge than in capturing more enemy troops.[98]

Most of the bridge targets were wooden structures easily destroyed by igniting fires underneath them. The Fairmont bridge spanning the Monongahela River was 615 feet long and supported by cast-iron tubular columns set on stone piers and was thus immune to destruction by fire.[99] Engineers, Lieutenant W.G. Williamson and Captain John Henderson, positioned three kegs of gunpowder underneath the iron piers and ignited them, but the explosions "did not do the slightest damage."[100] In the meantime, they were still being harassed by artillery shells and by the threat of an infantry assault.

Jones implemented a deception by directing Colonel Harman to feign an assault on Grafton, the base outpost of the threatening train-deployed Union forces. Their commander, Colonel James A. Mulligan, took the bait. Anticipating an attack on his home base, Mulligan ordered his troops to abort their offensive, withdraw, and return to Grafton by rail.[101] Their withdrawal and the cessation of hostilities provided Jones the time he needed to formulate an alternative plan to destroy the bridge.

Jones devised a plan to reduce the bridge's stability before setting off another series of powder-keg explosions. A work detail set fire to the wood crossties spanning the entire length of the bridge. Supervised by Jones and Captain Henderson, another detail poured gunpowder into the cast-iron tubular columns to give them a cannon-like effect.[102] Although the first round of blasting with this method failed, an ensuing one succeeded, and the magnificent structure toppled into the river. Jones expressed pride in the destruction of a primary target, second only to the Cheat River bridge at Rowlesburg. He reported that it had taken more than two years to construct the bridge at a cost of $486,333.[103]

During the Fairmont occupation, the Jones Brigade destroyed three secondary railroad bridges, seized one piece of artillery, and captured 260 prisoners along with 300 small arms. A foraging operation gathered additional horses and cattle. Jones reported his losses at three wounded to the enemy's twelve killed and many wounded.[104] He praised Colonel A.W. Harman, whom he credited for much of the success. Conversely, Jones reported, "Colonel [Jon Shac] Green again failed to execute the part assigned to him."[105]

Jones made some exceptions to General Lee's standing orders to respect private property. He ordered the burning of two mills that allegedly manufactured gunstocks, and also ordered the torching of a nonmilitary target, the Governor Francis H. Pierpont Library, "in retaliation for the like act on the part of the ambitious little man."[106]

Federal reports from the field regarding the capture of Morgantown and Fairmont frustrated the high command in Washington. General-in-Chief Halleck sent a scathing dispatch to General Schenck stating, "The enemy's raid is variously estimated at from

1,500 to 4,000. You have 45,000 under our command. If you cannot concentrate enough to meet the enemy, it does not argue well for your military disposition."[107] In a separate dispatch noting Jones's ability to maneuver his forces swiftly, Halleck sarcastically commented, "The enemy seems to march more rapidly than we move by rail."[108]

The temporary fall of Morgantown and Fairmont to the enemy further unsettled the local Union authorities. Appeals were sent to General Burnside in Cincinnati to dispatch any available troops for the protection of Parkersburg and Wheeling.[109] Gunboats were deployed to patrol the Ohio River.[110] Pennsylvania governor Andrew Greg Curtin sent a dispatch to President Lincoln requesting troops to thwart what he perceived as an imminent invasion into the Keystone State.[111] Recognizing Jones's actions as a diversion, Lincoln wired Curtin a response that he was overreacting.[112]

Having accomplished his objective at Fairmont, Grumble left his wounded in the hands of Southern sympathizers and marched his brigade southward along the West Fork River in search of Imboden's expeditionary force. The Union high command assumed Jones would return to Virginia proper by taking a direct route through Clarksburg. There, Federal troops under General Benjamin Roberts prepared to trap Jones in the region by obstructing his exit. Jones learned of the enemy's position and executed another deception by feigning a frontal assault on Clarksburg. Lacking a reconnaissance and failing to recognize that Jones was merely implementing a diversion, General Roberts kept his infantry bogged down behind defensive fortifications. Instead of attacking Clarksburg, Jones detoured his column eastward, back across the Monongahela River, and proceeded along Simpson Creek toward Bridgeport, a stockyard center for the B&O Railroad.

Bridgeport, Buckhannon and Weston

On the morning of April 30 Jones detached the First Maryland Cavalry to Bridgeport. The Marylanders took forty-seven prisoners and destroyed a second railroad bridge in addition to the one already torched by Union forces to deny its use to the raiders. They then seized a locomotive with an attached car, set the combination on fire, and ran it to the void over Simpson Creek.[113] The raiders also vastly increased their bounty of cattle in a foraging operation. For the time being, however, this prize would serve as an encumbrance.

At points east and west of Jones's position, Union infantry units stationed at Clarksburg and Grafton braced themselves for assaults that never came. Instead, Jones and his raiders drove their captured horses and cattle southward to Philippi. Anticipating that Jones might take this route, Union forces had damaged a bridge over the Tygart Valley River. Lieutenant W.G. Williamson led a detail that repaired the bridge joist and floor surface, allowing the raiders with their bounty of livestock to cross.[114] There may have been a sense of satisfaction to the Southern cause that the Jones Brigade briefly occupied Philippi as a respite. Two years earlier, Philippi had been the location of the first engagement in the Eastern Theater, which had been an overwhelming Union triumph.

On May 1, Jones detached the Sixth Virginia Cavalry under Colonel Harman to drive the captured livestock southeastward to Beverly, occupied by Imboden's force. Free of the encumbrance but significantly reduced in numbers, the main body of the Jones Brigade marched westward to Buckhannon.[115] By this time, exaggerated accounts of Jones's strengths and alleged atrocities had been further magnified. Francis H. Pierpont, assuming the title of "Governor of Virginia" (in exile) wired President Lincoln with a plea for more troops. Pierpont exclaimed, "From 5,000 to 7,000 rebels under Jones have got to Mannington in Marion County, [West] Virginia. They are conscripting, gathering horses, booty, and doing devilments generally"[116] In truth, Jones had considerably fewer than one-third of the numbers Pierpont alleged and was more than forty miles south of the location.

Exaggerated accounts of Jones's escapades grew to the point that Pennsylvania governor Curtin telegraphed Lincoln and Halleck declaring the "rebel force, estimated at 20,000, it is reported, under the command of Stonewall Jackson" was threatening Uniontown.[117] Jackson was more than two hundred miles to the east at Chancellorsville, and Jones, with well below 2,000 troops, was almost a hundred miles to the south of Uniontown. At Pittsburg, the authorities felt threatened and fortified their city.[118]

On May 2 Jones reached Buckhannon to rendezvous with Imboden for the first time on the joint mission. Having prior commission, Jones took command of the collective force. The combined brigades marched about fifteen miles into Lewis County and arrived at Weston on the following day.[119] The two brigadiers contemplated a combined assault on the Federal outpost at Clarksburg but aborted the idea after receiving word the enemy was well entrenched. Jones expressed aggravation that Imboden was bogged down with more than seventy wagons, which only served as an impediment.[120] Colonel A.W. Harman and the Sixth Virginia Cavalry left one company behind in Beverly to guard the captured livestock and marched his core detachment to Weston to join the collective Jones-Imboden force.

At Weston, during the three-day occupation, the raiders camped on the grounds of the lunatic asylum and combed the surrounding area for forage. Beneficiaries of the misinformation communicated among the various Federal field commanders, the expedition forces enjoyed another time of respite.

On a foraging detail in Lewis County, one of Jones's officers ventured to Jackson's Mill, a boyhood home of Stonewall Jackson and named for his uncle, Cummins Edward Jackson. He encountered an elderly woman who professed she had been a neighbor to young Thomas Jonathan Jackson. The officer reported back to Grumble that the woman stated to him, "I have been praying every day for the death of Tom Jackson, for this war cannot end while he lives."[121] Although the woman's remark seemed to imply hostility, it may have been stated in admiration of Jackson for his perseverance. Retelling the incident to Grumble, the officer added, "She exemplified by saying—when no one else would bring a log to his uncle's sawmill, he sent Tom and the log was sure to come."[122]

Unbeknownst to any of the parties at the time, the woman's prayers were already being answered. More than 200 miles to the east, Lieutenant General Thomas Jonathan "Stonewall" Jackson had just been accidentally and mortally wounded by his own troops at Chancellorsville. He would die in less than a week.

West Union, Harrisville and Cairo

On the morning of May 6 the Jones and Imboden combined forces separated. Imboden's brigade marched southward to occupy Summersville in Nicholas County. Jones led his column westward on the Parkersburg Pike to attack the Northwestern Virginia Railroad.[123]

Jones divided his command again and took the offensive. Colonel Harman led a detachment consisting of the Twelfth Virginia, the Eleventh Virginia, and the Thirty-Fourth (Witcher's Battalion) Virginia Cavalry forty miles eastward to West Union in Doddridge County, where they destroyed two bridges spanning Middle Island Creek.[124] They also captured and paroled nineteen prisoners. Harman's detachment then marched to Harrisville, where they captured and paroled seventy-five civilian members of the home guard. Jones and his force marched to Cairo, where they burned three bridges and a tunnel cribbed in wood, causing it to implode.[125] Without exchanging hostile fire, they captured and paroled twenty prisoners. Jones reported that at this stage he and his men had "traveled upward of 80 miles without unsaddling."[126]

Oiltown (Burning Springs)

May 9 was Grumble's thirty-ninth birthday. Whether this factored into his taking liberties is anyone's guess. His force encountered no resistance when it reached the Wirt County municipality of Oiltown (now Burning Springs). The town had been named for its many oil wells, which, at least according to Grumble, had been previously owned by Southern sympathizers before the wells were "appropriated by the Federal Government or Northern men."[127] Oil production, drawn and used extensively to provide lubrication for machinery and illumination, was at the height of its prosperity.[128] The spring thaw produced the waterway depths sufficient to transport the product up the Little Kanawha River to the Ohio River and then on to destinations in the Midwest. With production activity at its peak, the transport barges were fully loaded when Grumble's raiders seized control of the area and performed a spectacular demonstration of scorched-earth destruction.

Private John N. Opie noted that the two most combustible fluids known to science were coal oil and corn whiskey. General Jones ordered both commodities destroyed. Opie recalled, "They did it in the usual way—They drank the whiskey and fired the oil."[129] Jones proudly confirmed that he directed his raiders to set fire to "all the oil, the holding tanks, the barrels, pump engines, engine houses, and wagons—in a word, everything used for raising, holding, or sending it off" resulting in a " dense and jet black" smoke.[130] Raiders boarded the flatboats and, using axes, cut the containers, causing the oil to spill out onto the surface of the river before they set it to the torch. The vessels and contents exploded with sounds "almost equaling artillery" and spread the burning fuel all over the surface of the river. During daylight, the river was marked by the meanderings of black smoke "as far as the eye could reach," and by nightfall the Little Kanawha River was a blazing sheet of fire.[131] Private George Moffett doubted that the burning of Moscow during the Napoleonic Wars "equaled the scene presented" and described the blazing destruction as a "scene to give inspiration to Dante for a new description of his *Inferno*."[132] Private Opie further elaborated: "The current carried the flames over waterfalls, producing the most fantastic shapes and figures, resembling fiery demons, dancing upon the surface of the river, ever and anon disappearing in the darkness and again reappearing, when on line with one's vision. The men were greatly relieved when we left this scene of desolation, and many a man that night dreamed of hell or a personal demon."[133]

Reflecting upon the mass incendiary destruction reminiscent of a "brimstone lake," Captain Frank M. Myers borrowed the opening lines from *The Devil's Progress: A Poem* written by Thomas Kibble Hervey: "The Devil sits in his easy chair,/Sipping his sulphur tea,/And gazing out, with a pensive air,/O'er the broad bitumen sea."[134] Postwar accounts reflect that many of the raiders were appalled at the fiery destruction. Their commander, on the other hand, took euphoric delight in the desolation. Jones reported, "A burning river, carrying destruction to our merciless enemy, was a sense of magnificence that might well carry joy to every patriotic heart."[135] The torching of the petroleum reserves may have also marked an early transition to modern warfare. According to many historians, the action served as the first instance in which oil was targeted as a wartime objective.[136]

Return March

Oiltown marked the western extreme of the expedition. Jones's brigade encountered no resistance when it marched eastward through Glenville, Sutton, and Summersville, where they overtook Imboden's column driving the bounty of livestock in a homeward-bound movement. The combined forces proceeded on an uneventful southward march before arriving at the banks of the Gauley River. An anecdote details an instance in which an infantryman from Imboden's command was anxious about crossing the Gauley River and sought advice from a comrade, who, pointing to a man in a skiff near the shore, said, "Maybe that old fellow there will row you across." The infantryman approached the boatman and said, "Old man, I will give you a dollar to take me over the river." He was unaware that the "old man" was General Jones. Without identifying himself, Jones replied, "All right. Jump in." Enjoying the joke, Jones rowed the man across.[137] It was another of multiple instances in which Grumble's outward appearance deceived others into viewing him as someone other than a high-ranking officer.

After crossing the Gauley, the combined columns turned to the east through Lewisburg and White Sulphur Springs. At Lewisburg they received word of Stonewall Jackson's death. Captain Charles T. O'Ferrall wrote, "We had no conception of the momentous events that had been taking place in eastern Virginia. Jackson's death cast the deepest gloom over the brigade. All hoped and prayed that it was a false report, and yet, the information seemed so authentic as to leave no doubt of its truth."[138] Jackson's passing was devastating for Jones, who had lost his best friend and the one at the highest level of authority. The news clouded the spirits of the entire brigade and from that point "the march took on the character of a funeral procession."[139]

The Jones Brigade continued its march uncontested to Warm Springs in Bath County in Virginia proper, where they took advantage of the prewar luxuries nature provided.[140] By May 22 they arrived at their original base in Rockingham County.

Assessment

The joint mission was later deemed the "Jones and Imboden West Virginia Raid." Except for the failure to destroy the Cheat River bridge at Rowlesburg, Grumble met all of his objectives. He demonstrated admirable audacity and resourcefulness as a leader and as a strategist. In the long run, however, the expedition received mixed reviews. Militarily, the raid accomplished little. Politically, it was later judged an absolute failure.

The foraging of up to 3,000 head of beef cattle and 1,200 horses, grain and other provisions would sustain the Army of Northern Virginia on the pending incursion into Pennsylvania.[141] To General Lee, this part of the mission was more important than the destruction of Union military property and assets.[142]

The raid had served as a humiliation to the Union military, whose sole achievement was protecting the Cheat River Viaduct.[143] Consistently on the offensive, Jones had held the initiative throughout the entire expedition. By dividing and scattering his small brigade to threaten numerous targets simultaneously, he exaggerated the size of his force and thwarted any Federal attempt to launch a united force against him.[144] The Union forces, far superior in numerical strength and resources on their turf, remained on the defensive.

Within thirty days, the Jones Brigade marched nearly 700 miles and captured nearly 700 prisoners at the cost of modest losses. They destroyed a set of small arms for every prisoner, two locomotives with cars, sixteen railroad bridges, one tunnel, over 150,000 barrels of oil, an assortment of oil wells, and many river transport vessels related to the oil production.[145] Throughout the campaign, the men of the Jones Brigade held the "utmost confidence in their commander."[146] Revered on a level with Stonewall Jackson, Jones was described as brave "without being foolhardy, alert, cautious, and a good strategist, a leader that they would have followed blind-folded."[147]

Evaluating Grumble's performance, Lee reported to the inspector general: "General Jones displayed sagacity and boldness in his plans, and was well supported by the courage and fortitude of his officers and men."[148] In regard to the "injury" Jones rendered to the enemy, Lee commented that from that point on the Federals "will be induced to keep troops to guard the railroad who might be otherwise employed against us."[149] Throughout the remainder of the war the Federals had to dedicate men and resources to secure B&O Railroad lines, a frequent target of partisan rangers in the late stages of the conflict.

Notwithstanding all of the praise for its audacity, gallantry, and resourcefulness, doubts surfaced as to what the raid accomplished. More than forty years afterward, Private George H. Moffett, an outspoken Jones admirer, challenged the military purpose of destroying the petroleum fields at Oiltown.[150] Private John Opie deemed the same measure a "useless destruction of property and the culmination of a fruitless and unimportant raid."[151]

The raid's contribution to the Confederacy was far more temporary and psychological. Although main stems of the B&O Railroad were severed in multiple places, most were repaired and reopened within a relatively short time. Federal army engineers quickly directed the reconstruction of the bridges at Altamont, Oakland, Cranberry Summit, Newburg, and Independence.[152] Although timely reconstruction of the bridge at Fairmont was not possible, Federal authorities circumvented the damage by transferring passengers and cargo onto wagons and ferrying them across the Monongahela River on pontoon bridges.[153]

The raid caused noted political embarrassment to the emerging government of the future state of West Virginia by inciting panic at the Wheeling convention in progress at the time. A breathless messenger allegedly interrupted the conference, which was "discussing some matter of great importance," to announce that General Jones was approaching.[154] The scene erupted into one of bedlam, with members stampeding over each other to flee in different directions.[155] Governor Pierpont fled to Pittsburg.[156] In reality, the Jones expedition never came within fifty miles of Wheeling.

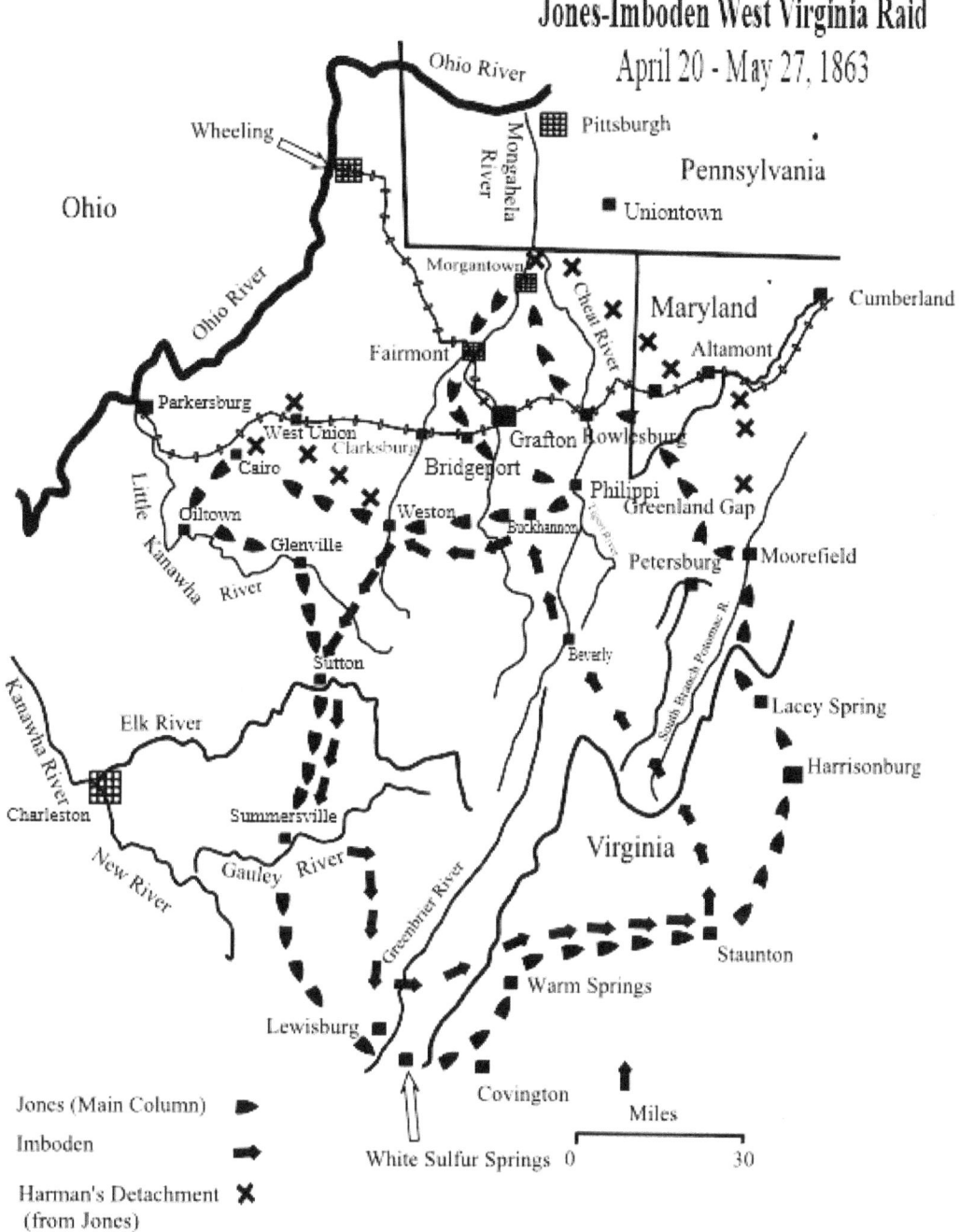

Jones and Imboden West Virginia Raid Map (sketch by author, 2016).

Aside from the temporary setback to the Pierpont government, the raid accomplished nothing politically. Contrary to Imboden's prediction, the number of recruits from the area was a major disappointment to the Confederate authorities. On the contrary, more than two hundred standing members of his force deserted during his occupation of Beverly.[157] Politically the raid did more to alter the allegiance of secessionist sympathizers, who were convenient foraging targets by the raiders. Unlike their Unionist counterparts, Southern sympathizers trusted the Confederate raiders to consider their loyalty and therefore took no precautions to protect their property. To their unpleasant surprise, the raiders were more interested in confiscating their forage than in receiving their moral support.[158]

During the occupation of Fairmont, a wealthy local secessionist allegedly rode out on his prize horse to greet General Jones as a liberator. Jones returned the favor by requisitioning the man's horse on behalf of the Confederate government. When the citizen protested and pleaded by citing his loyalty, Jones responded that he should gladly donate his horse to the cause he so much believed in.[159]

Imboden's objective and forecast of a pro–Southern uprising to bring the region back into the grasp of "old Virginia" never materialized. Once the expeditionary forces withdrew, the Wheeling Convention resumed with a greater resolve to publish to the world that on June 20, 1863, "West Virginia shall be and remain one of the United States of America." As for long-term effects of the raid, it could be said that the Jones and Imboden Raid did more "to crystallize local public sentiment in favor of the separate State of West Virginia than all other agencies combined."[160]

Moving On

More than a hundred miles to the east, the simultaneous Chancellorsville Campaign concluded on May 6 when Hooker's Army of the Potomac withdrew north of the Rappahannock and maintained a threatening presence in the region. Although circumstances demanded a high state of alert, the temporary respite allowed the Army of Northern Virginia's commander, Robert E. Lee, time to contemplate his next measures. Looking ahead, Lee was planning his second invasion of the North.

Lee also needed to address the strained personal relationship between Jones and Stuart. He considered reassigning Jones to Jackson's infantry Corps and command of the Stonewall Brigade, formerly commanded by Brigadier General Elisha Franklin Paxton, who had been killed at Chancellorsville on May 3.[161] Lee sensed that a transfer to Jackson's Corps might appeal to Jones, as he would serve under his friend, who at the moment was expected to recover from his wounds. The Stonewall Brigade, however, was an infantry unit. Jones had dedicated his entire military career to the cavalry and served in that capacity with distinction. Ultimately, Lee concluded that Jones was unlikely to desire the change.[162] In any event, Jackson's death on May 10 negated any possible incentive for Jones to favor the transfer. Shelving the idea, Lee reassigned Jones to Stuart's command.

Jones and his brigade encamped at Mount Crawford in Rockingham County to await further orders. He anticipated a time of reprieve for the men and, more importantly, for the horses. Jones, exhausted from the previous month-long campaign, proud of what he had accomplished, and saddened by Jackson's death, was not in the least enthusiastic about what lay ahead.

14

Brandy Station

On May 23 General Robert E. wrote to Jones congratulating him for his successful expedition. He also directed Jones to report to his old nemesis, Major General J.E.B. Stuart, at Culpeper Courthouse.[1] Understanding that the Jones Brigade deserved rest and recuperation, Lee communicated, "I desire you to join General Stuart by easy marches, as soon as you can, giving your men and horses rest and refreshment."[2]

Jones received Lee's communication on the following day; the content conflicted with his desires. Although Jones probably anticipated the termination of his seven-month-long status of autonomy, the concept of returning to Stuart's cavalry division was repulsive. Evaluating his recent accomplishment, he saw that he had requisitioned more than 3,000 head of cattle as well as grain that would help sustain the previously underfed Army of Northern Virginia. His foraging operations also added more than 1,000 horses as replacement mounts. Feeling that he had made a significant and final contribution to the cause, Jones tendered his resignation.[3] It is unlikely that he sincerely desired to terminate his service to the Confederacy. Resigning was a means of conveying his displeasure with being reassigned to Stuart's command. Well aware that Jones was acting on impulse and perhaps understanding the reasons, Lee withheld the resignation.[4] Out of reverence for Lee, Jones cast aside his personal differences for the time being.

Veneration for Lee had reached new heights. After a year of staving off multiple Federal offensives against Richmond, he had won his most impressive victory at Chancellorsville. With the Federal Army of the Potomac seemingly in retreat to Washington, D.C., Richmond appeared as secure as it had been at any time in the war.

Stuart, who had previously tried to dissuade Lee from promoting Jones in the first place, was equally unenthusiastic about the prospect of reuniting with Jones. Upon the conclusion of the recent Chancellorsville Campaign, Stuart conveyed to Lee his objections to the reassignment of Jones back to his cavalry division. Lee responded to Stuart, "Do not let your judgment be warped."[5] Jones's brigade was the largest in the cavalry division and had a proven combat record.

Lee's directive was part of an overall plan to consolidate and reposition the Army of Northern Virginia in preparation for its second major expedition to the North. In the aftermath of Chancellorsville, the main body of the Army of Northern Virginia was scattered along the south banks of the Rappahannock River, extending eastward to Fredericksburg. Lee directed Stuart to relocate his cavalry division headquarters northward from Orange Courthouse to Culpeper Courthouse and establish a new base of operations for the entire army. Longstreet's Corps of Infantry including Pickett's and Hood's divisions received orders to withdraw from southeastern Virginia and converge on Culpeper as well. Brigadier General Beverly Robertson and his cavalry brigade were called up from North Carolina. The Army of Northern Virginia infantry units that fought at Chancellorsville would march westward and join Stuart's cavalry. More than 70,000 Confederate troops would eventually congregate at Culpeper Courthouse. During the time of transition, Stuart's cavalry division served as the occupational force. Pending the arrival of Lee and the infantry corps commanders, Stuart was fully in charge.

Grumble would have preferred to have changed places with his West Virginia Raid associate, Brigadier General John D. Imboden, whose brigade remained on detached service to guard the western flank of the infantry's anticipated march down the Shenandoah Valley. Unlike Jones, Imboden and his brigade would be exempt from participating in what Stuart planned.

Lee had to take a cautious approach in relocating his army. Hooker's recently defeated Army of the Potomac did not retreat but repositioned itself just north of the Rappahannock River. It remained a formidable force that could turn on Richmond at any time. Lee was going to maneuver his revamped army beyond the Blue Ridge, across the Potomac, and into the Cumberland Valley. By threatening Philadelphia, Baltimore, and Washington, D.C., Lee would draw Hooker out of Virginia. Just as Lee anticipated, Hooker's Army of the Potomac commenced on a parallel march keeping itself between the Army of Northern Virginia and Washington.

From Mount Crawford, Grumble Jones and his brigade proceeded on a seventy-mile march to Stuart's new headquarters at Culpeper Courthouse, arriving in stages on June 3 and 4, with the second group driving the bounty of cattle. Jones was not in a festive mood, as reflected by his unaccepted resignation. He anticipated that upon his arrival his exhausted troops and mounts would receive a much-needed reprieve time. Stuart, however, had other plans. With the consolidation at Culpeper Courthouse, Stuart's cavalry division reached a milestone. Up to this point, Stuart's mounted troops had demonstrated clear superiority over their Northern counterparts in the Eastern Theater. The appeal of recent successes resulted in a mass enlistment of new and enthusiastic recruits with fresh mounts. The addition of Jones's and Robertson's brigades swelled the division to five brigades numbering 9,536 officers and enlisted men, the highest number Stuart commanded.[6]

Unlike the Shenandoah Valley, Culpeper County had not suffered the ravages of war. The current spring season brought an abundance of grazing grasses for the horses. Area farms had produced an overage of subsistence for the troops. Cattle and horses delivered by the recent Jones and Imboden expedition added to the surplus. The situation was in stark contrast to the beginning of the year when Lee's army neared starvation. With assumptions that the Army of the Potomac was in retreat, the Army of Northern Virginia seemed invincible. In spite of the recent loss of Stonewall Jackson, morale was at an all-time high.

Jones assumed that, following his latest accomplishment and with the present level of security, more time would be allotted for his men and, more important, the horses to recuperate. His division commander, Stuart, however, demanded and ordered a celebration.[7] The festivities would be another point of contention escalating the tensions between Stuart and Jones. While Stuart thrived on the pomp and pageantry of martial displays, Jones couldn't have cared less and was contemptuous of them. Since neither Lee nor any of the infantry corps commanders had yet to arrive, Stuart was bestowed with unchallenged authority. He ordered his cavalry division to perform an orchestrated military ceremony in a festival that would include a grand review. Announcements for the gala event were sent to Richmond and throughout central Virginia. Invitations were extended to government officials, dignitaries, journalists, and particularly Southern belles. Lodging arrangements were made at hotels and private residences.

Commencing the event of pomp and pageantry, banjo artist Sam Sweeney and his band performed at a ball held at the Culpeper County Courthouse on the evening of June 4,[8] a prologue to what would occur on the following day.

First Grand Review

The main event commenced on the morning of June 5 with an all-day parade on the plains between Culpeper Courthouse and Brandy Station, a depot established by the Orange & Alexandria Railroad.[9] Stuart led his staff, all in new uniforms, in a march through the streets onto the vast field that extended from the railroad tracks to the banks of the Rappahannock River. Railroad cars, horse-drawn carriages, and wagons encircled the parade ground and provided spectators with an elevated arena-style view. The entire cavalry division sat mounted on horses in a column that extended almost two miles.[10] Wade Hampton led the Carolinians, who were the most impressive regarding military primness.[11] In contrast, the squadrons of the Jones Brigade drew attention by the "graceful nonchalance of their riding." In spite of their casualness, these proud veterans of the recent expedition into West Virginia made a no less a distinct impression "with their warlike strength."[12] In his further description of the men of the Jones Brigade, Captain William N. McDonald wrote, "The riders like centaurs appeared almost one with their steeds. General Jones rode at their head, evidently proud of his command, but with a disdainful air, for he hated the *pomp and circumstance of war*."[13]

At ten o'clock, Stuart galloped out onto the field wearing a long black ostrich plume that waved gracefully from his black slouch hat, which was cocked to one side. He held a golden clasp-mounted battle flag.[14] Stuart and his staff continued past the entire line of the mounted division, rode to a small knoll, wheeled to an about-face, and formed a review station. Bands played patriotic songs while the two miles of cavalry joined in the march before the crowd.[15] After the entire cavalcade had passed the review station, it divided itself into units and maneuvered into various positions. In a mock battle, regiments charged at each other while the mounted artillery fired blank rounds.[16] The demonstration lasted until four o'clock.

That evening, a second dance was held at the courthouse, during which time Stuart and his cavaliers "romanced and charmed the local belles."[17] The common cavalry soldiers in the ranks, "unbidden to the dances," regarded the festivities as a bore and a burden.[18] Many "grumbled about the useless waste of energy, especially to the horses."[19] Lieutenant John Blue overheard Grumble Jones comment, "Stuart has had his horse show and sham fight, but … tomorrow, he would have a fight without the sham."[20] In further forecasting what would eventually come to pass, Jones angrily muttered, "No doubt the Yankees have two divisions of cavalry on the other side of the river. They have witnessed from their signal stations this show by which Stuart has exposed our strength and aroused their curiosity. They will want to know what is going on, and if I am not mistaken, they will be over early in the morning to investigate."[21] Jones's prophesy was not fulfilled the following morning. It would, however, take place the day after a second spectacle.

For Stuart, there was one missing but necessary element regarding the recently concluded grand review. General Lee, who had been delayed due to the uncertainty regarding Hooker's movements, had not yet arrived from Fredericksburg and was not present to bear witness.[22] Lee was the one spectator Stuart most desired to impress. Many of the officers agreed that "all the prologue and aftermath were enough of display."[23] To their dismay, Stuart scheduled a duplicate performance three days later, on June 8, to take place in the presence of Lee.[24] Unlike the first one, which extended to Brandy Station, the second performance would be limited to Culpeper Courthouse.

Second Grand Review

Stuart invited the newly arrived infantry corps and division commanders to accompany Lee at the second grand review. Typical of the rivalry between cavalry and infantry, there was some heckling from the infantrymen spectators near the commencement, but it promptly ceased with the emergence of Lee. Lee's presence also factored into toning down the theatrics. Conserving the stamina of the horses and the powder supply prohibited the mock battles or the firing of cannon. The parade was reminiscent of the pageant performed on June 5. General Lee sat on Traveler in a stationary position as the two-mile column of cavalry marched past. Stuart rode with a wreath of flowers draped around the neck of his horse.[25]

During the parade march, Stuart's desire for perfection came to light. First Sergeant George M. Neese of Chew's Mounted Artillery in the Jones Brigade rode at the head of his battery unit on a mule. In contrast to the distinguished-looking thousands of cavalry mounts, the mule had flickering ears estimated at a foot in length. Stuart dispatched an aide to Captain Chew with orders to remove Sergeant Neese and "his ear waving mule from the field." Neese sarcastically recalled, "I cared very little about the matter, but the mule looked a little bit surprised, and, I think, felt ashamed of himself and his waving ears, which cost him his prominent position in the grand cavalcade."[26] Neese took a more serious tone when he reflected, "No doubt General Stuart is proud of his splendid cavalry, and well he may be, for it certainly is a fine body of well mounted and tried horsemen, whose trusty blades have oft-times flashed in the red glow of battle's fiery tide and stemmed the deadly wave of war. But my mule, too, has heard the raging battle roar and the dreadful musketry roll and seen the screaming shell tear the sod to smithers around his feet. True, a mule is not built for the purpose of ornamenting a grand review or embellishing an imposing pageant, but as mine so willingly bears the hardships and dangers of the camp and field I thought it not indiscreet to let it play a little act in some of the holiday scenes of war."[27]

During the parade, Stuart viewed his ranks and noticed that members of the Jones Brigade were out of place and "loitering," as if dismissed or given an "at ease" command.[28] Stuart sent a courier, young Lieutenant Frank Robertson, to confront Jones and inquire why he was not in position for the next movement. Robertson found Jones and his staff "lying comfortably on the ground as if the review was the last and least" of their concern.[29] Robertson inquired as to why Jones's group was not mounted. Grumble roundly cussed him out for his troubles and sent him back to Stuart.[30] Once Robertson departed, however, Jones issued the order to mount up and fall in line. Stuart observed the encounter from a distance and took a mental note of the insolence.

Although not up to the spectacular grandstanding of the first review, the cavalry performed its second exhibition of martial demonstration in three days. Assumptions prevailed that Hooker's Army of the Potomac was retreating to Washington. Although it was known that a Federal cavalry unit remained in the area, it was assumed to be a token force intent only on covering Hooker's retreat. The Rappahannock River added to the sense of security. At the conclusion of the review, the men returned their camps to bivouac for the night. Orders were to pack all equipment and supplies in preparation for a march on the following morning. As planned, the cavalry would screen two infantry corps on their march toward the Potomac. Stuart established his temporary headquarters on the summit of Fleetwood Hill, situated approximately a half-mile east of Brandy Station, four miles west of Beverly's Ford, with a commanding view of the area. All of Stuart's supplies except for his tent were packed in wagons in preparation for a routine morning march. Jones's brigade camped at St. James Church with the task of securing the road to Beverly's Ford, two miles away, on the Rappahannock River. A forest enclosed the road for the first mile; the second mile was open country. Chew's horse artillery bivouacked at the edge of the forest in advance of Jones's main units.[31] Jones's Sixth Virginia Cavalry patrolled the open field to the river.

Jones's forecast following the first grand review would soon come to fruition. The festivities conducted at Brandy Station on June 4 and the second ceremony at Culpeper Courthouse on June 8 had in fact aroused Union curiosity on the east side of the Rappahannock. Union scouts reported the activity to their commander, General Alfred Pleasanton, who saw an urgency to ascertain the movements of the Army of Northern Virginia. Anticipating a Confederate cavalry assault on Hooker's retreating Army of the Potomac, Pleasanton planned a preemptive advance. To conceal their position and numbers, he prohibited the burning of campfires on the evening of June 8.[32]

Battle of Brandy Station

Pleasanton's Federal force consisted of 11,000 troops (8,000 cavalry and 3,000 infantry). A factor saving the Confederate cavalry from annihilation was that the Union troops had to be divided and funneled across the river at the two locations, six miles apart, Beverly's Ford to the north and Kelly's Ford to the south. The divisions of Colonel Alfred Duffie and General David Gregg formed the first wing that crossed at Kelly's Ford and then divided. Duffie's division executed a flanking maneuver toward Stevensburg while Gregg's advanced directly toward Brandy Station. Pleasanton accompanied the second wing, a cavalry division commanded by Jones's West Point classmate John Buford. They crossed at Beverly's Ford and would be the first to engage.

A state of pandemonium erupted at four o'clock in the morning of June 9 when, under cover of fog, Buford's division crossed the Rappahannock at Beverly's Ford. Major Cabell E. Flournoy was commanding 150 mounted pickets from Jones's Sixth Virginia Cavalry on patrol. Flournoy's squadrons charged into the Federal column, engaged in a fierce hand-to-hand fighting encounter, and suffered about thirty casualties before giving way to superior numbers.[33]

Reacting to the sound of small-arms fire, Jones mounted his horse and ordered the rest of his brigade into action. Many dashed "barefoot, hatless, and coatless" into the fight.[34] Federal sharpshooters, protected by the woods, fired at Jones and his Seventh

Virginia Cavalry. Jones's force dispersed the sharpshooters before encountering the main Union column. Heavily outnumbered, Jones was forced to fall back and divert his attention to his potentially exposed horse artillery. He rushed to that position and conveyed to Captain Preston Chew, "I'm not in command today, but do you see that gap in the woods yonder? I think the Yankees are bringing a battery in there. If they do, give 'em hell!"[35] As Jones predicted, the Federals set up an artillery battery that began firing. Chew's artillery fired canisters, cutting down hundreds of troops and repelling the Federal advance long enough for the rest of the brigade to regroup at St. James Church. Jones directed the Eleventh, Twelfth, and Thirty-Fifth battalions to join in a three-prong counterattack.

The Seventh Virginia moved to the left and joined Rooney Lee's Brigade. The Sixth Virginia veered to the right and merged with Wade Hampton's brigade. Jones led his Eleventh Virginia, Twelfth Virginia, and Thirty-Fifth Virginia to form a center column that reinforced the artillery. The situation turned into a melee. Jones's center column advanced into the open field and met a murderous volley of fire, followed by a charge of Buford's cavalry. The situation in the center then turned more chaotic, the momentum changing sides multiple times. Soldiers of the opposing armies intermingled. Jones had already saved the day at Beverly's Ford by buying time for the remainder of Stuart's cavalry division to respond.

The Sixth Pennsylvania charged through the melee toward Jones's artillery battery. Chew's Battery fired into the Federal advance, which continued despite casualties. Squadrons led by Jones and Hampton attacked the Federal column from the flanks, driving them back repeatedly until a deceiving lull fell over Beverly's Ford. A courier from Stuart arrived directing Jones and Hampton to fall back to Fleetwood Hill, a mile to the rear of their current position.[36] Undeceived by the apparent calm to his front, Jones suspected that the attack was spreading and would resurface elsewhere. Alarmed that a Federal flanking maneuver south of Beverly's Ford would threaten Fleetwood Hill, Grumble sent a courier to warn Stuart.

Aroused by the initial sound of gunfire at his Fleetwood Hill headquarters, Stuart utilized the high ground to direct counterattacks. During that time, he received the courier's message from Jones warning him about a possible flanking movement. "Stuart's pride and dislike of Grumble probably shaped his answer."[37] Stuart told the courier, who reported back to Jones, "Tell General Jones to attend to the Yankees at his front and I'll watch the flanks."[38] The courier returned to Jones to relay the response. Jones angrily replied, "So he thinks they ain't coming, does he? Well, let him alone; he'll damn soon see for himself."[39]

The worst-case scenario unraveled. Beverly Robertson's brigade failed to either check or stall General David Gregg's advance six miles downriver at Kelly's Ford. Consequently, Judson Kilpatrick's Federal cavalry veered southward and approached the southern slopes of Fleetwood Hill uncontested. Stuart found himself in the precarious position of being attacked from the rear while heavily engaged at his front. The commands of Jones and Hampton came to Stuart's aid. The movement, later deemed "the first true cavalry combat of the war" and ultimately the "largest" cavalry engagement of the entire war, further evolved into a chaotic situation of closely engaged hand-to-hand fighting for possession of Fleetwood Hill, which changed hands several times.[40] By this stage of the battle, artillery was ineffective, as the field "was covered with a mingled mass, fighting and struggling with pistol and saber like maddened savages."[41]

14. Brandy Station

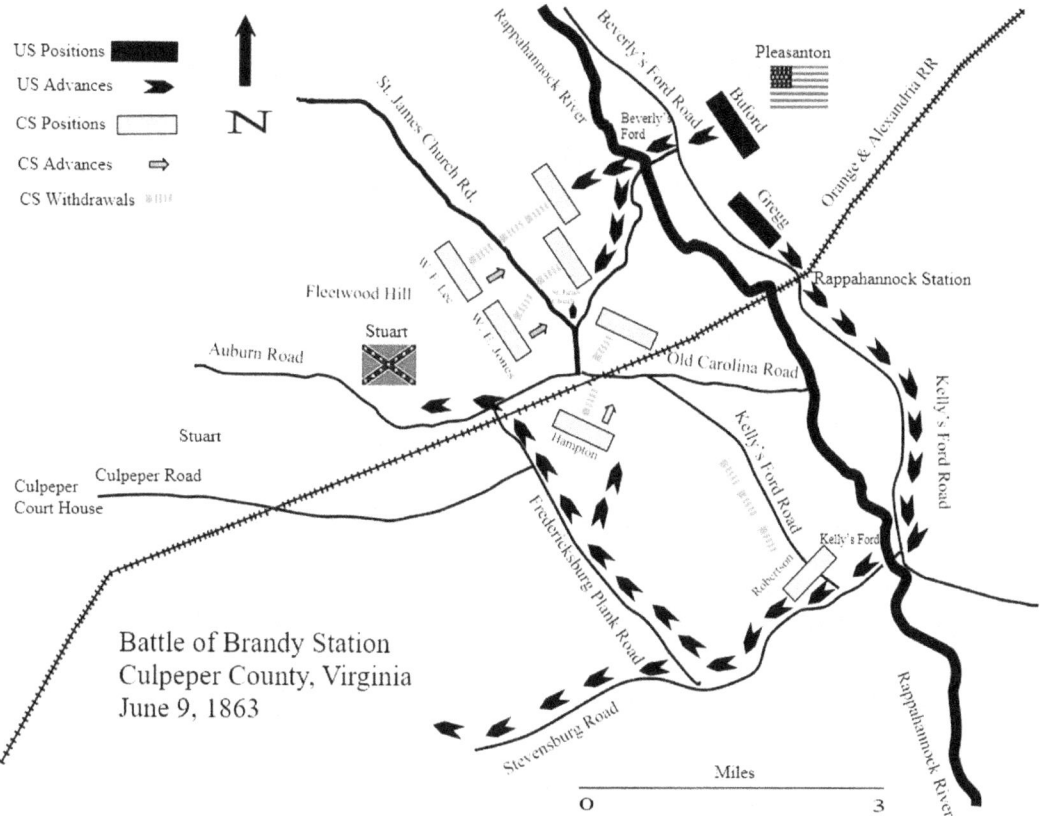

Battle of Brandy Station (sketch by author, 2015).

The Federals ultimately withdrew on their terms. By default, the Confederates held possession of the field. Stuart claimed a victory, but it was a hollow one and perhaps a draw at best.

Brandy Station was a paradox between June 5 and June 9 of 1863. Initially, the field extending from the railroad tracks to the Rappahannock River had been the stage for a demonstration full of pomp, pageantry, and mock battles. Four days later, it turned into a real ten-hour fight leaving a landscape of carnage: "Bluebottle flies swarmed over the bloody ground so thickly, and the hill was so littered with bodies of men and horses that tents could not be pitched."[42] While casualty statistics vary slightly, the Confederates were known to have sustained a loss of about 500, compared to Union losses of about 900, half being prisoners.

Aftermath

The Battle of Brandy Station was an anomaly that appealed to the romantics. Most cavalry engagements were comparatively small encounters involving troopers fighting dismounted and with carbines; their horses were merely means of conveyance. In this battle, about 20,000 horsemen engaged with the horse, sword, and pistol taking precedence over what had previously been conventional. It was a "passage of arms with romantic interest and splendor to a degree unequaled by anything the war produced."[43] Such tactics would become more prevalent later in the conflict and in the Indian campaigns following the Civil War.

Brandy Station was as much a surprise to General Alfred Pleasanton as it was to Stuart. Pleasanton's scouts had observed the colorful demonstration the previous day at Culpeper Courthouse and assumed that the Confederate cavalry would be encamped there instead of near the banks of the Rappahannock River.[44] Even after the battle, Pleasanton did not immediately realize its significance. He thought he had merely unmasked and thwarted a Confederate cavalry raid.[45]

Although battlefield statistics and final possession of the ground favored the Southerners, the Battle of Brandy Station was a moral victory for the Federals. An opinion by H.B. McClellan, "seconded by other Civil War historians," was that Brandy Station "*made the Federal Cavalry*," which up to that time had been "confessedly inferior to Southern horsemen."[46] For the remainder of the war, Union cavalry forces had the confidence to contend with their Confederate counterparts as no less than equals.

The events surrounding the circumstances at Brandy Station served as a public relations nightmare for Stuart. From the perspective of the general public, he had placed so much emphasis on the two grand reviews that he was ill-prepared for the unanticipated battle. An anonymous letter to President Davis declared the ceremony as a "monkey show and [Stuart] the monkey."[47] The same correspondence also implied philandering: "General S. loves the admiration of his class of lady friends too much to be a commanding general."[48] President Davis did not regard the circumstances as catastrophic. Instead, he wrote with a rather clever and playful admonition to Stuart: "Cease your attentions to the ladies and make them more general."[49] General Lee did not chastise Stuart like the public did.

The press, on the other hand, castigated Stuart for his vain conduct in holding the two reviews and his lack of vigilance that allowed the surprise attack. The *Richmond Dispatch, Richmond Enquirer,* and *Charleston Mercury* expressed noted criticism in their columns.[50] Not all of the media was critical, as the *Richmond Whig* praised Stuart for making the best of the situation and predicted his rebound.[51] However, the *Richmond Examiner,* in particular, published a scornful article assessing the battle at Brandy Station as a moral defeat for Stuart and the cavalry division. Without calling out Stuart by name, the June 12 article contained the following scathing remarks:

> The more the circumstances of the late affair at Brandy Station are considered, the less pleasant they appear. If this was an isolated case, it might be excused under the convenient head of accident or chance. But this puffed up cavalry of the Army of Northern Virginia has been twice, if not three times, surprised since the battles of December, and such repeated accidents can be regarded as nothing but the necessary consequences of negligence and bad management. If the war was a tournament, invented and supported for the pleasure of a few vain and weak-headed officers, these disasters might be dismissed with compassion. But the country pays dearly for the blunders, which encourage the enemy to overrun and devastate the land, with a cavalry which is daily learning to despise the mounted troops of the Confederacy. The surprise on this occasion was the most complete that has occurred.

In describing the outcome of the battle, the *Examiner* continued: "In the end, the enemy retired, or was driven, it is not yet clearly known which, across the river. Nor is it certainly known whether the fortunate result was achieved by the cavalry alone or with the assistance of Confederate infantry in the neighborhood." Near the article's conclusion, the

Examiner stated, "The only effective means of preventing the mischief it may do is to reorganize our own forces, enforce a stricter discipline among the men, and insist upon more earnestness among officers in the discharge of their very important duty."

Stuart tried to mask his humiliation. In his June 12, 1863, letter to his wife, he began, "God has spared me through another bloody battle and helped with victory our armies." He commented further: "The papers are in great error as usual about the whole transaction. It was no surprise. The enemy's movement was known, and he was defeated. We captured (3) pieces of Artillery that the Horse Artillery now have."[52] Continuing, Stuart wrote, "Our entire loss does not exceed 500 killed, wounded & missing."[53]

There were unfounded insinuations that the battle spoiled Stuart's plans for a raid beginning the following day, that captured documents from Stuart's headquarters revealed Lee's plan for the pending invasion, and that the Confederate infantry intervened to save the cavalry division from total defeat.[54] Stuart refuted the allegations: "The Examiner of the 12th *lies* from beginning to end. I lost no papers, no nothing except the casualties of battle. I understand the spirit and object of the detraction and can I believe trace the source. I will, of course, take no notice of such base falsehood."[55]

The level of accuracy regarding the media's assessment didn't matter. The Confederate cavalry division in the Army of Northern Virginia had performed two outrageous presentations of pageantry in a controlled environment only to be upstaged in a real fight. Stuart was embarrassed by the criticism and would resolve to restore his tarnished reputation. He made no apologies to his subordinates for the impairment caused by his arrogance. General Wade Hampton, whose brother was killed in the engagement, refrained from expressing any public criticism. The humiliation did nothing to improve the awkward relationship between Jeb Stuart and Grumble Jones. Stuart only nominally praised Jones individually for mitigating the damage. In his June 13 report, Stuart wrote that Jones, along with Wade Hampton and W.F. Lee, "were prompt in the execution of their orders and conformed readily to the emergencies arising." Later in the report, Stuart continued: "General Jones's brigade had the hardest fighting, all five regiments having been engaged twice."[56]

In his June 11 report, Grumble wrote, "My brigade bore the brunt of the action, both in the morning and evening, and lost severely in killed and wounded, but had the satisfaction of seeing the enemy worsted in every particular more than ourselves. We ended the fight with more horses and more and better small-arms than we had at the beginning. We took two regimental colors, many guidons, and a battery of three pieces. We took many prisoners, probably 250, as one regiment reports 122. Throughout the officers and men sustained their well-earned reputation for gallantry."[57] Jones would later recall that he observed his aide-de-camp, First Lieutenant Warren M. Hopkins, kill an enemy soldier with his bare hands.[58]

On the following morning, the infantry of the Army of Northern Virginia launched its northward march. The conclusion of the Battle of Brandy Station evolved into the beginning of the Gettysburg Campaign and the turning point of the war in the Eastern Theater of operations.

15

Gettysburg

Prologue to Invasion

The Battle of Brandy Station did not delay the advance of the Army of Northern Virginia. General Richard Ewell's II Corps of infantry spearheaded the expedition by fording the Rappahannock and crossing the Blue Ridge. Temporarily detached from the Jones Brigade, Elijah White's Thirty-Fifth Battalion, Virginia Cavalry (AKA the Comanches), served as escort. The corps of A.P. Hill and James Longstreet would soon follow. Recuperating from the Battle of Brandy Station and confronting the uncertainty regarding the Army of the Potomac's immediate intentions, Stuart's cavalry division delayed joining the march.

Upon entering the Shenandoah Valley, Ewell's Corps advanced on the Winchester garrisons under the command of Grumble's Shenandoah Valley nemesis, General Robert Huston Milroy. On June 14, Ewell's Corps routed Milroy's division, resumed its march into Pennsylvania, and served as a diversion. The collapse of the Upper Potomac Federal garrisons forced the authorities in Washington to withdraw the Army of the Potomac for defensive operations rather than, as Hooker suggested, conduct an advance on Richmond.[1]

On June 16 the cavalry division joined the expedition. The contest was a race to the Shenandoah Valley, with the Federals desiring to know the main body of the Army of Northern Virginia's position and Stuart's cavalry endeavoring to conceal its movements. Historians will always debate the performance of Stuart's cavalry division in the Gettysburg Campaign. Questions persist as to how well Stuart performed the primary tasks of serving as the eyes and ears of the Army of Northern Virginia. Few challenge the contention that there was an underachievement in regard to that particular aspect. However, detractors overlook the fact that the cavalry division successfully screened the Army of Northern Virginia's movements into the Shenandoah Valley and that the division successfully performed its task of protecting the infantry on its return march.

Jones cast his personal animosities toward Stuart aside to work with his division commander on their last campaign together. In a final evaluation of their executions, both performed with mixed results. Stuart's shortcomings would challenge his legacy. Grumble would not face the same level of scrutiny, but his performance is lesser known. Stuart's overall cavalry division would be only nominally engaged in the famous three days of clashes that occurred between July 1 and July 3 on what is now the Gettysburg National Battlefield. The major contests at Culp's Hill, Little Round Top, and Pickett's Charge were infantry clashes. For the cavalry, combat operations of the Gettysburg Campaign began when they joined the expedition one week after Brandy Station and did not conclude until the Army of Northern Virginia returned to Virginia on July 14. The cavalry actions thus involved a much broader sphere of both time and geography.

Cavalry Actions in Loudon County

Stuart divided his five-brigade cavalry division to screen the march of the Army of Northern Virginia from Culpeper into the Shenandoah Valley, where the Blue Ridge Mountains would provide a natural cover across the Potomac. The brigades of Beverly Robertson, Fitz Lee, and Rooney Lee (commanded by Colonel John Randolph Chambliss, Jr.) rode east of Longstreet's marching column. The brigades of Grumble Jones and Wade Hampton rode to the south and covered the rear of A.P. Hill's Corps, the last infantry unit to cross the Rappahannock.[2] As the two Confederate infantry corps marched westward, the Federal cavalry corps under Alfred Pleasanton conducted a series of attempts to penetrate the barriers that Stuart's cavalry division presented. The result was a series of cavalry clashes in Loudon County, Virginia, between Culpeper and the base of the Blue Ridge Mountains.

The psychological effects of the Battle of Brandy Station persisted. Pleasanton's Federal cavalry corps earned a profound degree of confidence, encouraging them to take the offensive. Although the cavalry clashes in Loudon County during the Army of Northern Virginia's march to Pennsylvania were relatively small compared to the momentous battle at Brandy Station, the engagements that occurred were frequent and furious.[3]

The first confrontation occurred on the afternoon of June 17 when Federal forces under General Judson Kilpatrick and David M. Gregg collided with Fitz Lee's brigade at the village of Aldie. Taking up defensive positions supported by mounted artillery, the Confederates repulsed a series of spirited mounted and dismounted Federal attacks. With inconclusive results, the Federals incurred 305 casualties and the Confederates lost between 100 and 119.[4] The second cavalry engagement transpired simultaneously about five miles west of Aldie at Middleburg when the brigades of Robertson and Chambliss surrounded and routed the First Rhode Island. Two days later, Gregg's Federal division arrived as reinforcements, and another inconclusive skirmish followed. Federal casualties were estimated at ninety-nine with the Confederates losing forty missing.[5] The Confederate units then withdrew farther to the west. The third action involved the Jones Brigade and took place on June 21 about eight miles west of Middleburg at Upperville. By this time, the main body of the Army of Northern Virginia was nearing the Shenandoah Valley. Pleasanton ordered a last, determined effort to penetrate Stuart's cavalry screen and locate the position of Lee's army.

Jones and his brigade occupied Union (later changed to Unison), Virginia, with Colonel John R. Chambliss commanding Rooney Lee's brigade. Stuart ordered them to retire gradually toward Upperville.[6] Meanwhile, General John Buford maneuvered his Federal cavalry toward the same location, arrived first, dismounted, and took cover behind a series of stone wall fences that lined the road. Jones and Chambliss reached Upperville to find that the stone fences provided barricaded protection for Buford's sharpshooters, "who fired with deadly effect into the almost helpless Confederate masses."[7] With the road situated between rows of stone fences, it was impossible for Jones to get his regiments into a formation.

John N. Opie starkly criticized Jones for his handling of the engagement at Upperville. The Jones Brigade charged the barricaded Union forces. Had matters gone according to plan, the horses would have jumped the stone wall, allowing Jones's mounted troops to penetrate the defenses and continue the momentum. Instead of jumping, the horses stopped and wheeled to the right. The turning maneuver denied the (mostly right-handed) troopers better access to their pistols. Unable to render an effective volley of fire, they received one from the Federals, which "uselessly" resulted in substantial losses.[8] Opie felt that in their part of the engagement they had been "decidedly worsted by the enemy," which was "assisted by the mismanagement on the part of General Jones."[9] Among the wounded in the Jones Brigade was Captain Charles T. O'Ferrall of Company I, Twelfth Virginia Cavalry. O'Ferrall received a gunshot wound to the chest that was initially diagnosed as fatal. Ultimately, however, he would recover and rejoin Jones a year later.

Jones reported his brigade's collective losses at fourteen killed, fifty-one wounded, and six missing between the Seventh Virginia, Eleventh Virginia, and Twelfth Virginia cavalry regiments.[10] He reported that the enemy took sixty-one wounded to two different field hospitals.[11]

In spite of Jones's setback, Hampton's and Robertson's brigades intervened to render the engagement at Upperville a tactical Confederate cavalry victory. The action thwarted the Union cavalry's final attempt to penetrate Stuart's barrier and allowed the Army of Northern Virginia to enter the Shenandoah Valley and cross the Potomac undetected. Pleasanton knew Lee's Army of Northern Virginia was maneuvering northward but he lacked specific knowledge regarding its position or destination.

The engagement at Upperville concluded combat operations in Loudon County. On the following day, the Federals withdrew and Stuart reestablished his cavalry division headquarters at Rectortown in Fauquier County. The Southerners regained the initiative and the momentum for the expedition into Pennsylvania.

Expedition into Pennsylvania

Under Lee's direction, once Stuart ascertained that the Army of the Potomac would march northward and not threaten Richmond, he was to divide his cavalry division to perform two different missions. Three brigades would advance into Maryland and take a position to the right of Ewell's Corps. The other two brigades would stay to the rear with the less glorious task of guarding the mountain passes through the Blue Ridge. Stuart had to decide which two brigades to exclude while the other three accompanied him on his expedition. It was a logical choice to leave behind Beverly Robertson, who was "unpredictable in battle."[12] Robertson's inexperienced brigade had failed to check the Federal advance at Kelly's Ford during the Battle of Brandy Station.[13] In what some historians regarded as highly controversial, Stuart elected to assign the W.E. Jones Brigade to the rear guard with Robertson.

Stuart felt he had a cohesive group commanded by the team of Hampton, Fitz Lee, and Chambliss. While Jones was on detached service in the Shenandoah Valley and his West Virginia Raid, the three selected brigades shared a past with Stuart on numerous operations, including the recent campaigns of Fredericksburg and Chancellorsville. In Stuart's mind, they "knew how to fight together."[14] Stuart further rationalized his decision by rating Grumble as "the best outpost officer in the cavalry division."[15] That faint praise, if one can use that term, was ambiguous, to say the least. Being excluded from Stuart's expedition should not have been a problem for Jones. Only weeks before, he had tendered his resignation (which Lee withheld) when ordered to return to Stuart's command. The slight to Grumble, however, was not so much his exclusion from Stuart's seemingly adventurous expedition; it was his assignment to serve with Robertson.

Of the two brigade commanders assigned to the rear guard, Grumble Jones was superior in combative skill and administrative efficiency. His brigade was the larger and more experienced. While Jones was participating in the Chambersburg Raid, conducting operations in the Shenandoah Valley, and leading his West Virginia Raid, Robertson was on a recruiting assignment in North Carolina, far from any of the action. While the officers carried equal rank, Jones possessed all of the superior qualifications. Robertson, however, had the *prior* commission and therefore held seniority. Thus, when the two brigades were ordered to work in conjunction, the far less distinguished Beverly Robertson held authority over the more proficient Jones.

Critics of Stuart's handling of the matter point out that he could have tactfully suggested that Robertson might work with Jones in a spirit of cooperation and "profit by counsel with the junior" officer.[16] Theories suggest that in Stuart's mind, the "numerical superiority" as well as the fighting experience of Jones's Brigade would persuade Robertson to "give full weight to Jones's suggestions and counsels."[17] Stuart did nothing of the sort. In a tone of detachment, he bluntly conveyed to Robertson, "You will instruct General Jones from time to time as the movement progresses or events may require, and report anything of importance to General Longstreet."[18] On June 24 Stuart reaffirmed his decision when he communicated to Robertson, "General, Your own and General Jones's brigades will cover the front of Ashby's and Snicker's Gaps, yourself, as senior officer, being in command."[19]

Ultimately, Jones's assignment with Robertson would prove to be a temporary measure and one of minimal consequence. There is no official record that he protested the awkward arrangement. Privately, however, he may have regarded Stuart's decision to place him under Robertson's command as a personal insult, and one he would not forget.

Stuart's Gettysburg Raid

The three-week period from the festivities at Culpeper Courthouse to the commencement of the Gettysburg Campaign challenged J.E.B. Stuart's legacy. The two grand reviews demonstrated his vanity. The surprise attack at Brandy Station revealed his momentary lack of diligence. His decision to leave Jones behind and under Robertson's command is reason to question his administrative judgment. It was for another reason, however, that the cavalry division under J.E.B. Stuart was most scrutinized for its pivotal role in the Army of Northern Virginia's failure at Gettysburg. Stuart's execution of his Gettysburg Raid would forever tarnish his image to at least some degree in the annals of Confederate history. His Gettysburg Raid was as spectacular a feat as his Chambersburg Raid the previous year. It covered more than 160 miles in one direction, most of it in enemy territory. His combat engagements were mostly triumphs; his few setbacks were inconclusive draws at worst. None could challenge Stuart's resourcefulness or his audacity. There are questions, however, as to what the incursion accomplished, particularly regarding the primary objectives of the Army of Northern Virginia.

Stuart had the brigades of Wade Hampton, Fitz Lee, and John Chambliss prepare three days of rations and rendezvous secretly on the evening of June 24 near Salem Depot (now Marshall) in Fauquier County. Transporting a minimum number of supply wagons, they would rely heavily upon foraging. Numbering about 2,000, the three-brigade detachment departed around one o'clock in the morning on June 25. Due to weather-related delays, it took four days to ride through Prince William and Fairfax counties just to reach and cross the Potomac into Maryland, by which time they had already exhausted their rations.[20]

Stuart's famished expeditionary force arrived in Rockville to receive a welcome from the citizenry sympathetic to the Southern cause.[21] By chance, a well-supplied and lightly guarded eight-mile-long Federal wagon train from Washington, D.C., approached their position. With minimal effort, Stuart's horsemen captured "125 of the best United States model wagons with splendid teams."[22] The wagons and accessories were brand new and fully stocked with provisions. Stuart's raiders also captured about 400 prisoners. Ironically, this small and easy victory would render Stuart's pre–Gettysburg raid a failure. Since the captured supplies were too valuable to abandon, they had to be transported for the remainder of the expedition and served as an impediment. The prisoners had to be paroled in a tedious and time-consuming task.

On the following day, June 29, Stuart's brigades defeated a small Federal detachment at Cooksville, Maryland, capturing 400 more prisoners. That triumph merely replaced the burden and negated the convenience of having released those at Rockville. At Hood's Mill, Stuart's raiders destroyed a trestle and nearby tracks of the Baltimore & Ohio Railroad. They then rode northward to Westminster, Maryland, and defeated a smaller force of the First Delaware. On June 30 Stuart's column encountered stiff resistance from General Judson Kilpatrick's division at Hanover, Pennsylvania. After disengaging, they detoured eastward to Dover in York County, Pennsylvania, on July 1. By that time, Lee's Army of Northern Virginia was beginning the three-day battle at Gettysburg.

After paroling the second group of prisoners, Stuart rode to Carlisle, Pennsylvania, with the intent of uniting with Ewell's Corps. Ewell, however, had already departed for Gettysburg, and Union forces under the command of Baldy Smith occupied the town.[23] Stuart demanded Smith's surrender and launched an artillery bombardment after he refused. After accomplishing nothing, Stuart conceded a stalemate to preserve his ammunition. Out of communication with Lee for eight days, he finally received a dispatch of the infantry's engagement at Gettysburg. At one o'clock on the morning of July 2, Stuart left his captured 125 wagons behind with a detachment and led the bulk of his force thirty miles southward to Gettysburg. It was said that Stuart arrived at Lee's headquarters at Seminary Ridge on the afternoon of July 2 with the enthusiastic confidence of a conquering warrior anticipating glorious praise. Instead, he was dressed down by his commander in a very awkward situation. According to legend, Lee austerely greeted his cavalry commander by saying, "Well, General Stuart, you are here at last!"[24]

Stuart was totally unaware that in regard to his specific objective he had failed his revered commander miserably. Lee would have preferred to have devised his strategy with the benefit of Stuart's intelligence regarding the strength and positions of the enemy. In the absence of information Stuart might have delivered, Lee delegated discretionary authority to his infantry corps and division commanders, who launched critical attacks at the Peach Orchard, Devil's Den, Little Round Top, and Culp's Hill. All of the frontal assaults failed, and the losses cost the Army of Northern Virginia its numerical superiority.[25]

In a last-ditch effort to salvage the campaign, Lee planned a final frontal assault, later called "Pickett's Charge," on the next day.

Jones and Robertson

The rear guard brigades of Beverly Robertson and Grumble Jones had their shortcomings as well. Their instructions were to shield the mountain pass at Ashby Gap until they observed Hooker's Army of the Potomac withdraw and then they were to join the expedition. The combined Jones and Robertson detachment failed to catch up with and unite with the infantry and did not cross the Potomac until July 1.[26] The Jones Brigade contracted for the second time in the campaign when the Twelfth Virginia Cavalry was detached for picket duty at Harpers Ferry. White's Thirty-Fifth Virginia Battalion had been previously detached to accompany Ewell's Corps spearheading the invasion.[27] Jones's downsized brigade consisted of the Sixth, Seventh, and Eleventh Virginia Cavalry regiments and Chew's Mounted Artillery, a collective strength of about 1,500. Jones arrived at Cashtown, about eight miles northwest of Gettysburg, on July 3, the day of Lee's final assault on Cemetery Ridge.

Pickett's Charge

The Army of Northern Virginia's frontal assault, now known as Pickett's Charge, was Lee's final effort to break the stalemate. Longstreet's Corps of 15,000 infantrymen marched across a half-mile open field from Seminary Ridge against Federal defenders behind improvised breastworks at Cemetery Ridge. Realizing that the measure was a gamble and having planned a contingency, Lee had positioned a supply wagon train stretching for several miles and parked in a meadow near Fairfield, eight miles southwest of Gettysburg. About seven miles due north of Fairfield at Cashtown, Jones positioned his Sixth, Seventh, and Eleventh Virginia Cavalry regiments along with Chew's Mounted Artillery to await further orders.

Pickett's Charge was a suicide mission that changed an inconclusive draw into a devastating failure. After his attacking force was repulsed at Cemetery Ridge with heavy losses, Lee had to alter his strategy to one of getting his defeated but still formidable Army of Northern Virginia out of enemy territory and back to Virginia. Evacuating more than 60,000 men from enemy territory was going to be a challenge, unlike that of the initial invasion march. With limited foraging opportunities and the need to sustain an army for what would amount to a twelve-day journey, the supply wagons served a vital a role. Manned by mostly noncombatant teamsters, the supply trains were attractive targets for the enemy. If they were captured, destroyed, or otherwise impeded, the Army of Northern Virginia could potentially be starved into submission. From his army's main line of battle at Seminary Ridge, Lee observed that his supply wagons were exposed, and he immediately dispatched orders for Jones to take proper measures.

Jones led his column on a seven-mile southward march toward Fairfield. About four o'clock in the afternoon, Luther Hopkins of the Seventh Virginia Cavalry heard a continuous rumbling sound and then observed the column of covered supply wagons stretching for miles. The column, proceeding on the same road that had brought it to Gettysburg, was facing the opposite direction. It was a sign that Lee's Army of Northern Virginia had been defeated for the first time.[28]

Battle of Fairfield

Two miles east of Fairfield approximately four hundred mounted troops from the Sixth U.S. Cavalry, commanded by Major Samuel "Old Paddy" Starr, rode toward the wagon train after receiving intelligence of its location from civilian scouts. A detachment led by Lieutenant Christian Balder spotted the lightly guarded supply train northbound on Fairfield-Orrtanna Road. Feeling that they had an easy target before them, Balder's unit initiated a charge that easily dispersed the few pickets.[29] Simultaneously, Jones and his 1,500 member brigade, coming from the opposite direction, arrived in the vicinity. Upon observing the Federal advance, Jones ordered his regiments to countercharge. Realizing that his troops were heavily outnumbered, Lieutenant Balder ordered his detachment to fall back to the safety of the main body of the Sixth U.S. Cavalry. Jones's forces, however, remained in "hot pursuit" and "screaming the Rebel yell to the top of their lungs."[30] The veteran Seventh Virginia Cavalry spearheaded the counterassault.

Starr's Sixth U.S. Cavalry dismounted and took cover behind fence railings on both sides of the road. The Seventh Virginia Cavalry entered a bottleneck and received a volley of carbine fire. With heavy losses and their momentum shattered, they halted and fell back, much to the disgust of Jones. Jones later reported that the retreat cost more men "than a glorious victory would have cost had the onset been made with vigor and boldness."[31] He further commented, "A failure to rally promptly and renew the fight is a blemish on the bright history of this regiment."[32] Jones then deployed the five cannons of Captain Preston Chew's mounted artillery. From a six hundred yard distance, they fired into the Union positions. Backed into a corner by the incoming shells, Lieutenant Balder's Union detachment rashly charged northward toward Jones's position.

Jones correctly interpreted his opponent's bold measure as one of desperation. Mounted on his horse, he shouted to Major Cabell E. Flournoy of the Sixth Virginia, "Shall one damn regiment of Yankees whip my whole brigade?"[33] Flournoy's horsemen drew their sabers and countercharged into the Union detachment. Standing members of the Seventh Virginia removed the rail fences, providing the charging Sixth Virginia the momentum of an open field. The Sixth Virginia routed their Union counterparts, forcing wounded Lieutenant Balder and Major Starr to surrender. Jones's troopers pursued the dispersed Federals, many of which abandoned their horses and fled on foot. The pursuit continued into the back streets between the buildings of Fairfield where frightened civilians scrambled for cover.[34] About a mile south of Fairfield, the Jones Brigade halted and marched exultantly back northward on the Fairfield-Orrtanna Road.

Jones's victory at Fairfield, Pennsylvania, although a minor engagement, was overwhelming. Starr's Union command suffered 50 percent casualties with six killed (including five officers), 23 wounded, and up to 203 captured (including an additional five officers).[35] Wounded Sixth U.S. Cavalry commander Samuel Starr lost an arm to amputation and was left behind when Jones withdrew. Lieutenant Balder died of his wounds. Jones's combined casualties were fifty-eight.[36]

Although the Fairfield engagement was minor and a resounding defeat for the Federals, they recognized its significance. The Sixth U.S. Cavalry was outnumbered four to one. Thirty-five years later, two Union noncommissioned officers received the Medal of Honor for valor demonstrated in the fight.[37] Jones's Fairfield triumph cleared the first major obstacle of retreat for the devastated Army of Northern Virginia. Had the Sixth U.S. Cavalry been properly reinforced, they would have captured the supply train and could have taken the high ground at Fairfield Gap. Lee's Army of Northern Virginia would have been without supplies, ammunition, or subsistence while having to fight its way back to the Potomac.

The Battle of Fairfield launched the final phase of the Gettysburg Campaign. The next twelve days would be a race to the Potomac between the retreating Army of Northern Virginia and the closely pursuing Army of the Potomac. The cavalry bore the task of escorting Lee's army's retreat as unmolested as possible.

Race to the Potomac

Lee's objective was to return his defeated army to Virginia to recuperate and fight another day. Not satisfied with the mere repulse of Lee's forces, the Lincoln administration recognized a rare opportunity to trap the Army of Northern Virginia in either Pennsylvania or Maryland and end the war in the Eastern Theater. Lincoln could not overemphasize the importance of this objective to the Federal field commanders.

The Army of Potomac commander, General George Meade, viewed the situation from a different perspective. Lee's army, although defeated, remained well supplied and formidable. Awed by the Southern valor during the three days of infantry clashes, particularly Pickett's Charge, Meade harbored concerns that if cornered the Confederate forces could march on Washington. To the dismay of Lincoln, Meade would take the cautious approach and balance the objectives of obstructing Lee's retreating forces while defending Washington in the event the enemy resumed the offensive.

Nature aggravated the misery of the fighters. The three days of infantry clashes between July 1 and 3 occurred during scorching heat. For the duration of the withdrawal, the combatants endured a blinding rainstorm that wreaked havoc at Monterey Pass on South Mountain and swelled the Potomac River barrier above flood stage. During the withdrawal, Lee's Army of Northern Virginia would be under constant surveillance by the Federal cavalry and pursued by the main body of the Army of the Potomac. To improve his chances, Lee committed a diversion. He divided his retreating army into two columns and directed each to take different routes to the common destination of Williamsport, Maryland, where they would cross the Potomac.

Taking a secondary route, Brigadier General John D. Imboden's Brigade escorted a seventeen-mile-long teamster-driven wagon train bearing most of the wounded.[38] Avoiding the rough terrain at Monterey Pass, they took the indirect cross-country route westward from Seminary Ridge through Cashtown and Marion, Pennsylvania, before turning due south into Maryland and on to Williamsport. It would be called the "march of the wounded."[39] Although a much longer route, it was deemed less likely to be impeded by enemy forces.[40]

The bulk of the Army of Northern Virginia would take the most direct route, a rough, forty-mile track through Fairfield Gap and Monterey Pass to Hagerstown, Maryland, from where they would proceed westward to Williamsport. The supply wagon trains that Jones saved at Fairfield would lead the way, followed by A.P. Hill's Corps serving as their escort. Behind Hill's Corps was Longstreet's Corps escorting Federal prisoners of war and hostages. Next in line came the train of supply wagons of Ewell's Corps, which departed Fairfield Gap at three o'clock in the morning on July 4. Ewell's Corps of infantry and artillery would bring up the rear. Stuart's cavalry division assumed the task of securing the mountain gaps against potential hostile threats.

Monterey Pass

Aside from the swollen Potomac River the Army of Northern Virginia would ultimately encounter, Monterey Pass presented the most challenging natural obstruction to the retreat. With its center situated in Franklin County, Pennsylvania, the area extends into three counties across the border with Maryland and thus along the Mason-Dixon Line.[41] There, the Fairfield Hagerstown Road snaked around the sides of the South Mountain Range atop steep cliffs and along deep gorges. The passage's extremely narrow width restricted marches to a single-file formation, and multi-configurations of sharp turns marked the way.[42] Aggravating the situation, the onset of heavy rains had washed out sections of the road and caused portions of it to collapse. As if the topographical and weather-related conditions were not hazardous enough, the maneuvering supply trains were about to encounter a Federal assault.

The Waynesboro (Pennsylvania) Emmitsburg (Maryland) Turnpike ran south of and almost parallel to the Fairfield Hagerstown Road. The two highways intersected at Monterey Pass. General Judson Kilpatrick, leading a cavalry division that included a Michigan brigade commanded by Brigadier General George Armstrong Custer, advanced on the Waynesboro-Emmitsburg Turnpike toward Monterey Pass. Upon their inevitable arrival, the Federals would pose an overwhelming threat to Ewell's lightly armed and unescorted convoy of wagon trains.

On the evening of July 4, Jones received intelligence of a Federal advance toward Monterey Pass and volunteered to go with his command "to its [the wagon train's] protection."[43] Stuart authorized Jones to proceed with the Sixth and Seventh Virginia Cavalry regiments plus Captain Preston Chew's battery. The Seventh Virginia was called back, and the Fourth North Carolina Cavalry, already on the road, took its place. Taking the Fairfield Hagerstown Road, Jones encountered obstacles in the way of broken-down wagons, washed-out portions of the road, run-off streams gushing over the road, and stragglers. He detached himself from his main column and, with his immediate staff, rendezvoused with the rear guard positioned on the Waynesboro-Emmitsburg Turnpike, just east of the junction of the two roads. The rear guard was a twenty-man company from the First Maryland Cavalry Battalion commanded by Captain George M. Emack, who had been urged to hold Monterey Pass at all hazards.[44]

Emack had already taken the initiative against overwhelming odds. He approached the Confederate convoy and instructed the teamsters to pick up their pace. Conceding that it would be impossible to save the entire train, he called for dividing it into multiple segments to mitigate exposure once the enemy did break through, an event that was inevitable.[45] He then returned to the intersection to await the Federal onslaught, he and his men wearing rubber ponchos that reduced their visibility. Kilpatrick's Division launched a frontal assault with Custer's Fifth Michigan, forcing Emack's company to exhaust its artillery ammunition. Although the firing resulted in no Federal casualties, the deafening sound echoed through the canyon, and the blinding flash of the blast brought a shock effect. Custer's Brigade disengaged and fell back down the slope of the mountain. More wagons passed through the junction and out of harm's way.

Emack's dismounted troopers took scattered positions on both sides of the Waynesboro-Emmitsburg Turnpike and awaited the second-wave attack. When it came, they fired their small arms under cover of total darkness in a masking deception that deluded the Federals into exaggerating the Confederate numbers.[46] At the same time, they had to conserve their ammunition. Jones and his staff arrived to find Emack's Marylanders facing an entire division of Federals. Their lone cannon had spent its last round, and their small-arms ammunition neared depletion. Jones later reported:

> Arriving, I found Captain G.M. Emack's company of the Maryland cavalry, with one gun, opposed to a whole division of Federal cavalry with a full battery. He [Emac] had already been driven back within a few hundred yards of the junction of the road. Not a half of the long train had passed. Darkness had just set in. This brave little band of heroes was encouraged with the hope of speedy reenforcements, reminded of the importance of their trust, and exhorted to fight to the bitter end rather than yield. All my couriers and all others were ordered to the front, directed to lie on the ground and be sparing of their ammunition. The last charge of grape was expended, and the piece sent to the rear. For more than two hours, less than 50 men kept many thousands in check, and the wagons continued to pass long after the balls were whistling in their midst.[47]

In preparation for Custer's third-wave assault, Kilpatrick launched an artillery bombardment, turning the scene into one of absolute bedlam. The combination of a raging, intense thunderstorm, total darkness, and the elements of battle set a stage for one of the most chaotic confrontations of the Civil War. Describing the barrage of Federal shells on the narrow mountain roadway, Lieutenant John Blue commented "the Yankees had the range and were making a kind of bowling alley of the pike."[48] A squad from the Sixth Virginia Cavalry maneuvered toward Jones's position only to confront the same obstacles. Commenting on the pandemonium, Private Luther W. Hopkins wrote the following:

> It was with great difficulty that we could get past the wagons in the darkness, and hence our progress was slow, but we finally worked our way up to the front and were dismounted and formed in line as best we could on either side of the road among the rocks and trees and then moved forward in an effort to drive the battery away from its position so we could guide our march. The only light we had to guide us was from the lightning in the heavens and the vivid flashes that came from the enemy's cannon. Their firing did not do much execution, as they failed to get proper range. Besides, we were so close they were firing over our heads, but the booming of the guns that hour of night, with the roar of the thunder, was terrifying indeed, and beyond description. We would wait for a lightning flash and advance a few steps and halt, and then for a light from the batteries and again advance.[49]

Jones, his staff, and Emack's company welcomed the reinforcements from the Sixth Virginia, but the measure only strengthened their collective numbers up to about 120 men facing an entire division. In a flanking maneuver, the First West Virginia Cavalry occupied the area of the Monterey Hotel west of Jones's position, providing the Federals the high ground for an attack against the approaching wagon train. About midnight, Custer's Michigan Brigade and the First West Virginia Cavalry launched the anticipated all-out, third-wave assault. Vastly outnumbered, the collective forces of Jones and Emack faced opposition to their front and rear.

The intensifying thunderstorm turned the scene even more chaotic. Only lightning flashes and gunfire blasts intermittently interrupted the total darkness. Custer's forces intermingled with Jones's men, rendering it impossible to distinguish friend from foe.[50]

Not knowing who was to one's side, verbal communication was minimized. In the darkness, some of the men addressed Jones as "General," to which he replied, "Call me Bill!" He did not want to let the enemy know that there was a general in the mix.[51] In the bedlam, Jones became separated from his company. Lieutenant John Blue later recalled the situation:

> We could not see the color of their clothes but was soon satisfied that they were blue. The other fellow, I feel sure were satisfied that there was a streak of gray got mixed up with them. They passed by the wagons without disturbing them for fear, no doubt, that the man at his elbow might quietly run him through if he should be imprudent enough to show by his actions where he belonged. Not a word was spoken. After we had passed the wagons, I dropped out of ranks as most of the command who had been mixed up with the blue coats had already done. I found my self in a body of timber and succeeded in getting a few rods from the road and waited with all the patience I could until day began to break when I moved further down the road. I soon discovered a column of cavalry moving on the highway. It was soon light enough to see that they were dressed in gray. I soon joined them and learned that we had politely escorted the Yankees until they had passed our train, and let them go without hindrance. But our general was missing. No one had seen him since daylight. We did not know what had become of him. (The) train now moved forward with our brigade in front.[52]

As anticipated, Kilpatrick's cavalry division broke through Jones's token resistance and wreaked havoc on a portion of Ewell's wagon train. The unfortunate teamsters found themselves in the wrong place at the wrong time. Many were captured. Some wagons with their teams fell over the cliff.

Jones was missing for several hours and presumed captured. A local newspaper covering the engagement reported his apprehension.[53] Even Captain Emack presumed the same.[54] Without their commander, the small detachment force resumed its march to Hagerstown. Fourth Lieutenant John Blue went on to write, "About nine o'clock we heard cheering in front which we could not account for, but soon learned that it was caused by the return of Gen. Jones. He had been mixed up with the Yankees the night before and did not succeed in getting away until near daylight."[55] During the mayhem, Jones had taken refuge in the cover of the woods. To avoid capture, he had crisscrossed the Mason-Dixon Line several times both concealed by and lost in the darkness.[56] Lieutenant Blue added, "He had followed a by-road and not acquainted with the country had found himself several miles from the line of march."[57] As for the feeling about their commander, Blue wrote, "No doubt he was glad to get back as we were to have him with us again."[58]

From a statistical perspective, the Battle of Monterey Pass was not only a Union triumph, but it was also one of the most one-sided victories of the war.[59] Kilpatrick claimed to have taken "1,360 prisoners, one battle flag, a large number of horses and mules, several hundred of the enemy's wounded being left upon the field."[60] The Federal gains were at a negligible cost of only five killed, ten wounded, and twenty-eight missing.[61] Those statistics, even if accurate, are somewhat misleading.

Kilpatrick's assault caused considerable damage to Ewell's supply train. However, the Federals saturated themselves beyond their capacity to take on more Confederate prisoners and plunder. Before disengaging, Kilpatrick's forces torched ammunition wagons they could not seize, setting up a mountaintop fireworks display visible for miles. Most of the prisoners were either noncombatant teamsters or scores of wounded being transported by ambulance who had to be paroled. Out of the multitude of supply wagons that advanced through Monterey Pass, Kilpatrick's Division disabled only a small portion of one train and not even the entire train.[62] Thus, although a marked setback, the engagement at Monterey Pass was not a catastrophic loss for the Confederates. For the record,

15. Gettysburg

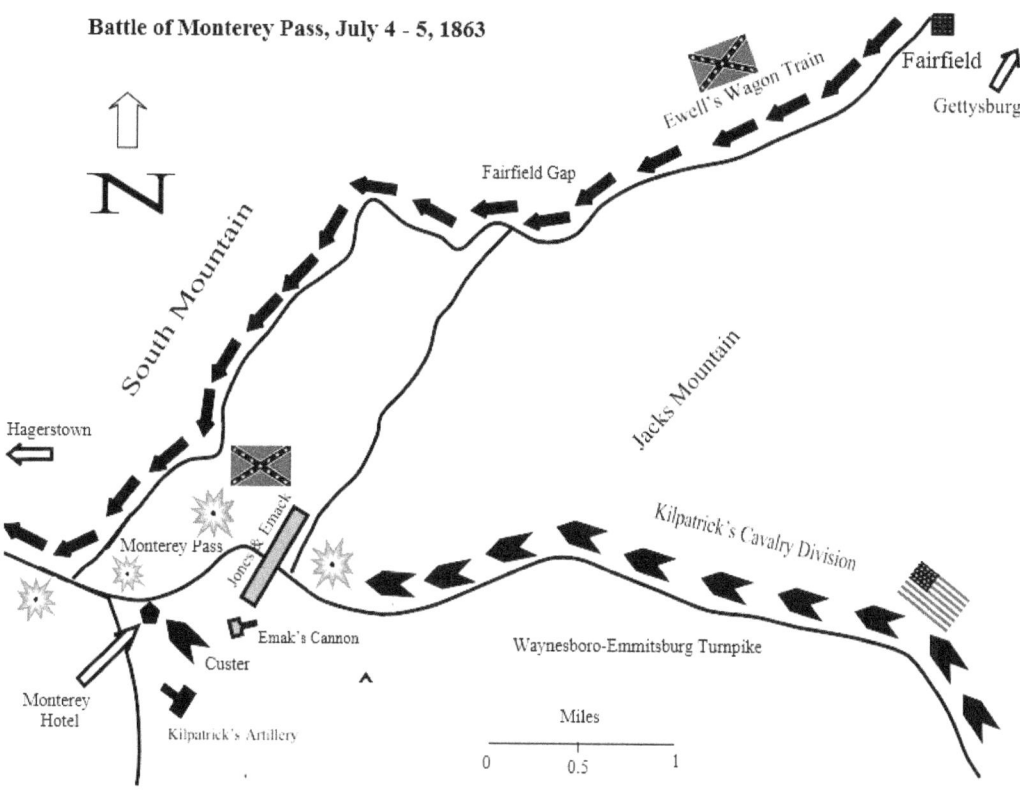

Battle of Monterey Pass (sketch by author, 2016).

Monterey Pass was the only battle in the Civil War fought on both sides of the Mason-Dixon Line. Although heavily outnumbered and almost out of ammunition while facing overwhelming odds, General Jones and Captain Emack bought time for most of the wagon train convoy to negotiate the pass. In spite of the losses, the vast majority of the supply wagons crossed South Mountain and would ultimately cross the Potomac. Soon after the engagement, the infantry and artillery units of Ewell's Corps marched the same route to Hagerstown uncontested.

The reunited Jones Brigade arrived at Hagerstown and joined the infantry units in establishing temporary defensive fortifications. Jones and his immediate staff then detached themselves to ride nine miles west to assess the situation at their next destination, Williamsport.

Williamsport

Williamsport, in Washington County, Maryland, was the point for the Army of Northern Virginia to cross the Potomac and enter the relative safety the river barrier provided. It was likewise the target of the pursuing Army of the Potomac in order to obstruct the Confederate retreat. By the time the lead groups of Ewell's wagon convoy arrived, Kilpatrick's and Buford's Federal cavalry units were already closing in.

On the morning of July 5 Jones and his staff reached Williamsport, after Ewell's wagon convoys but well ahead of Imboden's "march of the wounded," which had taken the alternate western route via Cashtown. After negotiating Monterey Pass, the wagon convoys had reached their next destination only to encounter a new chaotic situation. The same storm system that wreaked havoc on Monterey Pass had swollen the Potomac River above fording depth and partially swept away the pontoon bridges.[63] Kilpatrick's and Buford's cavalry were already nearby, and the bulk of Meade's Army of the Potomac was marching in their direction. The Army of Northern Virginia appeared trapped between the converging Union forces and the rising Potomac River.

Most of the personnel on hand were teamsters anxious to cross. Only one ferry boat was available, and it could conduct only seventy crossings in twenty-four hours. The teamsters were arguing among themselves as to which one should go first. Jones intervened to take control of the situation. He placed an armed picket at the crossing to regulate the flow of passengers. Then he armed the walking wounded, the capable fighters, and the teamsters with carbines and stationed them on the natural high ground and the tops of buildings. He directed that the wagons containing vital documents and the wounded receive priority.[64] He also remained on hand to direct the traffic flow and to command the defenses pending the arrival of Imboden's column. Within a relatively short time, he had restored order and established a formidable defense.[65]

Several roads converged upon Williamsport, providing the pursuing Army of the Potomac accessibility. However, the topographical features of high ground, rocky ridges, densely wooded areas, and marshy wetlands surrounding the region afforded the outnumbered and lesser capable Confederate fighters with formidable natural defenses. By the afternoon, Imboden's 5,000-unit wagon train arrived. Stretching seventeen miles, it produced a bottleneck effect, with masses of teamsters awaiting their turn to board the ferry. The situation would try their patience, but Jones had already restored order by establishing a formidable defense.

On the morning of July 6, Jones received a dispatch from Stuart, calling him back to Hagerstown. After turning the Williamsport defenses over to Imboden, Jones rode with his staff through enemy lines to Hagerstown and reunited with his brigade. Imboden, in turn, took advantage of the topography to deceive the enemy into overestimating his force's strength and fighting capability. They repulsed a joint attack by Kilpatrick's and Buford's cavalry units in an engagement later termed the "Teamster's Battle."[66]

Hagerstown and Vicinity

By the morning of July 6 General Jubal Early's Division of Ewell's Corps was bringing up the rear of the Army of Northern Virginia evacuation through Monterey Pass to reinforce the Confederate operations at Hagerstown. In a minor skirmish, Confederate infantry units drove Buford's cavalry from Hagerstown. Jones engaged the Eleventh Virginia Cavalry in a saber duel that expelled Kilpatrick's column as well. With Hagerstown secured, the Confederates occupied the College of St. James's campus as a base station and a field hospital.

Unfortunately, the minor Confederate successes forced Kilpatrick's and Buford's divisions to unite. Collectively, they could divert their attention to disrupting the fording operation and thus trap the Army of Northern Virginia on the Maryland side of the

Potomac. This development initiated a new round of confrontations switching the action back in the direction of Williamsport.

On the evening of July 7 Lieutenant Colonel Thomas A. Marshall led Jones's Seventh Virginia Cavalry on a scouting mission to Funkstown, Maryland, approximately three miles south of Hagerstown. Coincidentally, they encountered the Sixth U.S. Cavalry for the second time since the Battle of Fairfield. With their firearms rendered useless due to wet power, the mounted troopers used their sabers to rout their enemy.[67] An officer noted "the fallen lay thick along the road."[68] The Seventh Virginia pursued the fleeing Federals all the way to the outskirts of Buford's camp. Buford's forces counterchanrged, driving the Seventh all the way back to their starting point.[69]

It would be a stretch to call the Seventh Virginia Cavalry action at Funkstown a Confederate victory. At best, it was a draw. The Federals held the ground by the end of the contest. With that said, Grumble was proud of the Seventh Virginia Cavalry, "which availed itself of the opportunity of settling old scores." He added, "Sabers were freely used, and soon, 66 bloody-headed prisoners were marched to the rear, and the road of slumbering wrath was marked here and there by cleft skulls and pierced bodies. The day at Fairfield is nobly and fully avenged. The Sixth US Regular Cavalry numbers are among the things that were."[70] Jones's report of the annihilation of the Sixth U.S. Cavalry was an overstatement, but the Seventh Virginia Cavalry had performed well to solidify the Hagerstown defenses.

While torrential rains prohibited the Confederates from crossing the Potomac, they also impeded the pursuit by Meade's infantry. Lee needed more time for the swollen Potomac to recede. The Southerners had to hold the approaches to South Mountain at the town of Boonsboro, Maryland, where a new cavalry clash was about to take place. On July 8, with a break in the weather, Stuart launched a multi-pronged attack with the brigades of Fitzhugh Lee, Grumble Jones, John Chambliss, and Wade Hampton.[71] Due to the muddy conditions, the troopers dismounted and advanced on foot. Jones's brigade led the way by crossing the Beaver Creek Bridge to attack Buford's division.[72] Jenkins's cavalry brigade advanced from the west against Kilpatrick's. The combined attacks forced the Federal cavalry to establish defensive positions in the village of Boonsboro. Armed with artillery and Spencer repeating rifles, the Federals stalled Jones's advance. The engagement evolved into an inconclusive artillery duel. Stuart, however, had accomplished his objective by pinning the Federal cavalry down on the defensive. Simultaneously, Lee and his infantry corps extended their defensive positions at the College of Saint James all the way to the banks of the Potomac at Williamsport.

The Federal infantry arrived and counterattacked. Stuart's forces withdrew begrudgingly and inflicted sizeable casualties on the Federals.[73] By the end of the day the Federals held the field. Stuart's cavalry, however, had successfully screened the main body of the Army of Northern Virginia all the way to Williamsport and rendered the Battle of Boonsboro as a tactical Southern victory.

Crossing the Potomac

By July 10 Stuart's cavalry at Funkstown formed a crescent-shaped line of defense, with the Jones and Fitz Lee brigades manning the left wing.[74] The rocky terrain sheltered the troops from the artillery barrage and small-arms fire.[75] Stuart's defenses gradually gave ground while Meade's army gained reinforcements. Once again, Lee's army found itself wedged between an unfordable river and the full force of its adversary. Meade had another opportunity to trap Lee's army on the Maryland side of the Potomac. Fortunately for the Confederates, he remained cautious. For two more days, the Army of Northern Virginia dug more than a mile of earthworks in anticipation of an all-out frontal assault. Lincoln expressed optimism that Meade was finally going to render a decisive blow. Rather than advance, however, the over-cautious Meade awaited the arrival of more reinforcements. Stuart's cavalry maintained a picket line, while, well to the rear, the Army of Northern Virginia engineers directed the construction of pontoon bridges at Williamsport.

By July 13 the Army of Northern Virginia had established a formidable defensive line between the Potomac River and Stuart's cavalry holding the north (left) flank.[76] Meade remained cautious and refrained from ordering a frontal assault. Stuart's cavalry served as a rear guard while the Army of Northern Virginia infantry began its orderly crossing. The fording operation still encountered difficulties. Torrential rains further swelled the raging Potomac River and further deteriorated the roads leading to the crossing. In an act of deception, Stuart's staff officers rode up and down the lines engaging in loud conversation to deceive the Federals into believing the Confederates remained in their breastworks.[77] The regimental bands performed and masked the sounds of the evacuation.

The Jones Brigade led the way across the river on the night of July 13 and assumed the task of protecting Lee's forty-mile line of communication from the Williamsport fording operation to Winchester.[78] The rest of Stuart's cavalry remained on the Maryland side of the river to bring up the rear. Fording operations continued and would conclude about five miles downriver at Falling Waters, West Virginia, where the Federals made a final attempt to disrupt them. In a minor engagement, the Army of Northern Virginia sustained the loss of two cannons, the capture of 500 stragglers, and the mortal wounding of General James Johnson Pettigrew. However, the vast majority successfully forded the river.

At daylight on July 14 Meade finally ordered the all-out assault, but it was too late. The Federals found only empty rifle pits and unattended campfires. Lee's artillery, which had crossed over the previous evening, took the high ground and discouraged Meade from continuing the pursuit. Although severed from the Federal pursuit, the Army of Northern Virginia remained in enemy territory by being in West Virginia and not Virginia proper. Fifty mounted Federals detached from the First Connecticut Cavalry garrisoned at Harpers Ferry attempted to probe the Confederate lines. Jones's Twelfth Virginia Cavalry encountered and overwhelmed the unit, capturing two officers and twenty-five enlisted men.[79] Colonel A.W. Harman, who had just returned after recuperating from wounds suffered at Brandy Station, was captured in the engagement.[80] This minor engagement culminated the full evacuation of the Army of Northern Virginia. General George Meade had squandered an opportunity to end the war in the Eastern Theater. Lincoln vented his frustration by drafting a scathing letter to the Army of the Potomac commander, but he never sent it.

Stuart and his staff returned to The Bower to receive the Dandridge family hospitality. Jones led his brigade into camp near Charles Town (WV).[81] After a few days of reprieve, Stuart's cavalry division reconsolidated and marched southward through the Shenandoah Valley. They would ultimately cross the Blue Ridge and join the remainder of the Army of Northern Virginia in Culpeper County, the original base of operations and where they had launched their invasion.

16

Court-Martial

The Gettysburg Campaign officially concluded in late July, when Lee's Army of Northern Virginia established a tentative defensive position in Culpeper County. On July 30 Jones submitted his report on the campaign from his temporary headquarters at Rixeyville. He concluded, "In this campaign, my brigade participated in three battles and the affair at Boonsboro. It killed and wounded many of the enemy and captured over 600 prisoners."[1] By the middle of August, the Southerners had withdrawn farther southward to establish a new base of operations in adjacent Orange County, a measure that conceded all territory north of the Rapidan River.

Resuming its cautious pursuit, Meade's Army of the Potomac crossed into Virginia and took positions on the north banks of the Rappahannock River. Like their Southern counterparts, the Federals had gone full circle to occupy the same ground they had held before Lee launched his expedition into Pennsylvania. Following the Confederate withdrawal in mid–August, the Federals occupied Culpeper Courthouse. Although urged to press the offensive, the momentum had already been lost once the Southerners crossed the Potomac.

Other factors dispelled Federal ambitions to engage Lee's army for the time being. Meade had to dispatch troops to New York to restore order after the first draft lottery prompted a series of riots, leading to a declaration of martial law. The expiration of the terms of enlistments for scores of troops added to the attrition. The Lincoln administration had no other choice than to limit the Army of the Potomac's activity in Virginia to one of a "threatening presence."[2] Having suffered heavy losses at Gettysburg, both armies recoiled into defensive postures. The Army of Northern Virginia had incurred more than 28,000 combined losses in killed, wounded, and missing against more than 23,000 casualties for the enemy.[3] Skirmishes and minor combat engagements occurred throughout the region, but the overall conflict in the Eastern Theater settled into a long stalemate. The next major development in the East would not occur until Ulysses S. Grant assumed command eight months later.

Although the Army of Northern Virginia stood proud and defiant, Lee and his corps commanders portrayed a mood of devastation. In contrast, the demeanor of Jeb Stuart reflected a most positive assessment of the recent events and the situation at hand. From Hagerstown, while the secure withdrawal of Lee's army was still in doubt, Stuart wrote to his wife that he "had a grand time" in Pennsylvania. He boasted over the accomplishments of his raid, including the capture of "900 prisoners and 200 wagons & splendid teams."[4] On the following day he wrote, "General Lee's maneuvering the Yankees out of Va is the grandest piece of strategy ever heard of."[5] Stuart dwelled on how close they came to a victory while omitting the slightest hint that the expedition had been a devastating failure.

The rank and file did not share Stuart's celebratory mood. Conversely, he was the "subject of whispered criticism" regarding his overall handling of the recent events.[6] A long line of detractors, Longstreet among them, scrutinized Stuart's actions preceding the infantry engagements. Never admonishing Stuart publicly, Lee assumed all blame for the failure and offered his resignation to President Davis, who declined to accept it.

By all means, James Ewell Brown Stuart deserves his legendary place in the annals of the Confederacy. Many segments of his conduct in the Gettysburg Campaign support his stature. With that said, the overall Gettysburg Campaign highlighted Stuart's flaws. Censure was conveyed privately. Few if any were willing to rebuke the revered cavalry commander outwardly. Grumble Jones, however, was one of the exceptions.

After two months of suppressing growing animosities toward his commanding officer, Jones vented his long-constrained emotions in writing. On the same day he submitted his official report, Jones wrote a personal and confidential letter to Stuart. One can only guess as to the content, which may be one of the greatest mysteries of the Civil War. If it paralleled the stream of consciousness narrative device that he had drafted to Lieutenant Colonel William W. Loring in Texas a decade earlier, then Jones pulled no punches. Purely speculating, it seems likely that he freely and fluidly addressed much of the privately held criticism regarding Stuart's recent handling of matters.

Jones had plenty of personal grievances upon which to draw. He suspected Stuart of propagating unjust voting conditions in the 1862 field elections that cost him command of the First Virginia Cavalry.[7] Jones may have been aware of Stuart's efforts to thwart his promotion to brigadier general. He had the means to elaborate on the most embarrassing details of Stuart's direction of the festivities at Culpeper Courthouse only to be caught off-guard with the Federal cavalry advance across the Rappahannock at Brandy Station. Jones may have brought up the matter of his brigade's assignment to Beverly Robertson's overall command during the march to Pennsylvania. Containing his grievance as a private matter between himself and Stuart, Jones refrained from creating a public spectacle. Stuart, on the other hand, reacted to the insult by relieving Jones of command and placing him under "close arrest."[8]

Jones was not incarcerated but merely confined to the grounds within the outpost between Orange Courthouse and the banks of the Rapidan River. With no combat operations under way or immediately anticipated, little attention was drawn to the matter. Jones probably enjoyed the much-desired respite. Eight days passed before he offered a subtle protest.

On August 7 Jones submitted a letter to General Robert H. Chilton, assistant adjutant general for the Army of Northern Virginia, declaring that he had "been under close arrest for eight days without intimation as to the cause."[9] Jones reiterated that he had tendered his resignation to General Lee on May 24 (in response to Lee's directive to join Stuart at Culpeper Courthouse). Lee withheld the resignation, and Jones agreed to serve through the Gettysburg Campaign. He was willing to stand by his resignation but added that he desired to "remain in the service until his guilt or innocence in all matters affecting his official character" was determined and he requested "an early trial."[10] Following the standard protocol, Jones sent his plea up the chain of command to Stuart, who in turn forwarded it to the assistant adjutant general's office. Explaining his actions, Stuart informed the AAG that he had received a "very disrespectful letter from General Jones" and in response he had placed the brigadier under close arrest.[11] Without elaborating, Stuart added, "a list of charges will be furnished him [Jones] as quickly as possible."[12]

Three days later, a court-martial board of inquiry convened headed by Major General Henry Heth. Brigadier Generals Cadmus Marcellus Wilcox, Joseph Brevard Kershaw, Harry Thompson Hays, Stephen Dodson Ramseur, and Henry Harrison Walker served as ranking members on the panel.[13] On August 12, Stuart outlined the specific charges as follows:

1. Disobedience to orders
2. Conduct prejudice to good order and military discipline
3. Behaving with disrespect to his commanding officer

Jones looked forward to the trial as a defendant with nothing to lose. He anticipated that the worst possible outcome would be the acceptance of his resignation. He also knew that Stuart would have to address some embarrassing details if and when he prosecuted the case to the fullest. Both Jones and Stuart observed the gag order. Unfortunately for Jones, the trial could not convene quickly. Although no major combat operations were underway, August 1863 was an eventful month for the Army of Northern Virginia. Other administrative, political, and strategic challenges took priority.

One crisis plaguing Lee's army was the matter of mass desertions by soldiers who had fought valiantly at Gettysburg. A court-martial panel made an example out of one group. Twelve members from two companies of the Third North Carolina Infantry left camp without permission and headed south for their home state. A provost squad pursued and encountered the deserters attempting to cross the Fluvanna River near Scottsville, Virginia. A firefight ensued resulting in the death of the provost squad leader and two deserters. The remaining ten were apprehended and returned under guard to Montpelier Station in Orange County. They were tried, convicted, and condemned to die by firing squad. The execution on September 4 was a drawn-out and orchestrated ceremony witnessed by the entire division.[14]

Stuart filed his official report on the Gettysburg Campaign on August 20. He commended the Jones Brigade for its contributions while withholding praise for Jones individually. He applauded the Sixth and Seventh Virginia Cavalry regiments for their triumph at Fairfield, again without recognizing Jones. Stuart was most complimentary to Wade Hampton and the regimental commanders who accompanied him on his Gettysburg Raid. He singled out Fitz Lee as most deserving of praise and acknowledgment.[15]

After conferring, Lee and Stuart concluded that the cavalry brigades, even though reduced by attrition, were too large and should be limited to either three or four regiments, depending upon the numbers in each. A modest reshuffling would increase the number of cavalry brigades from five to seven and facilitate improved morale. The reorganization also called for the formation of two cavalry divisions to absorb the seven brigades. A newly appointed major general would command each division. Transforming five brigades into seven called for the creation of two new offices of brigadier general. The third position for brigade command was opened by relieving Beverly Robertson and reassigning him to the Second District of South Carolina.[16] From Stuart's perspective, the exit of Jones would open the potential fourth office of brigadier general.

Stuart recognized and desired to reward individual acts of valor and resourcefulness with promotions. His recommendations were a major factor prompting Lee's proposal to President Davis that Wade Hampton and Fitz Lee receive promotions to major general commanding the two newly formed cavalry divisions.[17] Wade Hampton and Fitz Lee received promotions to major general on September 1.[18]

As time progressed, the troops of the W.E. Jones Brigade grew more aware of their commander's absence from routine duties. Neither Jones nor Stuart disclosed any information, but it was impossible to quell the gossip. By September 1, leaks and rumors further fueled supposition, leading to false speculation. A partially accepted but incorrect assumption was that Jones had confronted Stuart after having been passed over for either of the two promotions to the rank of major general.[19] Stuart had placed Jones under "close arrest" on July 31, a day before Lee recommended organizing two new cavalry divisions.[20] Jones's arrest had also taken place an entire month before the promotions of Wade Hampton and Fitzhugh Lee received final approval. The content of Jones's communication to Stuart is not known and may never be known. However, under the circumstances, it seems highly unlikely that the issue of promotion was a contributing factor. Promotion within Stuart's cavalry would have conflicted with Grumble's personal objectives. He most desired to be separated from Stuart and if necessary would fall back on his resignation to achieve that outcome. Second on Jones's list of personal priorities was a reassignment to serve in Southwest Virginia. The emerging strategic situation was about to make that a distinct possibility.

Lee's successful withdrawal from Gettysburg salvaged a stalemate along the Rapidan. For the time being, Richmond appeared relatively safe. The more devastating loss to the Southern cause occurred a thousand miles away with the fall of Vicksburg, which coincidentally occurred one day following the climactic fight at Gettysburg. The momentum the Federals had gained at Vicksburg was likely to lead to an advance on Atlanta, and such an event "would wreck the Confederacy."[21]

The Confederacy found itself in the perilous situation of being engaged on three fronts. On the far left, General Joseph E. Johnston's army in Jackson, Mississippi, faced Grant's larger forces emboldened by their recent triumph that secured their control of the entire Mississippi River. In the center, Braxton Bragg's Army of Tennessee opposed Sherman's armies riding the same momentum that benefited Grant's forces. Manning the far right, Lee's Army of Northern Virginia, positioned in Orange County, stood against Meade's Army of the Potomac.

Southern leaders agreed that the Confederacy could not stay on the defensive but had to strike another offensive blow. While the Army of Northern Virginia recuperated, Lee and the Confederate high command sought an opportunity to turn the tide of the war in the West. They decided to detach Longstreet's Corps from the Army of Northern Virginia and deploy it to the center with Bragg's Army of Tennessee. The joined forces could then conduct a full-fledged assault against the Federals in that region. In early September, Major General James "Pete" Longstreet led three infantry divisions and a cavalry brigade on a southward march through the Carolinas into north Georgia.

Jones used his time under close arrest to catch up on administrative duties. He corresponded with the Confederate States auditor, W.E.S. Taylor, to address complaints regarding his horse requisitions in his West Virginia Raid. One resident of that region, considered to be part of Virginia and the Confederacy at the time, filed a grievance with the Confederate government regarding a lack of compensation for his seized horses. Jones was to provide vouchers to citizens whose livestock he had requisitioned. Responding to the complaint, Jones wrote to the auditor: "The horses were not taken by my order but with my sanctions which I regard as equivalent. Other horses were taken in the same way. The celerity of our movements made irregularities in impressments absolutely necessary. I have been anxious to get to Richmond to manage a general plan of settlement. I presume at least a thousand horses were taken in N.W. Va [Northwest Virginia]. I have forwarded a statement of this matter through Gen. Lee."[22] Jones probably regarded having to explain these details to the auditor as an aggravation. At best, the protesting West Virginians would recover Confederate script, which was diminishing in value each passing day in the South (and to an even lesser value in the newly established state of West Virginia).

On September 10, Jones wrote a detailed essay reflecting on his recollections of Stonewall Jackson at West Point. Grumble addressed his manuscript to the Reverend Robert Lewis Dabney, cleric professor at Hampden-Sydney College in Prince Edward County.[23] Dabney had a close prewar friendship with Jackson and later served as his reluctant chief of staff.[24] As one of Jackson's earliest biographers, Dabney authored the *Life and Campaigns of Lieut.-Gen. Thomas J. Jackson (Stonewall Jackson)* in 1866.

Requests a Leave of Absence

As time passed, Jones grew either emboldened or restless. He desired to attend to matters regarding his estate in Washington County, Virginia. On September 24 he submitted a letter from Orange Courthouse to General Robert H. Chilton of the assistant adjutant general's office requesting that the "limits of" his "arrest be extended to the entire state of Virginia."[25] Jones continued: "As the proceedings of the board in my case have to be reviewed by the Secretary of War, it will probably be some weeks before the result is known. Whilst I can be of no service here, I would be glad to attend to my private affairs at home. By using the telegraph and the railroad, I can return to my command within forty-eight hours after my presence may be required there."[26]

Chilton forwarded Jones's correspondence through the proper channels to Stuart, who, in an unwavering tone, responded with a rejection, declaring, "An officer in arrest should, in my opinion, have no indulgence in the nature of a leave of absence as the within would be. Gen. Jones present limits are deemed ample."[27] Three days later Stuart had given more thought to the matter and had a change of heart. If Jones received his requested furlough, he would be more than three hundred miles away. Stuart equally desired the separation. On September 28 Stuart directed his aide, H.B. McClellan, to write an amended reply: "Respectfully returned to Brig. Gen. W.E. Jones who is notified that, until further orders, the limits of Washington County, Va."[28]

With his request for a leave of absence granted, Jones took rail transportation to Glade Spring Depot and would remain there awaiting notice of the final disposition of his court-martial hearing. Without ceremony, it was a final severance from his brigade in the Army of Northern Virginia.

Southwest Virginia

While Jones was under close arrest, the strategic situation in Southwest Virginia was growing more unstable. Although no major campaigns had been fought in the region, the indirect effects of the war had devastated the economy and the morale of its citizenry.

Most of the able-bodied men were away serving in the Confederate armies. The Appalachian Mountains isolated the region while denying it convenient access to supplies and reinforcements. The proximity to Unionist regions of Kentucky, West Virginia, and East Tennessee exposed the locality and its vital mineral resources to raids. While Richmond appeared safe for the time being, Southern strategists were reassessing the potential exposure of the saltworks in Smyth County and the lead mines of adjacent Wythe County.

On September 1, 1863, Major General Samuel Jones assumed command of the Department of Southwest Virginia and found the region in a precarious situation. Two infantry regiments previously assigned to Saltville had transferred to Braxton Bragg's Army of Tennessee in north Georgia. Filling the void were several brigades scattered throughout Southwest Virginia and East Tennessee. General Sam Jones also received intelligence that 30,000 Federal troops had entered East Tennessee and were preparing an offensive against the saltworks and lead mines of Southwest Virginia.[29] Sam Jones relocated his headquarters to Abingdon to assume command of the District of Southwest Virginia and all troops in Tennessee east of Knoxville.[30] To concentrate a defense, he ordered troops stationed at Saltville and White Sulphur Springs to converge near Bristol to meet the anticipated Federal invasion.

On September 9 Federal forces captured the Confederate outpost at Cumberland Gap and prepared to follow up with an excursion into Southwest Virginia. On September 18 the Federal troops flanked Sam Jones's defenses at Bristol, advanced to their rear, and destroyed sections of the railroad. Satisfied with their accomplishment, the Federals withdrew to establish garrisons at Blountville and Carters Depot, from where they would launch their next major offensive. Sam Jones braced for the Federal attack that did not materialize. An event that occurred more than two hundred miles away spared the strategic situation in Southwest Virginia from an invasion. On September 19 Longstreet's divisions arrived at Chickamauga, Georgia, to form the left wing of Bragg's Army of Tennessee. On the following morning, Longstreet's Corps struck an opening in the Union lines, shattered two Federal divisions, and sent Rosecrans' Army of the Cumberland fleeing northward into Chattanooga, Tennessee.

Alarmed that their Knoxville garrison might be vulnerable to the victorious Southerners at Chickamauga, the Federal forces fell back. Without engaging in combat, Sam Jones won a small tactical victory, and his troops occupied the outposts that the Federals had abandoned. With Southwest Virginia momentarily safe from a Federal offensive, Sam Jones reestablished his Department of Western Virginia and East Tennessee Headquarters in Dublin, Virginia.

In a related development, Brigadier General James Deshler, CSA, was killed at Chickamauga while commanding an infantry brigade in Patrick Cleburne's Division. Deshler's promising career was reflected in part by his graduation from West Point in 1854 with an academic standing that surpassed classmates Jeb Stuart, Dorsey Pender, and Stephen D. Lee. Coincidentally, James's older brother, David T. Deshler, was in the Third Class with W.E. Jones and drowned while swimming in the Hudson River in the summer of 1845. In a conciliatory effort to place Grumble Jones in an agreeable position elsewhere, Lee proposed to President Davis the idea of assigning him to replace the deceased James Deshler in Bragg's Army of Tennessee. Jones was a qualified potential replacement, and as he was in Southwest Virginia it was geographically convenient. However, Deshler's brigade was an infantry unit. Jones had devoted his entire military career to the cavalry.

Other factors influenced Lee to shelve the idea of sending Jones to the Army of Tennessee. Notwithstanding the victory at Chickamauga, the situation for the Confederacy was getting more precarious elsewhere. General Burnside had more than 23,000 troops stationed between Knoxville and the upper East Tennessee counties adjacent to Southwest Virginia along with an uninterrupted supply route through the Cumberland Gap. Expanding Union influence in East Tennessee was reopening possibilities for an advance into Southwest Virginia, particularly the vital Smyth County salt mines situated within fifteen miles of Jones's home in Glade Spring. While the inaction around Richmond persisted, Southwest Virginia was emerging in strategic importance. With the verdict pending but predictable, Lee would recommend that the War Department transfer Jones to Southwest Virginia, where he had desired to serve from the beginning of the conflict.

The Verdict

Jones's trial (if one even took place) drew little attention. There appears to be no record of testimony or cross-examinations. The judicial panel observed "tight-lipped reticence."[31] Both Jones and Stuart seemed to take the position that the evidence stood for itself. Jones was neither going retract nor explain anything he mentioned in his written communication. Stuart was in the awkward position of wanting to keep the content confidential while he demanded Jones receive punishment for writing it in the first place.

Before the final disposition, Lee wrote to President Davis: "I consider General Jones a brave and intelligent officer, but his feelings have become so opposed to General Stuart that I have lost all hope of his being useful in the cavalry here. He tendered his resignation before the expedition to Pennsylvania, which I withheld. He has been subsequently tried by court-martial for disrespect, and the proceedings are now in Richmond. I understand that he says he will no longer serve under Stuart, and I do not think it would be advantageous for him to do so.[32] But I wish to make him useful."[33] Lee concluded by saying, "As soon as the proceedings of the court are published, I shall be obliged to relieve Jones from the command of his brigade, which in fact, has been without its commander ever since the army crossed the Potomac."[34]

On October 8 the court published its findings. The board found Jones "not guilty" of the first two charges of disobedience to orders and to conduct to the prejudice of good order and military discipline. The court found him "guilty" of the third charge of behaving with disrespect to his commanding officer. The sentence, which the panel regarded as "lenient," was a private reprimand from the commanding officer.[35] Officially Jones was "released from arrest and restored to duty."[36] The verdict did not mention Lee's call to relieve Jones from command of his brigade and transfer him out of the Army of Northern Virginia. However, it probably figured into the clemency.

On the following day, Samuel Cooper, adjutant and inspector general, issued a declaration that "the proceedings, findings and the sentence in the case of Brig. Gen. W.E. Jones have been received and duly approved."[37] Cooper followed up with Special Orders No. 240 directing Brig. Gen. W.E. Jones to proceed to Dublin Depot, Virginia, and report to Major General Samuel Jones, commander of the Department of Western Virginia, for assignment to the cavalry in his command."[38]

Going back to his leave of absence Jones had already separated from his brigade. Thus, there was no farewell ceremony marking his departure from the regiments he had commanded the previous year. Jones had led this group in Stuart's Chambersburg Raid, operations against Milroy in the Shenandoah Valley, the West Virginia Raid, Brandy Station, and Gettysburg. Within the brigade, he had commanded the Seventh Virginia Cavalry for an even longer period, beginning with the death of Turner Ashby.

There was a general "impression among the rank and file that Jones had been sacrificed to the animosity of General Stuart."[39] Speaking on behalf of most of the members of the brigade, Captain William N. McDonald wrote the following tribute:

> General Jones' connection with the brigade had much to do with the compactness of its organization. His great talent in this respect had been wisely exercised in increasing its efficiency. He looked after everything, and his close attention to details had affected many needed reforms. At first, he was regarded as a martinet, but afterwards, when better understood, he was greatly respected and loved by rank and file.
>
> Totally unlike Ashby, except in his modesty, which almost amounted to bashfulness, with neither superb horsemanship nor martial presence to impress the imagination of his soldiers, yet when the hour for action came the brigade felt itself always strong and ready to do its full part, and confident in the courage and ability of its leader. His personal appearance was not suggestive of the dashing brigadier, much less did it aspire to the pomp and circumstance of office. The faded slouch hat was decorated with no nodding plume, but while it served to conceal the baldness of his head it partly shaded a strong and noble brow. His features were plain, and the expression determined yet kindly. His eyes of steady blue glistened with intelligence, and at times his countenance glowed with a rather cynical humor. He was entirely self-adjusted in all his notions and opinions, and his remarks were almost always original and striking.
>
> In the confusion of ideas brought by the war, he was not tempted to forget the standard of truth and honesty he had set for his own guidance. And never was needle truer to the pole, than he, what he conceived to be his duty. His affection for his troops was deep and strong. He refused to fare better than they, and on the march, when necessary to bivouac in the rain he would not sleep himself under shelter, though a house might be within a few steps of him, but with his oilcloth around him would lie down in the rain or snow among his troopers. His contempt for all kinds of display perhaps made him go too far in the other extreme, especially in matters of dress. The insignia of his rank, if worn at all, was usually concealed by his coat collar, and he was frequently taken by his own men for a private in the ranks.[40]

Faced with a crisis in morale regarding one of the most distinguished cavalry brigades in the Confederate service, Stuart rose to the occasion with brilliance and charisma. He took into consideration that the W.E. Jones Brigade of the Army of Northern Virginia was already endowed with a reputation for personal bravery and outstanding leadership. Demonstrating sincere compassion, he rendered personal recognition all the way down "to the humblest private."[41] Stuart recommended that the Confederate high command appoint Fifth Virginia Cavalry commander Colonel Thomas Lafayette Rosser to the rank of brigadier general and command of the Jones Brigade. With his enlightened measures, Stuart won the hearts and minds of the men who had served under Grumble's leadership.

Having already established himself as part of the legacy of what would later be known as the "Laurel Brigade" and satisfied with the change, Jones moved on. The collective court-martial conviction and banishment from the Army of Northern Virginia served as the third major political and administrative setback for Jones. It was, however, a change that he welcomed.

17

Southwest Virginia and East Tennessee

Just before Brigadier W.E. Jones arrived at the Department of Southwest Virginia's headquarters at Dublin, security in the region was showing new signs of deterioration. Once again, the vital mineral reserves of Southwest Virginia appeared exposed to imminent attack from Federal forces occupying adjacent East Tennessee.

The Army of Tennessee's September 20 victory at Chickamauga was not as overwhelming as previously assumed. Instead of pressing the offensive, Bragg's army occupied Missionary Ridge and settled in for a siege. The Federal Army of the Cumberland regrouped and established defenses in Chattanooga, where they dug in and received sizeable reinforcements. General Ulysses S. Grant arrived to assume command of the reorganizing Federal forces, marking a reversal in the momentum. The emboldened Federals occupying Knoxville reevaluated their strategic situation. No longer having to divert forces to rescue their comrades in Chattanooga, they could expand their presence into upper East Tennessee and conduct offensive operations against Confederate targets in neighboring Southwest Virginia.

On October 10 General Ambrose E. Burnside's Army of the Ohio routed the cavalry brigade of Generals John Stuart "Cero Gordo" Williams and the infantry of Alfred E. "Mudwall" Jackson at the Battle of Blue Springs in Greene County, Tennessee. Both Confederate brigades retreated to Blountville. The result contributed to the rendering of the moniker "Mudwall" to General Jackson as a deliberate contra-distinction to his kinsman, the revered Thomas Jonathan "Stonewall" Jackson.[1] With this sudden adversity, the Confederates conceded their territory in Upper East Tennessee to the Federals, who were poised to march on into Southwest Virginia.

On the morning of October 11, 1863, General W.E. Jones reported to Major General Samuel Jones at the Dublin Headquarters.[2] Sam Jones was delighted to have Grumble and desired to place the newly arrived brigadier in command of the entire sphere of cavalry operations in Southwest Virginia and East Tennessee. Sam Jones immediately dispatched Grumble Jones to the front to take charge of the situation at Blountville.[3] On October 13 Jones assumed interim command of Williams' and Jackson's brigades and went to the region to direct a tentative stand and an orderly withdrawal toward Bristol.

During the withdrawal, Private George Dallas Mosgrove of the Fourth Kentucky Cavalry experienced his memorable first encounter with Grumble Jones. Mosgrove's interim brigade commander, Colonel Giltner, dispatched him as a messenger to Jones's quarters at an encampment outside of Bristol. Mosgrove's recounting suggests that Jones's quarters was a Sibley tent that he had marketed as a civilian contractor.[4] Mosgrove described the encounter as follows:

> [General William E. Jones] was an eccentric officer, who seemed to take pleasure in self torture, as if doing penance.
>
> At a point near Bristol, Tenn., I was sent to him with a message and found him lying on the ground, face downward, in a tent filled with smoke from a smoldering fire in the center. I involuntarily drew back. In muffled tones, the general called to me: "Lie flat down and the smoke won't hurt you." I dropped upon my hands and knees, crawled to him and delivered the message—about as ludicrous and undignified a scene as one could well imagine.
>
> General Jones had served with Stonewall Jackson, and rode a little trotting clay bank mare, to which he was much attached. He said the famous Stonewall had ridden the unpretentious-looking animal in the battles of Harpers Ferry, Sharpsburg, and Second Manassas. He was a small man, beyond middle life, exceedingly plain in dress, brave to a fault, cool and imperturbable.[5]

Jones and his two brigades gradually fell back to Abingdon, established a line of defense, and braced for a Federal offensive. The numerically superior Federals pressed their advance and took up positions in Southwest Virginia just north of Bristol. A major battle appeared imminent when the Confederates received an element of luck. The Union offensive halted and reversed course southward, back into East Tennessee.

The Southerners were beneficiaries of misinformation communicated among the Federal authorities between Chattanooga and Knoxville. General Grant had warned General Burnside that a detached force from Lee's Army of Northern Virginia was reinforcing the Department of Southwest Virginia.[6] Grant also misunderstood that Bragg's Army of Tennessee was threatening Knoxville. Union General J.M. Shackelford corresponded with a flawed report that Wade Hampton's cavalry division was joining W.E. Jones in Southwest Virginia.[7] Together, these erroneous reports exaggerated the Confederate strength and deluded the Union command into anticipating a Southern offensive against Knoxville on two fronts. The Union withdrawal conceded much of Northeast Tennessee. The Federals changed their objective from one of advancing on Southwest Virginia to defending their presence in and around Knoxville. The adjustment in Union strategy allowed the Confederate forces in Southwest Virginia to regroup and awarded Jones a moderate level of credit for repulsing a Federal offensive.

The Federals shifted their priorities to securing the Cumberland Gap, Bean Station, Morristown, and Bull's Gap to form a perimeter arch covering the East Tennessee & Virginia Railroad to Knoxville. In an impetuous command decision, Burnside ordered the establishment of an outpost at Rogersville, covering the eastern approaches of the Holston River Valley.[8] Two regiments, the Seventh Ohio Cavalry and the Second Tennessee (U.S.) Mounted Infantry, would man the Rogersville garrison, serving as the northeastern apex to the Federal defensive lines extending from Knoxville.

Grumble Jones had made a favorable impression by restoring order among the demoralized troops. Although the Confederates had conceded ground, the measure was temporary and they had seemingly thwarted a major invasion. The *Abingdon Virginian* expressed enthusiasm for Jones's arrival to the area: "It will be a source of gratification to many of our readers to learn, that Gen. Wm. E. Jones, by recommendation of Gen. R.E. Lee, has been assigned by the Secretary of War to the command of the cavalry forces in Southwestern Virginia and East Tennessee."[9] The article went on to expound upon Jones's background and his many accomplishments while serving in the Army of Northern Virginia. Praising Jones for his honor, gallantry, and discipline, the publication predicted that he would bring security and stability to the area.

In spite of his favorable debut, Jones's arrival placed Samuel Jones and the Department of Southwest Virginia into an unusual administrative dilemma. There were only two cavalry brigades within the department. Jones had assumed only interim charge over the brigade commanded by Old Cerro Gordo Williams, who would be restored to his position. Albert Gallatin Jenkins, who was on a temporary leave of absence, commanded the other mounted brigade. Mindful that Williams and Jenkins had received their commissions through political connections rather than by merit of their military backgrounds, Sam Jones regarded Grumble Jones's credentials as superior to either. Unfortunately, both Williams and Jenkins had received their commissions before Grumble Jones did and therefore held rank on him.[10] Sam Jones suggested that the high command in Richmond promote W.E. Jones to the rank of major general, a measure by which Grumble would assume command over all of the cavalry in the department.[11] For whatever reasons, however, the War Department would not consider the idea.

A graduate of Miami University in Oxford, Ohio, a veteran of the Mexican War, a lawyer, and a former member of the U.S. Congress, John Stuart "Old Cerro Gordo" Williams possessed a moniker reflecting his gallantry during the Mexican War. His military record with the Confederacy, however, was unimpressive, as indicated by his recent failure in Greene County, Tennessee. Albert Gallatin Jenkins, a former U.S. Congressman, had a war record that was more distinguished. Born in Cabell County (WV) in 1830, he had graduated from Jefferson College (now Washington and Jefferson College) in Canonsburg, Pennsylvania, in 1848 and Harvard Law in 1850. Upon secession, he resigned from his U.S. congressional seat and was elected as captain of the Border Rangers Militia. Rising to the rank of colonel, he commanded the Eighth Virginia Cavalry Regiment before being elected to the Confederate congress. He resigned from that congressional seat to accept the appointment to brigadier general in August of 1862. He led a raid into Ohio, marking the first Confederate invasion of the North. He was wounded in the Gettysburg Campaign, in which his brigade captured Chambersburg and participated in the rear-guard actions during the withdrawal.

Reorganization of the Cavalry Brigades

Contrary to what the *Abingdon Virginian* assumed and printed, Sam Jones could not appoint Grumble to command all of the cavalry units in Southwest Virginia. He therefore circumvented the administrative situation by organizing a new cavalry brigade that Grumble Jones would lead. In a reshuffling, he transferred selected regiments from the Williams and Jenkins brigades to organize the new W.E. Jones Brigade of the Department of Southwest Virginia. Grumble Jones would not have command over *all* of the cavalry brigades within the Department of Southwest Virginia, but his newly organized brigade would be the largest.

Sam Jones also called upon the area forces in West Virginia to consolidate at the Virginia-Tennessee border. He ordered the Eighth Virginia Cavalry Regiment at Princeton and the Thirty-Seventh Battalion Virginia Cavalry at Lewisburg to report to Abingdon."[12] He directed Captain J.G. Martin to call out the home guards of Washington County to assemble at Abingdon.[13] Completing the reshuffling deployment, he relocated his headquarters from Dublin back to Abingdon.

Formation of the W. E. Jones Brigade of Southwest Virginia

Six combat units formed the new W. E. Jones Cavalry Brigade of the Department of Southwest Virginia. The Eighth Virginia Cavalry Regiment, the Twenty-First Virginia Cavalry Regiment, the Twenty-Seventh Battalion Virginia Cavalry, the Thirty-Fourth Battalion Virginia Cavalry, the Thirty-Sixth Battalion Virginia Cavalry, and the Thirty-Seventh Battalion Virginia Cavalry gathered to form the new unit.[14] The new brigade's fighting reputation would pale when compared to the W.E. Jones Brigade of the Army of Northern Virginia. Most of the rank and file were unproven and undisciplined. The regimental officers had been elected based on their popularity, and many deficient officers retained their status due to the distance from the hostilities.

The Eighth Virginia Cavalry Regiment was commanded by Colonel James M. Corns, an architect and stonemason before the war from Wayne County (WV).[15] The regiment served under Albert Gallatin Jenkins in the 1862 Ohio expedition and during the Gettysburg Campaign.[16] After transferring to the Kanawha Valley, it engaged in the "Battle of White Sulphur Springs" before coming to Abingdon to form part of the W.E. Jones Brigade.[17] Representation from Virginia proper included Smyth, Nelson, Grayson, and Tazewell counties. Most of the members, James M. Corns among them, came from West Virginia and were thus fighting "in exile," as their homes were in Union hands.[18]

The Twenty-First Virginia Regiment had been organized out of companies that previously had formed the Virginia State Line, an all-volunteer force raised in localities where the Conscription Act was unenforceable.[19] It consisted mostly of young boys or old men to guard the Saltville saltworks. Most members were from the Southwest Virginia counties of Washington, Montgomery, Floyd, Smyth, and Russell.[20] They had no combat experience. Discipline was an issue. A short time earlier, the Washington County Court had filed a grievance with the regimental commander regarding stragglers and deserters who formed bands that plundered from private citizens.[21]

Commanding the Twenty-First Virginia Cavalry Regiment was Colonel William Elisha Peters. The Bedford County, Virginia, native had graduated from Emory and Henry College in 1848, taught at the New London Academy in Lynchburg, and took postgraduate studies at the University of Virginia. He had been a professor of classical languages at Emory and Henry over an eight-year span that included two years of study at the University of Berlin in Germany.[22] Although educated, he was unproven as an officer.

Grumble's eighteen-year-old former brother-in-law, Robert C. Dunn, was as a private in the Twenty-First Virginia Cavalry Regiment.[23] The younger brother to Jones's deceased wife, Eliza Margaret "Pink" Dunn Jones, had enlisted the previous summer.

The Thirty-Fourth Battalion Virginia Cavalry, commanded by Lieutenant Colonel Vincent Addison Witcher, had a proven combat record. Representation included the counties of West Virginia, Southwest Virginia, and Kentucky. The battalion served under Jones in his West Virginia Raid, transferred to the Jenkins Brigade, and served at Gettysburg. Impressed by Witcher's performance, Major General J.E.B. Stuart wrote a letter of commendation along with an endorsement for his promotion.[24] Witcher was from a prominent family in Pittsylvania County, Virginia. Before the war he had opened a law practice. He had earned the sobriquet "Clawhammer" because of a long, spike-tailed coat he "invariably wore."[25] Witcher's battalion impressed the comrades of other units. Private

George Dallas Mosgrove of the Fourth Kentucky wrote, "Having often heard of their *original methods* and invincible fighting qualities, our boys heartily welcomed their coming, and throughout the East Tennessee Campaign, Witcher's men were favorites of the entire division. They were good fellows to have around when we were in a predicament."[26]

There would always be friction between Grumble Jones and Witcher, who received his commission in a popular vote election. Witcher's endorsement from Grumble's nemesis, Major General J.E.B. Stuart, probably did not help to ease the strain. An antithesis to Jones, Witcher had earned a notorious reputation as one who operated outside of the normal rules of war.[27] Federal reports in 1862 described him as a murderer and his band as the most formidable of marauders.[28] There was an allegation that early in the conflict, Witcher assassinated an unarmed suspected Union sympathizer in Saltville, Virginia, execution style.[29] He and his band were also rumored to have murdered nine Unionists in Carter County, Tennessee.[30] Jones was probably aware of Witcher's notorious reputation, particularly the incident at Saltville.

The Thirty-Sixth Battalion Virginia Cavalry consisted of five companies organized by General Jenkins, who led them during the Gettysburg Campaign.[31] About fifty men deserted on August 10, 1863, before most were captured and returned to the ranks.[32] The regiment had transferred to Bath County before Sam Jones called it to Abingdon.[33] Captain Cornelius T. Smith commanded this unit.[34]

The Thirty-Seventh Battalion Virginia Cavalry was initially known as Dunn's Partisan Rangers after their commander, Colonel Ambrose C. Dunn. Consisting mostly of men from South Carolina, it was supplemented with troops from West Virginia.[35] Their service under Imboden as infantry during the Jones-Imboden West Virginia Raid marked their most significant combat experience. The regiment gained notoriety in that expedition when two hundred men deserted at Beverly in response to an order prohibiting them from seizing civilian horses for their personal use.[36]

The Twenty-Seventh Battalion Virginia Cavalry was originally known as Trigg's Battalion of Partisan Rangers.[37] When established, the unit was commanded by Colonel Henry A. Edmondson, who had gained notoriety in the antebellum years while serving in the U.S. House of Representatives. During the 1854 debates on the Kansas-Nebraska Act, he was arrested after having to be restrained from attacking an antislavery political opponent.[38] Composed of men primarily from Southwest Virginia, the Twenty-Seventh Virginia was untested. With Edmondson in poor health, Major Sylvester P. McConnell and Captain John B. Thompson assumed command.[39]

The collective units forming the new W.E. Jones Brigade had an official enrollment of about 1,500 and tended to fluctuate between 900 and 1,900. On average, about 1,200 were usually present for duty.[40] Desertions were common with rates running an average of 30 percent.[41] Jones's new brigade would bear the responsibility of defending a vast region of Southwest Virginia between the Cumberland Gap and the New River. Aside from a few exceptions, most of the troops were untrained, inexperienced, poorly equipped, and undisciplined. Jones had his work cut out for him.

Division of East Tennessee and Southwest Virginia

Coinciding with the formation of the W.E. Jones Brigade and the reshuffling of the Williams and Jenkins brigades, General Samuel Jones organized the Division of East

Tennessee and Southwest Virginia commanded by Major General Robert L. Ransom, Jr., from North Carolina. Ransom was an 1850 graduate of West Point who had served in the Old Army on the frontier and the Kansas Border Disturbances. His new division included the three Southwest Virginia cavalry brigades of Jones, Williams, and Jenkins. The brigades of Montgomery D. Corse and Gabriel C. Wharton composed the infantry. Six batteries of artillery rounded out the remainder.[42]

Generals Samuel Jones and Robert Ransom concluded that the most effective means to protect Southwest Virginia was to take the offensive in East Tennessee with a long-term objective to retake the Cumberland Gap. Capitalizing on the recent Federal withdrawal from Bristol that conceded ground in Sullivan County, Ransom's Division occupied and established headquarters at Blountville, where General William E. Jones and his recently formed brigade reported for duty.

On November 3, Ransom received intelligence of a detachment of two or three Union regiments encamped on Big Creek, four miles east of Rogersville.[43] Seizing an opportunity to strike a major blow against the Union presence in East Tennessee, Ransom formulated a plan to capture the force with an offensive operation executed by Grumble Jones. In an administrative maneuver, Ransom permanently relieved John Stuart Williams of his command and placed Colonel Henry L. Giltner as interim commander of the Williams Brigade to work in conjunction with Jones. This measure bypassed the issue of Williams outranking Jones, who would lead both brigades in a two-pronged offensive. Ransom directed the expeditionary force to prepare cooked rations and to take no supplies except ammunition.[44] He left the issue of an artillery battery up to Grumble's discretion. Jones chose to sacrifice firepower for mobility. The mission had to be expeditious to be successful.

Ransom's strategy was part of a broader plan. On November 4, under President Davis's direction, General Longstreet detached his corps from Bragg's Army of Tennessee at Missionary Ridge and launched an offensive from the southeast toward Knoxville. Simultaneously, Jones commenced his two-brigade march toward Rogersville from the north on November 5.

Battle of Rogersville

Intelligence gathered through spies, civilians, intercepted communications, and other sources informed General Ransom that the Union outpost at Rogersville was isolated and vulnerable. The garrison was manned by the Seventh Ohio Cavalry, the Second Tennessee (U.S.) Mounted Infantry, and the Second Illinois Artillery, all under the command of Colonel Israel Garrard.

Some of the Rogersville citizens performed a deception by inviting all of the Federal officers to a gala event at one of the public houses on the evening of November 5. Many officers attended and consequently were away from the outpost for the evening, and some for the entire night.[45] A steady rainfall inundating the area diminished the Federal's anticipation of enemy activity. Grumble utilized the inclement weather and the cover of darkness to conceal his movements and to enhance the element of surprise.[46]

Jones held overall command of his newly formed brigade and the Giltner Brigade, which consisted of the First Tennessee Cavalry, the Tenth Kentucky Cavalry, the Fourth Kentucky Cavalry, and the Sixteenth Georgia Cavalry. Ransom's plan called for the two

17. *Southwest Virginia and East Tennessee* 185

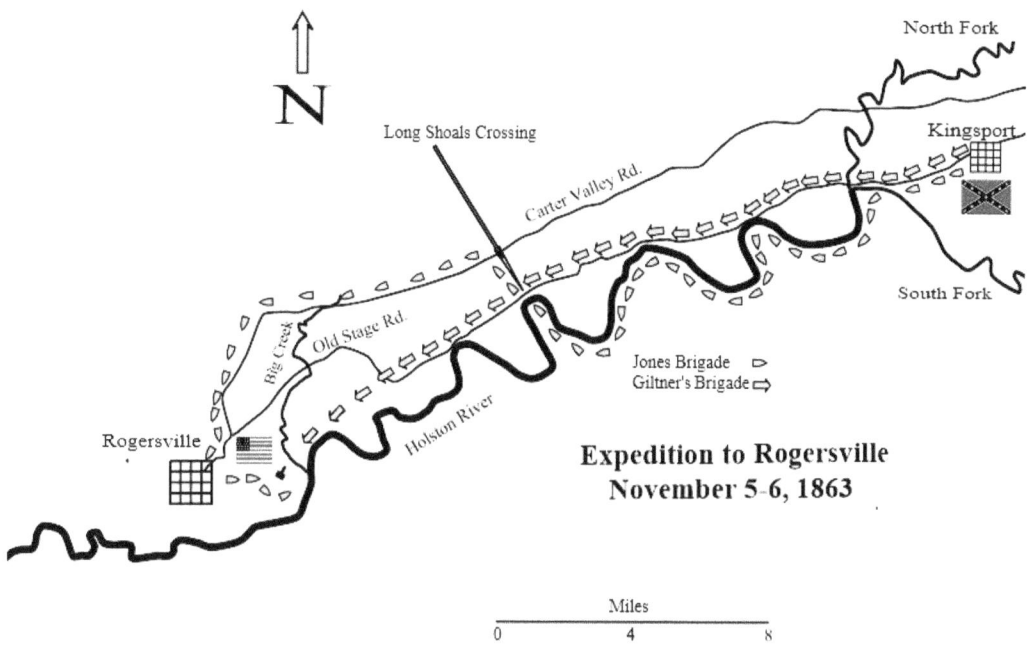

Expedition to Rogersville (sketch by author, 2016).

brigades to march along the Holston River from just west of Kingsport. Taking parallel routes, they would converge upon and surround the Federal encampment before making a simultaneous attack from different directions on Friday morning, November 6. With a combined force of about 3,000, the collective cavalry brigades doubled the enemy's strength. However, the enemy possessed four cannons, and Big Creek provided a natural barrier. Success depended on precise coordination between the two brigades that would be out of communication with each other until after the battle was joined.[47] It was a high-stakes gamble. If the mission failed, Southwest Virginia would be wide open for Union counteroffensive.

Giltner's Brigade forded the Holston at Kingsport and marched north of the river in a twenty-five-mile southwesterly direction toward Rogersville. The Jones Brigade advanced south of the Holston until crossing to the north side, twelve miles east of Rogersville at Long Shoals. Just north of the Long Shoals crossing, the two columns crossed paths on Old Stage Road. Giltner halted his column to allow the Jones Brigade to cross Old Stage Road and proceed to the parallel Carter Valley Road. The two brigades then proceeded in a southwesterly direction on parallel paths. The Jones Brigade had to travel a longer distance to reach the outskirts of the southwestern extreme of the Union encampment. Giltner halted his column a second time at Surgoinsville to allow Jones more time to reach his destination on the enemy's flank. At 4:30 a.m. the Giltner Brigade received fire from a Federal scouting party.[48] Although the element of surprise was partially lost, Jones's column remained concealed and continued to maneuver undetected past the enemy's position.

The main body of the Federal force camped along the west banks of Big Creek, just north of its confluence with the Holston River. Giltner was to attack from the east while Jones flanked the encampment and struck from the west. The Federals placed pickets on both roads east of their junction. While advancing on Carter Valley Road, the Jones Brigade encountered about fifty enemy home guards at the Kincade house. Jones directed his Eighth Virginia to surround the position, and they captured all but seventeen of the enemy.[49] Giltner's column encountered and overwhelmed a force of about the same number of pickets at C.C. Miller's (Yellow Store).[50] Union pickets who escaped fled to the main encampment and alerted Colonel Garrard of the attack. Utilizing Big Creek as a natural barrier, the Second Tennessee (U.S.) Mounted Infantry met Giltner's frontal assault and held his force at bay. However, they knew only Giltner's position and were unaware that the Jones Brigade had flanked their position and would attack their rear.

Jones divided his brigade behind enemy lines. He dispatched the Eighth Virginia Cavalry to Dodson's Ford to intercept any enemy units retreating to the east. He directed the Twenty-Seventh Virginia Cavalry to charge directly into Rogersville, where they captured about a hundred of the enemy. He sent Witcher's Thirty-Fourth Virginia Cavalry and the Thirty-Seventh Virginia Cavalry to Smith's Ford on Big Creek to apprehend any Union soldiers in flight. With Rogersville sealed off, Jones maneuvered the Twenty-Seventh Virginia to obstruct the area between the railroad and the Holston River. He held the Thirty-Sixth Virginia in reserve.[51]

Jones's maneuvers were so effective that his forces met only nominal resistance. Fifty-five home guards attempted a counteroffensive before Jones's aide-de-camp, Lieutenant Warren M. Hopkins, led a company to disperse it quickly.[52] Demoralized troops of the Seventh Ohio Volunteer Cavalry threw down their weapons and fled in a "perfect state of confusion."[53] In the turmoil of the battle there was an erroneous report among the Federals that Colonel Garrard had been killed.[54] The Confederates captured the Union artillery and turned the pieces on their enemy. Surrounded and cut off from any potential reinforcements, Major Daniel A. Carpenter of the Second Tennessee Mounted Infantry surrendered on behalf of himself and all Union forces present. Carpenter's capitulation concluded the Battle of Rogersville as an overwhelming Confederate triumph. Decrying an atrocity, Carpenter alleged that Private William Russell of Company A was shot to death after he and his squad had grounded arms.[55]

To the disgust of Jones, Colonel Garrard, his staff, and about half the members of the Seventh Ohio Cavalry escaped by swimming across the Holston River and fleeing to the nearest Union outpost, commanded by Colonel Shelby Harney at Morristown. Harney reported observing members of Garrard's staff galloping bare-headed, panic stricken, and demoralized into the town.[56] Harney's troops established a defensive position in preparation for a Confederate pursuit that did not materialize. He then yielded command to Garrard.[57]

Jones detached a detail to escort the masses of prisoners under guard to the rear. Other troops pleaded for permission to occupy Rogersville to rest and gather forage. Taking a cautious approach, Jones answered in his "fine soprano voice": "No, gentlemen. We had better be getting back to our base. It is better to make sure of the catch we now have than to risk losing it for a little rest and sleep. General Burnside is not far away. We will put more miles between us and his army. Then I think we can rest more securely."[58]

Humiliated but safe at Morristown, Garrard's report to General Burnside was brief and concise:

November 6, 1863
GENERAL: I was attacked this a.m. and totally defeated. I lost my guns and two-thirds of my command; rebel force not known, as they were continually sending their troops forward. I think the whole of the Second Tennessee is lost. About one-half of the Seventh [Ohio] Cavalry is lost.

The rebel cavalry was following us this side of Bull's Gap.

Very respectfully, your obedient servant, L. Garrard,
Colonel, Commanding[59]

Jones's execution of Ransom's plan was an overwhelming victory resulting in the capture of 850 prisoners, four cannons, two regimental colors, sixty wagons, and about a thousand transport animals.[60] Numbers of enemy killed and wounded were estimated to be between twenty-five and thirty. These gains were against modest losses of about a dozen Confederate killed or wounded.

The Union prisoners of war were marched on foot under guard by a Confederate mounted escort on a fifty-mile journey to Blountville. One prisoner recounted, "We were cavalrymen, and marching on foot made us very lame, and we could hardly hobble along."[61] From there, a cattle train would transport them to Richmond (Libby Prison or Belle Island) or other prisoner-of-war destinations, the most notable ultimately being Andersonville, Georgia.[62] Among the prisoners was twenty-year-old Sergeant John L. Ransom (no known relationship to the CSA division commander) of the Ninth Michigan Cavalry, serving on detached quartermaster duty at the outpost when the attack occurred. Imprisoned for a year, with most of the time at Andersonville, Ransom maintained a diary detailing life at the infamous camp. His *Andersonville Diary*, published in 1881, would become a primary source for Civil War researchers.

A negative aspect of the mission was looting. Of the nearly one thousand captured horses, only about three hundred were requisitioned; most were seized by the troopers as replacements. General Robert Ransom reported, "One Regimental flag was captured, but in some way lost. I regret that up to this time I have been unable to have accounted for more than about 300 animals, all told. I much fear they were appropriated by the men and have been sent off and sold. There is no other reasonable conclusion."[63] Other spoils were looted as well. The soldiers under Jones and Giltner felt entitled to fulfill their desperate need for garments, shoes, and equipment. Private George Dallas Musgrove of the 4th Kentucky Cavalry, Giltner's Brigade, elaborated on the subject of looting:

> The command had captured a rich Federal wagon train and, as usual, the boys appropriated to their own use everything they could lay their hands on. General Wm. E. Jones, in command at the time, issued an order that mules, coffee, sugar, and other "spoils of war" should be turned over to the quartermaster as Confederate States property, to be distributed, probably among troops who were strangers. This order caused a vigorous "kick" and indignant howl all along the lines of the rank and file, particularly those serving and inspired Major (Henry T.) Stanton to write the funny verses referred to. I can now only recall the concluding line of each stanza: "General Jones, here's your mule."[64]

There was qualified ecstasy for the victory. The Confederates had not experienced success in East Tennessee in the fall of 1863, and Rogersville was a rare exception. Secretary of War James Seddon wrote two days afterward, "I am happy to relieve in some measure the anguish inspired by the news I was constrained to communicate this morning by the more cheering intelligence of the within just received by me."[65] Seddon viewed Jones's victory as an encouraging contrast to the simultaneous Confederate defeat at Droop Mountain in West Virginia. President Davis was not so optimistic and responded, "This may affect the movements of the enemy in front of General Jones."[66] Davis agonized that the expedition into East Tennessee had left Southwest Virginia potentially exposed.[67]

Demonstrating his desire for perfection, William E. Jones conveyed discontent with portions of the outcome, particularly regarding Colonel Giltner's contribution. He considered the success as less than acceptable because significant numbers of the enemy, including Colonel Garrard, had escaped. Jones wrote:

> Had Colonel Giltner made a prompt and bold attack that would have discovered the position of the enemy before my dispositions were made, under the impression of his having abandoned his position, it is believed none would have escaped. The unaccountable delay, doubtless, has proved very detrimental to our interest.[68]

Jones also contradicted some of the boastful content of Giltner's report regarding the number of captured prisoners. Jones alleged that his detachment alone took 274 prisoners, and he credited 556 additional prisoners to the efforts of his Eighth Virginia Cavalry, led by Colonel James M. Corns.[69] Colonel Giltner, on the other hand, claimed that the forces under his command had captured 550 prisoners.[70] Rendering the matter even more awkward, the adjutant for the Department of Southwestern Virginia and East Tennessee asked Jones to endorse Giltner's account of the engagement. Jones answered:

> In reply to yours, enclosing a report of Colonel Giltner relative to the attack on the enemy near Rogersville, the 6th instant, I can say if by endorsement you wish me to confirm his statements, such is not in my power. My report will show you the affair appears to me in a different light from what it does to Colonel Giltner. As the report is not addressed to me, and is not sent through me, I presume it was not intended I should correct errors in it. I was under the impression I commanded this affair, and the statement of Mr. Watterson will show Colonel Giltner was of the same opinion before the fight.[71]

Agitated by the internal strife, General Ransom responded:

> The result of the expedition is the best proof that it was conducted well, and I am unwilling to create or sustain bickering or jealousy when there should be mutual good feeling.[72]

There was also a matter of missing prisoners. Of the 850 prisoners reported captured in the contest, only 775 arrived at the Divisional Headquarters at Blountville.[73] Most of the seventy-five unaccounted for had escaped. A selected few, however, received accusations as deserters from prior service to the Confederacy or as traitors and were dealt with accordingly.

Prisoner Dr. John Shrady, MD, of the Second Tennessee Mounted Infantry recounted his recollection of the alleged atrocity:

> Soon after our disaster, a Confederate captain rapidly selected from among his old neighbors five or six of our command, whom he claimed as deserters. The truth was that they had been "impressed" but had not yet been "mustered in" before their escape to our lines. We left them in the cold gray morning, a somber group around a burnt-out log fire under a close guard. Among them was poor Dabney, the bugler, the soul of our party, mimic, storyteller, and wit, with streaming eyes looking away from a hilarious life into the gloom beyond—and Lincoln, too, for we called him for his resemblance to the martyr President, straight and slender as a ramrod, with teeth set and his old, changeless battle face. Another was watching the curling clouds from a corn-cob pipe. The broken blue wreathes seemed mute emblems of crushed hopes, as they dissolved in the keen, frosty air. We never heard from them again—unflinching heroes all, beggars not even for their lives. The neighbor had gratified his malice, his patriotism, perhaps even his conscience, but our execrations fell upon the Judas, and our prayers went out with the victims.[74]

Major William Williams Stringfield of the Sixty-Ninth Regiment North Carolina Infantry (Thomas Legion) confirmed that "a painful example of discipline was made" of some of the Tennesseans captured at Rogersville and marched back to Blountsville. Stringfield recollected that three of the captured donning the "uniform of the enemy" were "court-martialed and shot at the stake."[75]

In contrast to the alleged cruelty, there were reported instances in which the victors showed empathy. Captain Theodore Allen of the Seventh Ohio Cavalry Regiment had suffered rib fractures in the engagement when his horse rolled over him. His companion, Lieutenant Albert A. Carr of the same regiment, was confined to the Rogersville camp hospital with a double rupture before the battle began. Both Federal officers were marching with the contingency of prisoners on foot toward Blountville under guard by a mounted Confederate escort detail when they paused to graze the horses in an open field. Exhausted, partially disabled with pain, and famished, Captain Allen approached the Confederate officer leading the prisoner escort detail and asked for relief. Allen later recalled, "Neither the Confederate soldiers or the prisoners had anything to eat. I remember making an appeal to a Confederate officer for some food. He told me that all he had to eat was two apples, but that he would be very glad to divide with me, which he did, giving me one apple and keeping one himself. I divided my apple with Lieutenant Carr."[76] Although his hunger was partially relieved, Captain Allen concluded that neither he nor his companion, Lieutenant Carr, were physically capable of continuing the long-anticipated march on foot. When it was apparent that the detail was going to resume the journey with a night march, he made an appeal to see the commanding officer. The Confederate officer escorted Captain Allen to General Jones, who showed remarkable compassion. Captain Allen later recollected the incident:

> I saw the General [Jones} and told him I was badly hurt, and that my companion, Lieutenant Carr, was suffering from a double rupture, and neither of us felt able to march all night on foot. I found General Jones to be a fatherly sort of man, and when he looked upon my condition, he expressed surprise that I had been able to walk as far as I had. He was very sympathetic and very kindly, and promised that he would send horses for Lieutenant Carr and myself, and he directed the guard who was with me to return to the prisoners' bivouac and to say to the officer of the guard that Lieutenant Carr and myself were not to be dispatched on foot with the other prisoners when the column took up its night march. About this time, a new officer of the guard appeared upon the scene for night duty, relieving the officer who had charge of us during the day. The officer of the old guard stated to the new officer of the guard that all the prisoners were to be marched out except Lieutenant Carr and myself, and that General Jones would furnish horses for us two. Just as this conversation was taking place, an orderly appeared on the scene from General Jones's headquarters with two led horses, which he stated were for Carr and myself. The officer of the guard turned to me and said, "Here are your horses."[77]

Notwithstanding the benevolence conveyed by General Jones, Captain Allen and his companion remained prisoners of war. Once they arrived at their destination in Blountville, they would be forwarded to either Libby Prison or Belle Island in Richmond. Mingled in with masses of other prisoners, they would be at the mercy of indifference. Allen concluded that they needed to escape while in pro–Union East Tennessee. On their mounts, Captain Allen and Lieutenant Carr intermingled with the inadequately outfitted Confederate cavalry company escorting the prisoner march. With wintry weather conditions and the absence of issued overcoats, the poorly clad mounted Confederates donned blankets that concealed their uniforms. Having received similarly woven blankets for their relief, Allen and Carr blended in with the escort detail. The duo took advantage of the darkness and a shift change between the officers to diverge from the marching column and escape through an open field. With the help of the Underground Railroad operated by East Tennessee Union sympathizers, Allen and Carr ultimately made their way to Federal lines.[78]

The Battle of Rogersville was a personal triumph for Grumble Jones, who was earning the same reputation he had previously acquired with the Army of Northern Virginia: competent fighter and capable leader. He also gained the admiration of his new body of troops, who took pride in their accomplishment and their eccentric commander's leadership. As a fellow Southwest Virginian, Grumble had something in common with the mountain men he commanded.

Jones withdrew his brigade from Rogersville and marched it northeast to Carter's Station (Greeneville), where they encamped and awaited further orders. To the Confederate high command, the victory at Rogersville was only the beginning of a major overall campaign to expel the pro–Unionist influence from East Tennessee. The next target was Knoxville. Its capture would sever Grant's supply lines at Chattanooga. Threatening Knoxville could draw Grant out of Chattanooga to relieve Burnside.

Campaign for Knoxville

The day before Jones launched his expedition to Rogersville, Longstreet commenced with marching his corps from Missionary Ridge toward Knoxville to confront General Burnside's main Army of the Ohio. Exercising caution and with the prospects for battle all along the way, it took almost two weeks for his forces to reach their ultimate destination. On November 12, Longstreet's Corps received reinforcements from General Joseph Wheeler's cavalry at Loudon, Tennessee, raising the Confederate numerical strength to about 15,000. During Longstreet's march, the situation for the Confederacy in Tennessee deteriorated. The besieged Federal forces at Chattanooga under Major General Ulysses S. Grant went on the offensive against Bragg's Army of Tennessee at Missionary Ridge. By the time Longstreet reached the outskirts of Knoxville, Bragg's force had been soundly defeated and driven out of Tennessee into north Georgia.

Longstreet requested reinforcements from the Division of East Tennessee and Southwest Virginia, but the only available units were the two cavalry brigades of Jones and Giltner.[79] Jones and the two brigades embarked from their Carter's Station encampment on a seventy-mile southwesterly march toward Knoxville to join Longstreet. Wintry weather conditions and the rough terrain hampered their progress, rendering it difficult to transport the supply wagons. Jones's force also bore the task of gathering forage for Longstreet's forces while in the hostile territory of pro–Union East Tennessee. Jones led his columns through Russellville, Morristown, Maynardville, and Strawberry Plains to reach the northern vicinity of Knoxville on November 28.

Longstreet hoped that the combined Confederate forces could strike from multiple directions and catch Burnside's troops outside of their fortifications. Instead, the Federals were well entrenched and anticipating action. Longstreet planned an assault against a salient on the northwest corner, named Fort Loudon by the Confederates and Fort Sanders by the Federals. Although he had been in a position to attack since November 20, he awaited more reinforcements and delayed his offensive until the 29th. Jones and his brigades served in a reserve capacity.

Longstreet's actions were not his usual strategy for tactical defense.[80] His ill-equipped infantry attempted to storm across a trench that he had underestimated in width and depth. Holding the high ground and supported by artillery, the Federal defenders poured a heavy fire into the Confederate ranks. After incurring more than eight hundred casualties, Longstreet aborted the attack and settled for a siege.

The stalemate presented Longstreet with a new dilemma. He had received an appeal from Braxton Bragg to fall back and reinforce the Army of Tennessee in Dalton, Georgia.[81] With doubts that the path would be open, Longstreet believed that measure appeared impractical.[82] Another option was to remain before Knoxville and draw a portion of Grant's forces that might otherwise engage against Bragg.[83] Although that measure required subsisting on dwindling supplies in a hostile region, it seemed to be the lesser bad alternative. Longstreet then received intelligence that General William T. Sherman's forces were advancing northward to relieve the Federals at Knoxville.[84] With that information, Longstreet conceded any ideas of taking Knoxville. Chattanooga was already lost, and the route to Dalton was blocked. In a state of humiliation on the evening of December 3, Longstreet ordered the withdrawal of his infantry corps from the lines before Knoxville and commenced on the gradual return march toward Virginia. Grumble Jones and his cavalry escorted the evacuation.

Not anxious to withdraw immediately, Longstreet implemented a strategy to gain control of Upper East Tennessee. The onset of winter impeded travel and minimized the chances for any major engagements. As long as Longstreet's Corps maintained a presence, the Federals had to be leery of a repeat offensive against Knoxville. As a diversion, Longstreet's presence secured the mineral reserves of Southwest Virginia from any threats in East Tennessee. The Federals resumed a defensive posture, conceding Upper East Tennessee while giving priority to protecting the vital supply lines at Knoxville and the Cumberland Gap. During Longstreet's gradual departure, the W.E. Jones Brigade would serve as a rear guard. Longstreet would not receive orders to move to central Virginia until April 11, 1864.[85]

On November 30, Longstreet directed Jones to move out on to the Maynardville Road to "annoy and distress the enemy as much as possible."[86] A day later they charged into Maynardville only to find that the enemy had withdrawn toward the Clinch River. Jones then positioned his force at Walker's and Black Fox fords.[87] They skirmished for several days and incurred modest losses before the Federals voluntarily withdrew. Achieving a stalemate was a somewhat remarkable feat, as their enemy possessed Henry 16-shot repeating rifles.[88]

Although the Federals withdrew, stragglers stayed behind. According to one source, a young black man in the Jones Brigade forded the river and brought back a Federal prisoner. Jones questioned the prisoner to learn the strength and positions of the enemy. Upon conclusion of the interrogation, the prisoner asked, "General, what are you going to do with me?" Jones replied, "You belong to that negro. He can do what he pleases with you." Pleading, the prisoner responded, "Oh my God General, don't leave me that way!"[89]

Resuming its rear-guard duty on the gradual withdrawal northward up the Holston River Valley, the Jones Brigade troopers occupied the abandoned Federal outpost at Morristown. On December 10 they were attacked by Federal forces under Colonel Israel Garrard, the commander Jones had humiliated a month earlier at Rogersville. Following a three-hour contest, the Jones Brigade withdrew.[90] In seeking a level of vindication for his earlier debacle, Colonel Garrard deemed the engagement a "gallant affair" that resulted in the expulsion of Jones out of Tennessee and into North Carolina.[91] Although Garrard may have slightly bested Jones in the engagement, he exaggerated his accomplishment. Jones did not flee into North Carolina but merely withdrew across the Holston River to rejoin Longstreet, who, approaching from Rogersville, planned another offensive.

Bean Station

On December 12, Longstreet received intelligence that a Federal division commanded by General James M. Shackelford occupied Bean Station and would not receive previously anticipated reinforcements from Chattanooga.[92] Seeking an opportunity to strike a major parting blow against the vulnerable Federals, Longstreet planned a three-pronged offensive. He would march his infantry corps on Bean Station via the road from Rogersville. A four-brigade cavalry division under the command of Major General William Thompson Martin would maneuver south of the Holston and cross below Bean Station. Jones would position his brigades on the north side of Clinch Mountain to obstruct the Federals' potential escape route through Bean Station Gap.[93]

According to Longstreet's assessment, his infantry reached their objective in a timely manner and surprised the enemy. Jones and his two brigades performed "their part admirably." However, the outcome fell well short of expectations. General Martin's four brigades mishandled their part of the mission and were therefore "of small service."[94] Recent rains had swelled the Holston River and limited Martin to crossing only a portion of his command, which he withdrew prematurely.[95] Out of communication with the other units, Jones retired from the gap after capturing a fleet of supply wagons. The outnumbered Federals escaped three miles south of Bean Station and regrouped behind the natural defenses at Blain's Crossroads. Longstreet ordered a pursuit, but the opportunity to capture the Federal force was already lost. Enraged by this most recent failure in the overall Knoxville Campaign, Longstreet brought charges against three of his subordinates (Jones was not among them). Culminating the action on the following day, the Jones Brigade was attacked at Powder Spring Gap in an inconclusive engagement lasting the entire day before nightfall terminated the action.

Falling short of achieving an overwhelming victory, Longstreet settled for occupying Bean Station. Although a modest consolation, the supply wagons Jones had captured would sustain the forces through the winter. Longstreet withdrew his infantry across the Holston and restored the railroad lines to Virginia. Well stocked with provisions and with secure access to the railroad, Longstreet placed his corps into winter quarters. The engagement at Bean Station concluded the Knoxville Campaign and Northeast Tennessee would remain under Confederate occupation for almost another year. Jones established his headquarters in familiar Rogersville to screen Longstreet's northern flank.

At Rogersville, on the morning of December 25, Jones was awoken by the sound of gunfire and a fresh three-inch snowfall. Members of the Thirty-Seventh Battalion, Virginia Cavalry, celebrated the white Christmas by firing off a few rounds. Not amused by the overt demonstration of unauthorized festivities, Grumble ordered the regimental commander, Major James R. Claiborne, and the men to saddle up and participate in a two-hour drill.[96]

Having conceded his aspirations to take Knoxville, Longstreet turned his attention toward the idea of seizing the Cumberland Gap back from Union hands. A successful recapture of the gap could sever the supply and reinforcement lines to Knoxville and open avenues for a possible invasion of Kentucky. On December 28, Longstreet sent orders to Jones to conduct a "sudden and well-concealed dash upon [the] Cumberland Gap with a view of obtaining possession of it."[97] The order seems to have shown an impetuous lack of realism on the part of Longstreet, but at the same time it allowed Jones the discretion to "secure definite information" before making his move.

The Cumberland Gap

With the outbreak of the Civil War reemerged the significance of the natural passage through the central Appalachians. Used by Native Americans for centuries, the trail received Anglo attention by the mid–1700s. Leading an expedition into the region, Dr. Thomas Walker named the passage after Prince William Augustus, the Duke of Cumberland. Establishing a migration route from current Wythe County, Virginia, renowned pioneer and American folk hero Daniel Boone blazed the Wilderness Road through the gap, leading to fifty years of mass westward migrations. The Wilderness Road was by no means a direct route, as to get through the Appalachians it ran approximately two hundred miles from Southwest Virginia southward into East Tennessee before curving northward into Kentucky. The Wilderness Road had been abandoned by the time of the Civil War, but with the outbreak of the war, a twelve-mile stretch of it became significant. With the gap running through Virginia, Tennessee, and Kentucky, the surrounding regions were very politically diverse and, consequently, divided in their allegiances.

The gap ran through Lee County, in Southwest Virginia, whose citizens voted not to secede but then cast their lot with the Confederacy once Virginia passed the ordinance. Although Tennessee seceded, the majority of residents of East Tennessee were pro–Union. Kentucky was a slave state that remained with the Union mostly due to a substantial Federal occupation that was especially formidable in areas near the Cumberland Gap.[98] The North viewed the gap as an access route to liberate pro–Union East Tennessee from the Confederacy and as a potential invasion route to target Southwest Virginia and its vital mineral resources.

Occupation of the Cumberland Gap changed four times between the two sides without a major battle for its control.[99] Notwithstanding its strategic importance, the gap had its limitations. The rugged topographical features along with general isolation rendered it an impractical region to which to deploy and supply large armies for extended periods of time. A year into the war, area farms were depleted of forage. Possession of the gap had most recently changed when a detachment force from General Ambrose E. Burnside's Knoxville-based Army of the Ohio forced the surrender of General John W. Frazer, who offered only token resistance. With the gap firmly in Federal hands, the pro–Unionists in East Tennessee received an uninterrupted route of supply and manpower.

Upon receipt of Longstreet's order, Jones comprehended the daunting task before him. The natural defenses provided a distinct strategic advantage to the Federal occupying force. Those same conditions, however, restricted the defenders in their capability to be self-sustaining or to receive supplies from distant centers in East Tennessee or Kentucky. Any Federal occupation force of significant numbers had to rely entirely upon foraging operations in the adjacent regions, already ravaged by two years of war. Politically, it was unfeasible for the Federals to forage in either pro–Union East Tennessee or Union-held Kentucky, as those resources were nearly exhausted. Their only viable option was to selectively pillage from the civilian residents of adjacent pro–Southern Lee County, Virginia, wedged between East Tennessee to the south and Kentucky to the north. Jonesville, the county seat, was situated only four miles from Harlan, Kentucky, and six miles from the border with Hancock County, Tennessee.

1864, Lee County, Virginia

By the fall of 1863, the matter of supplying the Federal forces occupying the Cumberland Gap neared desperation. Union raiding parties expanded their foraging operations against the civilians of Lee County and Jonesville in particular. Between October of 1863 and the end of the year, Federal raiders allegedly burned the Lee County Courthouse, Sim's Mill, and Franklin Academy.[100] These alleged atrocities produced nothing of strategic value but inflamed the local passions, adding incentives for the Confederate forces to take action. Jones and his brigade were called upon to liberate Lee County and to take up operations in Southwest Virginia.

In late December, Jones withdrew his force from Rogersville for the last time and commenced on a five-day, sixty-mile expedition march toward Jonesville. Enhancing his reputation by bearing the moniker "Old Night Hawk," he concealed his movements by conducting night marches during extreme weather conditions to minimize enemy anticipation of his eventual attack.[101] It was said that during his Lee County campaigns the Jones Brigade marched twenty-two days and nights without unsaddling their horses or pausing. Temporary halts were limited to feeding the horses or fighting the enemy.[102] On this march Jones led his brigade through Blackwater, Hunter's Gap, and Hurricane Ford, across the Clinch River, and over Powell Mountain. The expedition confronted not only a mountainous terrain but also subzero Fahrenheit temperatures. One man froze to death, and many suffered from frostbite.[103]

While Jones conducted his march, the Federals made their own move in Lee County. On January 1, 1863, Colonel Wilson C. Lemert, commander of Union forces at Cumberland Gap and Tazewell (TN), received intelligence of a Confederate detachment east of Jonesville.[104] Lemert directed Major Charles Beeres of the Sixteenth Illinois Cavalry, commanding a 400-man force including the Twenty-Second Ohio Battery, to attack the Confederate position. Major Beeres marched his regiment to Jonesville, where they encamped and waited for a favorable change in the weather. Locally, Beeres had earned a notorious reputation for waging war on civilians during his foraging operations.[105]

The Confederate troops near Jonesville were remnants of the Sixty-Fourth Mounted Infantry, which had escaped when the Federals captured the Cumberland Gap the previous September. The regiment's strength of approximately 130 men was commanded by Lieutenant Colonel Auburn L. Pridemore, who had led the unit from its origin. Reinforcements by a detachment from the Tenth Kentucky (CSA) Cavalry raised Pridemore's collective strength to about 230.[106] On the evening of December 30 Pridemore received a dispatch from Jones advising his expedition was in progress, his estimated time of arrival, and a plan of executing a coordinated assault against the Federals. Working in conjunction with Pridemore, Jones would have an overwhelming numerical advantage and the element of surprise.

Major Beeres, unaware that Jones was en route, assumed that his Federal force held numerical superiority. On the evening of January 2 he stationed pickets only to the east, where he knew his enemy to be. With temperatures below zero, he continued to await a break in the weather before launching his offensive.

Battle of Jonesville

The Jones Brigade crossed Powell Mountain and advanced on the Federal outpost from the west. Jones had directed Pridemore to attack from the east but only after the

Jones Brigade was already engaged.[107] Jones launched his attack at daybreak, catching Major Beeres and his Federal force, including the artillery, completely off guard. The Federals gave stubborn resistance, but with Pridemore's troops advancing from the east they were surrounded. Jones directed his forces to take cover while the Federals exhausted their ammunition. In desperation, the Federals fled out into the open. Jones's horsemen surrounded Beeres' troops and forced their surrender. At the cost of five killed and about twenty wounded, Jones captured 383 Union officers and enlisted men, three cannon, and twenty-seven wagons, each with a six-mule team.[108] Federal casualties in addition to the captured were ten killed and forty-five wounded.[109]

Jones was a benevolent victor regarding his enemy's wounded. He converted the home of a Union sympathizer, Andrew Milbourne, into a field hospital and authorized a black servant, George Martin, to pilot the enemy wounded into Kentucky.[110] Major Beeres and the other prisoners were marched under guard forty miles to Bristol, Virginia, to be transported by rail to detention facilities throughout the South.[111]

Jones declined personal credit for the victory. Major Beeres formally surrendered to Lieutenant Colonel Pridemore, who received Beeres' horse, sword, and pistols. Pridemore carried the tokens of his triumph through the remainder of the war.[112] At Bristol, Major Beeres was singled out, separated, and transferred to Abingdon, to be placed in irons and confined for sixteen days in the county jail.[113] He communicated with General Longstreet, who intervened to demand that Beeres receive the same treatment as other prisoners. Beeres was then transferred to and confined at Libby Prison in Richmond until May, when he was transported to Macon, Georgia. He was fortunate to be one of fifty prisoners transferred to Charleston, South Carolina, where conditions were vastly improved so as to prepare them for one of the last prisoner exchanges. Longstreet's intervention may have influenced his release by a prisoner exchange on August 8.[114]

In October 1864 Beeres visited Chicago while on a furlough and granted an interview to the *Chicago Tribune*. He recounted the details of his capture at Jonesville with an exaggerated account of the Confederate strength, which he contended to be two divisions.[115] Beeres spoke of the appalling treatment of Federal prisoners in Southern internment camps and expressed support for Lincoln over George McClellan in the pending election.[116] He rejoined his unit and participated in the Western Theater campaigns until the end of the war.

The Battle of Jonesville was to be known as the "Frozen Fight."[117] The victory prompted a new sense of optimism that Jones and his brigade might retake the Cumberland Gap. Exploring the possibility, Jones dispatched scouts, who returned with intelligence that the Federal occupation force was between 1,000 and 1,500 troops.[118] Word of Jones's recent triumph placed the Federals on high alert. Denied the element of surprise, Jones declined to launch an offensive.

The engagement at Jonesville was a major setback to the Federals occupying the Cumberland Gap. Two days following the engagement, Colonel Lemert commanding the outpost, reported that his force was down to only one day of rations.[119] Jones, on the other hand, reported that the captured bounty provided his men and horses enough subsistence to last them until March 1.[120]

Jones resumed the task of screening Longstreet's gradual withdrawal from East Tennessee back into central Virginia. He sent a detachment to Little War Gap near Rogersville to serve as an initial escort. Simultaneously, he led his main column into Harlan County, Kentucky, targeting a Federal supply train bound for the Cumberland Gap. A successful

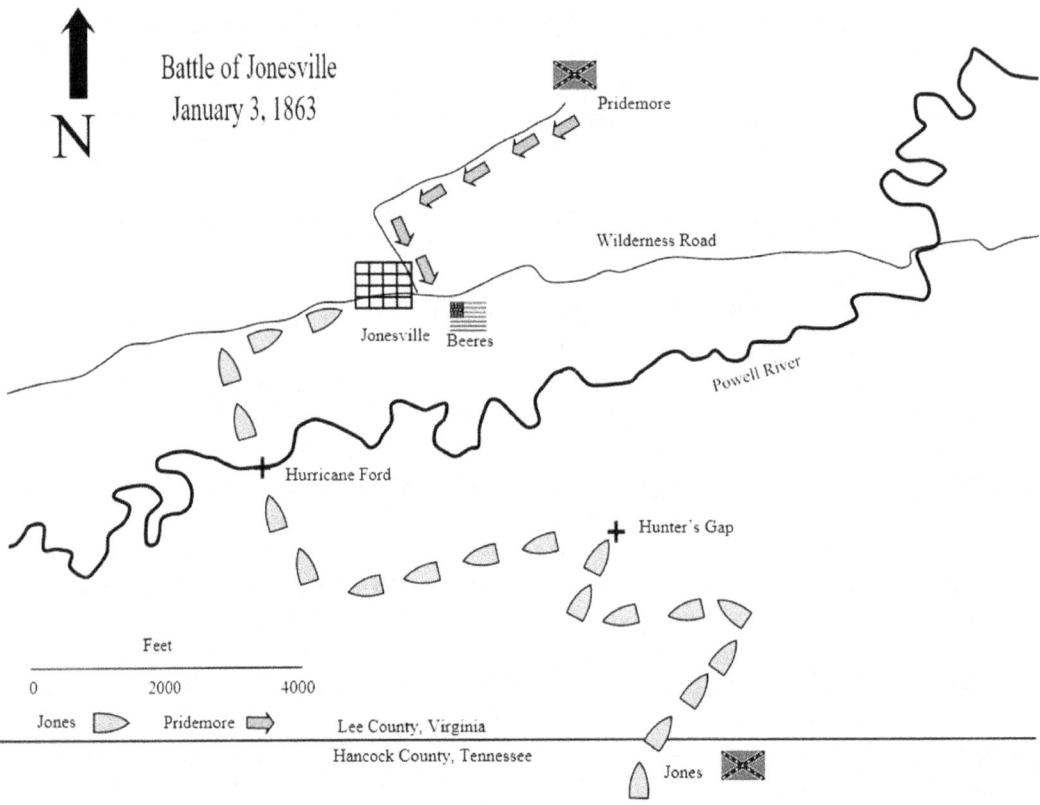

Battle of Jonesville (sketch by author, 2016).

expedition could have starved the enemy occupation force out of their garrison.[121] However, the Cumberland River had swollen beyond a fording level, and Jones aborted the mission. Captain George Williams of the 37th Virginia Battalion Cavalry later wrote, "This was the first raid General Jones had taken since he had been in command of the brigade that he did not accomplish his design."[122]

In late January, William E. Jones was recalled by the Department of Southwest Virginia commander, Major General Samuel Jones, for other duties, and Colonel James M. Corns assumed interim command of the brigade.[123] During Grumble's absence, Longstreet encouraged Corns and General John C. Vaughn to storm the Federal garrison at Tazewell (TN). Unable to coordinate an offensive, the measure failed. At the urging of Longstreet, Jones returned to resume command.[124]

On February 18, Jones positioned his force at Camp Robertson in Lee County.[125] Longstreet held ambitions that a united force of Jones, Vaughn, and Pridemore could capture the Cumberland Gap. From personal experience, however, Jones, knew that natural fortifications afforded a distinct advantage to undersized defensive forces. He also recognized the futility of storming the gap with cavalry alone. Without infantry and artillery, it would be impossible to execute a successful assault on the gap, which, contrary to Longstreet's assumption, was not undermanned. General Theophilus Toulmin Garrard (a cousin to Colonel Israel Garrard at Rogersville), commanding the District of the Clinch, held a formidable strength of 1,500 combined infantry, cavalry, and artillery personnel supported by four batteries.[126] Respecting Jones's judgment, Longstreet did not challenge his decision.

Jones reasoned that a direct frontal assault was not a practical strategy for dealing with the Federal forces occupying the Cumberland Gap. A more efficient measure was to harass their supply lines outside the protection the gap provided and to attack the Federal foraging details when they ventured out into Lee County. Such a strategy required diligence and patience, but in the long term it could deplete the occupying force by attrition and perhaps starve it into submission. An opportunity to implement this strategy was about to present itself.

Wyerman's Mill

On February 14, General Theophilus Toulmin Garrard dispatched a Federal foraging party into Lee County. Members included detached squads from the Second North Carolina (U.S.) Infantry and the Ninety-First Indiana Infantry. Serving as escort, the Eleventh Tennessee (U.S.) Cavalry, commanded by Lieutenant Colonel Reuben A. Davis, established an outpost at Wyerman's Mill on Indian Creek, about five miles southwest of Jonesville.[127] Colonel Davis notified General Garrard that he could observe enemy campfires at a distance and conveyed his apprehensions about exposure to a potential flanking movement. For whatever reason, Garrard did not react.[128]

On February 21, Jones led his brigade to Fulkerson's Mill and visited local attorney Ewing Litterell, the brother of Private William Litterell of the Twenty-Seventh Virginia Cavalry.[129] Familiar with the region, the Lee County brothers informed Jones that the Union position was vulnerable to a surprise attack.[130] Jones saw an opportunity to capture the entire force. Deploying his usual strategy, Jones used the darkness to conceal his movements with a night march. At midnight on the 22nd he positioned a detachment from the Thirty-Sixth Battalion, Virginia Cavalry, just below the crossing of Indian Creek at Wyerman's Mill. He placed the Thirty-Fourth Battalion, Virginia Cavalry, out on the Wilderness Road, approximately four miles east of their target, with orders to attack the front pickets as soon as they heard the firing from the rear. He placed all the other units west of the Union position. Jones had his enemy virtually enclosed between his divided brigade and the natural barrier of Indian Creek. At dawn, he launched his surprise attack.

Not all went according to plan. Most of the enemy infantry managed to escape. Overall, however, the mission was a success. At the cost of three killed and seven wounded, Jones captured 256 prisoners, eight wagons, a cache of small arms, and about a hundred horses. He reported that thirteen of the prisoners were "runaway slaves."[131]

Lieutenant James W. Orr of the 37th Virginia wrote, "There were quite a number of negro troops on the Federal side who suffered severely."[132] There is some question as to whether or not a massacre occurred.[133] The sensitive matter of treatment of prisoners of war was a contested issue between the two sides of the Civil War. The South took the position that any and all black soldiers, even those donning the Federal uniform, would be regarded not as prisoners of war but as rebellious or fugitive slaves. It appears improbable that any of the black captives at Wyerman's Mill were actually in uniform. There were no Union reports of black troops engaged. More than likely, former slaves were employed by the Union forces as laborers.[134]

Lieutenant Colonel Reuben A. Davis, the commander of the Federal detail, was

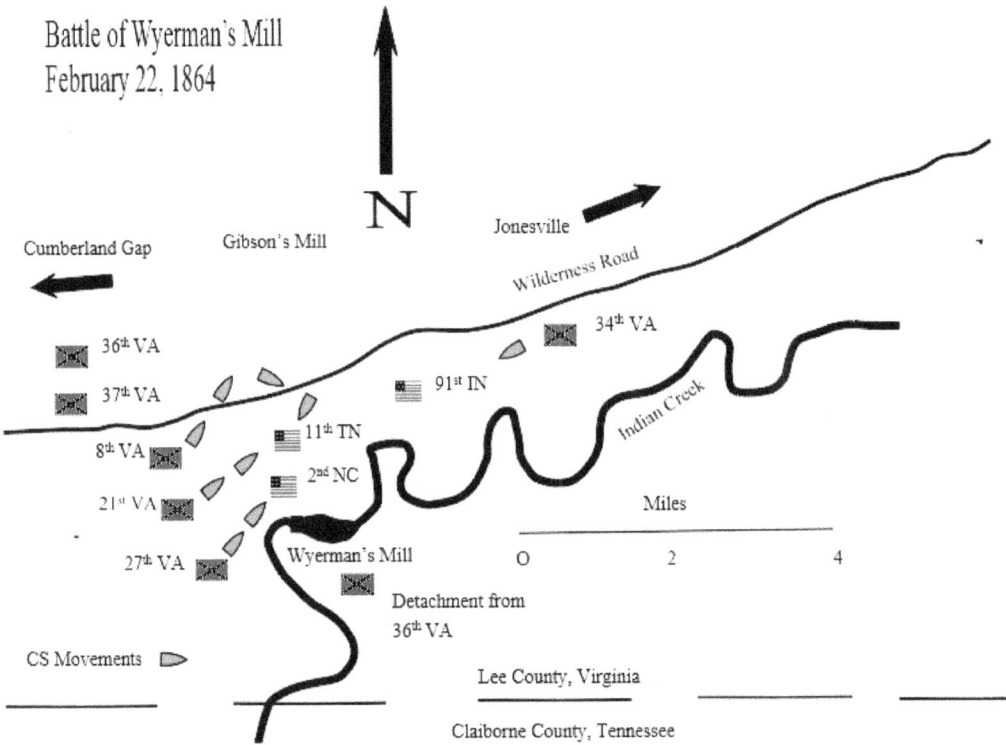

Battle of Wyerman's Mill (sketch by author, 2016).

among the captured. He also received a gunshot wound to the hip, resulting in an ammunition round being lodged in his groin.[135] In spite of his wound and impairment, Davis escaped and made his way to rejoin the Federal lines.[136]

Two days later General Garrard reported that Lieutenant Colonel Davis had been surprised while entirely surrounded before being captured along with a company of the Second North Carolina (U.S.) Mounted Infantry. A company of the Ninety-First Indiana Infantry fought their way through the lines to escape, at the cost of three casualties. Garrard added that four officers and about sixty enlisted men of Davis's battalion and seven men of the Second North Carolina (U.S.) Company, successfully escaped. Garrard acknowledged that Colonel Davis was severely wounded and captured before escaping.[137]

There is irony regarding the Federal authorities' handling of Lieutenant Colonel Reuben A. Davis. The fact that he was wounded, still managed to escape, and returned to the Federal lines might lead one to surmise that his exploits were heroic. Apparently, that was not the case. Garrard blamed Davis for the defeat. Six months later, Davis received a formal discharge based upon an adverse report by a board of examination accepting his prior resignation on account of incompetency.[138] Davis would survive the war but died in 1895 from an infection of the wound incurred at Wyerman's Mill.[139] The treatment of Davis is in stark contrast to that of Major Charles Beeres, the Federal commander at Jonesville. Beeres, who was not injured, had surrendered and managed to be exchanged due to influential connections. He ultimately received a hero's welcome.

In regard to his casualties, Jones reported Captain C.E. Burks of Peter's Twenty-First Virginia Cavalry Regiment among the three killed. In a posthumous and rare tribute to any officer of his brigade, Jones described Burks as "a most gallant and excellent officer."[140]

Jones's victory at Wyerman's Mill denied the Federal force occupying the Cumberland Gap access to potential forage once again in Lee County. It also placed the Federal authorities in a high state of alert. Jones anticipated that his most recent success negated the element of surprise regarding any new offenses he might plan in the short term. Instead of launching a new expedition, he loaded up the captured supplies and marched the bulk of his brigade to Ball's Bridge.[141] Jones detached the Thirty-fourth Cavalry Virginia Battalion to escort the 256 prisoners under guard through Jonesville and on to Bristol, Tennessee.

Jones's final combat action in the Longstreet tenure took place at Panther Spring Gap on March 5. In a minor engagement, he attacked a foraging party from the Third Tennessee (U.S.) Infantry. Officially recorded reports indicate the four-hour engagement resulted in Federal casualties of up to three killed, one "badly wounded" and twenty-two captured.[142] Following the encounter, Jones and his brigade encamped at Morgan's Farm in Lee County.

For the remainder of the winter Longstreet held on to his ambitions about retaking the Cumberland Gap and following up on it with an invasion of Kentucky. Maintaining a presence in Lee County, however, was turning into a liability, as forage was rapidly being depleted. By mid–March, the Confederate authorities in Richmond shelved the idea of a Kentucky invasion.[143] On April 11 Longstreet received his orders to return his corps to rejoin Lee's Army of Northern Virginia in central Virginia.[144] Longstreet and Jones apparently had a good working relationship. Although critical of most of his subordinates, Longstreet praised the Jones Brigade for its contribution to the siege of Knoxville and Bean Station. Longstreet may have held a bias in the Jones and Stuart dispute.

In contrasting the inglorious Southern campaigns in Tennessee, the *Richmond Whig* compared Jones's exploits in East Tennessee and Southwest Virginia to Stonewall Jackson and his Shenandoah Valley Campaign.[145] Keeping the Federals on the defensive, Jones forced them to concentrate on defending their presence in the region and to relinquish plans of any offensive operations toward the mineral reserves in Southwest Virginia. Recognized for his accomplishments, Jones was appointed as commander of the Department of Southwest Virginia, a remarkable title for a brigadier general.

Enjoying a brief time of reprieve, Jones followed up on personal matters during the latter half of March 1864. The March 19 edition of the *Abingdon Virginian* published an advertisement in which he offered his prize racehorse, named "John Red," at his Washington County farm for stud services. John Red was an offspring of the celebrated Red Eye and had been bred by a Thoroughbred Margrave mare. John Red was also the first item on the inventory of personal property regarding the estate of W.E. Jones following his death.

With Longstreet's withdrawal, the Jones Brigade no longer needed to conduct cavalry escort or foraging operations in East Tennessee or Lee County, Virginia. Longstreet's departure also signaled the termination of Confederate ambitions toward Knoxville or the Cumberland Gap. As the spring of 1864 approached, Confederate authorities concluded that the next threat to the mineral reserves in Smyth and Wythe counties would not come from East Tennessee but from West Virginia. Pridemore's Sixty-Fourth Virginia Mounted Infantry and the Twenty-Seventh Virginia Battalion were detached to secure

Lee County. While the main body of the Jones Brigade marched to Saltville in Smyth County, Grumble Jones was temporarily detached to Bristol, Tennessee, on an urgent and sensitive administrative matter.

Dissension Within the Ranks

The aftermath of Grumble's victory at Wyerman's Mill unveiled an element of dissension regarding the Thirty-Fourth Battalion Virginia Cavalry, commanded by Lieutenant Colonel Vincent Addison Witcher. The professional relationship between Grumble Jones and Witcher had been strained from the beginning. Although Grumble valued Witcher's capabilities as a fighter, he was cognizant of the Clawhammer's dark side. Witcher carried a reputation and was demonized by both sides as a bushwhacker. Witcher did not take part in the Battle of Wyerman's Mill. He was in Bristol serving as a witness in a court-martial trial.[146] From Grumble's perspective, the Thirty-Fourth Battalion of Virginia Cavalry had performed well in the absence of the unit's commander, whose service was expendable.

Other factors escalated tensions between Jones and Witcher. By March 1864 the main armies of the Confederacy were granting leaves of absence to the rank and file to boost morale, clamp the hemorrhage of desertion, and relieve the excess burden of sustenance. With Lee County ravaged by the forces of both sides, members of the Jones Brigade suffered from deprivations. Significant numbers from the ranks were from the counties of West Virginia, eastern Kentucky, or pro–Union East Tennessee. Jones declined to grant furloughs to those particular individuals because their homes were "within enemy lines."[147] Witcher and members of other units filed a petition requesting a transfer back to the Albert Gallatin Jenkins Brigade. Witcher wrote that he would have "no hesitancy in saying that if Gen. Jones succeeds in carrying out his policy; every border man of [his] command will desert."[148]

In the aftermath of Wyerman's Mill, Grumble had detached a squadron of the Thirty-Fourth Battalion, Virginia Cavalry, to escort the 256 Federal prisoners to Bristol. Already situated in Bristol serving on court-martial duty, Lieutenant Colonel Witcher met the detachment upon its arrival. Their standing orders were to deliver the prisoners to the provost officers and then return to their post in Lee County. Witcher, however, redirected his men to accompany him on an expedition to the Southwest Virginia counties of Tazewell, Russell, Wise and Buchanan for the alleged purpose of rounding up suspected deserters. Witcher claimed that he had requested permission to conduct the expedition. When he did not receive a prompt reply, he took the initiative. His detachment did not return to their post until early April.[149]

During the time of Witcher's unauthorized expedition, the *Abingdon Virginian* printed a brief story bearing the headline "Outrageous Conduct." Dated March 18, 1864, the publication reported that while on furlough the men under Witcher's command passed through Russell County and requisitioned the only workhorse of Mr. Lewis Horton, who had thirteen sons serving in the Confederacy. The article attributed the maddening influence of liquor to the men's atypical behavior.[150] It is probable that Jones, who had a good relationship with the *Abingdon Virginian*, learned of the alleged incident either by reading the article or from other sources.

Immediately upon Witcher's return, Jones placed the battalion commander under arrest, preferring charges of two counts of absence without leave, two counts of conduct prejudicial to good order and military discipline, and two counts of disobedience to orders. The court-martial was held on April 25, 1864 in Bristol. The reported incident in Russell County did not factor into the prosecution. In his defense, Witcher cited his health problems along with the logistics regarding the topography and distance between Bristol and Jonesville. The court panel and some of the prosecution witnesses were sympathetic to Witcher because he was a highly revered officer and had conducted himself well in the trial. The circumstantial evidence, however, was overwhelming. Witcher was convicted on all counts on the first two charges of absence without leave and conduct prejudicial to good order and military discipline. He was acquitted on both counts of disobedience to orders.[151] The court sentenced Witcher to be suspended from rank and pay for two months and to receive an official reprimand.

To the probable chagrin of Grumble Jones, the judicial panel asked the presiding judge, Major General Simon Bolivar Buckner, to remit the sentence in light of the defendant's gentlemanly, soldierly, manly, and frank "acknowledgment of his error."[152] No immediate action was taken. However, the issue would come up again two months later, following Grumble's death.

State of the W.E. Jones Brigade

On April 24, while Jones was away serving as a prosecution witness in Bristol, Major General Robert Ransom inspected the W.E. Jones Brigade at its encampment seven miles north of the saltworks in Smyth County.[153] Ransom's "rough notes" and his adjutant's narrative constituted the assessment report filed with President Davis's advisor, General Braxton Bragg. The report described the general condition of the Jones Brigade as deplorable.

The junior staff of officers received the harshest criticism. Overall, there was "not a fair commander among" them.[154] In Jones's absence, Lieutenant Colonel Alphonso Cook of the Eighth Virginia Cavalry had assumed interim command. Cook had been second in command of the Eighth Virginia Cavalry, previously commanded by Colonel James M. Corns, who was deemed a "drinking blackguard," relieved of duty, and replaced by Captain John P. Sheffey.[155] Three regimental or battalion commanders, Lieutenant Colonel Witcher among them, were under arrest.[156] Colonel Ambrose C. Dunn of the Thirty-Seventh Battalion, Virginia Cavalry, had been "cashiered" on the day of the Battle of Rogersville.[157] The only positive note, far short of an endorsement, referred to the Twenty-First Virginia Cavalry Regiment commander, Colonel William E. Peters. Ransom judged Peters to be "a gentleman, but ignorant of military duty."[158] The commentary concluded that all the other officers were of "no account."[159] Discipline and efficiency appeared lacking. Present for duty were 66 officers and 887 enlisted men, while 169 were absent without leave. Except for the Eighth Virginia Cavalry, there were no schools or lessons in tactics for the units. Company and battalion drills were "rare." The troops were unfamiliar with tactics.[160]

The report outlined problems with supplies and armaments. Many troopers were barefooted. Some companies were armed only with sabers. Firearms were either in short supply or in poor condition. Accouterments and other means of record keeping were nonexistent. There was a shortage of mounts, and some of the available horses had back sores due to defective saddles. The horses on hand required up to three weeks of rest and grazing before they would be ready for a campaign. The bulk of the brigade was about to transfer to Wythe County, and the report recommended a reorganization during that time.

Ransom bestowed minimal praise upon the brigade that had been triumphant in combat actions at Rogersville, Jonesville, and Wyerman's Mill. The brigade never tasted outright defeat. Ransom explained the nominal success by crediting General W.E. Jones. In spite of the brigade's many deficiencies, the report applauded Jones for his effort to purge incompetent officers and suggested implementing the measure by consolidating units. Rationalizing the seemingly pathetic state of affairs Ransom added, "The work during the winter has been constant and hard." Finally, he remarked, "Jones ought to be promoted; notwithstanding all his grumbling, he is a fine officer."[161] It was the second official recommendation to promote Jones to major general.

A Shift in Federal Strategy

On March 2, 1864, Lieutenant General Ulysses S. Grant assumed command of all Union forces. Grant devised a three-pronged plan to divide and conquer the overall South. Sherman would apply pressure on Joseph Eggleston Johnston's Army of Tennessee, based at Dalton in north Georgia. General Nathaniel Banks would advance on Mobile, Alabama, to secure the Gulf Coast. The third and most complex measure would occur in Virginia with its divide-and-conquer approach.

In Virginia specifically, Grant would launch his Overland Campaign from the north with his Army of the Potomac deploying a strategy of relentless hammering against Lee's Army of Northern Virginia, based along the Rapidan River. To the east, Benjamin Butler's Army of the James was to advance toward Richmond along the north banks of the James River. To the west, General Franz Siegel would proceed up (in a north to south direction) the Shenandoah Valley from Martinsburg, West Virginia, against General John C. Breckinridge and the Army of the Valley District. Finally, Grant's plan called upon General George Crook, commander of the Kanawha District, to sever the Virginia-Tennessee Railroad between Lynchburg and East Tennessee.

Smyth County and Wythe County

Having withdrawn from Lee County, the W.E. Jones Brigade took up operations in Smyth County with the emphasis on guarding the local saltworks and the lead mines of adjacent Wythe County. Saltville produced an estimated two-thirds of the Confederacy's much-needed salt supply, while the mines at Wytheville turned out 150,000 pounds of lead each month.[162]

Following the trial of Lieutenant Colonel Witcher, Jones rejoined his brigade near Saltville. While Jones was en route from Bristol, the Federals partially met their objectives in Southwest Virginia. On May 9, at Cloyd's Mountain in Pulaski County, Federal forces under General George Crook defeated the Confederate forces commanded by Albert Jenkins, who was mortally wounded and captured. Crook's army then occupied Dublin Station and destroyed sections of the Virginia-Tennessee Railroad, including the bridge spanning the New River at Central Depot (now Radford, Virginia). As part of Crook's offensive, General William W. Averell launched a cavalry raid on Saltville, only to be repulsed by Brigadier General John Hunt Morgan's well-established defenses. Altering his objective, Averell turned northward toward the lead mines at Wytheville.

Reunited with his brigade, Jones marched northward to joined forces with Morgan. The two mounted units raced to Wytheville to save the lead mines from capture. Recognizing Jones's abilities as a commander, Morgan willingly served as his subordinate.[163] On May 10, Jones's and Morgan's combined 4,500-man force reached Crockett's Gap (AKA Crockett's Cove) to confront Averell's dismounted cavalry, which was drawn up in a defensive line.[164] Jones ordered a dismounted frontal assault that routed Averell's forces in what was later designated the Battle of Cove Mountain. Morgan wrote to his wife, euphorically describing the engagement, and stated if they had two more hours of daylight, they would have captured the entire force.[165] Jones won what was to be his final victory, and Averell retreated to the protection of Crook's infantry in West Virginia.

John Hunt Morgan was a celebrated Mexican War veteran from a prominent Lexington, Kentucky, family. The successful and wealthy merchant organized a militia group that was absorbed into Confederate service with the start of the Civil War. He served with distinction in the 1862 Shiloh Campaign and was appointed brigadier general by the end of the year. His escapades included the Stones River Campaign and several raids into Kentucky, one of which captured Lexington. His activities then extended into Indiana and Ohio. His actions earned him the CSA Thanks of Congress.[166] In July 1863, however, he was defeated for the first time and captured. Four months later, Morgan added to his charisma by escaping from the Ohio State Penitentiary. His action at Crockett's Gap was his first combat experience since his escape.

A False Sense of Security

The withdrawal of General George Crook's Army of the Kanawha District turned matters deceptively quiet in Southwest Virginia. The Confederates could not claim total victory for Jones's Wythe County triumph, as Crook's and Averill's forces had accomplished their primary mission to destroy the New River Bridge. However, the Wytheville lead mines were relatively secure, and priority shifted to the saltworks. Jones returned his brigade to Saltville, reestablished his headquarters, and resumed his title of commander of the Department of Southwest Virginia. Morgan positioned his brigade headquarters at Abingdon.

Saltville was a convenient location for Jones, as it was situated less than fifteen miles from his estate near Glade Spring. From the beginning of the conflict he had desired to serve in Southwest Virginia, and he was currently operating in his domain. As the spring season progressed, however, both Jones and Morgan felt that they had exhausted their effectiveness in Southwest Virginia. They saw the futility in occupying a region where forage and supplies were dwindling. Both expressed desires to pursue other ambitions. Morgan planned another expedition into Kentucky while Jones reset his sights on East Tennessee. On May 17 Jones submitted a report to General Samuel Cooper requesting the authority and troops to launch a second offensive against Knoxville. Grumble added, "I feel assured, from the reports made by my scouts; Knoxville and all east of that point can be taken by the troops under my command."[167] The war front, however, was rapidly evolving in central Virginia and drawing attention away from Tennessee.

At his Saltville headquarters, Jones received daily dispatches on the developments occurring at a rapid pace in the campaigns between Lee and Grant around Richmond. The first half of May 1864 was costly for Confederate operations at the Wilderness and Spotsylvania Courthouse. The Army of Northern Virginia was fighting for its own survival as well as that of the Confederate central government in Richmond. Concluding that he would be needed to rejoin Lee's Army of Northern Virginia, Jones relinquished his ambitions of venturing back into East Tennessee. Conversely, General Morgan was bound and determined to launch his expedition into Kentucky at the earliest opportunity.

It was said that Jones returned to his headquarters at the end of one day and anxiously inquired from his adjutant, Captain Walter K. Martin, of the latest developments regarding the campaigns near Richmond. Martin responded, "General Stuart has been killed."[168] Jones was said to have paced back and forth staring at the ground in silence. In a posthumous and final tribute to his old nemesis, he replied, "By God Martin! You know I had little love for Stuart, and he had just as little for me, but that is the greatest loss that army has sustained since the death of Jackson."[169]

Stuart was not the only casualty. While confronting Grant's Overland Campaign, Lee had lost more than half a dozen generals killed, wounded, or captured. In addition to the action around Richmond, a new crisis was emerging in the Shenandoah Valley. Surmising that he was going to be needed elsewhere to the east, Jones concluded that his time in Southwest Virginia was coming to an end.

18

The Shenandoah Valley— May 1864

During Jones's final month in Southwest Virginia, a major event occurred more than 200 miles to the north at New Market in the Shenandoah Valley. General Franz Sigel (U.S.), the commander of the Department of Western Virginia, failed Grant miserably in his mission to sever the Virginia Central Railroad in and around Staunton.

It took two weeks for Sigel's 5,000-man force to advance seventy-five miles from Martinsburg. On May 15, the Department of Western Virginia commander, John C. Breckinridge (CSA), along with the brigades of General John C. Echols, General Gabriel Wharton, Imboden's cavalry, and a reserve regiment of VMI cadets, confronted Sigel's army at New Market. While Sigel failed to engage all of his regiments, Breckinridge ordered all of his forces, including 247 VMI cadets, into the fight. In a coordinated assault, Breckinridge drove Sigel's forces from the field in humiliating retreat to Cedar Creek, north of Strasburg. Reasoning that the upper (southern) Shenandoah Valley was secure, Breckinridge and his divisions withdrew to unite with the Army of Northern Virginia at the North Anna River. The regiment of VMI cadets transferred to serve in the defense of Richmond.[1] Having to consolidate as many forces as possible to confront Grant's imminent threat to Richmond, the Southerners conceded the lower (northern) Shenandoah Valley to the Federals.

To the Northern troops, Sigel's debacle at New Market spurred outrage. At this third-year stage of the war, control of the upper valley appeared just as elusive to the Federals as it had been following Jackson's Valley Campaign of 1862. To the Southern troops under Breckinridge, there was a sense of pride that immortalized the VMI cadets in particular. In reality, the Confederate victory at New Market was mostly a psychological boost that lacked strategic significance.[2] Unlike previous campaigns, the Confederate victory at New Market failed to expel the Federal presence in the valley. The Federals regrouped at Cedar Creek as an army of occupation. For the Confederacy, the triumph resulted in a dangerous sense of complacency.

With Breckinridge's withdrawal, security of the upper Shenandoah Valley rested with Brigadier General John D. Imboden's modest-sized cavalry brigade, various bands of partisan rangers, and scattered groups of the home guard. These measures could offer only token resistance to the impending threat at hand.

Hunter Takes Command

Grant relieved Sigel of command of the Department of Western Virginia and replaced him with sixty-one-year-old Major General David Hunter, a West Point graduate and Mexican War veteran. Hunter was the son of an ardent patriot of the Revolutionary War and the grandson of a signer of the Declaration of Independence.³ In 1861 he had accompanied President Lincoln on his inaugural train ride to Washington.⁴ Politically and ideologically, Hunter was the antithesis of Grumble Jones.

As Segil's replacement, Hunter commanded the newly organized Army of the Shenandoah which Grant directed to occupy the Shenandoah Valley and disrupt the impending harvest.⁵ According to the plan, Hunter would ultimately unite with General George Crook's army en route from West Virginia. The collective force would then destroy the railroad centers at Staunton, Gordonsville, Charlottesville, and Lynchburg.

Following an abolitionist and anti-secessionist agenda, Hunter developed a reputation as one who fought outside of the conventional rules of war, measures that did not go unnoticed by the South.

General David Hunter, circa 1863 (courtesy Library of Congress).

The Confederate congress branded him as a "felon to be executed if captured."⁶ Comrades and enemies alike referred to him as "Black Dave" (he dyed his mustache black and wore a dark wig) and "a human hyena."⁷

In spite of their ideological differences, Jones and Hunter had similarities. Both were West Point graduates and career soldiers. Hunter's checkered life in the Old Army included several duels and a court-martial conviction (with a sentence of dismissal that was remitted by President John Quincy Adams).⁸ Each man near mid-career had resigned his commission in the U.S. Army to pursue private ventures.⁹ Like Jones, Hunter possessed an irascible personality, a violent temper, and a past marked by bitterness and contention.¹⁰ Both generals emphasized pride and discipline. While taking the offensive in enemy territory, both took stern measures to mitigate the abuses of foraging.

Unlike Jones, Hunter had friends in high places, including the military hierarchy, the U.S. Congress, and the president. He had served on Grant's administrative staff in the Western Theater and presided over the court of inquiry investigating the failed Chickamauga Campaign.¹¹ With his recent appointment, Hunter's ties with the lieutenant general strengthened. Hunter took command of an army that had been demoralized and lacked discipline. The Federals had branded the Shenandoah Valley with a stigma of defeatism going back to the beginning of the war. Jackson's Shenandoah Valley Campaign of 1862 and the Ewell Corps' route of Robert Huston Milroy's force in the Second Battle of Winchester were two examples. What had happened at New Market was the latest in a series of setbacks, and Hunter was determined to reverse the trend.

Unlike Jones, Hunter was not highly revered by his troops. While willing to wage war on civilians, he took extreme measures to control foraging. Private Charles H. Lynch of the Eighteenth Connecticut Infantry wrote in his diary that they could stand just about anything but hunger and found it strange that they could not forage in the enemy's territory.[12] Hunter was also willing to torch the property of innocents in response to guerrilla attacks.

Hunter sought to purge many of the officers who had served under Sigel. Exceptions included Captain Henry Algernon DuPont, who had graduated from West Point at the top of his class in 1861.[13] Lieutenant John Rogers Meigs's qualifications also impressed the new commander. Another officer meeting Hunter's approval was his cousin Lieutenant Colonel David Hunter Strother, whom he appointed as chief of staff. Hunter established his headquarters at Cedar Creek, the point of refuge where Sigel's defeated army regrouped. Hunter's main base of operations and supply source was forty miles to the rear at Martinsburg. His supply lines were overstretched and an inviting target to partisan rangers.

Hunter's Raid Begins

On May 23 Hunter received confirmation that Breckinridge's divisions had withdrawn from the valley to join Lee's Army of Northern Virginia near Richmond.[14] Hunter ordered his soldiers to travel light, limiting each to one pair of replacement footgear, a hundred rounds of ammunition, and a minimal supply of rations.[15] His army would sustain itself by *controlled* foraging. With an initial collective strength numbering near eight thousand along with twenty-four cannons facing nominal resistance, Hunter had a seemingly unobstructed path to Staunton. According to the plan, when Hunter's Army of the Shenandoah united with Crook's Army of the Kanawha District, the combined armies would resume the expedition against targets in central Virginia.

Hunter delayed the launch of his expedition to allow the supply trains from Martinsburg time to arrive. Well to the rear of his forward Cedar Creek base, Confederate partisans attacked an escorted wagon train passing through the village of Newtown, resulting in minor casualties. Addressing the guerrilla-style warfare to his rear with a clear message to ward off future attacks, Hunter issued his retaliation order and dispatched a mounted squad to Newtown. The unit torched three homes owned by suspected secessionists and issued Hunter's declaration of future reprisals in response to any new attacks.[16]

Word of the burnings and Hunter's retaliation order spread throughout the valley. A four-member citizen committee from Newtown appealed for clemency, contending that only one of the three burned dwellings belonged to an ardent secessionist. Hunter's chief of staff, Colonel David Strother, met with the committee members and advised that to protect the innocent they must identify the attackers. The group named several individuals who remained at large, along with a Mrs. Wilson, a widow who granted partisans access to her *rented* home as a point of rendezvous. Strother ordered Mrs. Wilson's arrest and evicted her daughters. Federals then seized her personal property, brought it out to the street, and set it ablaze.

On May 26 the main body of Hunter's army commenced its march from Cedar Creek. Approximately five miles ahead at Fisher's Hill, five Union scouts were killed. In reprisal, Hunter ordered the burning of a nearby farmhouse suspected of being a haven for the bushwhackers.[17] Two days later, a Federal scouting party burned the house of a man suspected of having assisted in the murder of Federal stragglers during Sigel's retreat from New Market.[18]

Alarm over Hunter's scorched-earth policies continued to precede his advancing column. Within his ranks, however, there were voices of moderation. Captain George M. Ellicott refused to burn a suspected bushwhacker's house when he discovered a woman and three children occupied it. Hunter reprimanded Ellicott but spared the structure.[19] Hunter reversed his order to burn the Hollingsworth Hotel in Woodstock after learning it had served as a hospital caring for wounded Union soldiers following the battle of New Market.[20]

On May 29, well to the rear of Hunter's main column, a second incident occurred in Newtown. Major Harry Gilmor (CSA) and 150 partisan rangers attacked a lightly escorted sixteen-unit wagon supply train coming from Martinsburg. Gilmor's guerrillas confiscated four of the wagons and destroyed the others. Federal losses included nine wounded enlisted men, one mortally wounded officer, and nine missing.[21] Hunter dispatched a 200-man mounted detail to back-track to Newtown and burn the entire village as a reprisal.

Anticipating Hunter's retaliatory measures, Major Gilmor prepared a message outlining that in his assault he took prisoners, which accounted for the nine missing. Gilmor met with the Federal detail commander under a flag of truce and passed on his written threat to execute the prisoners if the village was burned. Hunter's order was not implemented.[22] Hunter's staff soon counseled their commander that the partisan attacks were more a nuisance than a threat, and his retaliations only enflamed animosities and provoked countermeasures. Hunter had a seemingly clear path and enforcing reprisals was a distraction. However, his actions had already drawn the attention of the Confederacy, from partisan rangers in the field all the way to the high command.

Hunter's raid up the Shenandoah Valley prompted public outrage and posed an imminent threat to Robert E. Lee's primary sources of sustenance. Lee had to concentrate on Grant's movements and did not have an immediate solution. Acknowledging the crisis at hand on May 25, Lee communicated the following to Secretary of War James Seddon:

> Since I withdrew Breckinridge from the Valley, there is no general commander. General Jenkins has since died. A good commander should at once be sent to that brigade. I do not know who is senior in that department. Is Morgan there? W.E. Jones I believe, belongs to East Tennessee. The case is urgent. I shall return General Breckinridge as soon as I can.[23]

Two days later, the matter turned more pressing. John D. Imboden, commander of the token resistance forces in the region, sent a dispatch to R.E. Lee:

> General Hunter commands the forces advancing upon me. He occupied Mount Jackson at noon today. His cavalry outnumbers ours two to one; his infantry four to one; his artillery four to one. He is moving on my flank and will compel me to fall back. There is no point this side of Mount Crawford where I can successfully resist him, and there it is very doubtful, though I will do my best.[24]

Lee was bogged down against Grant at the North Anna River (AKA Hanover Junction) and could not spare Breckinridge's division or other detachments from the Army of Northern Virginia. Lee replied to Imboden: "Keep the commanding officer in Southwestern Virginia informed of enemy's movements in this district, and cooperate in driving him back."[25]

On May 30, Hunter's Army of the Shenandoah reached and occupied New Market in a measure of symbolic significance. Reaching the milestone negated all that Breckinridge had accomplished during his victory only fifteen days earlier. Aside from the token resistance by small groups of cavalry or bands of partisan rangers, Hunter stood virtually unopposed with no formidable opposition before him. For the first time in the war, the Confederacy was about to lose control of the entire Shenandoah Valley. On May 31, Imboden issued the following to the citizens of the area:

> The Genl Commanding this District has this moment notified me that "every man who can fire a Gun is urgently required at Mount Crawford—He says: I see no reason why Magistrates & Constables should not fight for their homes in a pinch like this. A man should be ashamed to claim such a pitiful exemption. If it becomes necessary to make them fight, I will declare martial law in this district until the danger is over & make every man shoulder his musket. A man who will deliberately refuse to defend his home, wife, & children for a few days ought to be forced into the ranks. IF KILLED, THE LOSS IS TRIFLING.
>
> Beverly Randolph
> Major Commanding[26]

Imboden's desperate appeal rounded up the assembly of the Augusta and Rockbridge reserves under the command of Colonel Kenton Harper, Captain George Chrisman's Rockingham Reserves, Captain H.B. Harnsberger's Rockingham Reserves, and Captain James C. Marquis's Augusta Battery. Many recruits were men over the age of forty-five and boys younger than eighteen. Imboden's 1,200-man cavalry fell back from New Market to Lacey Spring and on through Harrisonburg before taking a stand near Mount Crawford at the North River to await reinforcements. Hunter had an opportunity to bypass Imboden and move on Staunton while avoiding a frontal assault but chose to rest his army at New Market.

Southwest Virginia

On May 29 Imboden wired the following to Jones at Saltville: "Enemy, 7,000 strong, advancing from Mount Jackson; also reported by signal corps in force at McDowell today. Is it possible for you to aid me?"[27] Jones wanted to come to Imboden's immediate aid, but the measure would expose the saltworks to a Federal offensive. Jones also needed clarification from the Confederate high command before he could make such a commitment. For the time being, he made preparations and awaited orders.

On the same day, General Morgan wrote to Braxton Bragg that he and his brigade would be departing Abingdon on a raid into Kentucky on the following day.[28] The tone of Morgan's correspondence suggests he was not *requesting* authorization but issuing a declaration. Justifying his actions, Morgan claimed that area sustenance and supplies were depleted to the point that his men would starve in ten days. He alleged to have reliable information that Federal forces from Kentucky were preparing an offensive targeting the saltworks and lead mines of Southwest Virginia. Morgan contended that the best way to defend those resources was to attack and thereby create a diversion.

Two days later Morgan submitted a report from Russell Courthouse stating he had already launched his expedition. He alleged that he had consulted with Jones and he had received approval from the Department of East Tennessee commander, Major General Simon Bolivar Buckner, to follow through on his plan.[29] Witcher's Thirty-Fourth Battalion, Virginia Cavalry, accompanied Morgan's expedition force as an escort.[30] The authorities in Richmond were dismayed, but it was too late to reverse what Morgan had already set in motion.[31]

In hindsight, Morgan's culpability comes into question. There is no confirmation that Jones granted Morgan his consent. In fact, Jones "would be in dire straits if Morgan left" and was therefore "reluctant to give his consent. But the command structure was confusing, and it was not certain that he [Jones] possessed the authority to disapprove."[32] Also, if Buckner had granted Morgan permission, Jones was powerless to do anything about it. In any event, Morgan would be of no help when he might have made a difference.

In Morgan's defense, his expedition may have placed Union troops in southeastern Kentucky on the defensive and thereby thwarted an advance on Saltville or Wytheville. Also, there are no indications that Jones sought Morgan's direct help in the Shenandoah Valley. Jones primarily wanted Morgan to protect the Southwest Virginia mineral reserves. As a diversion, Morgan's expedition may have been the best measure under the circumstances.

On May 30 Jones was visiting his family plantation on the Middle Fork of the Holston River for what would turn out to be the last time. At nearby Glade Spring Depot, he received the following dispatch from Lee: "Get all the available forces you can and move at once to Imboden's assistance to defend Valley; enemy said to be advancing by Mount Jackson and McDowell. Call out the reserves to hold your lines with what forces you leave behind."[33] Having already anticipated Lee's order, Jones was anxious and ready to respond accordingly.

19

Return to the Valley

In the Shenandoah Valley, only General John D. Imboden's 1,200-man cavalry brigade obstructed Hunter's path. It contained the Eighteenth Virginia Cavalry Regiment, led by the brigadier's brother Colonel George W. Imboden. A second brother, Captain Francis Marion Imboden, commanded a company within the regiment. Imboden's brigade also included Colonel Robert White's Twenty-Third Virginia Cavalry, Captain Sturgess Davis's Maryland Battalion, and Captain John H. McClanahan's Battery of artillery. Able to present only token resistance against Hunter's much-larger force, Imboden deployed delaying tactics before falling back to Mount Crawford to await whatever reinforcements Jones would bring.

John D. Imboden's background has been addressed in previous chapters. His working relationship with Jones went back to operations in the Shenandoah Valley, their West Virginia Raid, and the defense of Williamsport during the withdrawal from Gettysburg. Although there is nothing to suggest they had a friendship, they shared a spirit of working cooperation.

Lieutenant Colonel Charles T. O'Ferrall, who had served in the Jones Brigade of the Army of Northern Virginia via the Twelfth Virginia Cavalry, was reunited with Grumble almost a year after sustaining a near-fatal gunshot wound at Upperville. Following his recovery, he received a promotion to lieutenant colonel and organized a battalion that was absorbed into the Twenty-Third Virginia Cavalry.[1]

Captain John Newton Opie also had prior service under Jones as a private in the Sixth Virginia Cavalry in the Jones Brigade of the Army of Northern Virginia. Wounded in a post–Gettysburg skirmish in October 1863, Opie took up residency in Staunton to recuperate.[2] He received a commission and organized a company of mounted infantry attached to Colonel George W. Imboden's Eighteenth Virginia Cavalry.[3]

A Gathering and Mobilization of Forces

Jones assumed the overwhelming task of gathering as many troops as possible from Southwest Virginia and East Tennessee, transporting them an average distance of 250 miles to the Shenandoah Valley and assembling them into a fighting force to confront Hunter's Army of the Shenandoah. Jones was in a race for Staunton in order to establish a line of defense before Hunter's army could arrive against only token opposition. Hunter had a four-day head start, and his current position at New Market was less than fifty miles distant.

Jones had one advantage in the railroads. Unfortunately, rail transportation provided no direct route. The Virginia-Tennessee Railroad could transport the troops the first hundred miles to Salem to transfer and ride the next sixty miles to Lynchburg. From Lynchburg, they would ride the Virginia Central Railroad seventy miles to Charlottesville, where they would connect to the final, forty-mile link to Staunton. Traveling by rail, Jones and the forces at his immediate disposal conducted a journey of more than 270 miles. Although some forces were closer, units stationed near Bristol would have to travel more than three hundred miles.

Further complicating the mobilization were the results of the recent engagement at Cloyd's Mountain in Pulaski County. The armies of Generals George Crook and William Averell had destroyed overland sections of the Virginia-Tennessee Railroad, including the bridge spanning the New River. Timely repairs restored the overland rails, but it was not possible to reconstruct the bridge. The damage restricted all forces west of the New River to riding the rails to the location of the lost bridge, exiting the rail cars, marching on foot, fording the New River, boarding another train, and riding to Salem to connect on another link to Lynchburg. The logistical problems did not end there. Traveling by rail meant going without the horses. Thus, cavalry units riding the train would ultimately have to fight as infantry.

Jones called upon scattered units he had never worked with to fight alongside those with whom they were equally unfamiliar. In the pending engagement, Jones would command four brigades, two of which were infantry and a third that was converted from cavalry to infantry. It would be the largest force he had ever commanded in his career as a soldier.

In assembling his army, Jones started with the forces at his immediate disposal stationed around Glade Spring and extending to the garrison at Saltville. All would take rail transportation to the Shenandoah Valley. Jones also called upon all available units from elsewhere in Southwest Virginia and East Tennessee to take the same route.

Richard Henry Brewer Battalion

Stationed at nearby Glade Spring were five hundred mounted troopers commanded by Major Richard Henry Brewer from Annapolis, Maryland, an 1858 graduate of West Point.[4] He had served the Old Army in California under his early mentor, General Albert Sidney Johnston. When the Civil War broke out Brewer joined his revered commander and cast his lot with the Confederacy, while his home state elected not to secede. He rose to the rank of lieutenant colonel and led a battalion of Mississippi and Alabama cavalry that covered the withdrawal of General Leonidas Polk's Corps in the April 1862 Shiloh Campaign. Cited for gallantry, Brewer was promoted to full colonel, but in June of 1862 he contracted typhoid fever. Assuming he would not recover, he tendered his resignation.[5] But by August Brewer had recovered both his health and his ambitions. He traveled to Richmond, settled for the appointment of first lieutenant to restart his career, and served Brigadier General William Dorsey Pender as a volunteer aide.[6] For his gallant service at Second Bull Run and Antietam, Brewer received commendations from Pender and his division commander, Major General Ambrose Powell Hill.

Brewer sent appeals up the hierarchy requesting command of a regiment. In early

1863, he returned to the Trans-Mississippi Department to serve on the staff of Lieutenant General Polk and acquired the rank of major. Generals Pender, Hill, Polk, Wheeler, and Wharton wrote to the secretary of war endorsing Brewer's unconventional promotion to brigadier general, which skipped the usual progression.[7] President Davis's chief advisor, Braxton Bragg, declined approval, and Brewer remained a major. In April of 1864 Brewer served on the staff of General Ransom with the Department of East Tennessee. By the end of May, he commanded a mounted battalion assigned to Jones and the Department of Southwest Virginia. Brewer was a proven cavalry leader whose ambitions had been battered. In regard to both combat and administrative experience, he may have been the most qualified officer on Jones's staff. In spite of his disappointments, he apparently accepted his reduced rank dutifully.

Richard's brother, Dr. Charles Brewer, was a close friend and the brother-in-law of J.E.B. Stuart. Their friendship was to the level that, after having been mortally wounded in battle, Stuart directed he be transported to Dr. Charles Brewer's home for final care. Brewer was from a family deeply divided in allegiance. His parents and three brothers sided with the Union. A fourth brother died fighting for the Confederacy.

Brewer and his battalion left their mounts behind and boarded the train in Glade Spring along with Jones, his staff, and the Thomas Legion. In the Shenandoah Valley they would perform as infantry.

Thomas Legion

Stationed at Saltville was the Thomas Legion of Cherokee Indians and Western North Carolina Highlanders, temporarily detached from the Sixty-Ninth North Carolina Infantry. Lieutenant Colonel James R. Love, Jr., commanded the estimated four hundred troops.[8] Love was the son of an American Revolutionary War hero and founder of Waynesville, the county seat of Haywood County, North Carolina. He was an Emory and Henry College graduate and served in the North Carolina legislature. The legion served with distinction in the Battle of Seven Pines in 1862.[9] More recently they had served in Ransom's division during operations in East Tennessee and Longstreet's siege of Knoxville.

Second in command was Major William W. Stringfield, the son of a Methodist minister and educator instrumental in the founding of the Holston Conference. Stringfield was a student at Strawberry Plains College in pro–Union East Tennessee when the war erupted. He served the Confederacy in various capacities before ultimately being reassigned to the Thomas Legion.

During their encampment at Saltville, the Thomas Legion received its long-anticipated, desired orders to return to western North Carolina. Jones assured Colonel Love that his legion would receive their transfer as soon as they resolved the threat in the Shenandoah Valley.[10] The Thomas Legion boarded the train, which made its first stop at Glade Spring Depot to unite with Jones, his staff, and the Brewer Battalion before continuing eastward. They rode the Virginia-Tennessee Railroad to the location of the burned-out New River bridge, where they bivouacked for the evening and spent the entire next day fording the New River. They then marched to and camped at Central Depot (now Radford). On the following day they boarded a train bound for Lynchburg and arrived on the evening of June 1.

Forty-Fifth Regiment, Virginia Infantry

Encamped just west of the destroyed railroad bridge spanning the New River was the Forty-Fifth Regiment, Virginia Infantry, commanded by Colonel William Henry Browne. Most of the companies that formed the regiment were from Tazewell, Wythe, Grayson, and Carroll counties in Southwest Virginia. Browne's regiment had fought valiantly at Cloyd's Mountain, where they also assumed the unpleasant detail of burying the dead.[11]

William Henry Browne, a twenty-five-year-old Tazewell County, Virginia, native, was a West Pointer who did not graduate. After attending the academy for three years with notable classmates Alonzo H. Cushing and George Armstrong Custer, he followed the example of upperclassman Thomas L. Rosser and resigned after Virginia seceded.[12] He joined Confederate service as captain of Company G of the Forty-Fifth Virginia Infantry before rising to the rank of colonel and command of the entire regiment.[13] Browne would command the Second Brigade of the about-to-be-organized Army of the Valley District, and his Forty-Fifth Regiment, Virginia Infantry, would serve as the core unit.

Upon receipt of its orders to join forces with Jones, the regiment forded the New River, marched to Central Depot, and boarded the eastbound train to Lynchburg. They would ultimately ride to Charlottesville and on to Staunton.

Sixtieth Regiment, Virginia Infantry

The Sixtieth Regiment, Virginia Infantry, had fought at Gaines Mill in the Seven Days' campaigns of 1862. Most recently, serving in Albert Jenkins's brigade, its members had fought valiantly at Cloyd's Mountain and afterward, encamped near Christiansburg on the east side of the New River.

Commanding the regiment was forty-one-year-old Colonel Beuhring H. Jones, from Kanawha County, (West) Virginia. Before the war, he had practiced law in Fayette County before migrating to Missouri. At the outbreak of the Civil War he resided in Greenbrier County, West Virginia. He commanded the Sixtieth Virginia Infantry, also known as the Wise Legion, from its origin. In the about-to-be-organized Army of the Valley District, B.H. Jones would command the First Brigade, and the Sixtieth Virginia Infantry would serve as the core unit.

Unimpeded by the destruction of the New River Bridge, the regiment marched to Christiansburg, where it boarded the train along with the Lewisburg Battery of Captain Thomas A. Bryan. Approximately 1,300 personnel and six cannons boarded the cars, which arrived in Lynchburg via Salem on the evening of June 1 and joined Jones's units from Glade Spring and Saltville[14] All would then ride the rails from Lynchburg to Charlottesville and then on to Staunton.

Thirty-Sixth Regiment, Virginia Infantry

The Thirty-Sixth Regiment, Virginia Infantry (not to be confused with the Thirty-Sixth, Virginia Cavalry, W.E. Jones Brigade in Southwest Virginia), had recently fought at Cloyd's Mountain. John C. McCausland had commanded this regiment from its beginning until he was promoted to brigadier general to replace the deceased Albert Jenkins. The veteran unit had participated in multiple engagements and was one of the few regiments to escape capture at Fort Donelson in 1862. Lieutenant Colonel William Estill Fife, a Charleston, (West) Virginia, native and Virginia Military Institute graduate, commanded the unit.[15]

With the call to come to the Shenandoah Valley, the unit was detached to join Grumble Jones's new army. Unimpeded by the loss of the New River bridge, the members took rail transportation from Christiansburg to Salem, where it connected to join Jones at Lynchburg. Like the others, they would take the same rail route through Charlottesville and on to Staunton.

Forty-Fifth Battalion, Virginia Infantry

The Forty-Fifth Battalion, Virginia Infantry (not to be confused with the Forty-Fifth Regiment, Virginia Infantry), was a 150-man unit composed mostly of mountaineers from Logan and Wyoming County, West Virginia. The battalion had been formed principally from members of the First Cavalry Regiment, Virginia State Line. The original roster included sixteen Hatfields and nine McCoys, whose postwar family feud earned them lasting infamy in American folklore.[16] Lieutenant Colonel Henry Beckley commanded the unit that had seen recent action at Cloyd's Mountain. Positioned east of the New River bridge and therefore unimpeded by its destruction, the unit marched to Central Depot, boarded the train to Salem, and reconnected to Lynchburg. Like all the other units, they would make their way through Charlottesville and on to Staunton.

Vaughn's Brigade

On May 29 at Bristol, Brigadier General John C. Vaughn received emergency orders from Grumble Jones to gather all available forces and hurry to Staunton.[17] Vaughn gathered elements of the First Tennessee Cavalry, the Third Tennessee Mounted Infantry, the Thirty-Ninth Tennessee Mounted Infantry, the Forty-Third Tennessee Mounted Infantry, the Fifty-Ninth Tennessee Mounted Infantry, the Twelfth Tennessee Cavalry, the Sixteenth Tennessee Cavalry, the Sixteenth Georgia Cavalry, the Sixtieth Tennessee Infantry, the Sixty-First Tennessee Infantry, and the Sixty-Second Tennessee Infantry.[18] Many of these units were ultimately consolidated.

General Vaughn was a Mexican War veteran and a merchant before the Civil War. He had been a delegate to the 1860 Democratic convention in Charleston, South Carolina, and was present during the bombardment of Fort Sumter. He commanded a regiment at First Bull Run. As a secessionist in pro–Union East Tennessee, his family endured personal suffering throughout the conflict. Appointed to brigadier general in the fall of 1862, he commanded a brigade at Vicksburg, where he surrendered and was exchanged. He raised a cavalry brigade in East Tennessee, served with Grumble Jones in Ransom's Division, and joined Longstreet in the unsuccessful siege of Knoxville.

Vaughn would be second in command to Jones in the about-to-be-formed Army of the Valley District. General Ransom's recent inspection report described Vaughn's Brigade as being "in deplorable condition," which he attributed to its commander. Ransom further depicted the unit as "almost a band of marauders," their arms, equipment, and clothing "all poor."[19] Declaring that Vaughn had "no idea of discipline," Ransom recommended reassigning the brigadier to an infantry division "under a strict officer."[20] Finally, Ransom suggested disbanding Vaughn's brigade altogether and consolidating the units into other brigades. Before this came to pass, the crisis in the Shenandoah Valley erupted and saved the status quo. The calling of Vaughn's Brigade to the valley reflects the level of desperation behind it.

Vaughn's cavalry members dismounted and boarded the Virginia-Tennessee Railroad at Bristol, taking the same routes and confronting the same obstacles as Jones, the Thomas Legion, and the Brewer Battalion did. Vaughn's Brigade rode to the destroyed New River bridge, exited the rail cars, forded the river, and marched to Central Depot to board a second train, which transported them to Salem. After connecting to Lynchburg, they rode the rails to Charlottesville and Staunton. Most members of Vaughn's Brigade would fight the coming battle as infantry.[21] At about half strength, this contingency would add a thousand men to the Army of the Valley District.[22]

The W.E. Jones Brigade of Southwest Virginia

None of the estimated 1,100 troops on hand forming the W.E. Jones Brigade, Department of East Tennessee and Southwest Virginia, boarded the trains heading for Staunton via Lynchburg. Instead, they marched toward Staunton on their mounts at a much slower pace. Departing from their scattered encampments in Southwest Virginia on May 25 it took them twelve days to reach the area, and they were no closer than Buchanan in Botetourt County by the time the Battle of Piedmont concluded.[23] Theory suggests that Jones wanted to allow the unit the option to reverse course in case Federal forces advanced against the saltworks or the lead mines.[24] Although not engaged in the Battle of Piedmont, the former W.E. Jones Brigade of East Tennessee and Southwest Virginia would play a significant role in its aftermath.

Lynchburg and Staunton

By June 1 Jones, his staff, and the accompanying units from Southwest Virginia arrived in Lynchburg, where he received the following telegram from Imboden:

General:
This will be handed to you by gen'l means of Shenandoah who goes to meet you at my request and will state to you fully the condition of affairs in the Valley. I am holding out every inducement I can to Hunter to follow me up as far as Mount Crawford. If he does not, and you can get him "on a run," we can ruin him. He is playing devilish cautious, however, and may not take the bait. Col. [William L.] Jackson telegraphed me last night that the enemy in Greenbrier was moving, he believed in the direction of Staunton. If I can, with North River in my front, hold Hunter, till you thrash Crook and Averell, we can pay our respects to Hunter.

Yours Respectfully,
J.D. Imboden
Brig. General[25]

Jones and his accompanying forces remained in Lynchburg for three days, during which time other units traveling by rail converged. Jones canvassed the area hospitals, guard outposts, and other sources to impress able-bodied men into the service of his newly formed army. On the night of June 2, Jones telegraphed Imboden that he would arrive at Staunton within twenty-four hours.[26]

Three separate trains transported the troops from Lynchburg to Charlottesville, where three separate trains connected all to their final destination at Staunton. A collective 3,800 arrived in Staunton by June 3. While Jones's mass mobilization effort was in progress, covering an average distance of 250 miles, Hunter's Army of the Shenandoah had advanced only twenty-five miles, from New Market to the outskirts of Harrisonburg, arriving on June 2. Jones and his scattered units reached Staunton well ahead of Hunter, whose army occupied Harrisonburg.

Hunter's scouts reported Imboden's presence just across the North River at Mount Crawford. Unaware that Jones would bring reinforcements, they inaccurately estimated the Confederate strength at 2,500. Assuming they outnumbered their opponents by a three-to-one margin, Hunter's forces were poised to strike.

Mount Crawford

From Staunton, Jones led his 3,800 troops on an eighteen-mile night march and arrived at Imboden's Mount Crawford headquarters on the morning of June 4.[27] Having the prior commission, Jones assumed overall command.

Mount Crawford afforded the outnumbered Southerners a strategic advantage. Situated on high ground in the most direct path up the Shenandoah Valley, the natural defenses included the rain-swollen North River as a barrier. In all previous major valley campaigns, the undersized Southern forces had utilized the natural defenses to their advantage and had always prevailed. However, Imboden's confidence gave way to apprehension when he inspected the troops Jones brought with him. Detailing his account of the battle two decades later, Imboden wrote:

> To my dismay, I learned from officers in command of the detachments arriving that no large organized body of troops was on its way to join me except Vaughn's small Tennessee brigade of cavalry. Jones had cleaned out the hospitals from Lynchburg to Bristol of convalescents, and gathered them together with depot guards along the railroad, aggregating all told less than 2,200 men. The largest organization was not more than a battalion, not a single complete regiment was coming on, except, as stated, Vaughn's brigade of about 800 men. Mostly they were companies and parts of companies.[28]

Further elaborating on his disappointment, Imboden added:

> Perhaps at no time during the war were such heterogeneous materials brought together so suddenly and compacted into harmonious and obedient bodies of troops. I have often thought this incident proved most strikingly the devoted patriotism of our Confederate soldiers. Here, without acquaintance with each other, in the face of the enemy, and a desperate battle impending at any moment with overwhelming odds, some 2,200 men and officers, without a murmur of objection, accepted the situation and with alacrity stepped into the ranks and "touched elbows" with strangers and obeyed orders from, to them, unknown and unfamiliar lips.[29]

Charles T. O'Ferrall seconded Imboden's assessments. The executive officer of Colonel Robert White's Twenty-Third Virginia Cavalry wrote, "He [Jones] brought with him Vaughn's Tennessee Brigade, and some odds and ends of different regiments, which had been hastily gathered together, and a regiment of some reserves or home guards."[30] Imboden's and O'Ferrall's evaluations deserve credence in part, but Jones also brought proven veterans. Their physical appearance as underfed, poorly clothed, and inadequately equipped did not accurately reflect their fighting capabilities. Imboden emphasized their underdog status as a means of explaining the ultimate defeat.

Reserves

Area residents also answered Imboden's call. Two improvised regiments of reserves led by Colonel Kenton Harper and Colonel William H. Harman joined forces with Jones. Both Harper and Harman were veterans of the Mexican War and distinguished citizens of Staunton.[31] William H. Harman served in Jackson's Shenandoah Valley Campaign and was the brother of Asher Waterman Harman, former commander of the Twelfth Virginia Cavalry in the W.E. Jones Brigade, Army of Northern Virginia.

Another notable officer of the reserves was Lieutenant Monroe Blue, a cousin to Lieutenant John Blue of the Sixth Virginia Cavalry. The Hampshire County (West) Virginia, native had already earned a reputation for daring. Arrested as a spy in Martinsburg in May of 1863, he was incarcerated at Johnson's Island, Ohio.[32] On February 9, 1864, he and a contingency of fellow prisoners were being transported by rail to Point Lookout, Maryland. Near Cumberland he leaped from a moving transport car and landed on an embankment of snow. After he wandered for two days, Southern sympathizers provided him sanctuary, and he eventually joined a group of his former unit on furlough. He accompanied the unit to the Shenandoah Valley and participated in Breckenridge's victory at New Market.[33] Following the battle, he came to Staunton, joined Harper's Reserves, and was appointed the commander of Company K.[34]

Organization of the Confederate States Army of the Valley District

The forces from Southwest Virginia, East Tennessee, General Imboden's Brigade, and the local reserves gathered at Mount Crawford, where Jones organized the Army of the Valley District as follows:

CS Army of the Valley District
Commanding: Brigadier General William E. Jones

First Brigade
Commanding: Colonel Beuhring H. Jones
60th Regiment, Virginia Infantry, commanded by Captain James W. Johnston
36th Regiment, Virginia Infantry, commanded by Lieutenant Colonel William E. Fife
45th Battalion, Virginia Infantry, commanded by Lieutenant Colonel Henry Beckley
Lewisburg Battery, commanded by Captain Thomas A. Bryan
Estimated Combined Strength: 1,300[35]

Second Brigade
Commanding: Colonel William Henry Browne

Thomas Legion, commanded by Lieutenant Colonel James Love, Jr.
45th Regiment, Virginia Infantry, commanded by Lieutenant Colonel Alexander Davis
Brewer's Battalion, commanded by Major Richard Henry Brewer
Estimated Strength: 1,500[36]

Vaughn's Brigade
Commanding: Brigadier General John C. Vaughn
1st Tennessee, commanded by Colonel James Carter
39th Tennessee, commanded by Major Robert McFarland
43rd Tennessee, commanded by Colonel James W. Gillespie
59th Tennessee, commanded by Colonel William L. Eakin
12th Tennessee Battalion, commanded by Major George W. Day
Estimated Strength: 1,000[37]

Imboden's Brigade
Commanding: Brigadier General John D. Imboden
18th Virginia Cavalry, commanded by Colonel George W. Imboden
23rd Virginia Cavalry, commanded by Colonel Robert White
Captain Sturgess Davis's Maryland Battalion
Captain John H. McClanahan's Battery
Estimated Strength: 1,200[38]

Reserves
Colonel Kenten Harper's Augusta and Rockbridge Reserves
Colonel William H. Harman's Augusta Reserves
Captain George's Rockingham Reserves
Captain H.B. Harnsberger's Rockingham Reserves
Captain James C. Marquis's Augusta Battery
Estimated Strength: 600[39]

The Confederate States Army of the Valley District had an estimated combined strength of 5,600 troops and sixteen cannons. They would be confronting David Hunter's Army of the Shenandoah with 7,766 troops and twenty-four cannons.[40] Although they would be facing a force of greater size and firepower, the natural fortifications of Mount Crawford would level the odds.

To ascertain Hunter's movements, Imboden dispatched his Eighteenth Virginia Cavalry Regiment on a scouting mission beyond the North River. They would discover that matters were not going according to plan. Hunter was not committing to a straight-line advance; he was executing a major flanking maneuver to the east.

Hunter Changes Course

A native of Martinsburg and a former landscape artist familiar with the topography of the Shenandoah Valley, Hunter's chief of staff, Colonel David H. Strother, persuaded his commander to change course. Strother recognized that an undersized force could utilize the natural fortifications of Mount Crawford to present a formidable opposition. Strother suggested that by diverting eastward, Hunter's army could avoid a costly direct frontal assault, leaving an open path to Waynesboro, Charlottesville, and Lynchburg. Isolating the supply center at Staunton would be just as effective as its capture or destruction and could demoralize the enemy without a fight.[41]

On the morning of June 4, Hunter diverted his army in a southeasterly direction toward Port Republic undetected.[42] As a diversion, he detached a cavalry unit to feign a march on Staunton. Initially, the deception succeeded, as Imboden's advance scouts perceived it as a frontal assault. Although it was a successful diversion, Hunter's overall maneuver did not go according to plan. To reach Waynesboro required fording the rain-swollen North River. In a tactical error, Hunter had detached his chief engineer on the cavalry demonstration to deceive the Confederates. No other members of Hunter's engineering staff knew how to assemble the canvass pontoons, and their awkward attempt took time.[43] Futility led to frustration. An impatient bugler from the Fifteenth New York Cavalry tried to ford the rising river and drowned.[44]

Hunter's engineers could not complete the construction of the pontoon bridge until late in the evening. Venting their frustration, they torched a nearby woolen factory. Aborting the advance on Waynesboro, Hunter directed his force to bivouac and resumed the march the following morning with a flanking maneuver back toward Staunton.[45]

Mount Crawford Rendered Obsolete

Imboden's scouts reported the disquieting intelligence that Hunter's army was not advancing directly up the valley but deploying a flanking maneuver via Port Republic. Hunter could then march on Staunton from either the south or east. Jones and Imboden had to alter their defensive strategy.

Cognizant of Imboden's familiarity with the region, Jones looked to his subordinate for guidance. Imboden sketched a map detailing the topographical features.[46] He recommended that the CS Army of the Valley District establish new defensive fortifications on Mowery's Hill, situated on the farm of George W. Mowery, eight miles northeast of Staunton and three miles south of New Hope. Similar to Mount Crawford, the high ground of Mowery's Hill provided a strategic advantage to an undersized force. Decades later, Imboden would write, "When he [Jones] fully understood me, he, without hesitation, concurred in my views."[47] Imboden proposed that he would position his brigade at Hunter's front to delay the Federal advance, allowing Jones and Vaughn time to occupy Mowery's Hill and establish defenses. Imboden added, "All this was agreed to, and at his request, I furnished him guides from the Augusta reserves."[48]

About three o'clock on the afternoon of June 4 Jones and Imboden evacuated Mount Crawford, marching their brigades southward on the Valley Pike a few miles before parting ways. As planned, Jones and the main body of the CS Army of the Valley District continued southward toward Mowery's Hill. Imboden led his detached brigade on an advanced scouting mission eastward to Mount Meridian. That evening, Jones and his forces camped just north of Mount Sidney to resume their southward march on the following morning. A mounted courier arrived bearing a telegram from General Lee informing Jones that no reinforcements would come to the valley for several days, and within that time frame Crook's Army of the Kanawha District would unite with Hunter.[49] Lee urged Jones to engage Hunter's forces before they could unite with Crook's.[50] Grumble stuffed the correspondence into his pocket without revealing the contents.[51]

Surmising that time was not on his side, Jones did not have the luxury of waiting

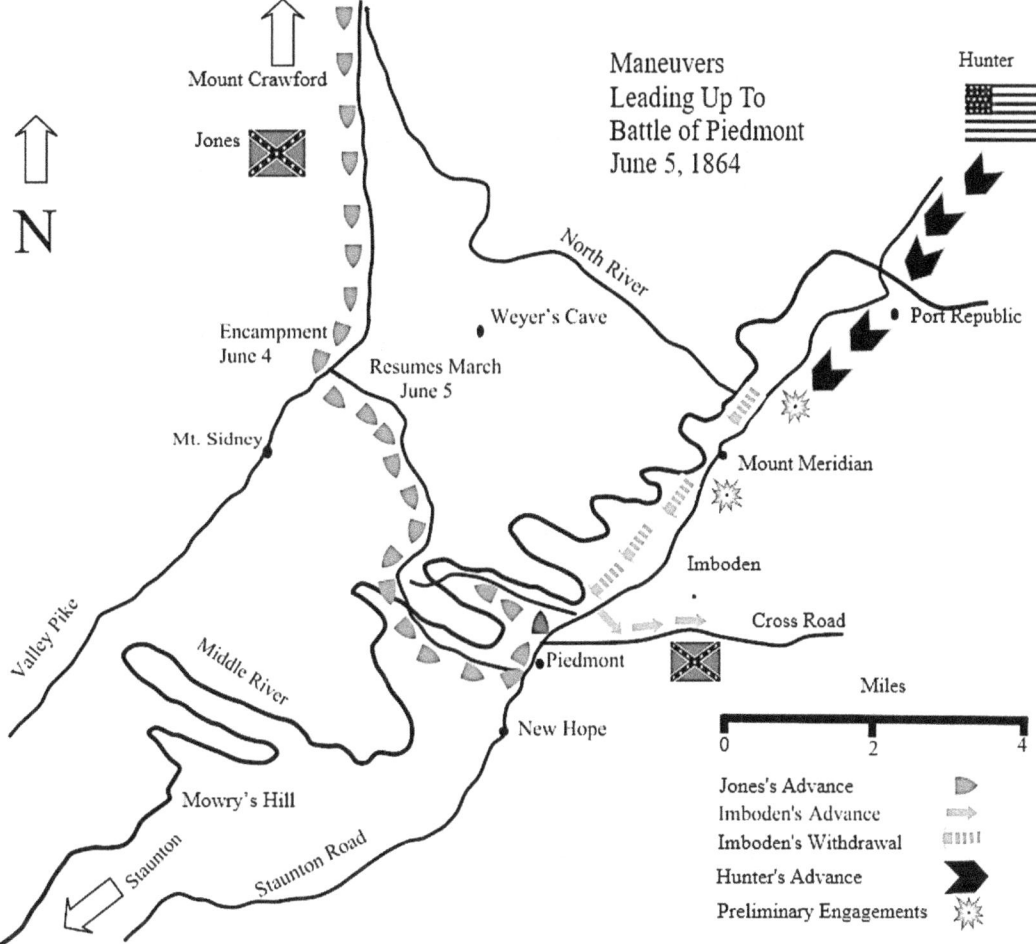

Maneuvers to Piedmont (sketch by author, 2016).

for Hunter to attack. Hunter held numerical superiority with his Army of the Shenandoah alone. Hunter had the option to delay battle, bypass Jones's stationary defenses at Mowerey's Hill, await the arrival of Crook's reinforcements, and then march on Staunton with an even more formidable force.[52] The planned strategy of a defensive position on Mowerey's Hill was now obsolete. Jones had to take the offensive by maneuvering his army outward and engage Hunter wherever he might find him.

Out of touch, Jones could not inform Imboden of his sudden change in plans. In preparations for the morning march, Jones and his forces bivouacked near Mount Sidney in the rain without shelter, blankets, or rations.[53] It would be the last night of his life.

Jones's Final March: June 5, 1864

Early on the morning of June 5 Jones and his three brigades broke camp near Mount Sidney and marched in an eastwardly direction. After fording the Middle River they arrived at the outskirts of the village of Piedmont, situated thirteen miles east of Staunton, a mile north of New Hope, and about nine miles south of Port Republic. Piedmont was a hamlet consisting of about a dozen houses along Staunton Road (also called East Road), which connected New Hope and Port Republic. Prosperous farms surrounded the area marked by rolling hills along with contrasting thick forest and open fields. The winding Middle River, with its distinctive curves and steep embankments, formed the western boundary. Four miles north of Piedmont at Mount Meridian, Imboden did not anticipate Jones's maneuver. He assumed that Jones would act according to their previously derived plan and march his column southward to establish defenses on Mowery's Hill.

From Port Republic, Hunter had commenced on his march toward Staunton with the intent of delaying battle until he could unite with Crook's army coming from West Virginia. Hunter knew of Imboden's token resistance at Mount Meridian but was unaware that Jones and his forces were in the area. The Battle of Piedmont was about to begin.

20

The Battle of Piedmont—June 5, 1864

Jones and his three brigades arrived at the village of Piedmont during a lull in the battle already in progress. Although the combat operations had initially engaged four miles away, the action was rapidly approaching the immediate ground Jones was about to occupy.

Earlier that morning, Imboden's Eighteenth Virginia Cavalry embarked on a scouting mission and engaged the leading Federal advance force at Mount Meridian, south of Port Republic. A Federal countercharge routed the regiment, capturing Captain Francis Marion Imboden in the process and sending it on a retreat southward.[1] The Federals continued their pursuit, and General Imboden barely escaped.[2]

Colonel Robert White's Twenty-Third Virginia Cavalry, Captain Sturgess Davis's Maryland Battalion, and Captian John Opie's mounted reserves intervened to check the Federal pursuit momentarily. Imboden's demoralized brigade regrouped at the outskirts of Piedmont and established a *temporary* defensive position.

Feeling that a battery of artillery plus about five hundred infantry would stall the Federal advance, Imboden dispatched a courier to find Jones and request a reinforcement detachment.[3] Before the courier even left Imboden's sight, Jones suddenly appeared on the scene. By coincidence, Jones's forward expedition and Imboden's retreat had arrived at the same location. Jones's presence surprised Imboden, who until that moment had assumed his commanding officer was establishing a defensive position four miles southward at Mowery's Hill. Although baffled, Imboden regained his composure to report the disastrous results of his engagement at Mount Meridian, his estimate regarding the enemy's strength, and suggestions on how to stall its advance.

Jones replied that he already anticipated what Imboden needed and was acting accordingly. He assured Imboden that a battery of Captain John McClanahan's artillery and Major Richard Henry Brewer's dismounted infantry would arrive in minutes. Jones further astonished Imboden by advising that "*all* of his troops" were just behind him by a few hundred yards. Imboden imagined that Jones had been misled by his guides or had simply lost his way to his destination. Jones directed Captain McClanahan to deploy an artillery battery. Brewer's Battalion also moved into position to form a temporary defensive line. Almost two decades later, Imboden wrote for the *Confederate Veteran* in 1883 this account of the dialogue:

Imboden exclaimed, "My God General! You are not going to fight here, and lose all the advantage of position we shall have at Mowery's Hill?"

Jones apparently angrily replied, "Yes! I am going to fight right here, if Hunter advances promptly to the attack. If he don't, I will go over there and attack where he is." Jones then pointed to the Federal position.

Imboden protested, "We have no advantage of ground here, and he out numbers us nearly three to one, & will beat us."

Jones angrily replied, "I don't want any advantage of ground, for I can whip Hunter anywhere!"

Imboden responded, "General! I will not say you cannot whip him here, but I will say, with the knowledge I have of his strength, that if you do, it will be at the expense of a fearful loss of life on our side, and believing we have no right to sacrifice the lives of our men where it is possible to avoid it, as it is now, if you will even yet fall back to Mowery's Hill, I enter my solemn protest against fighting here today."

Jones turned to Imboden and said, "By God sir! I believe I am in command here today!"

Imboden replied, "You are sir! And I now ask your orders and will carry them out as best I can; but if I live, I will see that the responsibility for the day's work is fixed where I think it belongs."[4]

The conversation was interrupted when Lieutenant Carter Berkeley arrived with a two-cannon section of McClanahan's Battery. Berkeley's guns fired on the approaching Union cavalry and drove it back out of range. Imboden recalled that the action seemed to bring a calming effect to Jones, "for he was brave to a fault, and I believe enjoyed the roar of the battle field."[5]

Formation of a Line of Battle

Jones marched two of his two infantry brigades on the Cross Road from the west where it intersected with the Staunton Road, just south of Piedmont. The two brigades then established a line of battle just north of the Cross Road and just west of the Staunton Road.

Jones's legacy would receive criticism for selecting the outskirts of Piedmont as the battlefield. Realistically, he lacked other options, as he had to engage Hunter wherever he found him. The chosen battlefield also had its merits. Although not the high ground Imboden preferred at Mowery's Hill, it provided other natural defenses. To the extreme left (west) of the line of battle was an eastern loop of the Middle River with sixty-foot vertical cliffs aligning the banks and prohibiting an enemy left flanking movement.[6] Rail pasture fences along with the topography of forest and sloping hills provided the defenders some protection and concealment. Unfortunately, some of those features would also serve the opposition.

Major Brewer's battalion and Berkeley's artillery joined to establish an advance temporary defensive line providing Jones the time to organize his main line of battle. To the rear of Brewer and Berkeley, Jones aligned his First and Second Brigade units into a crescent-shaped formation that extended from the Staunton Road to the bluffs of the Middle River.[7] For two hours Brewer's battalion and Berkeley's batteries checked the Union probes. Federal artillery then fired on Berkeley's outnumbered cannons and forced them to draw back. Ultimately, Brewer's battalion withdrew into the main lines of the Second Brigade, but it had bought time for Jones. In the center, Jones's infantry had a wide-open field of fire. Behind his lines was a wooded area that offered cover and concealment.

Grumble approached the First Brigade commander, Colonel Beuhring H. Jones, and directed him to form a line of battle perpendicular to the Staunton Road, with his extreme left extending to the bluffs of the Middle River.[8] Colonel Jones led his brigade, consisting of the Thirty-Sixth Virginia Infantry, the Sixtieth Virginia Infantry, the Forty-Fifth Battalion, Virginia Infantry, and the Lewisburg Battery, through the woods to a clearing in the center and the bend in the river to the left. Colonel Jones formed his line of battle just in front of the wooded area, behind the pasture fence rails, and with a five-hundred-yard open field to their front.[9]

Positioned just to the right of the First Brigade was Colonel Henry Browne's Second Brigade consisting of the Thomas Legion, the Forty-Fifth Virginia Infantry Regiment, and Brewer's Battalion. Browne's Second Brigade manned the far right, extending the lines to the Staunton Road. The "Boy Battery," a group of Augusta County teenage boys serving as reserves and commanded by Captain James C. Marquis, occupied the Staunton Road. To their rear were the reserves commanded by Colonel Kenton Harper and Colonel William Henry Harman. Vaughn's Brigade of Tennessee Regiments, numbering about a thousand and serving as dismounted infantry, were positioned about a quarter of a mile east of the Staunton Road and the Boy Battery's position. Jones intended to keep this group in reserve. To the extreme right, he placed Imboden's Cavalry, which earlier in the day had initiated the battle before falling back. Jones directed Imboden's mounted forces to protect his right (east) flank. Optimistically anticipating a victory, he also intended to deploy Imboden's mounted forces to pursue the Federals in retreat.

Within two hours Jones appeared to have established a secure line of battle extending from the Middle River to the Staunton Road. With the Middle River protecting his left flank and Imboden's cavalry securing the right, Jones's First and Second Infantry brigades were well positioned to confront multiple Federal assaults on the center. Whether intentional or accidental, there was one major flaw in General Jones's design. To the right of the Staunton Road was an unoccupied gap, estimated in length from a quarter of a mile to six hundred yards, between Marquis's Boy Battery and Vaughn's Brigade. This void would factor into the outcome of the battle.

During a lull, Jones and Imboden rode their mounts parallel to the battle lines between the Staunton Road and the Middle River's high east banks. Jones joked to his staff, "Gentlemen, I don't want any of you killed, and I don't want to be killed myself today."[10] While riding up and down the lines to the cheers of the infantry, their spirits were high, and Jones in particular was gleeful. As he passed the ranks that included regulars, old men, and boys, he repeated shouts of encouragement, "Aim low, boys! Aim low, and hit 'em below the belt. And be sure you *see* them before you shoot. Aim low and make every shot tell!"[11]

According to Imboden, Jones's final orders were, "Move your men back. You will find Vaughan dismounted just back of the village. Dismount your men, sending your horses to the rear in the woods, and take position on Vaughan's right. You see that hill over there (pointing toward the round hill), throw out flankers to the foot of that hill, and protect my right flank. Hunter will try to turn my position *there,* and if you can prevent *that,* it is all I shall ask of you. I'll attend to the rest of the field."[12] Imboden responded with a final salute and promised to comply with the orders. It was the last time he ever saw General Jones. Both Imboden and Vaughn would contend that Jones's specific orders granted no discretion.

Jones took a position to the rear of the Thomas Legion's right flank, just west of the Staunton Road and on the crest of an elevated plateau that afforded a view of the battlefield.

Battle Resumes

On the Confederate left, Colonel B.H. Jones's First Brigade successfully repulsed two frontal assaults, pinning down the Federal forces. Private Lynch of the Eighteenth Connecticut Infantry described close calls. The intense firing caused some of his comrades to fall, blew the stock off of his musket, and pierced a tin cup hanging from his haversack.[13] The First Brigade then received two hours of artillery bombardment of grape and canister from DuPont's battery. Artillery shells that failed to make direct hits struck the fence rails and shattered trees. Splintering fragments of wood injured many Confederates who escaped harm by direct shrapnel. To Colonel B.H. Jones's surprise, he received reinforcements from Vaughn's Tennessee Brigade, using the woods as cover. He questioned the necessity of the maneuver and surmised they had misunderstood an order.[14] With the artillery bombardment, Vaughn's reinforcements merely entered harm's way and suffered significant casualties.

Even at this advanced stage of the battle, Hunter remained clueless regarding the strength of his opponent. Assuming that he was merely facing Imboden's cavalry brigade and a group of unorganized reserves, he ordered a series of frontal assaults that served only as costly probing missions. DuPont's batteries maintained pressure by firing a barrage of artillery shells into the Confederate left wing. DuPont then directed his fire on the Confederate right, particularly in the Marquis Boy Battery, killing six, wounding one, and forcing their withdrawal.[15] This measure widened the gap between the Second Brigade and Vaughn's Brigade.

After departing from Jones, General Imboden rode toward the extreme right to join his brigade manning the eastern flanks. As he passed through the village of Piedmont, he observed the main body of Vaughn's Brigade manning their position as reserves. Realizing that he had ridden through an unoccupied gap up to six hundred yards wide, Imboden immediately recognized "a most dangerous and, as the result showed, [a] fatal mistake in the formation of our lines."[16]

The Federals, however, remained unaware of the void and therefore failed to exploit it. All points indicated that Jones was going to prevail. Observing the Federal position from a distance, Major William W. Stringfield of the Thomas Legion concluded that Hunter was about to give up. Disheartened by the many repulses, Hunter directed his teamsters to reverse the course of the supply wagons in preparation for a retreat.[17]

Although at least four of his assaults had failed, the most recent one had provided Hunter with knowledge regarding the broad gap between Jones's infantry brigades in the center and Vaughan's left flank.[18] The observation marked the turning point in the battle. In a final measure, Hunter called for one more advance specifically targeting the unoccupied gap. Federal infantry used the depressions in the landscape to conceal their movements and maneuvered undetected.

Federals Breach the Gap

While manning the far right, Imboden and his standing cavalry brigade observed the Federal maneuvers invisible to Jones. Imboden later admitted that he and Vaughan could have checked the last enemy flanking movement, and *if* they had engaged, they would have prevailed. Both brigadier generals, however, stood firm that Jones's specific orders granted no such discretion. Vaughn's men pleaded for permission to advance upon or fire into the Federal mass, but their targets were out of range. Allegedly Jones finally dispatched couriers to Vaughn and Imboden to charge into the horde up to half a mile away.[19] If the couriers arrived at all it was too late.[20] In sheer frustration, the two cavalry brigades helplessly stood by as spectators to observe the melee.[21] The collective 1,600 to 1,800 forces under Imboden and Vaughn never fired a shot.

From behind the Thomas Legion, Jones could see that his left flank was secure. The estimated six-hundred-yard gap between the Thomas Legion and Vaughn's dismounted cavalry, however, ultimately aroused his attention. He dispatched a courier to Colonel Jones, directing him to detach half of his command to fill the gap.[22] Colonel Jones responded accordingly and directed Vaughn's reinforcements to reverse course and join in filling the gap, but they would not arrive in time to prevent disaster.

Colonel Joseph Thoburn's Brigade, consisting of the Twelfth West Virginia, the Fifty-Fourth Pennsylvania, the Thirty-Fourth Massachusetts, and the Fourteenth Pennsylvania, stormed the gap. Riding his horse between the lines, Jones comprehended the gravity of the situation and called out to the Thomas Legion, "Brave Carolinians, I'll bring you help!"[23] He quickly returned to the scene with the Thirty-Sixth and Sixtieth regiments, but it was too little and too late. Colonel Kenton Harper's reserves also charged in from the south in a futile attempt to repel the assaults, which were now spreading along all the lines.

The scene of Jones's final moments probably resembled some artists' renditions of Custer's Last Stand at Little Big Horn. Colonel Jacob M. Campbell of the Fifty-Fourth Pennsylvania Regiment recalled, "Here for a short time a most desperate struggle took place, bayonets and clubbed guns were used on both sides, and many hand to hand encounters took place."[24] In a coordinated action the Union infantrymen charged Brewer's right flank. Jones rode up and down his battle lines encouraging his forces, but their momentum was failing. Major Brewer fell mortally wounded, and his leaderless troops fled. Jones rode into their midst and shouted for an officer to take command and reverse the tide.[25]

Lieutenant Monroe Blue of Harper's Augusta and Rockbridge reserves answered Jones's plea. He dismounted from his horse and shouted, "General, I will lead them! Boys, follow me, and we will soon have them on the run!" Like Lewis Armistead during Pickett's Charge, Blue placed his hat on his saber, dashed forward, and led Brewer's troopers back into the fight.[26] Blue shouted, "New Market! New Market! Remember New Market!"[27] Numbers of Brewer's troops joined in the chorus to rally their comrades and taunt their foes.

Blue's heroics drew the attention of an officer with the Fifty-Fourth Pennsylvania who, upon observing the Confederates reorganize, shouted to his troops, "Boys, shoot that officer before he starts a rally!" The Fifty-Fourth Pennsylvania fired a volley into Blue's advancing troops, disrupting their formation. Private Thomas Evans claimed to have fired the shot that struck Blue in the neck.[28] Blue spun around, dropped his sword, and fell dead on the field. The Thirty-Fourth Massachusetts and the Fourteenth Pennsylvania then fired into Blue's reserves. Those who were not killed or wounded lost their composure and fled. All hope of rallying Brewer's Battalion died with Monroe Blue.[29]

Observing his lines collapse, Jones galloped forward in a last-gasp attempt to rally

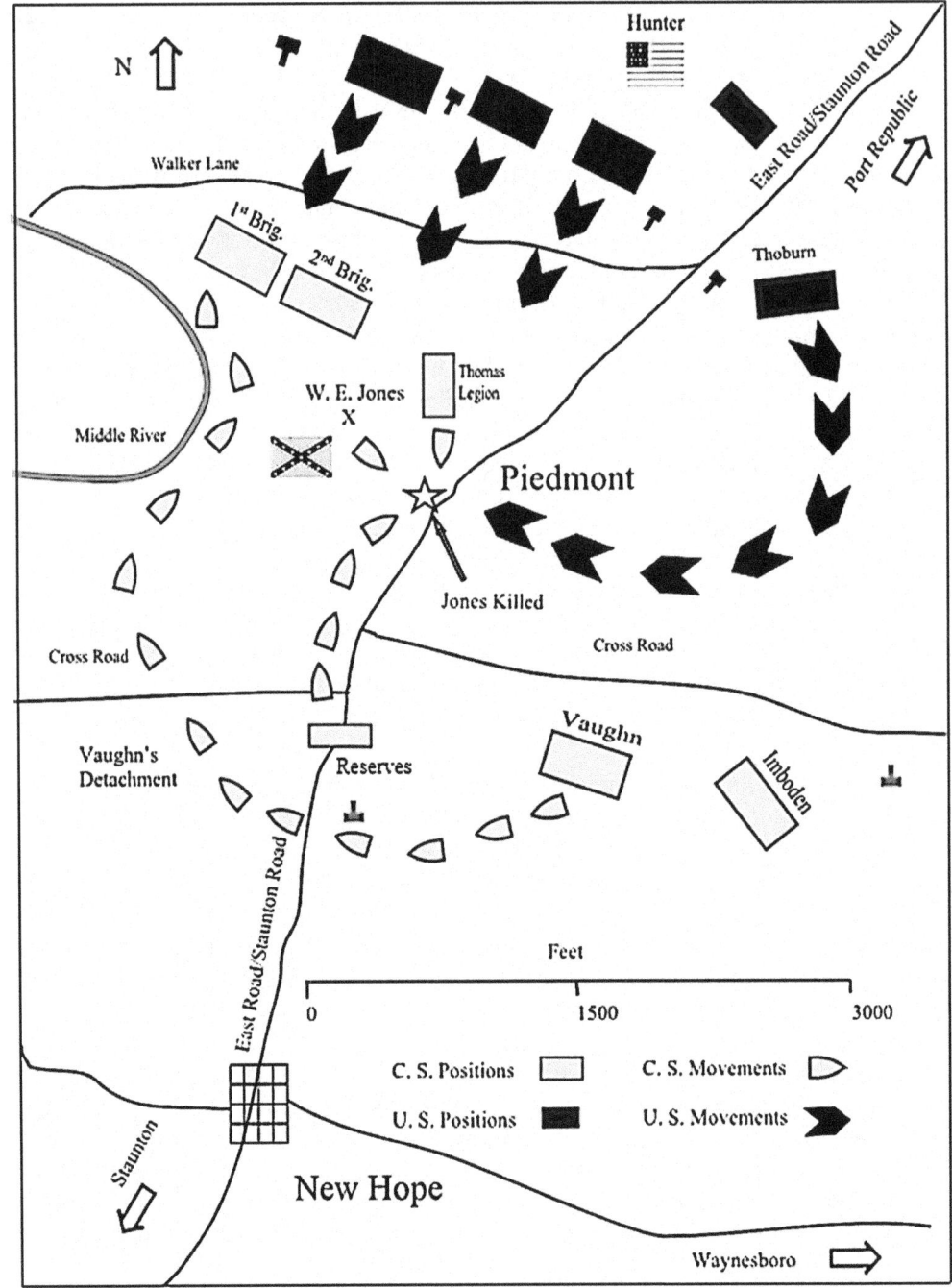

Battle of Piedmont (sketch by author, 2016).

his disintegrating army. Mounted high on horseback over the level of the infantrymen and shouting, he drew the attention of the standing members of the Fourteenth Pennsylvania, the Thirty-Fourth Massachusetts, and the Fifty-Fourth Pennsylvania. The three regiments raised their muskets and fired at Jones and his followers. A round of ammunition struck Jones in the center of his forehead, killing him instantly.

Jones's adjutant, Captain Walter K. Martin, added to the panic by wailing, "General

Jones is killed! We have no leader now!"[30] Captain Robert Doyle, a retired lieutenant colonel, tried to resume the rally, but he was shot down and died as well.[31]

Although General Jones's death was a clear indication as to the eventual outcome, the CS Army of the Valley District continued to fight for basic survival. Without capitulating, most of the troops fought their way out to avoid capture. There were only two open routes of retreat: the Staunton Road southward to New Hope or to ford the Middle River to the west. Vaughn's and Imboden's brigades had a headstart, taking the Staunton Road southward. Vaughn's Twelfth Tennessee, McClanahan's artillery battery, and the Thomas Legion checked the Federal cavalry pursuit.

The forces on the left wing had a greater challenge. Their only avenue of escape was to flee westward into the Middle River. The sixty-foot bluffs and the flowing river that had protected them from a flanking action suddenly obstructed their retreat. Significant numbers, however, fought until the last moment before jumping down into the river. From the top of the bluffs, Federal infantry fired down and killed as many as ninety men.[32] In contrast to the cruelty, some Federals filled their canteens and comforted the wounded.

The Battle of Piedmont had lasted ten hours, resulting in more casualties than Jackson's two-month-long Shenandoah Valley Campaign of 1862, which involved three times as many troops engaged.[33] Proportionally, it was one of the bloodiest battles in the war. With its conclusion, a Union army stood as the undisputed victor in the upper Shenandoah Valley for the first time.

21

Piedmont Aftermath

The Battle of Piedmont settled into as a mop-up operation for the victors. The Southerners attempted to escape, the largest contingency retreating well south of New Hope and heading eastward toward Rockfish Gap. The Federals gathered prisoners and tended to the wounded on both sides. A dying Confederate infantryman declared that before the battle, General Jones informed his unit that the Yankees would kill any surrendering Rebel.[1]

Some Federals sought commemorative relics by stripping deceased Confederate officers of buttons and equipment. Private Thomas Evans of the Fifty-Fourth Pennsylvania returned to the location where he shot Lieutenant Monroe Blue, whose saber would be an attractive souvenir. Upon arrival, he found that others had beaten him to the prize. He observed his regimental commander, Colonel Jacob M. Campbell, grieving over Blue's body. Although they were enemies, Colonel Campbell had befriended Blue's family while his unit was garrisoned in Hampshire County, West Virginia.[2]

A nearby farmhouse was converted to a field hospital. Notable Confederate officers Colonel William Henry Browne and Major Richard Henry Brewer were among the wounded prisoners of war. Colonel Browne seemed to have only minor wounds when he received a visit from former West Point associate, Captain Henry Algernon DuPont. Anticipating that his past acquaintance would transfer to a prisoner of war camp, DuPont tendered Browne the last ten dollars in his immediate possession and wished him well. To his surprise, Browne died of his wounds a short time later.[3] Major Brewer had received a musket ball through one of his lungs, and after lingering under the care of captured Confederate surgeons for two weeks, he died on June 20.[4]

From Staunton on the evening of June 5, Colonel Edwin G. Lee sent the following report to his cousin and commander of the Army of Northern Virginia:

> We have been pretty badly whipped. General W.E. Jones killed. General Vaughn in command. Falling back toward Fishersville. He asks that you hurry the reinforcements promptly. I fear Staunton will go.[5]

Staunton would fall within twenty-four hours. Anticipating the calamity, Edwin G. Lee made preparations to evacuate.

The Body of Jones

Dozens of Federals claimed to have fired the shot that killed General Jones, prompting a veteran to quip, "If every boy who later claimed to have shot him had put a bullet in him, why he would have been so heavy it would have taken a four horse team to have moved his body off the battlefield."⁶ Jones's corpse was in Federal hands. Colonel David Strother recorded in his diary:

> At three p.m., the enemy were routed and in full retreat. The cavalry came in with the report that the Rebel General Jones was killed and brought some papers and small articles taken from his body to prove the statement. The General [Hunter] desired me to go down and verify it beyond a doubt. I found a crowd around a body coarsely clothed in a dirty grey suit without any military trappings or insignia about it. He had a pair of fine military boots well worn and fine woolen underclothes perfectly clean and new. His hands were small and white, and his features, high white forehead, brown beard, and long hair indicated the gentleman was a man of the upper class. I concluded that this was truly the body of the General. Just then, four Rebel prisoners came up with a stretcher to carry the body to burial under the orders of the provost marshal. I asked each of these men if they recognized the body. They said, "Yes, that is the body of our commander, General William E. Jones."
>
> Meanwhile, (Major Theodore F.) Lang visited his pockets and got some curious papers from it. One contained a memorandum in figures giving a summation of his forces at seven thousand men and sixteen guns. The other was a letter to General Jones from General Imboden.⁷

Among the Confederates captured was Colonel Beuhring H. Jones, commander of the First Brigade. While under Federal guard, he wrote what he knew about Grumble's death and inserted some poetic verse:

> Our gallant Gen. (Wm. E. Jones) was killed a short distance in the rear of the 2nd Brigade in the woods. I have not the means of ascertaining the precise moment of his death. It was certainly near the termination of the battle and probably while anxiously waiting [for] the arrival of the troops ordered from the left, with the intention of putting them in position to oppose the expected flank movement of the enemy. There is melancholy satisfaction of believing that the fatal missile found our lamented Chieftain while his countenance was yet flushed with the cheering anticipation of victory for:
>
>> T'were sad to think that in his dying hour
>> He saw confusion and the beaten rout
>> Saw clouds upon his country's banner lower
>> And heard the hated Northmen's triumphant shout
>
> A more gallant soldier, or more ardent & inflexible patriot, never laid his life, a voluntary sacrifice upon the alter [sic] of liberty. Learning after the battle had ended, that a body had been found in the woods on the battle field, supposed to be that of Gen. Jones, I sent a man guarded by Yankees to identify it. It proved to be that of Gen. Jones and was decently interred in a garden a few hundred yards from the battlefield.⁸

Private Charles H. Lynch of the Eighteenth Connecticut observed Grumble's body and commented, "I saw the dead commander lying on the field, he having been shot through the forehead. I saw the flag of truce when the Confederates came for the body. I spoke to the escort, they telling me who the dead general was."⁹

Hunter's forces camped on the battlefield and celebrated their triumph. The veterans of New Market had redeemed themselves and had verily "wiped out the disgrace" of that earlier defeat.¹⁰ For the first time in three years of war, the Federals had prevailed in a full-fledged campaign in the upper Shenandoah Valley. Hunter faced no resistance during his mission to disrupt the railway and communication centers at Staunton. The path seemed equally clear all the way to the primary railroad center at Lynchburg.

Hunter reported the Confederate losses at over a thousand prisoners including sixty officers in addition to more than six hundred killed or wounded. Those figures appear to be reasonable estimates. Exaggerating, he alleged that the Confederates lost an equal amount by desertion following the battle. He reported his own losses at five hundred killed or wounded.[11] For Hunter to admit that estimate was significant, "in view of his proneness to minimize" reports of his casualties.[12] Historians have concluded that Hunter's forces sustained losses estimated at 150 dead, 650 wounded, and 75 missing.[13]

Word of Hunter's victory at Piedmont was welcomed by the Lincoln administration, which two days earlier had received notice of a calamity 130 miles to the east at Cold Harbor. Lee's Army of Northern Virginia had repulsed Grant's ill-advised frontal assault, resulting in 7,000 Federal losses.

Incident at Mowery's Hill

Command of the CS Army of the Valley District passed to Brigadier General John C. Vaughn, who shifted to a strategy of orderly withdrawal. The Southerners retreated through New Hope and established a temporary encampment at Fishersville. Before continuing their escape eastward through Rockfish Gap, Vaughn deployed a bloodless delaying tactic. On the morning of June 6 he directed Lieutenant Colonel Charles T. O'Ferrall to approach the Federal pickets under a flag of truce, request a conference with General Hunter, and deliver his written request for the bodies of General Jones and other deceased officers. Vaughn's underlying objective was to prompt administrative delays on the part of Hunter and stall his potential pursuit.[14]

O'Ferrall set out with two ambulances and a three-man squad and met a detachment from the Twenty-First New York Cavalry commanded by Major Charles Otis at Mowery's Hill. O'Ferrall asked to deliver the written communication directly to Hunter, who was about four miles north at Piedmont.[15] Major Otis dispatched a mounted courier to deliver the message, and while waiting for his return engaged in a frank conversation with O'Ferrall regarding the battle of the previous day. O'Ferrall recalled that Otis, acting neither exultant nor boastful, conceded "all of Hunter's front[al] attacks had been badly worsted, and that Hunter was preparing to withdraw and retire when he learned of the gap in our lines; that he then determined, to find the movement which I have described, and fortunately for them it was successful, and won the fight for them; that its success was a matter of wonderment with him and the Federal officers who knew of the position and proximity of our cavalry."[16]

During the ninety-minute wait for the courier to return, an awkward moment occurred when a civilian horseback rider approached. The soldiers from both sides were unaware that the rider was the elderly George W. Mowery, owner of the land upon which Mowery's Hill was situated. Assuming that the Union soldiers were prisoners, Mowery, in "vigorous style," shouted, "The damn Yankees. The [every] last one of these infernal rascals should be taken and strung up on that limb!" He then pointed to a large tree limb that extended over the Staunton Road.[17] Embarrassed and desiring to mitigate the animosity, O'Ferrall called out to Mowery, "You should not talk that way; you should not abuse prisoners—men who are helpless. You evidently think these men are prisoners, but they are not—we are all here under a flag of truce."

Realizing his error, Mowery changed his demeanor. "His face grew ashy pale, and he seemed to become limp and almost to reel in his saddle." He regained his composure, reversed his direction and said, "Good-day, gentlemen," and sped away "with his coat-tails standing straight out behind him."[18]

A short time later, the courier returned with a reply: "General Hunter declines to see the rebel officer. He must send forward his communication at once, or return to his lines."[19] O'Ferrall responded to Otis by declaring, "Major, this is discourteous and un-soldier-like treatment. I cannot see why he declines to see me. I believe I will retain my communication and return to my lines." Otis responded, "Hold on. I will try him again." Otis issued his own written communication and dispatched the courier a second time on a fresh horse.[20] After a much shorter interval, the courier returned bearing a written memo that stated the following:

> The rebel's General Jones and Colonels Brown(e) and Doyle are dead and have been decently buried. All the rebel dead have been decently buried, and the wounded are being well cared for. The bearer of this communication must return to his lines forthwith.
>
> David Hunter,
> Maj. Genl, Commanding U.S. Forces[21]

Before departing to return to the Confederate lines, O'Ferrall shook hands with Otis, who had forever earned his admiration and respect. As for Hunter, O'Ferrall recalled his "ungentlemanly, un-soldier-like, and unfeeling" manner were simply "in keeping with the character of the man."[22]

Blame

As with any catastrophic failure, it was human nature to assess blame. The authorities in Richmond and the participants in the field found plenty to spread around to Generals Morgan, Vaughn, Imboden, and even Jones himself. Morgan's expedition into Kentucky drew criticism from the Confederate high command. Five days after Piedmont, General Braxton Bragg commented, "It is a most unfortunate withdrawal of forces from an important position at a very critical moment."[23] Adding to Bragg's remarks, Secretary of War Seddon could only add, "Unfortunately, I see no remedy for this movement now."[24] Four weeks later on July 2, General Braxton Bragg called out General Morgan a second time by reporting to President Davis:

> The accounts received so far do not indicate any satisfactory results of the movement into Kentucky by General Morgan. Should he ever return with his command, it will as usual be disorganized and unfit for service until again armed, equipped, and disciplined. The large number of prisoners we always lose by these raiding expeditions has been the source of great evil, placing us, in that respect, at the mercy of a cruel foe. Had this force been with us in the Valley of Virginia, we should probably not have to regret a defeat there and mourn the loss of one of our most gallant leaders [W.E. Jones], who fell striving to save that invaluable region from devastation.[25]

Grumble Jones made his share of mistakes. Two decades later Imboden published his written account, attributing the overconfidence and stubbornness of Grumble Jones as major factors. Other explanations include his inexperience in leading such a large force and his failure to deploy effectively his artillery manned by inexperienced crews who were no match against the Federal cannons directed by the most capable Captain Henry A. DuPont. Captain John Opie assessed blame on Jones, who, in his opinion, "had selected a most miserable position for the coming battle. Instead of occupying a line of hills, where his artillery would have full play upon the advancing enemy, he placed his army in a level woodland, where his artillery would have no sweep."[26] Jones's greatest error was leaving the large gap in his line of battle between his infantry and the cavalry brigades of Vaughn and Imboden. Also, by having ordered Vaughn and Imboden to restrict their activity to guarding his right flank, Jones failed to engage a third of his army. Decades after the battle, former Lieutenant Colonel Charles Triplett O'Ferrall wrote the following:

> There was most outrageous bungling at Piedmont; I am sure General Jones never intended to leave a gap in his line; I am sure somebody failed to obey his orders.[27] It is always disagreeable to me to criticize a fellow officer, condemn him for any act of commission or omission, but truth forces me in this instance to lay blame at the door of General Vaughn for our defeat at New Hope [Piedmont]. He ranked General Imboden, and sat quietly on his horse, awaiting orders, in spite of Imboden's persistent desire and eagerness of the men to move upon the enemy. General Vaughn did not lack personal courage, and he would have led his men anywhere without wavering for an instant if he had been ordered, but his judgment must have taught him what orders he should have had and that his failure to receive them was the result of a mistake, oversight, inability, or want of knowledge, and he should have acted upon his own judgment and responsibility.[28]

To a somewhat lesser degree, Imboden shared the blame with Vaughn. His brigade guarded the extreme right and was further distant, and Vaughn outranked him. Captain John Opie shared O'Ferrall's sentiments on Vaughn's culpability but gave equal blame to Imboden. Decades later, Opie wrote, "Had Vaughn and Imboden, at this time, attacked the advancing column in flank, or advanced at the left half wheel, Hunter would have been surrounded by fire and water; but these two generals stood by, silent spectators of this flank movement, absolutely regardless of orders from General Jones."[29]

Sixty years after the battle, former Sergeant Milton Wylie Humphreys of the First Brigade, Captain Thomas A. Bryan's Lewisburg Battery, supported the criticisms levied against Vaughn and Imboden. Having served the entire war as an artillery gunner, the Greenbrier County, (West) Virginia, native held a bias toward his specialty. By the time he published his account he was a prominent scholar of classical languages at several universities but also maintained his interest on the subject of artillery. Humphries defended Grumble Jones for his selection of the battle site, "which happened to be an excellent one." Humphries went on to state "the battle was won through the efficiency of DuPont and lost through the inactivity, however caused, of Vaughn and Imboden"[30]

Historians who studied the battle generally cast equal blame on Imboden and Vaughn for their collective failure to act at the critical moment when the Federals stormed the gap.

Postmortem

Hunter's expedition up the Shenandoah Valley including the Battle of Piedmont and beyond would later be deemed the Lynchburg Campaign. Ironically, what began as an overwhelming Federal triumph evolved into a disastrous failure with nearly catastrophic results.

Hunter's Army of the Shenandoah marched unopposed into Staunton and eventually united with Crook's Army of the Kanawha (later named the Army of West Virginia). During his Staunton occupation, Hunter paroled the Confederate wounded and had the able-bodied prisoners marched to camps in Ohio. After destroying the railroad complex, he "liberated" the incarceration chambers of the jails, prisons, and the Western State Lunatic Asylum, leaving the town at the mercy of the inmates.[31] Hunter withdrew from

Staunton on June 10 and in doing so abandoned his wounded to the mercy of the next occupying force.

Against nominal resistance, Hunter's combined force converged upon Lexington and the highly symbolic target of the Virginia Military Institute. Following several acts of plundering, they torched most of the campus structures and the home of Governor John Letcher. They then turned their attention to the adjacent campus of Washington College, where they committed some looting but spared the buildings. Hunter's army crossed the Blue Ridge at the Peaks of Otter and ultimately arrived in the vicinity of the Lynchburg, a most valuable transportation hub and hospital district. Poised to strike a fatal blow against the Confederacy Hunter turned cautious, and the anticipated battle for Lynchburg never took place.

The CS Army of the Valley District regrouped east of the Blue Ridge, received reinforcements, and made its way to Lynchburg to reorganize into a corps under the command of Jubal A. Early. Confronted with an exaggerated perception regarding the strength of Early's forces, Hunter terminated his expedition and withdrew through the mountains into West Virginia. Early then went on the offensive. Utilizing the railroads he transported his forces to retake Staunton unopposed. Wounded Federals whom Hunter left behind in hospitals were captured and transported to various prison camps including Camp Sumter in Andersonville, Georgia. Many of them would not survive.

At Staunton, Early reorganized his 10,000-man infantry into two corps with two divisions each.[32] The cavalry brigades of Vaughn, Imboden, McCausland, Mudwall Jackson and the former W.E. Jones Brigade of the Department of Southwest Virginia were reorganized into a 4,000-troop division under General Robert Ransom. On June 27 the collective infantry and cavalry launched perhaps one of the most ambitious and desperate expeditions of the war. Negating all of Hunter's prior gains, they retook the lower Shenandoah Valley and followed up with the South's final invasion of the North, threatening Washington and Baltimore. Appropriately, the expedition was later termed Early's Washington Raid. By some accounts, this was the real "high-water mark" of the Confederacy.[33] Although Early's forces had not pursued Hunter, they did not forget his atrocities. In Maryland, Early levied combined reparations on Hagerstown and Frederick exceeding $200,000. Early's raiders also burned the home of U.S. postmaster general Montgomery Blair. Other reprisals included the capture and burning of Chambersburg, Pennsylvania.

Hunter returned to the valley but was unable to respond decisively to Early's offensive. Grant relieved him of command and replaced him with Major General Phillip Sheridan, who launched his Shenandoah Valley Campaign, which lasted from August 1864 until March 1865. Sheridan reversed the momentum of Early's campaign and brought a level of devastation to the valley beyond parallel. In the major engagements, he routed Early's forces at Winchester, Tom's Brook, Cedar Creek, and Waynesboro. By the time of the last action, the war in the Eastern Theater was nearing a conclusion.

After conquering the Shenandoah Valley, Sheridan's forces united with Grant's Army of the Potomac in the pursuit of Lee's Army of Northern Virginia, which was attempting to join General Joseph E. Johnston's Army of Tennessee in North Carolina. Sheridan routed the Confederate forces at Five Forks on April 1 and at Sayler's Creek on April 6. With no hope of escaping, Lee's half-starved Army of Northern Virginia surrendered at Appomattox Courthouse on April 9, 1865.

Fought ten months before Appomattox, the Battle of Piedmont was not by any stretch a turning point in the Civil War. Conversely, it was a link in a chain of events that prolonged the conflict. There is an ambivalent sense of futility regarding the battle in which Grumble Jones sacrificed his life. To the South, it was a catastrophic failure that lost control of the upper Shenandoah Valley for the first time in the war. To the North, Piedmont was merely the opening salvo of the Lynchburg Campaign, which combined with the backlash was a disastrous failure with near-catastrophic consequences. The Battle of Piedmont bore the stigma of waste and failure from the perspective of both sides. It is thus one of the most overlooked combat engagements of the American Civil War.

The Legacy of William E. Jones

With the body of Grumble Jones in Federal hands, looting Union soldiers took souvenirs in the way of his buttons, insignia, personal papers, and even his wallet. Confederate prisoners buried their commander in a garden near the battlefield. After the war, his body was exhumed and reinterred at Old Glade Presbyterian Church Cemetery in Glade Spring, Virginia. He lies in the Dunn family section next to the grave of his wife, Eliza Dunn Jones, who preceded him in death by a dozen years and who was also reinterred after her initial burial in Texas. If there was any formal ceremony with his reinterment, it was not recorded.

Graves of Eliza Jones and William E. Jones, Old Glade Presbyterian Church Cemetery (photograph by author, 2014).

In 1872 Memphis resident Robert Campbell Jones visited Washington County, Virginia, to serve as the administrator of the estate of his brother William Edmondson Jones.[34] Grumble did not leave a will. By that time, Robert Campbell Jones was the only surviving member of the immediate family. However, multiple nieces and nephews, many of them minors, were legally entitled beneficiaries to the estate. On January 8, 1877, Jones's 450-acre farm was sold by Washington County commissioner John A. Buchanan to Robert Craig. Via a friendly suit, the proceeds went toward the benefit of Robert Campbell Jones and multiple surviving nieces and nephews.

Grumble Jones was revered by the men under his command. However, he left a mixed legacy. One theory suggests his long-term dispute with the highly revered legend J.E.B. Stuart tarnished his reputation. If there is truth to that assessment, it is only in part and a minor one at that. Other factors caused his historical obscurity. Most of the anonymity can be attributed to the circumstances and results surrounding Grumble's final stand at Piedmont.

As for timing, the Battle of Piedmont occurred only three weeks following the Battle of New Market, the most celebrated single Southern victory in the Shenandoah Valley. Piedmont was a much larger conflict than New Market, but it lacked the distinguishing features such as the regiment of VMI cadets. Piedmont took place within two days of the carnage at Cold Harbor, more than 100 miles to the east, an engagement that almost cost Lincoln the 1864 presidential election. Piedmont also preceded a highly significant chain of events in Early's Washington Campaign and Sheridan's Shenandoah Valley Campaign, the latter of which hastened the war toward a conclusion.

Grumble Jones's legacy suffered mostly from the fact that Piedmont was a resounding defeat for the Southern cause, the South losing control of the upper Shenandoah Valley for the first time. It was the only battle that Jones ever lost decisively, and one for which he paid with his life. Grumble's adversary at Piedmont, Major General David Hunter, had a superior supporting cast, more troops, more artillery, and a strategic distance advantage from the outset. As valiant and remarkable as Jones was in his effort, the final evaluation was based on the end results. In an unjustified historical assessment, Grumble's defeat to a mediocre and reviled commander like Hunter tarnished his legacy with a stigma of failure.

From the Federal perspective, the Battle of Piedmont was the triumphant beginning of the miserably failed Lynchburg Campaign. Aside from attrition in the way of Southern casualty losses, the contest contributed nothing toward bringing the war to a conclusion. Hunter's repulse at Lynchburg abbreviated Federal control of the valley to less than two weeks and negated any strategic advantage his victory acquired. Hunter's retreat also left Washington, D.C., potentially exposed.

The carnage at Piedmont exceeded that of New Market and any action in Jackson's legendary 1862 Shenandoah Valley Campaign.[35] Three months after the Piedmont engagement, General John B. Gordon (CSA) visited the battlefield and remarked "never, not even in the Wilderness or Spotsylvania, had he seen forest so devastated."[36] The combined events that followed, however, rendered the Battle of Piedmont one of diminished and forgotten significance. Some historians still refer to the Battle of Piedmont as a mere "skirmish."

Marshall Moore Brice published an account of the Battle of Piedmont in 1965, the final year of the Civil War Centennial. His research involved interviews with locals, and he noted, "Practically everyone knows that a battle was waged there, but some are not

Historical Marker of Piedmont Battlefield (photograph by author, 2014).

sure whether it was against the British or the Yankees. It was a big battle, all will agree, and there was much carnage, but many are uncertain as to which side won."[37]

The battlefield has not been preserved as either a national or state park, but it has not been lost to development either. It remains an agricultural region in Augusta County, and most of the battlefield is on private property. A bronze plaque mounted on a stone base positioned near the place where Jones fell offers a token element of commemoration. Those with only a casual interest in the Civil War, however, know little about the battle.

It is said that history is written by the winners. History is also told by the survivors. Grumble chose to reside alone in Washington County, Virginia, after his immediate family migrated westward. His wife preceded him in death by a dozen years; he never remarried, and he fathered no known issue. By the turn of the century only one of Grumble's six siblings was still living, and he was more than five hundred miles away. Like many who did not survive the Civil War, Grumble Jones faded into historical oblivion. For a multitude of reasons his legacy remains mixed and is relatively obscure.

Epilogue

U.S. Army of the Shenandoah

Once celebrated for his overwhelming triumph in the Battle of Piedmont, General David Hunter found himself scrutinized politically, militarily, and by the press for his debacle at Lynchburg. His retreat negated all gains and placed Washington, D.C., at risk.

Under Grant's orders, Hunter and his combined forces returned from their West Virginia sanctuary to the Shenandoah Valley to serve as a diversion and to disrupt the region's capacity to provide sustenance. Hunter exploited the opportunity to satisfy his personal vendettas by ordering the torching of the homes of political adversaries including his cousin Andrew Hunter.[1] While these actions served no practical military or strategic purpose, they motivated Early's raiders to retaliate in like kind. Responding to the harsh criticism, Hunter blamed his subordinates for his failures and deemed himself a wrongly labeled scapegoat.[2] On August 8, 1864, he resigned from his command, which allowed Grant to appoint Sheridan as his replacement. He requested but was denied another field command and served out his army career in an administrative capacity.

Hunter performed as an honor guard at the state funeral of President Lincoln and accompanied his body to Springfield, Illinois. He then presided over the commission that tried the assassination conspirators. He retired from the U.S. Army in 1866 and died in 1886 in Washington, D.C., at the age of eighty-four. To Southerners, particularly residents of the Shenandoah Valley, Hunter was one of the most reviled figures in the war.

Hunter's chief of staff, Colonel David Hunter Strother, resigned from the army after Sheridan replaced his superior. Immediately following the war he received a commission of brevet brigadier general and served as adjutant general for Francis H. Pierpont, who had been appointed by President Andrew Johnson as governor of the restored state of Virginia.[3] Strother followed Governor Pierpont's policy of clemency and reconciliation for Virginians (and West Virginians) who had served the Confederacy. During the Lexington occupation in the Lynchburg Campaign, Strother had influenced General David Hunter's decision to torch the campus buildings at Virginia Military Institute. Following the conclusion of the war, however, he served on the VMI board of visitors and actively promoted its reconstruction.[4] In 1866, Strother returned to his home in Berkeley Springs, West Virginia, and authored "Personal Recollections of the War," published in *Harper's Monthly*. In 1879 President Rutherford B. Hayes appointed him as general consul to Mexico, a position he held until retiring in 1885. He lived the remainder of his life in Charles Town, West Virginia, where he died in 1888 at the age of seventy-one.

Hunter's artillery officer, Captain Henry Algernon DuPont, directed his batteries to fire with such precision as to turn the tide in the Battle of Piedmont. He went on to receive the Medal of Honor for his gallant and meritorious service at the battles of (Third) Winchester and Fisher's Hill during Sheridan's Shenandoah Valley Campaign.[5] Remaining with the U.S. Army for ten years after the war, DuPont settled in his home state of Delaware and became president of the Wilmington & Northern Railroad and served two terms in the U.S. Senate. He authored several publications on military science and reminiscences on his Civil War experience. *The Campaign of 1864 in the Valley of Virginia and the Expedition into Lynchburg,* published in 1925 and a reference source for this biography, was among his works. He lived to the age of eighty-eight, dying in 1926.

Confederate States Army of the Valley District

General John C. Vaughn participated as a brigade commander in Early's Washington Raid before returning to East Tennessee to lead guerrilla-style actions against occupying Federals. He stood by President Davis and was the last Confederate general in the Eastern Theater to surrender.[6] He returned to East Tennessee to face political vindictiveness and financial hardship. Vaughn overcame most adversities and served in his state legislature before settling in Georgia. He died at the age of fifty-one in 1875, leaving a mixed legacy.

During Early's Washington Raid, Brigadier General John D. Imboden contracted typhoid fever, was relieved and served out the war supervising the prisoner system. After the war, the Augusta County native settled near Grumble Jones's home in Washington County. There he involved himself in land development and transportation as a premier expert on mineral exploitation, an inventor, and a designer. His company acquired the community of Mocks Mill, which ultimately evolved into the incorporated town he named Damascus. He authored numerous articles on the Civil War but sought a legacy reflecting his contributions to humanity and not his war record. Upon his death in 1895 he was buried, according to his wishes, in Damascus in a grave marked with the inscription, "J.D. Imboden, Founder of Damascus." Three years later, however, his remains were exhumed and reinterred at Hollywood Cemetery in Richmond, among 18,000 Confederate veterans.[7]

The First Brigade commander, Colonel Beuhring H. Jones, captured at Piedmont, was a prisoner of war confined at Johnson's Island in Ohio beyond the conclusion of the war.[8] When finally granted clemency, he was "physically and financially ruined" upon his return to Greenbrier County, West Virginia.[9] To rebuild his life he published *The Sunny Land; or, Prison Prose and Poetry Containing the Productions of the Ablest Writers in the South, and Prison Lays of Distinguished Confederate Officers,* to which he was the primary contributor. Describing the horrific life of a prisoner, his most acclaimed poem detailed evading starvation by ingesting rats. His bleak outlook reversed itself in 1870 when Southern sympathizers of his state gained political momentum against the Radical Republicans.[10] Seemingly vindicated, he served as assistant secretary of the West Virginia Constitutional Convention and died while serving at his post, on March 18, 1872, at the age of forty-nine.[11]

While on furlough, Major William W. Stringfield of the Thomas Legion visited the convalescent hospital at Emory and Henry College, where his family had taken refuge.[12]

He arrived on October 8, 1864, six days after the nearby First Battle of Saltville, to confront the notorious Confederate guerrilla Champ Ferguson, who was conducting a racially motivated massacre of the wounded Union soldier patients at Wiley Hall. Unarmed, Stringfield, Professor Edmund Longley and Dr. James B. Murfree looked down the barrel of Ferguson's revolver at point-blank range. Ferguson relented but departed with a vow to return and murder more victims (he did not return to carry out his threat).[13] After the war Stringfield testified against Ferguson, whom Federal authorities arrested for war crimes. His testimony led to Ferguson's conviction and execution by hanging in 1865.

Stringfield ultimately moved to western North Carolina, where he clerked for a U.S. congressman, ventured into private business, and served several terms in the state legislature. He was active in Civil War veterans' movements and published his memoirs. In 1900 Stringfield wrote a history of Love's regiment for the publication *Histories of the Several Regiments and Battalions from North Carolina in the Great War, 1861–1865*. He died in 1923 at the age of eighty-five.

Charles Triplett O'Ferrall served in the defense of Lynchburg, Early's Washington Raid and partisan actions against Sheridan's Shenandoah Valley Campaign during which he sustained a severe wound for the second time. He recovered and returned to duty in time to disband his Twenty-Third Virginia Cavalry when the war concluded. He returned to Morgan County, West Virginia, and received an indictment. Francis Pierpont, serving as governor of the "Reorganized State of Virginia," intervened to effect O'Ferrall's full pardon by President Johnson. O'Ferrall stood forever in gratitude to the Fairmont Unionist, whose library Grumble Jones ordered torched during his West Virginia Raid.

In 1868 O'Ferrall earned a law degree at Washington College under the college presidency of Robert E. Lee. He served two terms in the state legislature, six years as a Rockingham County judge, and six terms in the U.S. House of Representatives. Elected Virginia governor in 1894, he implemented active measures to enforce right-to-work laws during miner strikes and to prevent racially motivated mob lynchings.[14] In 1904 he published his autobiography, *Forty Years of Active Service; Being Some History of the War Between the Confederacy and the Union and of the Events Leading Up to It*. O'Ferrall died in 1905 in his sixty-fifth year and is buried with his spouse at Hollywood Cemetery in Richmond. Of Jones, Governor O'Ferrall wrote, "General Jones was a superior brigade commander, [and] he took the best care of his men and shared their hardships and discomforts; he was alert, untiring, and as a fighter, he was not excelled by any officer in the army.[15]

John Newton Opie served as a private under Jones in the Sixth Virginia Cavalry and as a captain of a reserve company in the CS Army of the Valley District at Piedmont. At the conclusion of the Battle of Piedmont, he served with the regrouped forces in the defense of Lynchburg and Early's Washington Raid. During Sheridan's Shenandoah Valley Campaign, Opie was captured and remained a prisoner of war until exchanged shortly before Appomattox.[16] After the Civil War he graduated from the University of Virginia Law School and served in the Virginia House of Delegates and the Virginia State Senate.[17] He authored *A Rebel Cavalryman with Lee, Stuart, and Jackson*, which was published in 1899 and is a source in this biography. Opie died in 1906 in his sixty-second year at his home in Staunton and is buried there in Thornrose Cemetery.

W.E. Jones Brigade, Army of Northern Virginia

Jones's replacement, Brigadier General Thomas Lafayette Rosser took the unit originally known as the Ashby Cavalry Brigade and later as the W.E. Jones Brigade to new heights, meriting it the official title of the "Laurel Brigade."[18] The Laurel Brigade served as Early's primary cavalry unit during his Washington Raid and distinguished itself in actions against Sheridan, earning Rosser the moniker "Savior of the Valley."[19] Promoted to major general, Rosser served as the brigade's division commander. Rejoining Lee's Army of Northern Virginia during the Appomattox Campaign, the unit participated in multiple engagements in the final days of the war. Never surrendering, Rosser's division committed the last offensive action by Lee's army when it charged through the Federal lines before Appomattox Courthouse and disbanded after receiving notice of the surrender.

Lieutenant John Blue, whose writings served as a source in this biography, was from Hampshire County, West Virginia, as was his cousin Monroe Blue, who died heroically at Piedmont. John Blue had served under Grumble Jones in actions from Orange Courthouse to Gettysburg. He was captured in an engagement after Grumble Jones had already parted ways with the Army of Northern Virginia. He spent the remainder of the Civil War as a prisoner of war at Johnson's Island, Point Lookout, and Fort Delaware.[20] He participated in a failed escape plot that involved walking on the ice-covered surface of frozen Sandusky Bay to Canada and nearly froze to death.

Following his release and parole, Blue returned to Hampshire County, where Confederate veterans faced discrimination in regard to political and property rights, inducing him to contemplate migrating to South America. His fortunes changed with the 1870 state elections, which reversed the political climate to a pro–Southern position. Thirty-five years after the end of the war he wrote about his recollections. He entered politics in 1892 and served as county assessor. On June 30, 1903, during his second term, he died of a heart attack at the age of 69 "while quietly rocking on his front porch." His obituary, printed in the July 1 *Hampshire Review*, described him as a "plain, blunt man, of more than ordinary intelligence and sense."[21]

Jefferson County, (West) Virginia, native William Lyne Wilson participated in Jackson's Shenandoah Valley Campaign and Jones's operations in the Shenandoah Valley, with the latter action including a brief time as a prisoner of war before being exchanged. He served under Jones in the West Virginia Raid and at Brandy Station. After Jones had transferred out of the Army of Northern Virginia, Wilson served under Tom Rosser in the main engagements leading up to and including the Petersburg and Appomattox campaigns.

After the conclusion of the war, Wilson joined the faculty at his alma mater, Columbian College. According to legend, it was said that during his first few weeks of presiding over his classroom he defiantly wore his Confederate uniform. In addition to teaching, he also acquired a master's degree and a law degree from the institution. He opened a law practice in Jefferson County with a former Twelfth Virginia Cavalry comrade, George Baylor. He held various political offices on the local level until 1882, when he served as the third president of West Virginia University. The latter was a highly ironic situation, as West Virginia University had been "established at the height of Radical Republican rule" and was situated in Morgantown, a strongly pro–Union area of the state. The institution assumed an anti-clemency policy after its establishment and restricted enrollment of students from the southern and eastern counties that "espoused the Confederacy."[22] Adding to the irony was Wilson's personal history of having been, two decades earlier, an active participant in the dual occupation of Morgantown during the Jones West Virginia Raid, in which he requisitioned livestock from residents.

Wilson's tenure as president of West Virginia University was brief. During his first academic term he was nominated as the Democratic candidate for the U.S. House of Representatives in the Second West Virginia District. With only three weeks to campaign against a political opposition eager to exploit his involvement as an alleged horse thief in the Jones West Virginia Raid, Wilson won the election by a close margin. Taking office in 1883, he was reelected five times and served until 1895. As an opponent to protectionism, he coauthored the Wilson-Gorman Tariff Act. In favor of the gold standard, he sought to repeal the Sherman Silver Purchase Act of 1893. He also chaired the House Ways and Means Committee. Following his congressional reelection defeat in 1894, Wilson served as postmaster general in the cabinet of President Grover Cleveland until 1897. He then served as president of Washington and Lee University and died at his post in 1900. He was buried in Charles Town, West Virginia. A stretch of U.S. 340 between Charles Town and Harpers Ferry is named the William L. Wilson Freeway in his honor.

W.E. Jones Brigade of East Tennessee and Southwest Virginia

The brigade that Jones led through his East Tennessee and Southwest Virginia campaigns did not arrive in time to participate in the Battle at Piedmont. However, it served a vital role in the defense of Lynchburg and Early's Washington Raid. As part of General John McCausland's division, the unit captured and burned Chambersburg, Pennsylvania, on July 30. The brigade's combat fortunes turned on August 7 when it was routed by the Federals at Moorefield, West Virginia, marking the beginning of Sheridan's Shenandoah Valley Campaign. Decimated by losses over a three-month span, the unit was reorganized several times, ultimately serving alongside the Laurel Brigade in General Rosser's division. Like the Laurel Brigade, the unit did not surrender but broke out from Appomattox Courthouse before disbanding.

The Twenty-First Virginia Cavalry commander, Colonel William Elisha Peters, reinforced his mixed reputation by refusing to execute McCausland's order to burn Chambersburg, where only noncombatants resided. The town was torched, and Peters was arrested. He was, however, released, and the charges were dropped.[23] At Moorefield, Peters sustained severe wounds that Federal reports concluded were fatal.[24] However, he survived the war and served as a professor of classical languages at the University of Virginia. He died in 1906 and is buried in the Sheffey family cemetery in Marion, Virginia.

Grumble's brother-in-law, Private Robert Campbell Dunn of the Twenty-First Cavalry Virginia Regiment, was captured during Sheridan's Shenandoah Valley Campaign on September 13, 1864, at Opequon Creek and spent the remainder of the war at Camp Chase in Ohio.[25] Surviving captivity and the war, he lived out his life in Glade Spring until his death in 1907 at the age of 61. He is buried in the Dunn section at Old Glade Presbyterian Church.[26]

Lieutenant Colonel Vincent Addison Witcher and his battalion accompanied part of General John Hunt Morgan's Kentucky expedition. To Witcher's astonishment, he received notice that on June 28, 1864, he was "dropped" from the rolls of the Provisional Army of the Confederacy by the War Department as punishment for his court-martial conviction, which Jones had prosecuted.[27] Officers of influence appealed to President Davis requesting leniency for the sake of the cause, and Witcher's dismissal was revoked on August 9, 1864.[28] No explanation detailed either the original departmental action or the reversal. Once restored to command, Witcher gained more autonomy following General Morgan's death in September. Witcher committed partisan-style raids in West Virginia, Southwest Virginia, and East Tennessee in measures Secretary Seddon regarded as plundering acts of depredation.[29] At the end of the war Witcher disbanded his battalion and was paroled at Greensboro, North Carolina. He moved to Utah, where he was said to have joined the Mormon Church for political reasons. He ultimately returned to Pittsylvania County, Virginia, to live out the remainder of his life. He died at the age of seventy-five in 1912.

Washington Mounted Rifles

Jones was the first mentor to John Singleton Mosby, who evolved into one of the most fascinating characters of the Civil War. Mosby's partisan actions not only prolonged the life of the Confederacy, they probably also persuaded the victorious Federals to amend their postwar policies toward the conquered South. Following Lee's surrender at Appomattox, Mosby disbanded his Forty-Third Battalion, Virginia Cavalry. Unlike most Confederate soldiers in the regular armies, he and his followers were denied pardons. A report falsely linked Mosby to the Lincoln assassination.[30] Only an intervention by General Grant in 1866 permitted the former ranger to return to a relatively peaceful lifestyle.[31]

Mosby's successful law practice in his wartime home of Warrenton, Virginia, drew Northern resentment. Southerners in turn branded him as a turncoat when he staunchly supported President Grant's 1972 reelection. The former adversaries developed a friendship lasting until Grant's death in 1885. Adding to his social isolation, Mosby was widowed in 1876. He further alienated die-hard Southerners when he supported Republican candidate Rutherford B. Hayes, whom Grant endorsed as his successor. In 1878 President Hayes appointed Mosby as consul to Hong Kong, where he remained in the form of protective exile until the 1885 inauguration of President Grover Cleveland.[32]

Through former President Grant's influence, Mosby landed employment in San Francisco as an attorney for the Southern Pacific Railroad. By the late 1880s, publishers solicited him to write and he produced *War Reminisences* and *Memoirs*. In his writings Mosby was complimentary towards Jones while overtly laudatory toward Stuart.

President William McKinley appointed Mosby as a special agent with the General Land Office. President Theodore Roosevelt appointed him as assistant attorney in the Justice Department. He spent his final years touring the lecture circuit in New England and died in 1916 at the age of eighty-two. His former rangers served as his pallbearers at a state funeral in Warrenton, where he was buried next to the graves of his wife, his two sons who had died in infancy, and his first son, John S. Mosby, Jr., who had died the previous year. Biographer Virgil Carrington Jones wrote that Mosby lived a long life but, by doing so, had outlived his fame. V.C. Jones called his death at age eighty-two "fifty-two years too late to bring him the glory he deserved."

Warren M. Hopkins remained at Grumble's side from the formation of the Washington Mounted Rifles until Jones's death at Piedmont. Hopkins served as Jones's aide-de-camp in the First Virginia Cavalry, the Seventh Virginia Cavalry, the W.E. Jones Brigade of the Army of Northern Virginia, the W.E. Jones Brigade of the Department of Southwest Virginia, and with the CS Army of the Valley District. Following Grumble's death, Hopkins joined the staff of Jones's replacement, Brigadier General Bradley Tyler Johnson, until being appointed colonel to command the newly organized Twenty-Fifth Virginia Cavalry, serving in that capacity until the end of the war. Following the war, Hopkins settled in Abingdon, Virginia. He died in 1875 at the age of thirty-five and is buried in Sinking Springs Cemetery.[33]

Thomas Benjamin Estill Edmondson, who accompanied Grumble Jones to Texas in 1852, enrolled in the Washington Mounted Rifles and remained with the unit as Second Company D of the First Virginia Cavalry for the duration, reaching the rank of third-lieutenant. He was killed in action at Todd's Tavern during the Spotsylvania Courthouse Campaign on May 7, 1864, at the age of thirty-three and is buried at Old Baptist Cemetery Annex in Washington County.

Following Stuart's death in May of 1864, staff officer William Willis Blackford was appointed lieutenant colonel and executive officer of the First Virginia Regiment of Engineers, serving in that capacity until the Army of Northern Virginia surrendered at Appomattox. After the war, Blackford was an engineer for the Lynchburg & Danville Railroad and the Baltimore & Ohio Railroad. Between those times, he operated a sugar plantation in Louisiana before returning to Virginia to serve as a professor of engineering at Virginia Polytechnic Institute. Upon retiring, Blackford acquired property in what was then Princess Anne County (now Virginia Beach). He died in 1904 at the age of seventy-four and is buried in Sinking Springs Cemetery in Abingdon. *War Years with Jeb Stuart,* his memoirs, were compiled and published after his death under the guidance of Dr. Douglas Southall Freeman.

Dr. William Logan Dunn, Grumble's brother-in-law, had received an education at "old field schools," Emory and Henry College, Jefferson Medical College (now Sidney Kimmel Medical College at Thomas Jefferson University), and Richmond Medical College to follow the professional path of his father.[34] He enrolled as a private in the Washington Mounted Rifles, which was mustered into the First Virginia Cavalry, and served as assistant surgeon in Mosby's Forty-Third Battalion, Virginia Cavalry. Dunn's reputation as a combatant flourished to the point that Mosby considered him to be "too fond of fighting" and sought his replacement with a surgeon who "took more pride in curing than killing."[35]

Dunn was captured in November of 1863 and later exchanged. As an assistant surgeon, he was instrumental in the care and saving the life of Mosby, who suffered a near-fatal gunshot wound in late 1864. Dunn remained under Mosby's command until the unit disbanded. He practiced medicine in Washington County, served as a surgeon for the Norfolk & Western Railroad, and was president of the Abingdon, Virginia, Academy of Medicine. He received recognition in articles published in various medical journals.[36] During visits from the legendary Mosby in their later years, the two frequently paid their respects to Grumble Jones's grave at the Old Glade Presbyterian Church Cemetery.[37] Dunn resided in Glade Spring until his death in 1922 at the age of eighty-three. He is buried in Old Glade Presbyterian Church Cemetery in the Dunn Family section and in close proximity to the grave of Grumble Jones.

The Antebellum Years

John Buchanan Floyd, a states-rights advocate, former governor of Virginia, and former U.S. secretary of war, organized a brigade and received a commission of brigadier general in the Confederate service. He commanded Fort Donelson in 1862 when General Ulysses S. Grant launched his campaign to open routes of invasion along the Tennessee and Cumberland rivers. Floyd escaped capture, but Fort Donelson fell, marking one of the early major setbacks for the Confederacy. The campaign initiated the rise of Grant to prominence and for all practical purposes ended Floyd's military career.[38] Floyd returned to Washington County, where he died in 1863 of natural causes. He is buried in Sinking Springs Cemetery in Abingdon.

Grumble's personal dislike of Jeb Stuart paled when compared to his contempt for his Old Army commander, William Wing Loring. Remaining with the Old Army, Loring served in the Utah Expedition and traveled abroad to study European military tactics. In May of 1861 he resigned to serve the Confederacy, ultimately acquiring the rank of major general. The celebrated hero of the Mexican War and lauded Old Army administrator on the western frontier served the Confederacy with less distinction. Following an administrative dispute with Stonewall Jackson, Loring transferred to the Western Theater, where he participated in the Vicksburg, Atlanta, and Franklin and Nashville campaigns. Following the Civil War, he was a New York bank consultant. Loring then went abroad to serve the Khedive of Egypt in the Abyssinian campaign before returning to New York as a man of means. He authored an account of his time in Egypt titled *A Confederate Soldier in Egypt*, published by Dodd, Mead & Company. He frequently traveled to lecture on his military career and was in the process of writing his autobiography when he died of a sudden illness in 1886.

Grumble's former business client Major Henry Hopkins Sibley served the Old Army on the Texas frontier, during the Kansas Border Disturbances, and on the Utah Expedition. Upon the secession of his home state of Louisiana, he resigned his commission, joined the Confederacy with the rank of brigadier general, and commanded the Department of New Mexico. His ill-fated expedition to secure New Mexico and Arizona tarnished his CSA legacy. Like Loring, after the war Sibley went abroad to serve the Khedive of Egypt. Returning to America, he settled in Virginia. In spite of his prior inventions and engineering skills, he was financially strained. Sibley petitioned for relief after learning that his former partner, William Wallace Burns, received royalties for his half interest in the Sibley tent, produced in mass numbers.[39] The U.S. War Department did not agree Sibley was so entitled. Unlike Burns, who remained loyal to the Union, Sibley had joined the rebellion and had contributed to the increased demand for his tents. It was therefore illogical that he should profit from his wrongdoing.[40] Sibley tried to pursue the matter legally, but ultimately, a congressional subcommittee rejected his claim. Sibley died so impoverished in 1886 that his grave remained unmarked for seventy years.[41] He may be the only nonfictional character in the Clint Eastwood western film *The Good, the Bad, and the Ugly*. In the production, his character has no speaking lines but is seen once and mentioned several times.

No tragedy took a greater emotional toll on William E. Jones than the drowning death of his wife in 1852 on the Texas coast. Calamities befell the individuals associated with the shipwreck and upon the region in later years.

In 1875, a major hurricane destroyed the Texas coastal towns of Saluria on Matagorda

Island and Indianola on the mainland. Indianola survived the 1875 storm but had lost its significance before a second storm in 1886 finished it off for good. Neither municipality exists today. Had Grumble not reinterred Eliza's remains from Saluria, they would have rested in an unmarked grave forever. The 1875 storm took the lives of more than four hundred people, including Captain William Nichols, the coastal pilot who had initiated the rescue of the passengers and crew of the steamship *Independence*. Captain Nichols, his wife, and infant child perished when a storm surge obliterated their home in Saluria.[42] Years later his commemorative silver cup, awarded to him in appreciation by the passengers, was found washed up on the shoreline of Matagorda Island. It was returned to surviving members of his family.

According to legend, the hair of fellow steamship *Independence* passenger Stephen Minot turned white as he witnessed his family drown.[43] Resuming his solitary migration to Gonzales, he remarried, fathered a new family, and lived a prosperous life, dying at the age of eighty-six in 1898.

Commemorative Silver Cup (courtesy Matthew C. Schulte, 2017).

Grumble's two most distinguished West Point classmates, John Buford and John C. Tidball, served the Union in the Civil War. Distinctive on the mythological level, Old Bison McLean supported neither side.

Jones fought Buford in multiple combat engagements between Brandy Station and the Gettysburg Campaign. Buford's cavalry division occupied the high ground at Gettysburg, setting the stage for the turning point in the war. Contracting an illness from exhaustion and exposure, he died in December of 1863 at the age of 37.

Brevetted five times for gallant and meritorious conduct, John C. Tidball participated in most of the major campaigns in the Eastern Theater from First Bull Run to Appomattox, achieving the rank of brevet major general. During that time, he also served as commandant of the cadets at West Point. After the war he remained in the smaller-sized Regular Army with the reduced rank of captain and served twenty-five additional years, including duty in the recently acquired territory of Alaska. Retiring in 1889 with the rank of colonel at age sixty-four, Tidball lived until his eighty-first year, dying in 1906. In 1895 he wrote an unpublished manuscript titled "Getting Through West Point by One Who Did and for Those Who Want to Know," a significant resource for this biography. He originated the tradition of playing taps at military funerals and was the last surviving member of the West Point class of 1848.[44]

Legend has it that upon his expulsion from West Point, Thomas Frelinghuysen McKinney "Old Bison" McLean drifted to the West and pursued the life of "a thorough Indian in all habits and ways" in New Mexico and Arizona.[45] Allegations emerged that he attacked antebellum U.S. forces and raided settlements in those regions.[46] An anecdote surfaced that an Apache chief showed McLean a secret gold mine in Arizona, the "Lost Yuma," which is still being sought in modern times.[47] Other rumors suggested that McLean joined different tribes and held grudges against everyone associated with West Point for denying his graduation and withholding his commission.[48] During Reconstruction, U.S. Army officers familiar with McLean at West Point reported frequent sightings of him.[49] Conflicting accounts of his demise also arose. One source indicated that following the 1872 Battle of the North Fork of the Red River in Texas, a body matching Old Bison's description was among the warrior dead.[50] The most spectacular theory came from multiple sources, although many were anonymous. Tidball wrote, "At the time of the Custer massacre, it was said, and by many believed, that Sitting Bull was none other than Bison McLean."[51] The stories originated almost immediately following the calamity at Little Big Horn on June 26, 1876. Public outcry demanded inquiries as to how a savage could have defeated Custer, a seasoned veteran and West Point graduate. Speculation transpired regarding the possible credibility that Chief Sitting Bull had graduated from the academy, was fluent in French (a part of the curriculum at the antebellum USMA), and was familiar with Napoleon's tactics.[52] The question was then asked, "Could the dark, hairy cadet known as Bison have been, in fact, this omnipotent Sioux?"[53]

Another account, apparently originating from a letter written by someone familiar with McLean's relatives in Missouri and published in the *St. Louis Republican* shortly after Little Big Horn, indicated that Bison was killed by rival Indians in Arizona in 1870.[54] Most of the details regarding the life of Thomas F.M. McLean following his dismissal from West Point were in the way of speculation, rumor, and hearsay. His legacy remains one of tragedy and mystery. His ultimate fate may never be known, a factor that is in keeping with the man and the myth.

The family of Robert and Catherine Moffett Edmondson Jones was enshrouded in mystery and tragedy. Although Grumble Jones died at the age of forty, he lived a longer life than five of his six siblings. James W. Jones, the youngest of the seven children, migrated to Arkansas with his mother and two siblings in 1851. He enlisted in the Twenty-Third Arkansas Infantry in March of 1862 but received a disability discharge a month later.[55] He died three weeks following his discharge at the age of twenty-eight.[56] He left behind two sons, who lived to the ages of thirty-nine and twenty-nine. His younger son was named after his uncle, William Edmondson Jones.

The only sister among Grumble's siblings was Sarah Eliza Jane Jones, who migrated with her mother and two brothers to Crittenden County, Arkansas. She married Jefferson Greer in Memphis, Shelby County, Tennessee in 1851.[57] The couple had two daughters, one of whom died as an infant, followed by Jefferson Greer's death shortly afterward. Sarah Eliza Jane married Reuben T. Redman and with him bore four more children. She died in 1869 at the age of thirty-seven.[58]

The only family member to live beyond their forty-first birthday was Robert Campbell Jones, who also migrated to Arkansas. He was a Confederate veteran and represented Crittenden County in the Arkansas legislature.[59] As a married but childless man of wealth and prestige, this sole survivor of the family brought about an element of closure in 1876. He had the remains of Catherine Moffett Edmondson Jones, James W. Jones, Sarah Eliza

Jane Jones Greer Redman, Jefferson Greer, and Virginia Greer exhumed from their original burial sites in Crittenden County, Arkansas, and reinterred at the family plot at Elmwood Cemetery in Memphis.[60] Robert Campbell Jones lived to the age of seventy-eight, dying in 1908, and is buried along with his wife, who had survived him, and the other members of his family at the Jones plot in Elmwood Cemetery, more than 500 miles from Grumble's burial site at Glade Spring. Grumble Jones remains separated from his immediate family in death, as he was in life.

Chapter Notes

Chapter 1

1. Howard Vance Jones, "The Edmondson (Edmiston) Family at King's Mountain" The Historical Society of Washington County, Virginia *Bulletin,* Abingdon, VA, 2007, 60.

2. Lyman C. Draper, *King's Mountain and Its Heroes, History of the Battle of King's Mountain, October 7th, 1780 and the Events Which Led to It.* Peter G. Thomson, 1881, Cincinnati, 403. Note: Howard Jones, a noted genealogist on the Edmondson/Edmiston family, contends that Colonel William Edmondson fathered fourteen children between the first two wives and a fifteenth by a third wife who is unknown.

3. Howard Vance Jones, 60. Howard Jones notes that the officials did not agree on the division between Maryland and Pennsylvania at the time.

4. *Ibid.*
5. Draper, 402.
6. *Ibid.*
7. *Ibid.*
8. *Ibid.*, 403.
9. *Ibid.*, 404.
10. *Ibid.*
11. Deed Book 7, 218, Washington County Clerk's Office, Abingdon, VA.
12. Mabel Abbott Tucker and Jane Warren Waller, *Lincoln County, Tennessee Bible Records,* Vol. ii, Lincoln County, TN, Pioneers, Batavia, IL, 1971, 71–72.
13. *Ibid.*
14. George J. Stevenson, *Increase in Excellence: A History of Emory & Henry College 1836–1968,* Appleton-Century-Crofts, Division of Meredith Publishing Co., New York, 1963, 6.
15. *Ibid.*
16. *Ibid.*
17. *Ibid.*, 8.
18. *Ibid.*
19. Frank Richardson, *From Sunrise to Sunset, Reminiscence,* King Printing Co., Bristol, TN, 1910, 10.
20. Tucker and Waller, 71.
21. Will Book # 6, 347, Will of Robert Jones, Washington County Clerk's Office.
22. Stevenson, 9.
23. *Ibid.*
24. *Ibid.*, 27.

Chapter 2

1. Stevenson, 39
2. *Ibid.*, 35, 39, 50.
3. *Ibid.*, 7.
4. *Ibid.*, 50.
5. *Ibid.*, 70.
6. *Ibid.*, 51.
7. *Ibid.*, 59.
8. *Ibid.*, xiii in Foreword.
9. *Ibid.*
10. *Catalogue of the Officers and Students Emory & Henry College, Washington County, VA,* 1840. James C. Moses, Knoxville, TN 1843; printed in the Virginia Office, Abingdon, VA, 1842. Note: Edmondson replaced the Reverend Arnold Patton, who served the post from 1836 to 1839. Stevenson, 48 (n). This source will be abbreviated to *Catalogue of Emory & Henry College.*
11. *Catalogue of Emory & Henry College,* 1838–1839.
12. *Ibid.,* 1839–1840.
13. Stevenson, 3.
14. *Ibid.*, 4.
15. *Ibid.*
16. Emory & Henry was an all-male institution until 1899. In 1918 it merged with Martha Washington Collge, a Methodist affiliated all-female school in Abingdon.
17. *Ibid.*, 73.
18. *Catalogue of Emory & Henry College,* 1840–41.
19. *Ibid.*
20. Stevenson, 70.
21. *Ibid.*, 72.
22. *Catalogue of Emory and Henry College,* 1841–1842, 2–3.
23. *Ibid., 1842–1843,* 11.
24. *Ibid.*
25. U.S. Military and Naval Academies, Cadet Records and Applications, 1805–1908, Record for William Edmondson Jones.
26. *Catalogue of Emory & Henry College, 1842–1843.*
27. *Ibid.*

28. Stevenson, 169.
29. *Ibid.*
30. *Ibid.*, 170.
31. "Hermesian Society Literary Minutes, 1854–59, Constitution, Members, 1841–53; Chickasaw Members" Emory & Henry Archives, Emory, VA.
32. Stevenson, 206. Stuart left Emory & Henry in 1850 after two years to attend the United States Military Academy at West Point.
33. Tucker and Waller, 72.
34. *Catalogue of Emory & Henry College, 1871–72*, 5; William E. Jones and Joseph H. Price received diplomas as the graduating class of 1846.

Chapter 3

1. Tucker and Waller, 72.
2. *Ibid.* John C. Tidball, *Getting Through West Point*, 16–17. Unpublished manuscript by John C. Tidball in 1895 reflecting on his time as a cadet at West Point 1844–1848. USMA Archives. This source will be abbreviated to *Getting Through West Point*.
3. Charles William Dabney Collection (#1412), University of North Carolina at Chapel Hill, NC, Special Collections: W. E. Jones Manuscript from Rapidan Station, September 10, 1863. This source will be abbreviated as the Charles W. Dabney Collection (#1412).
4. *Ibid.*
5. *Getting Through West Point*, 90.
6. *Official Register of the Officers and Cadets of the U.S. Military Academy*, West Point, NY, June 1848. This source will be abbreviated to *Official Register of Officers and Cadets* designated by the year.
7. *Getting Through West Point*, 26–27.
8. *Ibid.*, 45.
9. Charles W. Dabney Papers (#1412). Note: This is W. E. Jones's spelling of McLean's first middle name. John C. Tidball in his *Getting Through West Point* stated that "Freeman" was his middle name. USMA archives only show the initial "F" for the first middle name.
10. James S. Robbins, *Last of Their Class: Custer, Pickett, and the Goats of West Point*. Encounter Books, New York, 2006, 129.
11. *Getting Through West Point*, 124.
12. *Ibid.*, 125.
13. Charles W. Dabney Papers (#1412). W. E. Jones attributed the unusual pronunciation of McLean's first middle name earned the moniker "Bison." Tidball recalled the first middle name as "Freeman" and attributed the moniker to McLean's physical appearance, and the fact that he was from Missouri, which he understood to be the "Land of the Bison."
14. *Ibid.*
15. Charles W. Dabney Papers (#1412).
16. *Ibid.*
17. *Getting Through West Point*, 51.
18. *Ibid.*, 44.
19. *Ibid.*, 50.
20. *Getting Through West Point*, 50.
21. *Ibid.*, 51.
22. *Ibid.*
23. *Ibid.*
24. *Ibid.*
25. Eugene C. Tidball, 18.
26. Charles W. Dabney Papers (#1412).
27. *Getting Through West Point*, 81
28. *Ibid.*, 84.
29. *Official Register of Cadets,* June 1845
30. Charles W. Dabney Papers (No. 1412).
31. *Ibid.*
32. *Getting Through West Point*, 89.
33. *Ibid.*
34. *Ibid.*
35. *Getting Through West Point*, 90
36. *Ibid.*, 91–92.
37. *Ibid.*, 104.
38. Charles W. Dabney Papers (#1412).
39. *Getting Through West Point*, 116–117. Note: John Young Mason (1799–1859) served as Secretary of the Navy under President John Tyler from March 26, 1844, to March 4, 1845.
40. *Ibid.*, 118.
41. Charles W. Dabney Papers (#1412).
42. *Getting Through West Point*, 152.
43. *Ibid.*, 151.
44. *Official Register of Officers and Cadets*, 1845, 13–14.
45. *Getting Through West Point*, 31.
46. *Getting Through West Point*, 116.
47. *Ibid.*, 101.
48. *Ibid.*, 101–102.
49. *Ibid.*, 76.
50. *Getting Through West Point*, 77–79.
51. *Ibid.*, 79.
52. *Ibid.*
53. *Ibid.*, 77.
54. *Ibid.*
55. *Ibid.*
56. *Ibid.*, 78.
57. *Ibid.*, 77.
58. *Ibid.*
59. Robbins, 13 Note: Although most assumed Havens was Irish, the source places his ancestry in Wales.
60. *Ibid.*
61. *Getting Through West Point*, 102.
62. *Ibid.*, 35.
63. *Ibid.*, 40.
64. *Official Register of Officers and Cadets*, June 1845, 16.
65. *Ibid.*, 47.
66. .*Ibid.*, 47–48.
67. *Getting Through West Point*, pt. 2, 47–48.
68. *Official Register of Officers and Cadets*, June 1845, 19
69. *Official Register of Officers and Cadets*, June 1845, 13.
70. *Ibid.*, 18.
71. Charles W. Dabney Papers (#1412).
72. *Ibid.*

73. *Official Register of Officers and Cadets*, June 1845, 13
74. *Ibid.*, 17.
75. *Getting Through West Point*, pt. 2, 51.
76. *Ibid.*
77. *Ibid.*, 51–52.
78. Charles W. Dabney Papers (#1412).
79. *Ibid.*
80. *Ibid.*
81. Stonewall Jackson, *The Man, the Soldier, the Legend*. Macmillan Publishing, New York, 1997, p. 39.
82. *Ibid.*
83. *Getting Through West Point*, 128.
84. *Ibid.*, Note: Tidball referred to the location as "Geo's Point." *Official Register*, 1845 shows David T. Deshler finished his Fourth Class year ranked 14/54. Lehigh County Historical Society, *History of Lehigh County, Pennsylvania and a Genealogical and Biographical Register of its Families*, Lehigh Valley Publishing, Allentown, PA, 1914, 241.
85. *Ibid.*
86. *Ibid.*, 126.
87. Gilder Lehrman Institute, William E. Jones Collection, GLC02711.13, New York. William E. Jones letter to Robert C. Jones, dated August 30, 1845.
88. *Official Register of the Officers and Cadets*, June 1845, 11.
89. *Ibid.*, 56.
90. *Ibid.*, 11–12.
91. *Getting Through West Point*, pt. 2, 52
92. *Ibid.*, 54.
93. *Ibid.*
94. *Official Register of the Officers and Cadets*, June 1846, 11.
95. *Ibid.*, 11.
96. Charles W. Dabney Papers (#1412).
97. *Getting Through West Point*, 128.
98. *Ibid.*, 127–128.
99. *Ibid.*, 128–129.
100. *Ibid.*, 129.
101. *Ibid.*, 130
102. *Ibid.* In the antebellum days, the Plain was referred to the relatively flat area of the main campus in contrast to the varied hilly terrain of the upper Hudson River Valley.
103. *Ibid.*
104. *Ibid.*
105. Charles W. Dabney Papers (#1412).
106. The United States declared war on Mexico on April 25, 1846.
107. *Getting Through West Point*, pt. 2, 65.
108. *Ibid.*, 66
109. *Official Register of Officers and Cadets*, June 1846, 17.
110. *Ibid.*, 7.
111. James I. Robertson, 45.
112. George Francis Robert Henderson *Stonewall Jackson and the American Civil War*, Grossett & Dunlap, New York, 1943, 12.
113. Minutes of the Board of Trustees, Emory & Henry College, Emory, VA, 1846. The 1887 Alumni Catalogue mistakenly records the diploma as an "M.A."
114. *Catalogue of Emory & Henry College 1871–1872*.
115. Charles W. Dabney Papers (#1418)
116. *Getting Through West Point*, pt. 2, 130.
117. Robbins, 130.
118. *Getting Through West Point*, pt. 2, 131.
119. Robbins, 130.
120. *Getting Through West Point*, pt. 2, 68.
121. *Official Register of Officers and Cadets*, June 1847, 7.
122. *Ibid.*
123. *Ibid.*
124. *Getting Through West Point*, pt. 2, 90
125. *Ibid.*, 131.
126. Charles W. Dabney Papers (#1412).
127. *Getting Through West Point*, pt. 2, 95
128. *Official Register of Officers and Cadets*, June 1847, 10.
129. *Ibid.*, 9.
130. *Ibid.*, 11.
131. *Ibid.*
132. *Getting Through West Point*, pt. 2, 95
133. *Ibid.*, 132
134. *Getting Through West Point*, pt. 2, 132.
135. *Ibid.*
136. *Ibid.*, 131.
137. *Official Register of Officers and Cadets*, June 1848, 7.
138. *Getting Through West Point*, pt. 2, 102.
139. *Official Register of The Officers and Cadets*, June 1824, 6; *Getting Through West Point*, pt. 2, 102.
140. *Getting Through West Point*, pt. 2, 102–103.
141. *Official Register of Officers and Cadets*, June 1848, 7.
142. *Getting Through West Point*, pt. 2, 109.
143. *Ibid.*
144. *Official Register of Officers and Cadets*, June 1848.
145. *Getting Through West Point*, pt. 2, 113.
146. *Official Register of Officers and Cadets*, June 1848, 7.
147. *Getting Through West Point*, pt. 2, 106.
148. *Official Register of Officers and Cadets*, June 1848, 7.
149. *Getting Through West Point*, pt. 2, 115.
150. *Getting Through West Point*, pt. 2, 115
151. *Ibid.*, 134.
152. *Ibid.*
153. *Official Register of Officers and Cadets*, June 1848, 8.
154. Charles W. Dabney Papers (#1412).
155. Evan S. Connell, *Son of the Morning Star: Custer and the Little Big Horn*, North Point Press, San Francisco, CA, 2011, 224.
156. Eugene Tidball, 50, *Official Register of Officers and Cadets*, June 1848, 8.

157. *Getting Through West Point*, pt. 2, 121.
158. *Ibid*. Crows Nest is a mountain along the west bank of the Hudson River on the northern edge of West Point.
159. *Official Register of Officers and Cadets*, June 1848, 8. *Getting Through West Point*, pt. 2, 122. Tidball wrote the names of the three including their given nicknames and then crossed them out. The names, however, remain legible, and the *Official Register* confirms the dismissals.
160. *Ibid*.
161. *Ibid*.
162. Lorraine Netrick Abraham, "Levi Sheftall D'Lyon, A Preliminary Biography," Manuscript prepared at Armstrong College, Savannah, GA, 1992, 24–25.
163. *Official Register of Officers and Cadets*, June 1848, 8.
164. Charles W. Dabney Papers (#1412), *Official Register of Officers and Cadets*, June 1848, 8 confirms McLean as the fourth cadet dismissed and noted that he, in particular, was "deficient in conduct."
165. Robbins, 131.
166. *Official Register of Officers and Cadets* June 1848, 11. George Washington Cullum, *Biographical Register of the Officers and Graduates of the U.S. Military Academy at West Point*, Vol. II, Riverside Press, Cambridge, MA, 1891, 460–461 states that in 1865, Morris was brevetted major general in the U.S. Volunteers for gallant and meritorious service in the Battle of the Wilderness. He also invented a repeating carbine.
167. *Getting Through West Point*, pt. 2, 122–123.
168. *Official Register of Officers and Cadets*, June 1848, 7.
169. *Ibid.*, 20.
170. *Getting Through West Point*, pt. 2, 156.
171. *Official Register of Officers and Cadets*, June 1848, 20.
172. *Getting Through West Point*, pt. 2, 156.
173. *Ibid.*, 156–57.
174. *Ibid.*, 155–156. This comment, written long after the Civil War, probably referred to John Baker "Texas Jack" Omohundro and William F. "Buffalo Bill" Cody who served as frontier scouts after the Civil War and gained legendary fame performing in western dramas. They were further popularized as dime novel characters.
175. *Ibid.*, 119.
176. *Ibid.*, 136.
177. *Ibid.*, 138.
178. *Ibid*.
179. *Ibid.*, 144.
180. National Archives, U.S. Military Service Record on W. E. Jones. Letter from W. E. Jones to R. Jones; Adjutant General, dated August 21, 1848. This source will be abbreviated to National Archives.
181. *Ibid*. W. E. Jones *Oath of Allegiance*, August 22, 1848.

Chapter 4

1. William Wessels, *Born to Be a Soldier: The Military Career of William Wing Loring of St. Augustine, Florida*, Texas Christian University Press, Fort Worth, 1971, 17–18.
2. David Dary, *The Oregon Trail: An American Saga*, Alfred A. Knopf, New York, 2004, xiii.
3. John C. Fremont had led two smaller expeditions westward in the early 1840's to earn the sobriquet, *The Pathfinder*.
4. Mary Lee Stubbs and Stanley Russell Connor, *Army Lineage Series, Armor-Cavalry*, Part I, Regular Army and Army Reserve, Office of the Chief of Military History, United States Army, Washington, D.C., 1969, 10.
5. Dary, 2.
6. Gilder Lehrman Institute, W. E. Jones Papers. Letter drafted by W. E. Jones at Fort Ewell, TX, dated August 4, 1852, 1
7. Raymond W. Settle, *The March of the Mounted Riflemen from Fort Leavenworth to Fort Vancouver, May to October 1849 as recorded in the journals of Major Osborne Cross and George Gibbs and the official report of Colonel Loring*, University of Nebraska Press, Lincoln and London, 1940, 16.
8. University of Texas at Arlington Archives, Special Collections, Arlington, Texas Manuscript, dated March 27, 1849, by C. H. Ogle, Brvt. 2nd Lt., 1st Dragoons, Officer of the Guard.
9. Gilder Lehrman Institute, W. E. Jones Papers. Letter drafted by W. E. Jones at Fort Ewell, TX, dated August 4, 1852, 3.
10. Major Osborne Cross, *March of the Regiment of Mounted Riflemen to Oregon in 1849*, Ve Galleon Press, Fairfield, WA, 1967, 125–127.
11. Settle, 277.
12. Charles E. Rosenberg, *The Cholera Years, The United States in 1832, 1849, and 1866*, The University of Chicago Press, 1962, 115.
13. *Ibid.*, 3.
14. Cross, 11.
15. *Ibid*.
16. Cross, 3.
17. *Ibid.*, 29
18. *Ibid.*, 25
19. *Ibid.*, 115.
20. Wessels, 25.
21. *Ibid.*, 26.
22. *Ibid.*, 31–32.
23. *Ibid.*, 44.
24. *Ibid.*, 48
25. *Ibid.*, 53
26. *Ibid.*,
27. *Ibid.*, 74.
28. *Ibid.*, 71; Wessels, 30.
29. Cross, 75.
30. *Ibid.*, 88; Settle, 203 (n).
31. Wessels, 31.
32. Cross, 125–27.

33. Wessels, 31.
34. Settle, 22.
35. *Ibid.*
36. Wessels, 36.
37. *Ibid.*
38. *Ibid.*
39. Gilder Lehrman Institute, W. E. Jones Papers. Letter drafted by W. E. Jones at Fort Ewell, TX, dated August 4, 1852.
40. Cullum, 212.
41. National Archives, W. W. Loring U.S. Military Service Record, Letter from Lt. Col. W. W. Loring, dated July 2, 1851, on the Steamer Falcon to General Robert Jones in Washington, D.C.
42. *Ibid.*
43. *Getting Through West Point*, pt. 2, 135.
44. Charles William Dabney Papers (#1412).
45. National Archives, Washington D C, U.S. Military Service Record of W. W. Loring, Letter from Loring, dated July 2, 1852, on the Steamer Falcon to General Robert Jones in Washington, D.C.
46. Wessels, 31.

Chapter 5

1. Tucker & Waller, 71.
2. ShEby County, Tennessee Archives, Memphis
3. Historical Society of Washington County, Virginia papers, Abingdon, VA, Unfiled Court Records, Washington County, Compiled by D. E. Brown, Deeds, 1782–1875.
4. Diana Powell, *Pioneer Families of Washington County, Virginia*, 2005–2013, 2893. Her source: Emily Dunn Bible, *Virginia Genealogical Society Quarterly*, Vol. 15, # 4, 7. Jones, William E., Glade Spring Presbyterian Church Cemetery inscription on Eliza's monument.
5. Robert Wooster, *Soldiers, Sutlers, and Settlers: Garrison Life on the Texas Frontier*, Texas A&M University Press, College Station, TX, 1987, 73.
6. Historical Society of Washington County, Virginia, Unfiled Court Records, Washington County, Virginia, Vol. 2, pt. 2, 2.
7. National Archives, U.S. Military Service Record of W. E. Jones.
8. Steve Johnston, Private Collection, Chilhowie, VA.

Chapter 6

1. Arnold J. Barto III, *A Matagorda Bay Magnetometer Survey & Site Test Excavation Project*, Texas Antiquities Committee Publication No. 9, Austin, TX, 1982, 13.
2. *Ibid.*, 44
3. Brownson Malsch, *Indianola, The Mother of Western Texas*, State House Press, Austin, TX,1988, 61.
4. *Ibid.*
5. *Ibid.*
6. Mabel Morris Mayfield, "Texas Ghost City May Live Again as a State Park," *Houston Chronicle*, Editorial Section, January 15, 1933, 8.
7. Malsch, 292.
8. John Henry Brown, "Wreck of the Independence, Distressing Loss of Life," *Indianola Bulletin*, Indianola, TX, April 1, 1852. This source will be abbreviated to *Indianola Bulletin*.
9. Malsch, 72.
10. Reverend J. W. E. Airey, Lifetime Chaplain of the National Frontiersmen's Association, article"Tragic Drowning of Two Women at Old Indianola Enshrouded in Mystery" *The Houston Chronicle*, Sunday, April 19, 1936.
11. Brown, *Indianola Bulletin*.
12. Charles Eldridge, Manuscript: "Indianola Letter," University of Texas, Archives, Austin. Note: This is an unpublished manuscript, dated March 30, 1852. *Independence* passenger Eldridge of Mt. Carmel, Illinois wrote a personal eyewitness account of the wreck in a letter to his friends, 1–2.
13. *Ibid.*
14. *Ibid.*, Brown, *Indianola Bulletin*.
15. Eldridge, "Indianola Letter," 2.
16. *Ibid.*, 4.
17. *Ibid.*, 5.
18. *Ibid.*
19. Brown, *Indianola Bulletin*.
20. Eldridge, "Indianola Letter," 6–7.
21. *Ibid.*, 7.
22. Avery.
23. Eldridge, "Indianola Letter," 6.
24. *Ibid.*
25. *Ibid.*, 8.
26. *Ibid.*
27. *Ibid.*, 9.
28. *Ibid.*, 12.
29. *Ibid.*
30. *Ibid.*, 16.
31. Brown, *Indianola Bulletin*.
32. *Ibid.*
33. Malsch, 75. Source assumes missing body was a daughter.
34. Airey, 38.
35. Gonzales County Marriage License Records, Gonzales, TX.
36. Douglass Southall Freeman, *Lee's Lieutenants, Vol. II, Cedar Mountain to Chancellorsville*, Charles Scribner's Sons, New York, 1945, 410.
37. Thomas W. Colley, "Brig. Gen. William E. Jones," *Confederate Veteran*, Vol. XI January 1903 to December 1903, Reprinted 1987–1988, Broadfoot Publishing Co., Wilmington, NC, 266.
38. Carolyn Ryburn, Private Collection, Glade Spring, Virginia, Letter from W. E. Jones at Fort Merrill, TX, to Jane Ryburn Dunn at Glade Spring, VA, dated June 1, 1852.
39. Dobbie Edward Lambert, *Grumble: The W. E. Jones Brigade, 1863–1864*, Lambert Enterprises, Wahiawa, HI, 1992, 3.

40. John W. Thomason, *JEB Stuart*, University of Nebraska Press, Lincoln Nebraska, 1994, 73.
41. Virgil Carrington Jones, *Ranger Mosby*, University of North Carolina Press, Chapel Hill, NC, 1944, 33.
42. Colley, 266.

Chapter 7

1. There is no conclusion as to how Jones earned the nickname but this is one theory.
2. Tidball, 75.
3. Thomas Smith, *The Old Army in Texas, A Research Guide to the U.S. Army in Nineteenth-Century Texas*, Texas State Historical Association, Austin, 2000, 95.
4. National Archives, U.S. Military Service Record of W. E. Jones.
5. M. L. Crimmins, *The Southwestern Historical Quarterly*, Vol. 51, July 1947 to April 1948, "Notes and Documents, W. G. Freeman's Report on the Eighth Military Department," Texas State Historical Association, Austin, 1948, 350.
6. *Ibid.*, 351.
7. Smith, 64.
8. Crimmins, 252.
9. *Ibid.*
10. *Ibid.*, 253.
11. *Ibid.*, 254.
12. *Ibid.*
13. *Ibid.* Note: The "Col" referred to in this correspondence is more than likely not W. E. Jones's commanding officer but Colonel Robert Buchanan Edmondson, 1808–1872, father of Thomas Benjamin Estill Edmondson who accompanied the couple on the Steamship *Independence* and remained in Texas as a sutler. Source: Diana Powell, http://www.ramblingroots.com/RYB-p/p2272.htm.
14. Carolyn Ryburn, Private Collection, report card from the institution.
15. Roger J. Judd, Private Collection, Fairbury, Nebraska, Jackson, Letter from Thomas Jonathan in Lexington, VA, to Lieut. W. E. Jones, U.S. Mounted Rifles, dated March 24, 1855.
16. Carolyn Ryburn, Private Collection, Letter from William E. Jones at Fort Ewell, TX, to Jane Ryburn Dunn at Glade Spring, VA, dated August 21, 1852.
17. *Ibid.*
18. *Ibid.* Letter from W. E. Jones at Fort Ewell, TX, letter to Jane Ryburn Dunn at Glade Spring, VA, dated December 26, 1852.
19. Jonathan Wild was one of the most infamous criminals of Great Britain in the 1720s. As a revered public figure, he gained power by manipulating the press and the nation's fears. His villainy was finally exposed, and he was publicly hanged in 1725. His name developed into a symbol of corruption, hypocrisy and a frequent reference in satire. *Peter Simple* is a fiction novel published in 1834 by Frederick Marryat about a British midshipman during the Napoleonic Wars of the early nineteenth century. Told in the first person by the title character, the narrative recounts his odyssey from naïveté to heroism. Written by a veteran officer of the Royal Navy, the novel was a best-seller that was popular with West Point cadets.
20. *Ibid.*, 8.
21. Wooster, 85.
22. *Ibid.*, 111.
23. *Ibid.*, 85.
24. Carolyn Ryburn, Collection Jones, Letter from W. E. Jones at Fort Merrill, TX, to Jane Ryburn Dunn at Glade Spring, VA, dated June 1, 1852.
25. Crimmins, 352.
26. Wooster, 195
27. Carolyn Ryburn, Private Collection, Letter from W. E. Jones at Fort Ewell, TX, to Jane Ryburn Dunn at Glade Spring, VA, dated June 13, 1853.
28. Carolyn Ryburn, Private Collection, Letter from W. E. Jones at Fort Merrill, TX, to Jane Ryburn Dunn at Glade Spring, VA, dated June 1, 1852.
29. Wooster, 45.
30. *Ibid.*, 64.
31. Carolyn Ryburn, Private Collection, Letter from W. E. Jones at Fort Ewell, TX, to Jane Ryburn Dunn at Glade Spring, VA, dated May 1, 1852.
32. *Ibid.*
33. Annette Martin Ludeman, *La Salle County, South Texas Brush Country*, 1856–1975, Texas County History Series, Nortex Press, No. Quanah, TX, 1975, 2.
34. M. L. Crimmins, 255–256.
35. Wooster, 110.
36. Carolyn Ryburn, Carolyn, Letter from W. E. Jones at Fort Merrill, TX, to Jane Ryburn Dunn at Glade Spring, VA, dated June 1, 1852l.
37. *Ibid.*, Letter from W. E. Jones at Fort Ewell, TX, to Jane Ryburn Dunn at Glade Spring, VA, dated August 21, 1852.
38. *Ibid.*, 111
39. Crimmins, 255.
40. *Ibid.*
41. Wooster, 59.
42. *Ibid.*
43. *Ibid.*, 94.
44. *Ibid.*, 188.
45. University of Texas at Arlington Archives, Lieutenant William E Jones report from Galveston, TX, January 18, 1853.
46. *Ibid.*
47. *Ibid.*
48. Wooster, 52.
49. Cullum, 212.
50. Randy Steffen, *United States Military Saddles, 1812–1943*, University of Oklahoma Press, Norman, 1973, 61
51. Cullum, 212.
52. Carolyn Ryburn, Private Collection, Letter from W. E. Jones in New Orleans, LA to Dr. Samuel Dunn in Glade Spring, VA, dated May 8, 1855.
53. *Ibid.*
54. National Archives, U.S. Army file on W. E. Jones.

55. Carolyn Ryburn, Private Collection, Letter from W. E. Jones in New Orleans, LA, to Dr. Samuel Dunn in Glade Spring, VA, dated May 8, 1855.
56. Washington County District Clerk, Will Book 6, 347.
57. National Archives. U.S. Military Service Record on W. E. Jones.
58. Tucker and Walker, 70.
59. Wooster, 58. His source: Letter from Robert E. Lee to Mary Custis Lee, dated August 18, 1856. The letter is part of Francis Raymond Adams, Jr. "An Annotated Edition of the Personal Letters of Robert E. Lee, April 1855–April, 1861" (Ph.D., diss; University of Maryland, 1955, 156–157.
60. *Ibid.* His source: R. E. Lee letter, dated November 1, 1856, to Fitzhugh Lee.
61. National Archives, U.S. Military Service Record of W. E. Jones. Letter from W. E. Jones in Camp Crawford, NM, to Lt. Col. W. W. Loring in Santa Fe, NM, dated September 4, 1856.
62. *Ibid.*, U.S. Military Service Record of W. W. Loring. Report from Lt. Col. W. W. Loring in Santa Fe, NM, to the U.S. War Department in Washington, D.C., dated September 5, 1856.
63. *Ibid.* Letter from W. A. Nichols, Assistant Adjutant General, Department of New Mexico, Santa Fe, NM, to W. E. Jones in San Elizario, TX, dated October 26, 1856.
64. *Ibid.* Letter from W. E. Jones in San Elizario, TX, to Secretary of War Jefferson Davis in Washington, D.C., dated November 10, 1856.
65. *Ibid.* Letter from W. E. Jones in San Elizario, TX, to Major W. A. Nichols, Assistant Adjutant General, Department of New Mexico, Santa Fe, NM, dated November 14, 1856.
66. *Ibid.* Letter from W. E. Jones in San Elizario, TX, to Major W. A. Nichols, Assistant Adjutant General, U.S. Army, Department of New Mexico, Santa Fe, NM, dated November 19, 1856.
67. *Ibid.* Report by Lt. Col. W. W. Loring in Santa Fe, NM, to the Adjutant General, Department of New Mexico, Santa Fe, NM, dated November 27, 1856.
68. *Ibid.* Report from R. E. Lee in Brownsville, TX, to the Department of New Mexico Headquarters in Santa Fe, NM, dated December 20, 1856.
69. Gilder Lehrman Institute. William E. Jones Collection Letter from B. Williams in San Antonio, TX, to S. C. Greenhow in Richmond, VA, dated December 20, 1856.
70. National Archives, U.S. Military Service Record of W. E. Jones. Report from Colonel Samuel Cooper, Assistant Adjutant General, U.S. Army, Washington, D.C. to Secretary of War, Jefferson Davis, Washington, D.C., dated January 15 to January 27, 1856.

Chapter 8

1. Charles Pinnegar, Charles, *Brand of Infamy: A Biography of John Buchanan Floyd*, Greenwood Press, Westport, CT, 2003, 53.
2. Pinnegar, 59
3. United States Patent Office, "William E. Jones of the United States Army, Saddletree" Specification of Letters Patent No. 11,068, dated June 13, 1854.
4. Steffen, 61.
5. British Office of Patents, no. 1892, Printed by George Edward Eyre and William Spottiswoode, Printers to the Queen's Most Excellent Majesty, 1858, 2.
6. *Ibid.*
7. *Ibid.*, 1
8. *Ibid.*
9. National Archives R.G. 92, Entry 225, Consolidated Correspondence File, Letter from W. E. Jones to Secretary of State, John B. Floyd, dated January 23, 1858. The Pennsylvania Historical Society, Philadelphia, provided the address information on Lacey & Phillips.
10. Steffen, 62.
11. *Ibid.*
12. Mark R. Wilson, "The Extensive Side of Nineteenth-Century Military Economy: The Tent Industry in the Northern United States during the Civil War," *Enterprise and Society 2*, Oxford University Press USA, 2001, 299.
13. *Ibid.*
14. National Archives, Fort Riley Resolution, November 12, 1855, Jerry Thompson, *Henry Hopkins Sibley, Confederate General of the West*, Texas A&M University Press, College Station, TX, 1996, 130.
15. *Ibid.*, Records of Quartermaster General's Office, William Wallace Burns "History of My Connection with the Sibley Tent" National Archives, R.G. 92, Thompson, 131.
16. *Ibid.*
17. *Ibid.*
18. Thompson, 133.
19. Gilder Lehrman Institute William E. Jones Collection, Contract between W. E. Jones and Henry H. Sibley, dated March 9, 1857.
20. Library of Virginia, W. E. Jones Papers, Letter from Solomon Parrett to W. E. Jones, dated May 12, 1857.
21. Wilson, 302.
22. National Archives, R. G. 92, Consolidated Correspondence File, Letter from W. E. Jones in Baltimore, Maryland to Secretary of War, John B. Floyd in Washington, D.C., dated March 25, 1857
23. "Bleeding Kansas" was the term applied to the violence-torn Kansas Territory, where a five-year border war erupted between pro-slavery and abolitionist factions following the Kansas-Nebraska Act of 1854. The Act left the issue up to popular sovereignty and opened the territory to mass migrations from both sides.
24. Thompson, 142.
25. *Ibid.*, 146 and 148.
26. National Archives, R.G. 92, Consolidated Correspondence File, Letter from T. S. Jesup to Charles Thomas, February 8, 1858.
27. National Archives R. G. 92, Consolidated Cor-

respondence File, Records of the Office of Quartermaster General, Entry 225, Letter from W. E. Jones to Thos. S. Jesup, dated January 20, 1858.

28. *Ibid.*, Letter from W. E. Jones in Philadelphia to John Buchanan Floyd in Washington, D.C., dated January 23, 1858.

29. *Ibid.*

30. *Ibid.*

31. *Ibid.*

32. *Ibid.*, Letter from T. S. Jesup to Secretary of War John B. Floyd, dated February 5, 1858

33. *Ibid.*, Letter from E. I. Baily to H. H. Sibley, April 14, 1858.

34. *Ibid.*, Letter from F.J. Porter to H. H. Sibley, April 15, 1858.

35. *Ibid.*, Letter, Jim Bridger to H. H. Sibley, April 15, 1858.

36. Library of Virginia, W. E. Jones Papers, Letter from John H. Landell in Newark, NJ, to W. E. Jones in St. Louis, MO, dated March 19, 1859.

37. *Ibid.*

38. *Ibid.*

39. National Archives R. G. 92, Consolidated Correspondence File, Records of Quartermaster General's Office, Letter from Charles Thomas in Philadelphia to T. S. Jesup in Washington, D.C., dated February 8, 1858.

40. Carolyn Ryburn, Private Collection, Jones Letter from W. E. Jones at Fort Ewell, TX, to Jane Ryburn Dunn at Glade Spring, VA, dated June 13, 1853.

41. Library of Virginia, William E Jones Papers, Drafted essay manuscript to an unknown London-based newspaper editor, not, dated.

42. *Ibid.*

43. *Ibid.*

44. "Fire Eaters" were extremist Southern politicians who advocated secession with violence and complete animosity towards the abolitionists. Due to their extreme viewpoints, they were denied important government positions in the new Confederacy.

45. Library of Virginia, Jones, William E., Drafted essay manuscript to an unknown London-based newspaper editor, not, dated.

46. *Ibid*

47. *Ibid.*

48. *Ibid.* Note: the "Hottentot" was a negative European term applied to the Khoikhoi, a culture of South African nomadic tribesmen related to the Bushmen. European colonist regarded them as a primitive savage group.

49. *Ibid.*

50. *Ibid.*

51. *Ibid.*

52. *Ibid.*

53. Gilder Lehrman Institute, Institutional Collection, William E. Jones Collection GLC02711, Paris Order and Bill of Lading, January 10, 1859.

54. *Ibid.*

55. Lewis Preston Summers, *History of Southwest Virginia, 1746–1786 and Washington County, 1777–1880*, J. Hill Printing Company, Richmond, VA, 1903, 753.

56. National Archives R. G. 92, Consolidated Correspondence File, 50th U.S. Congress, Senate Bill 583 for the relief of personal representatives of Henry H. Sibley, deceased, regarding the use of the Sibley Tents by the Army of the U.S.

57. *Ibid.*, W. W. Burns, "History of My Connection to the Sibley Tent."

58. *Ibid.*

59. *Ibid.*

60. *Ibid.*

61. *Ibid.*

62. Library of Virginia, W. E. Jones Papers, Letter from Charlotte Sibley to W. E. Jones, dated October 27, 1860.

Chapter 9

1. Pinnegar, 94.

2. *Ibid.*

3. Mark Mayo Boatner III, *The Civil War Dictionary*, David McKay Company, Inc. New York, 1959, 286.

4. The Historical Society of Pennsylvania, Philadelphia, PA, Gratz and Dreer Collections, Letter from W. E. Jones in Abingdon, VA, to Virginia Governor John Letcher in Richmond, VA, dated May 11, 1861.

5. Gilder Lehrman Institute, William E. Jones Collection GLC02711.25, letter from John B. Floyd in Washington, D.C., to Virginia Governor Henry Wise in Richmond, VA, dated November 26, 1859.

6. Library of Virginia, Richmond, Virginia William E. Jones Papers, Undated manuscript circa 1860.

7. *Ibid.*

8. Lieut. Col. W. W. Blackford, C.S.A. *War Years with Jeb Stuart*, Charles Scribner's Sons, New York, 1945, 11, 13

9. *Ibid.*, 13.

10. *Ibid.*

11. *Ibid.*, 14.

12. *Ibid.*

13. *Civil War Times Illustrated*, "Grumble Jones, A Personality Profile," Historical Times, Inc., Gettysburg, PA, 1968, 36.

14. Blackford, 14.

15. *Ibid.*

16. Gilder Lehrman Institute: William E. Jones Collection GLC09285, Drafted essay, dated December 1860.

17. Virgil Carrington Jones, 1944, 33.

18. National Archives, CS Military Service Record on W. E. Jones. Jefferson Davis was Secretary of War in the cabinet of President Franklin Pierce and had ultimately received the resignation of 1st Lt. W. E. Jones from the U.S. Mounted Rifles in December of 1856.

19. James Buchanan Ballard, Personal Collection, William E. Jones, an undated and unpublished essay on the Virginia Conference circa 1861.

20. *Ibid.*

21. *Ibid.*

22. Virgil Carrington Jones, 1944, 33.

23. John S. Mosby, *The Memoirs of John S. Mosby*, J. S. Sanders & Co., Nashville, TN, 1995, 16–17 (n).

24. James I. Robertson, Jr., "The Virginia State Convention of 1861," *Virginia at War*, 18.
25. National Archives, CS Military Service Record on W. E. Jones, letter from W. E. Jones in Richmond, VA, to President Jefferson Davis in Richmond, VA, dated April 28, 1861.
26. The Historical Society of Pennsylvania, Gratz and Dreer Collections, Philadelphia, PA, letter from W. E. Jones in Richmond, VA, Letter to Virginia Governor Letcher in Richmond, VA, dated April 29, 1861.
27. United States War Department, *The War of Rebellion, A Compilation of the Official Records of the Union and Confederate Armies*, Prepared under the direction of the Secretary of War by Robert N. Scott, Government Printing Office, Washington, D.C. 1880–1900, Vol. 2, 823. Note: This source will be abbreviated to *O. R. (Official Records)* from this point. Unless stated otherwise, all units are Series I.
28. VMI Archives.
29. The Historical Society of Pennsylvania, Gratz and Dreer Collections, Philadelphia, PA, letter from W. E. Jones in Abingdon, VA, to Virginia Governor Letcher in Richmond, VA, dated May 11, 1862.
30. Virgil Carrington Jones, 1944, 37.
31. *Ibid*., 35.
32. *Ibid*.
33. Colonel John S. Mosby, *Mosby's Memoirs*, J. S. Sanders & Co., Nashville, 1995, 23.
34. *Ibid*., 37.
35. *Ibid*.
36. National Archives, CS Military Service Record on Thomas B. Edmondson, Mosby, 22.
37. National Archives, CS Military Service Record on William Logan Dunn.
38. Emory & Henry Archives, Minutes of the Board of Trustees, May 13, 1861, George J. Stevenson, 92.
39. *Ibid*.
40. Virgil Carrington Jones, 1944, 41, 43.
41. *Ibid*., 43
42. *Ibid*., 44.
43. *Ibid*.
44. Burke Davis, *JEB Stuart, The Last Cavalier*, The Fairfax Press, New York, 1988, 52.
45. *Ibid*.

Chapter 10

1. Cullum, 212, 374. While Jones served at Fort Duncan at Eagle Pass, Stuart served at Fort McIntosh at Laredo.
2. Tidball, 51; Thomason, 21; Davis, 27. According to legend, out of concern that a higher class ranking would place him into the elite Corps of Engineers, Stuart slowed his academic pace to reduce his class standing.
3. Davis, 41.
4. Blackford, 17.
5. Virgil Carrington Jones, 1944, 45.
6. Davis, 54.
7. Boatner, 99.
8. Davis, 64. Jubal Early expressed this opinion.
9. Note: According to Boatner, Patterson was criticized for his failure to engage and mustered out of the Army on July 27, 1861.
10. Virgil Carrington Jones, 1944, 46.
11. Note: While Jones had served eight years in the U.S. Mounted Rifles, the U.S. was not at war with other nations. Although he may have experienced skirmishes with Apache and Comanche Indian tribes, he had not been exposed to artillery fire.
12. Mosby, 48.
13. National Archives, C. S. Military Service Record on Robert Swan, Letter from Brigadier General W. H. Whiting to Secretary of War, George Wythe Randolph, dated July 21, 1862.
14. Jones, Virgil Carrington, 1944, 48.
15. Mosby, 49.
16. *Ibid*.
17. *Ibid*., 50.
18. George Cary Eggleston, *Southern Soldier Stories*, an Edited Reprinting of the 1898 Classic, SCS Publications, Fairfax VA, 1998, 102.
19. *Ibid*.
20. Virgil Carrington Jones, 1944, 50.
21. Mosby, 85.
22. Virgil Carrington Jones, 1944, 51.
23. *Ibid*., 51.
24. Robert J. Driver, Jr. *1st Virginia Cavalry*, 1st Edition, H. E. Howard, Inc., Lynchburg, VA, 1991, 20.
25. Virgil Carrington Jones, 1944, 51–52.
26. *O.R. Vol. 5*, 181.
27. *Ibid*.
28. *Ibid*.,
29. Richard L. Armstrong, *7th Virginia Cavalry*, 1st Edition, H. E. Howard, Inc., Lynchburg, VA, 1992, 172.
30. McClellan, Henry B. McClellan, *I Rode with Jeb Stuart, The Life and Campaigns of Major General J.E.B. Stuart*, De Capo Press, Bloomington, IN, 1958, 320.
31. *O.R Vol. 5*, 181.
32. Eggleston, "Old Jones and the Huckster" *Southern Soldier Stories*, 178–180.
33. Mosby, 23
34. Virgil Carrington Jones, 54.
35. *Ibid*., 55, Mosby, 102
36. Cheat Mountain took place from September 10 to 15 of 1861. By February, Lee was an advisor to President Davis in Richmond.
37. Blackford, 60.
38. Virgil Carrington Jones, 1944, 57.
39. *Ibid*.
40. *O.R. Vol. 12*, 415.
41. National Archives, CS Military Service Record on W. E. Jones, Letter from W. E. Jones in Bealton, VA, to CS Secretary of War, G. W. Randolph in Richmond, VA, dated March 24, 1862.
42. Virgil Carrington Jones, 1944, 57.
43. *Ibid*.
44. Blacktord, 62.
45. Virginia Historical Society, Richmond, VA, H.B. McClellan Papers, MSS1st923u15–20, Stuart, J.E.B.,

letter to his wife, Flora Stuart, dated January 29, 1862, from Centerville, VA.
  46. Blackford, 62.
  47. *Ibid.*, 51
  48. *Ibid.*
  49. Gilder Lerhrman Institute, W. E. Jones papers.
  50. Jones, Virgil Carrington, 1944, 57.
  51. *Ibid.*, 57–58.
  52. Mosby, 109.
  53. Virgil Carrington Jones, 1944, 59.

Chapter 11

  1. Freeman, *Vol. 1*, 309.
  2. Thomas A. Ashby, M.D. *Life of Turner Ashby,* The Neal Publishing, New York, 1914, 39.
  3. *Ibid.*, 57–58.
  4. *Ibid.*, 87.
  5. Freeman, *Vol. 1*, 309.
  6. Ashby, 106–107.
  7. Boatner, 739.
  8. *O.R. Vol. 12*, pt. 1, 704.
  9. Ashby, 187.
  10. *Ibid.*, 264.
  11. Boatner, 742.
  12. *O.R. Vol. 12*, pt. 1, 712.
  13. Ashby, 216.
  14. *Ibid.*
  15. William N. McDonald, *A History of the Laurel Brigade, Originally the Ashby Cavalry of the Army of Northern Virginia and Chew's Battery,* The John Hopkins University Press, Baltimore, MD, 2002, 76.
  16. National Archives, CS Military Service Record on W. E. Jones.
  17. MacDonald, 169.
  18. *Ibid.*
  19. Armstrong, 38.
  20. Dan Oates, *Hanging Rock Rebel, Lt. John Blue's War in West Virginia and the Shenandoah Valley,* Burd Street Press, Shippensburg, PA, 1994, 110.
  21. *Ibid.*, 111.
  22. *Ibid.*, 113.
  23. *Ibid.*
  24. *Ibid.*
  25. *Ibid.*
  26. *Ibid.*
  27. *Ibid.*
  28. *Ibid.*
  29. *Ibid.*, 114.
  30. Armstrong, 39, 191 Major Thomas Marshall was a prisoner of war and exchanged the following month. He returned to the Seventh Virginia Cavalry and served with distinction until killed in action on November 12, 1864, during Sheridan's Shenandoah Valley Campaign. He is buried at Stonewall Cemetery in Winchester beside Turner Ashby. Thomas Marshall was the grandson of Chief Justice John Marshall.
  31. *O.R. Vol. 12*, pt. 2, 112. Oates, 114. Note: Lieutenant Blue stated they were "outnumbered at least five to one."
  32. Oates, 115; National Archives CS Military Service Record on W. E. Jones
  33. *O.R. Vol. 12*, pt. 2, 114.
  34. Oates, 115.
  35. *O.R. Vol. 12*, pt. 2, 112.
  36. *Ibid.*, 113.
  37. *O.R. Vol. 12*, pt. 2, 181–182.
  38. *O.R. Vol. 12*, pt.3, 926. Note: Jackson's letter to Lee is not in the *O.R.* The content can be reconstructed from Lee's reply.
  39. On March 23, 1862, Garnett had ordered a withdrawal from an impossible situation during the rout at Kernstown. Jackson ordered his arrest. During his court martial trial, Garnett vehemently defended his record and his honor in a cross-examination challenging Jackson's credibility. The trial proceedings were suspended upon reports of Union General John Pope's advance, and Garnet was released. Before the trial could be resumed, Jackson died at Chancellorsville and became a legend. Unable to ever officially clear his name, Garnett was killed during Pickett's Charge at Gettysburg.
  40. *O.R. Vol. 12*, pt. 3, 926.
  41. *O.R. Vol. 12*, pt. 2, 239.
  42. Robertson, 1997, 534
  43. *Ibid.*
  44. *Ibid.*, 537.
  45. *O.R. Vol. 12*, pt. 2, 725.
  46. *Ibid.*
  47. *O.R. Vol. 12*, pt. 2, 727.
  48. *Ibid.*
  49. Davis, 189.
  50. *Ibid.*
  51. Freeman, *Vol. 2*, 285.
  52. *Ibid.*
  53. *O.R. Vol. 19*, pt. 2, 52.
  54. Davis, 221; *O.R.* Vol. 19, pt. 2, 52.
  55. Davis, 222–223.
  56. Freeman, *Vol. 2*, 302.
  57. Boatner, 814.
  58. *O.R. Vol. 19*, pt. 2, 54.
  59. *Ibid.*
  60. Freeman, *Vol. 2*, 304.
  61. Longacre, 152.
  62. Longacre, 151.
  63. Robertson, 1997, 626, 900.
  64. Virginia Historical Society, Richmond, Virginia, H. B. McClellan Papers, MSS1st923994 Letter from J. E. B. Stuart to R. E. Lee, dated October 24, 1862.
  65. Armstrong, 172.
  66. *O.R. Vol., 19*, pt. 2, 705, Virginia Historical Society, Henry B. McClellan Papers, Richmond, VA.
  67. *O.R. Vol. 19*, pt. 2, 712.
  68. Freeman, *Vol. 2*, 281.

Chapter 12

  1. National Archives CS Military Record on Warren M. Hopkins
  2. *Ibid.*

3. Frank M. Myers, *The Comanches: A History of White's Battalion Virginia Cavalry, Laurel Brig., Hampton's Div., A.N.V.C.S.A.* Kelly, Piet & Co., Baltimore, Maryland, 1871, 116.

4. John N. Opie, *A Rebel Cavalryman with Lee, Stuart, and Jackson*, W. B. Conkley Company, Chicago, 1899, 45.

5. Festus, Summers, *The Baltimore and Ohio in the Civil War*, Stan Clark Military Books, Gettysburg, PA, 1993, 17.

6. Robertson, 1997, 642.

7. *Ibid.*, 642, 643

8. *O.R. Vol. 21*, 1080–1081.

9. Freeman, *Vol. 2*, 409.

10. David L. Phillips, Editor, and Rebecca L. Hill, Chief Editor, *War Stories: Civil War in West Virginia*, Gauley Mount Press, Leesburg, VA, 199.

11. In 1863, Petersburg was an unincorporated town in Hardy County in what would later become the state of WV. It is not to be confused with the City of Petersburg, VA, on the Appomattox River south of Richmond. In 1866, Grant County was formed out of Hardy County, WV, and Petersburg became the county seat.

12. N Jonathan A. Noyalas, thesis submitted to the faculty of the Virginia Polytechnic Institute and State University, "My will is absolute law: General Robert H. Milroy and Winchester, Virginia," 2003, Blacksburg, VA, abstract.

13. Spencer C. Tucker, *Brigadier General John D. Imboden, Confederate Commander in the Shenandoah*, The University Press of Kentucky, Lexington, KY, 2003, 11–12.

14. *Ibid.*, 20–21.

15. *Ibid.*, 68.

16. *Ibid.*, 70–71.

17. *Ibid.*, 72.

18. *Ibid.*, 102.

19. *Ibid.*, 107.

20. *OR Series III, Vol. 2*, 944.

21. *OR Series II, Vol. 5*, 810.

22. *Ibid.*, 811 *The Crisis* was a Northern newspaper Publishing established by Samuel Medary of Ohio and known for its opposition to the Lincoln administration's policies. Often comparing President Lincoln to King George III, the publication promoted States Rights and Peace Democrats AKA Copperheads who opposed the war policy for a negotiated settlement.

23. *OR Vol. 21*, 875.

24. *OR Vol. 21*, 1080. Jones does not mention Withers by his name other than that the prisoner of war was a major with the Tenth (West) Virginia Infantry Regiment. The National Archives U.S. Military Service Record shows that Major Henry H. Withers of the Tenth West Virginia Regiment was captured by the Confederates on December 23, 1862, at Strasburg.

25. *OR Series III, Vol. 3*, 8.

26. *Ibid.*

27. *Ibid.*, 9. On May 13, 1862, the state legislature of the reorganized government at Wheeling approved the formation of a new state and applied to Congress for admission into the Union. On December 31, 1862, President Lincoln signed an enabling act conditionally admitting West Virginia to the Union pending the adoption of a state constitution and a public referendum. A convention convened on February 12, 1863, and a revised constitution was adopted on March 26, 1863. On April 20, 1863, President Lincoln issued a proclamation admitting the state of West Virginia to the Union at the end of sixty days. West Virginia officially became an independent state admitted to Union on June 20, 1863.

28. *OR Series III Vol. 3*, 9–10.

29. *OR. Vol. 21*, 1080. General John Pope had aroused Southern animosity before the Second Manassas Campaign, by calling for harsh treatment of Southern sympathizers in occupied portions of Virginia. Benjamin Franklin Butler earned infamy while occupying New Orleans when he ordered the hanging of a citizen who pulled down the U.S. flag over the mint. He followed up with his "Woman Order" inciting international outrage. Butler confiscated monetary funds from the Dutch consul and earned the moniker "Spoons" for allegedly looting silverware. Political indignation escalated until he was recalled on December 16, 1862, and replaced by Nathaniel Banks.

30. *OR, Vol. 21*, 179. National Archives U.S. Military Service Record on Henry H. Withers who was exchanged on April 26, 1863.

31. Noyalas, 1. Possession of Winchester changed from seventy-two to ninety-six times during the Civil War.

32. *Ibid.*, 18.

33. Joseph Warren Keifer, *Slavery and Four Years of War, Vol. 1and 2, A Political History of Slavery in the United States Together, with a Narrative of the Campaign and Battles of the Civil War in Which the Author Took Part: 1861–1865*, Filquarian Publishing, Lexington, KY, 1899, 226.

34. F. N. Boney, *John Letcher of Virginia, The Story of Virginia's Civil War Governor*, University of Alabama Press, 1966, 183.

35. Noyalas, 23; Boatner, 552.

36. *OR Vol. 21*, 1080.

37. As previously outlined, Petersburg, WV, not to be confused with the City of Petersburg, VA, became the county seat for newly formed Grant County after the Civil War.

38. *O.R. Vol. 21*, 747.

39. *Ibid.*

40. *Ibid.*

41. *Ibid.*

42. *Ibid.*, 748.

43. *Ibid.*, 747.

44. Festus, Summers(Editor), *A Borderland Confederate*, Greenwood Press, Westport, CT, 1973, 41.

45. *OR Vol. 21*, 948

46. *OR Series III Vol. 3*, 13–14.

47. Lambert, 67.

48. Myers, 103–104; *Civil War Times Illustrated*, 37.

49. *Ibid.*, 605–606.

50. Charles T. O'Ferrall, *Forty Years of Active Service; Being Some History of the War Between the Confederacy and the Union and of Events Leading up to It.* The Neale Publishing, New York and Washington, 1904, 53–54.
51. *Ibid.*, 54.
52. *Ibid.*
53. *Ibid.*
54. OR Series III Vol. 3, 10.
55. *Ibid.*, 10–11.
56. *Ibid.*
57. *Ibid.*, 11.
58. *Ibid.*, Vol. 21, 978.
59. *Ibid.*
60. OR Vol. 21, 948.
61. *Ibid.*, Vol. 25, pt. 2, 64.
62. *Ibid.*
63. *Ibid.*, Vol. 21, 1092.
64. Roger Judd, Private Collection, R. E. Lee confidential letter to W. E. Jones, Camp Valley District, February 2, 1863.
65. OR Vol. 25, pt. 2, 84.
66. *Ibid.*, 106.
67. Roger Judd, Private Collection, R. E. Lee confidential letter to W. E. Jones, Camp Valley District, February 2, 1863
68. Noyalas, 30.
69. Armstrong, 46.
70. O.R. Vol. 2, pt. 1, 32.
71. Oates, 174.
72. O.R. Vol. 25, pt. 1, 27.
73. *Ibid.*, 28.
74. *Ibid.*
75. *Ibid.*, pt. 2, 641.
76. *Ibid.*, 646.
77. *Ibid.*, 654.
78. *Ibid.*

Chapter 13

1. O.R. Vol. 25, pt. 2, 652–653.
2. *Ibid.*
3. O.R. Vol. 25, pt. 2, 685; Virgil Carrington Jones, Virgil Carrington, *Gray Ghost and Rebel Raiders,* Galahad Books, New York, 1956, 163.
4. O.R. Vol. 25, pt. 2, 711.
5. National Archives CS Military Service Record on William G. Williamson, Engineers, Provisional Army of the .Confederate States document, dated April 20, 1863.
6. *Ibid.*
7. O.R. Vol. 25, pt. 1, 99.
8. *Ibid.*, 122; Festus, Summers, 1993, 135.
9. O'Ferrell, 57.
10. *Ibid.*, 58; John Bigelow, Jr., *The Campaign of Chancellorsville: A Strategic and Tactical Study*, Yale University Press, New Haven, CT, 1910, 460.
11. Following the Civil War, Grant County was formed out of Hardy County and Petersburg became the Grant County seat.
12. *OR Vol. 25*, pt. 1, 114.
13. *Ibid.*; Myers, 121.
14. O.R. Vol. 25, pt. 1, 114.
15. McDonald, 120.
16. George Baylor, *Bull Run to Bull Run or Four Years in the Army of Northern Virginia,* R. F. Johnson Publishing Co., Richmond, VA, 1900, 136–137.
17. *Ibid.* Baylor identified the individual as Sergeant Major James Henry Figgat.
18. George H. Moffett, "The Jones Raid Through West Virginia" *Confederate Veteran,* Vol., XIII, January 1905 to December 1905, Reprinted 1987–1988, Broadfoot Publishing, Wilmington, NC, 449.
19. O.R. Vol. 25, pt. 1, 116.
20. Darrell L. Collins, *The Jones-Imboden Raid, The Confederate Attempt to Destroy the Baltimore & Ohio Railroad and Retake West Virginia*, MacFarland & Co., Inc. Jefferson, NC, 2007, 65.
21. O.R. Vol. 25, pt. 1, 108–109.
22. Collins, 67.
23. *Ibid.*, 69.
24. O.R. Vol. 2,5, pt. 1, 129.
25. *Ibid.*, 109.
26. Baylor, 137.
27. O.R. Vol., 25, pt. 1, 109.
28. *Ibid.*
29. *Ibid.*
30. *Ibid.* Note: Captain Wallace was referring to the legendary Colonel James Adelbert Mulligan, who organized the 23rd Illinois, also known as the "Irish Brigade."
31. Myers, 122.
32. *Ibid.*
33. *Ibid.*
34. *Ibid.*
35. O.R. Vol. 25, pt 1, 135; Myers, 124. Note. CS Military Service Record with the National Archives indicates that Private T. E. Tippett was wounded at Spotsylvania Courthouse on May 16, 1864, and died at the General Hospital in Charlottesville on June 29, 1864. Captain Frank A. Bond disputed this version in his article published in the *Confederate Veteran* Vol. XVII, January 1909 to December 1909, Reprinted 1987–1988, Broadfoot Publishing, Wilmington, NC., 499. Bond contended that Sergeant. Edward Johnson of his First Maryland Cavalry stormed the barricade and forced the surrender.
36. *Ibid.*, 121. In his report, Jones recommended Private W. Alexander Buck of Company E, Seventh Virginia Cavalry for a commission for this act of valor. National Archives, CS Military Service Record on W. A. Buck, Private, Company E, Seventh Virginia Cavalry documents that he was wounded and captured at Fairfield, Pennsylvania during the Gettysburg Campaign and confined at DeCamp General Hospital, David's Island, New York Harbor. Remaining a POW for the remainder of the war, he was paroled at Winchester, Virginia, April 26, 1865.
37. O.R. Vol. 25, pt. 1, 110.
38. Myers, 124.

39. Oates, 177; McDonald, 122–123.
40. *O.R. Vol. 25*, pt. 1, 124; McDonald, 123.
41. *Ibid.*
42. McDonald, 123; Myers (pp. 260–261) Myers distinguishes "bushwhackers" from "Swamp Dragons." According to Myers, "bushwhackers" were civilians armed with sporting rifles while "Swamp Dragons" were armed by the Federal Government but acted in their interest as outlaws.
43. *O.R. Vol. 25*, pt. 1, 110.
44. *Ibid.*, 117, Jones' report, dated May 26, 1863, revised the casualty figures from his report of May 4, 1863, contained in *O.R. Vol. 25*, pt. 1, 114. Collins, 75 states that the Compiled Service Records in the National Archives shows the Confederate losses at nine killed and thirty-eight wounded.
45. O'Ferrall, 56; National Archives, CS Military Service Record on Private James Flynn of the Twelfth Virginia Cavalry.
46. *O.R. Vol. 25*, pt. 1, 110. In Captain Wallace's report, he acknowledged six Union wounded. *O.R. Vol. 25*, pt. 1, 117.
47. *Ibid.*, 107–108.
48. *Ibid.*, 108.
49. *Ibid.*
50. *Ibid.*, 114.
51. Oates, 178.
52. *O.R. Vol. 25*, pt. 1, 117.
53. Robert W. Black, *Cavalry Raids of the Civil War*, Stackpole Books, Mechanicsville, PA, 2004, 49.
54. *OR Vol. 2*, 239.
55. Festus, Summers, 1993, 128.
56. *O.R. Vol. 25*, pt. 1, 114.
57. *Ibid.*, 117.
58. *Ibid.*
59. *Ibid.*
60. *Ibid.*
61. Opie, 110.
62. Myers, 124; Black, 49.
63. Myers, 129.
64. *Ibid.*, 125.
65. *O.R. Vol. 25*, pt. 1, 114.
66. Baylor, 137.
67. *Ibid.*, 138; McDonald, 125
68. *O.R. Vol. 25*, pt. 1, 126.
69. *Ibid.*, 114.
70. Oates, 178.
71. *Ibid.*, *O.R. Vol. 25*, pt. 1, 132. National Archives CS Military Service Records show records of soldiers named John Dailey as a private in Company D of the Eleventh Virginia Cavalry, Company D of the Sixth Virginia Cavalry, and Company D of the Seventh Virginia Cavalry. Whether the sets of records are the same or different individuals is not known. There is no mention that the individual had the title of "doctor" or "surgeon" while serving in the regiment.
72. Oates, 178.
73. Baylor, 138.
74. Festus, Summers, 1993, 132.
75. National Archives CS Military Service Record on William L. Wilson indicates he held the rank of sergeant major when he received his parole on April 19, 1865.
76. Festus, Summers, 1962, 59.
77. *Ibid.*, Festus, Summers, 1993, 132; Note: Senator Willey served as a U.S. Senator from Virginia from 1861–1863 along with Senator John Carlisle. He served as the first U.S. Senator from the new state of West Virginia from 1863–1871.
78. Festus, Summers, 1993, 133.
79. *O.R. Vol. 25*, pt. 1, 126.
80. *Ibid.*
81. Baylor, 138.
82. *Ibid.*, 138; Festus, Summers, 1993, 133.
83. Bigelow, 465.
84. Summers, 132.
85. *O.R. Vol. 25*, pt. 1, 126; Wilson, 59; Summers, 132–133; Collins, 101. National Archives, CS Military Service Record on William I. Rasin. The CS Treasury reimbursed Rasin $525.00 for his horse killed in action.
86. Tucker, 128; Summers, 132.
87. *Ibid.*
88. Baylor, 138. The allegation surfaced while Wilson was conducting his first campaign for the House of Representatives in the fall of 1892. Wilson won the election by a close margin in spite of it.
89. *O.R. Vol. 25*, pt. 2, 296–297.
90. *Ibid.*, 296.
91. *Ibid.*, 281.
92. *Ibid.*, 298.
93. *Ibid.*, 296.
94. *Ibid.*, 297.
95. *Ibid.*, 280.
96. *O.R. Vol. 25.*, pt. 1, 114.
97. *Ibid.*, 118.
98. *Ibid.*
99. Festus, Summers, 1993, 134; *O.R. Vol. 25*, pt. 1, 118.
100. *O.R. Vol. 25*, pt. 1, 123.
101. *Ibid.*, 110.
102. Festus, Summers, 1993, 134–135; *O.R. Vol. 25*, pt. 1, 122–123.
103. *O.R. Vol. 25*, pt. 1, 118.
104. *Ibid.*, 119.
105. *Ibid.*
106. *O.R. Vol. 25*, pt. 1, 120.
107. *Ibid.*, pt. 2, 295.
108. *Ibid.*, 280.
109. *Ibid.*, 295.
110. *Ibid.*, 299.
111. *O.R. Vol. 25*, pt. 2, 346.
112. *Ibid.*, 347.
113. *O.R. Vol. 25*, pt. 1, 119; *O.R. Vol. 25*, pt. 1, 133.
114. *Ibid.*, 123.
115. *O.R. Vol. 25*, pt. 1, 119.
116. *Ibid.*, pt. 2, 345.
117. *Ibid.*, 347.
118. Boatner, 445.
119. *O.R. Vol. 25*, pt. 1, 102, 119.
120. *Ibid.*, 119.

121. Charles William Dabney Papers #1412.
122. *Ibid.*
123. *O.R. Vol. 25*, pt. 1, 120.
124. *Ibid.*
125. *Ibid.*, 120.
126. *Ibid.*
127. *Ibid.*
128. *Ibid.*
129. Opie, 126.
130. *O.R. Vol. 25*, pt. 1, 120.
131. *Ibid.*
132. Moffett, 450–451.
133. Opie, 127.
134. Myers, 130. Note: Although he used the lines, Myers did not acknowledge the author, Thomas Kibble Harvey, or the title, *The Devil's Progress, A Poem*, published by Lupton Relfe, London, 1849.
135. *O.R. Vol. 25*, pt. 1, 120.
136. Dwayne Yancey, "Rebel First of the Slick Fighters," *Roanoke Times & World News*, Roanoke, VA, January 31, 1991, B-1, B-3. The source was comparing this incident of the Jones WV Raid to Saddam Hussein's setting the Kuwaiti oil wells ablaze during Operation Desert Storm. Source provided by Carolyn Ryburn, Private Collection, Glade Spring, VA.
137. McDonald, 170.
138. O'Ferrall, 62.
139. Myers, 132.
140. Wilson, 64–65.
141. Tucker, 134.
142. Virgil Carrington Jones, 1956, 163.
143. Tucker, 135.
144. Festus, Summers, 1993, 139.
145. *O.R. Vol. 25*, pt. 1, 120.
146. Moffett, 450.
147. *Ibid.*
148. *O.R. Vol. 25*, pt. 1, 121.
149. *Ibid.*
150. Moffett, 450. Note: Private Moffett served in Company F of the Eleventh Virginia Cavalry Regiment. Before the war, he was a resident of Pocahontas County (West) Virginia. In the post-war years, he was a resident of Parkersburg, West Virginia.
151. Opie, 128.
152. Festus, Summers, 1993, 139; *O.R. Vol. 25*, pt. 2, 281, 376.
153. *Ibid.*
154. McNeil, John A. "The Imboden Raid and Its Effects," *Southern Historical Society Papers*. Vol. XXXIV, Richmond, VA, 1906, 311.
155. *Ibid.*
156. *O.R. Vol. 25*, pt. 2, 345.
157. *Ibid.*, 102. Imboden attributed the mass desertions to his troops' reaction to his order prohibiting the seizure of horses for personal use.
158. Bigelow, 472.
159. *Ibid.*
160. McNeil, 312.
161. *O. R. Vol. 25*, pt. 2, 789.
162. *Ibid.*

Chapter 14

1. *O.R. Vol. 25*, pt. 2, 819–820.
2. *Ibid.*, 820.
3. National Archived, CS Military Service Record on William E. Jones.
4. *O.R. Vol. 29*, pt. 2, 771.
5. *Ibid.*, 789.
6. McClellan, 293.
7. *Ibid.*, 303.
8. *Ibid.*
9. Freeman, *Vol. 3*, 2.
10. George M. Neese, *Three Years in the Confederate Horse Artillery*, The Neale Publishing, New York, and Washington, D.C., 1911, 201.
11. McDonald, 131.
12. *Ibid.*
13. *Ibid.*
14. Neese, 201–202.
15. *Ibid.*, 203.
16. *Ibid.*
17. *Ibid.*
18. Freeman, *Vol. 3*, 3.
19. McDonald, 132.
20. Oates, 198.
21. *Ibid.*, 197.
22. Freeman, *Vol. 3*, 2.
23. *Ibid.*, 3.
24. *Ibid.*, 2.
25. Davis, 305, Virginia Historical Society "Southern Lady" Letter to President Davis.
26. Neese, 205.
27. *Ibid.*
28. Freeman, *Vol. 3*, 4.
29. *Ibid.*
30. *Washington County News*, February 20, 1969.
31. McClellan, 262.
32. *Ibid.*, 264.
33. McDonald, 134; McClellan, 265.
34. Davis, 306; McClellan, 266.
35. Neese, 209.
36. McDonald, 138.
37. Freeman, *Vol. 3*, 8.
38. Myers, 137.
39. *Ibid.*
40. Boatner, 80.
41. Davis, 306.
42. *Ibid.*, 310.
43. Blackford, 215.
44. Borcke, Heros von, and Scheibert, Justis, *The Great Cavalry Battle of Brandy Station*, translated from the German with historical commentary by Stuart T. Wright and F. D. Bridgewater, Palaemon Press Ltd, Winston-Salem, NC, 1976, 19–20.
45. *Ibid.*, 21.
46. Boatner, 80–91, McClellan, 294.
47. Virginia Historical Society Letter signed "A Southern Lady" in Culpeper County, Virginia to President Jefferson Davis, undated.
48. *Ibid.*

49. *Ibid.*, Davis, 311.
50. Freeman *Vol. 3*, 51.
51. *Ibid.*
52. *Ibid.*
53. Virginia Historical Society, Richmond, VA, J. E. B. Stuart, letter to his wife, Flora, dated June 12, 1863, from Camp Farley. The Battle of Brandy Station was also known as the Battle of Fleetwood Heights.
54. Boatner, 81.
55. Virginia Historical Society, Richmond, VA, J. E. B. Stuart, letter to his wife, Flora, dated June 12, 1863, from Camp Farley.
56. *O.R. Vol. 27*, pt. 2, 683.
57. *O.R. Vol. 27*, pt. 2, 750.
58. National Archives CS Military Service Record on Warren M. Hopkins, Letter from General W. E. Jones to Major General Samuel Cooper, dated December 22, 1863.

Chapter 15

1. Boatner, 332.
2. McClellan, 298.
3. Freeman, *Vol. 3*, 53.
4. Boatner, 6.
5. *Ibid.*, 548.
6. McDonald, 149.
7. *Ibid.*, 151.
8. Opie, 149–150.
9. *Ibid.*, 150.
10. *O.R. Vol. 27*, pt. 2, 751.
11. *Ibid.*
12. Freeman, *Vol. 3*, 59.
13. Davis, 307.
14. Freeman, *Vol.3*, 59–60. Note: Rooney Lee was wounded at Brandy Station, and Colonel John Chambliss replaced him as brigade commander.
15. McClellan, 318.
16. Freeman, *Vol. 3*, 60
17. McClellan, 318.
18. *Ibid.*, *O.R. Vol. 27*, pt. 3, 927, Freeman, *Vol. 3*, 60.
19. *Ibid.*
20. Davis, 325.
21. Freeman, *Vol. 3*, 66.
22. *O.R. Vol. 27*, pt. 2, 694.
23. *Ibid.*, 697.
24. Thomason, 440; Davis, 334. Davis acknowledges the Anne Bachman Hyde Papers, University of North Carolina that elaborate on the meeting. Davis states this is the most detailed account of the meeting.
25. Davis, 334.
26. *Ibid.*
27. McDonald, 153.
28. Luther M. Hopkins, *From Bull Run to Appomattox, A Boy's View,* Sprinkle Publications, Harrisonburg, VA, 1914, 103.
29. Petruzzi, 29.
30. *Ibid.*
31. *O.R. Vol. 27*, pt. 2, 752.
32. *Ibid.*
33. Petruzzi, 30.
34. *Ibid.*
35. McClellan, 348; *O.R. Vol. 27*, pt. 2, 752. Jones reported his forces took a fewer number of prisoners at 184.
36. Petruzzi, 33.
37. *Ibid.*, 33. Note: German-born Sgt. Marten Schwenk received the Medal of Honor in 1899 for rescuing an officer in the Rebel rout. Sgt. George Platt received the same honor in 1899 for his valiant rescue of the 6th U.S. Cavalry's flag at Fairfield.
38. Eric J. Wittenberg, David Petruzzi, and Michael F. Nugent, *One Continuous Fight: The Retreat from Gettysburg and the Pursuit of Lee's Army of Northern Virginia, July 4–14, 1863*, Savas Beatie, New York, and El Dorado Hills, CA, 2008, 6.
39. *Ibid.*, 51.
40. *Ibid.*, 5.
41. The Mason and Dixon Line, a.k.a. Mason-Dixon Line, had been surveyed during the time of Colonial America between 1763 and 1767 by Charles Mason and Jeremiah Dixon to resolve a border dispute between four states. Distinguished as a demarcation forming the boundaries of Maryland, Pennsylvania, Delaware, and West Virginia (then part of Virginia), it came to represent the cultural border between North and South.
42. Wittenberg, et al., 5.
43. *O.R. Vol. 27*, pt. 2, 753.
44. Wittenberg et al., 59.
45. *Ibid.*, 59.
46. *Ibid.*, 60.
47. *O.R. Vol. 27*, pt. 2, 753.
48. Oates, 270.
49. Hopkins, 105–106.
50. *Ibid.*, 106.
51. *Ibid.*
52. Oates, 205.
53. Hopkins, 107.
54. Wittenberg, et al., 68.
55. *Ibid.*
56. John A. Miller, *The Battle of Monterey Pass, Pennsylvania's Second Largest Battle, July 4th–5th, 1863*, Friends of the Monterey Pass Battlefield, Inc., Waynesboro, PA, not dated, 22
57. Oates, 206.
58. *Ibid.*
59. Wittenberg, et al., 74.
60. *Ibid.*, 72.
61. *Ibid.*, 74.
62. *Ibid.*, 72.
63. Hopkins, 107.
64. Wittenberg, et al., 93.
65. *O.R. Vol. 27*, pt. 2, 753
66. Wittenberg, et al., 139.
67. Marshall McDonald Papers, 1777–1926, Perkins Library, Duke University, Durham, NC, Report of Lt. Charles H. Vandiver, William T. Leavell, and A. H. Edward.

68. *Ibid.*
69. *Ibid.*
70. *O.R. Vol. 27*, pt. 2, 754.
71. Wittenberg et al., 174, Note: Hampton was wounded, and Laurence Baker assumed temporary command of his brigade.
72. *Ibid.*, 176.
73. *Ibid.*, 187.
74. *Ibid.*, 208.
75. *Ibid.*, 209.
76. *Ibid.*, 269.
77. *Ibid.*, 272.
78. McDonald, 164; Wittenberg et al., 274.
79. *O.R. Vol. 27*, pt. 2, 754.
80. *Ibid.*, 767. National Archives CS Military Service Record on A. W. Harman documents he remained a prisoner of war until exchanged in February 1865.
81. McDonald, 165.

Chapter 16

1. *O.R. Vol. 27*, pt. 2, 754.
2. Wittenberg, et al., 347.
3. Boatner, 339. His source: Livermore, Thomas L. *Numbers and Losses in the Civil War in America, 1861–65*, Houghton Mifflin, Boston, 1901.
4. Virginia Historical Society, Richmond, Virginia, Stuart, J.E.B., letter to Flora, dated July 12, 1863, from camp near Hagerstown, MD.
5. *Ibid.*
6. Davis, 350.
7. Gilder Lehrman Institute, William E. Jones Collection, Jones letter of resignation to Secretary of War, G. W. Randolph, dated April 28, 1862.
8. National Archives, CS Military Service Record on W. E. Jones, Assistant Adjutant General report, dated August 7, 1863, on the Court Martial of Brigadier General W. E. Jones.
9. *Ibid.*
10. National Archives, CS Military Service Record on W. E. Jones Assistant Adjutant General report, dated August 7, 1863.
11. *Ibid.*
12. *Ibid.*
13. *Ibid.* Captain W. W. Kirkland of the 21st NC Regiment and a Captain W, Shroeder also served on the panel
14. Jayne E. Blair, *Tragedy At Montpelier, The Untold Story Of Ten Confederate Deserters From North Carolina*, Heritage Books, Westminster, Maryland, 2006, 71-99.
15. *O.R. Vol. 27*, pt. 2, 709.
16. Boatner, 702; *O.R. Vol. 27*, pt. 3, 1068–1069.
17. *O.R. Vol. 27*, pt. 3, 1068–1069.
18. National Archives, C. S. A. Service Records on Wade Hampton and Fitzhugh Lee. Both appointments were retroactive to prior dates.
19. McDonald, William N., *A History of the Laurel Brigade*, John Hopkins University Press, Baltimore, MD, 2002, 168. Davis, 351-352 states "Jones was incensed at Jeb's failure to urge his promotion, and an explosion followed."
20. *O.R. Vol. 27*, pt. 3, 1068–1069. Lee corresponded to President Davis on August 1, 1863, recommending the formation of two cavalry brigades along with the promotions of Wade Hampton and Fitz Lee to the ranks of major general to command them.
21. Freeman, *Vol. 3*, 221.
22. National Archives. C. S. A. Military Service Record on W. E. Jones.
23. Charles William Dabney Papers (#1412).
24. Robertson, 360.
25. Roger Judd, Private Collection, Letter from W. E. Jones to General R. H. Chilton, dated September 24, 1863, from Orange C.H.
26. *Ibid.*
27. Judd, Private Collection, Reply letter from Stuart, dated September 25, 1863.
28. *Ibid.*
29. *OR Vol. 30*, pt. 2, 603.
30. *Ibid.*
31. Freeman, *Vol. 3*, 213; McDonald, 168.
32. *O.R. Vol. 29*, pt. 2, 771–772.
33. *Ibid.*
34. *Ibid.*
35. National Archives, W. E. Jones CS Military Service Record, Court Martial Proceedings.
36. *Ibid.*
37. *O.R. Vol. 29*, pt. 2, 779.
38. *Ibid.*
39. McDonald, 169.
40. *Ibid.*, 169–170.
41. *Ibid.*

Chapter 17

1. George Dallas Mosgrove, *Kentucky Cavaliers in Dixie, Reminiscences of a Confederate Cavalryman*, University of Nebraska Press, Lincoln, 1957, 65.
2. *O.R. Vol. 30*, pt. 4, 740.
3. Lambert, 43.
4. A unique quality of the Sibley Tent was that a campfire could be contained inside of it.
5. Mosgrove, 85.
6. *O.R. Vol. 31*, pt. 1, 745.
7. *Ibid.*, 745–746.
8. Theodore Allen, "The Underground Railroad and the Grapevine Telegraph, An Escaping Prisoner's Experience—1863," *Sketches of War History 1861-1865*, Papers prepared for the Commandery, State of Ohio, Military Order of Loyal Legions of the United States (MOLLUS), Vol. 6, Cincinnati, Ohio, Monfort & Co., 1908, 152.
9. Charles B. Coale and George R. Barr, "Gen. Wm. E. Jones," *Abingdon Virginian*, Abingdon, October 16, 1863.
10. John Stuart Williams received his commission to Brigadier General in April 1862. Albert Gallatin Jenkins received his appointment to Brigadier in August 1862. W. E. Jones received his appointment to

Brigadier in September 1862. Via prior commissions, Williams and Jenkins held rank on Jones.
11. *O.R. Vol. 30*, pt. 4, 740.
12. *OR Vol. 30*, pt. 4, 750.
13. *Ibid.*
14. *O.R. Vol. 31*, pt. 1, 454.
15. Jack L. Dickinson, *8th Virginia Cavalry*, H.E. Howard, Lynchburg, VA, 1986, 17
16. *Ibid.*, 38–39.
17. *Ibid.*, 40–41.
18. Lambert, 169.
19. Wallace, 79.
20. John E. Olson, *21st Virginia Cavalry*, H. E. Howard, Lynchburg, VA, 1989, 3.
21. *Ibid.*, 8.
22. Olson, 78.
23. National Archives, CS Military Service Record on Robert C. Dunn.
24. National Archives, CS Military Service Record on Vincent A. Witcher.
25. Scott Cole, *34th Virginia Cavalry*, 2nd Edition, H.E. Howard, Inc., Lynchburg, VA, 1993, 5.
26. Mosgrove, 69–70.
27. Brian D. McKnight, *Contested Borderland, The Civil War in Appalachian Kentucky and Virginia*, The University Press of Kentucky, 2006, 98.
28. *O.R. Vol. 16*, pt. 2, 182, 644.
29. McKnight, 98.
30. *Ibid.* His Source: Ellis, Daniel, *Thrilling Adventures of Daniel Ellis*, Harper & Brothers, New York, NY, 1867, 289–305 (Knox County Library). Samuel W. Scott and Samuel, Angle, *History of the Thirteenth Regiment Tennessee Volunteer Cavalry*, W. Ziegler & Co., Philadelphia, 338–340. This source indicates that Colonel V. A. Witcher, Jr., a nephew of the Thirty-Fourth Battalion Virginia Cavalry commander, was responsible for this atrocity deemed "The Massacre at Limestone Cove."
31. J. L. Scott, *36th and 37th Battalions Virginia Cavalry*, H.E. Howard, Inc. Lynchburg, VA, 1986, 2.
32. *Ibid.*, 6.
33. *Ibid.*
34. *Ibid.*, 7, *O.R. Vol. 31*, pt. 1, 454.
35. Lambert, 34.
36. Tucker, 134.
37. Wallace, 83–84.
38. Michael A. Morrison, *Slavery and the American West, The Eclipse of Manifest Destiny and the Coming of the Civil War,* University of North Carolina Press, Chapel Hill, North Carolina, 1997, 153–154.
39. Lambert, 34.
40. *Ibid.*
41. *Ibid.*
42. *O.R. Vol. 31*, pt. 1, 454.
43. *Ibid.*, Vol. 31, pt. 1, 561.
44. *Ibid.*
45. John L. Ransom, *John Ransom's Andersonville Diary: Life Inside the Civil War's Most Infamous Prison* Berkley Books, New York, NY, 1986, 4.
46. G. D. Ewing, "Battle of Rogersville or Big Creek, TN.," *Confederate Veteran,* Vol. 30, 1922, Broadfoot Publishing Co., Wilmington, NC, 1922, 386.
47. Lambert, 48.
48. *O.R. Vol. 31*, pt. 1, 564.
49. *Ibid.*, 559.
50. *Ibid.*, 562.
51. *Ibid.*, 559
52. *Ibid.*
53. *Ibid.*, 552.
54. *Ibid.*
55. *Ibid.*, 553. National Archives, U.S. Military Service Record of Private William Russell confirms that he, as a member of the Second Tennessee Mounted Infantry was killed in action at Rogersville, Tennessee on November 6, 1863.
56. *O.R. Vol. 31*, pt. 1, 555.
57. Lambert, 55.
58. Ewing, 386.
59. *O.R. Vol. 31*, pt. 1, 551.
60. *Ibid.*, 555.
61. Ransom, 4.
62. Camp Sumter at Andersonville would be established February of 1864 and begin to receive prisoners via transfer.
63. *O.R. Vol. 31*, pt.1, 557.
64. Mosgrove, 92–93. Note: Major Henry T. Stanton had served as an adjutant to CS Generals John S. "Cero Gordo" Williams, John Hunt Morgan, and John Echols. Upon the conclusion of the war, he was paroled at Greensboro, NC. Referred to as the "Poet Laureate of Kentucky" he authored *Poems of the Confederacy* (published by John, Morton & Co., Louisville, KY in 1900). His poem ridiculing the Grumble Jones order was not among those selected for the publication.
65. *O.R. Vol. 31*, pts. 1, 556.
66. *Ibid.*
67. Lambert, 56.
68. *O.R. Vol. 31*, pt. 1, 560.
69. *Ibid.*
70. *Ibid.*, 565.
71. *Ibid.*, 557.
72. *Ibid.*
73. *Ibid.*
74. John Shrady, M.D. "Reminiscences of Libby Prison," *Magazine of American History*, Vol. XVI, July—December 1886, New York, 90–91. National Archives USA Military Service Record on Surgeon John Shrady confirm he was captured at Rogersville on November 6, 1863, and released on November 28, 1863, from prison in Richmond.
75. W. W. Stringfield, "Sixty-Ninth Regiment" *Histories of the Several Regiments and Battalions from North Carolina in the Great War 1861–1865*, Vol. III, Edited by Walter Clark, Nash Brothers, Goldsboro, NC, 1901, 742.
76. Allen, 152.
77. *Ibid.*, 153.
78. *Ibid.*, 166–167. Note: Lieutenant A. A. Carr, however, died from his injuries soon after completing his escape. There is a dramatization of this event in McVey Multimedia, Inc.'s 2007 movie, *Freedom*, 2007.

79. Lambert, 59.
80. *Ibid.*, 62.
81. *O.R. Vol. 31*, pt. 3, 760.
82. Freeman, *Vol. 3*, 296.
83. *O.R. Vol. 31*, pt. 1, 461.
84. *Ibid.*, 462.
85. *O.R. Vol. 51*, pt. 2, 1076–1077; Freeman, *Vol. 3*, 336.
86. *O.R. Vol. 31*, pt. 3, 769.
87. Lambert, 64.
88. James D. Sedinger, West Virginia Division of Culture and History, *War Time Reminiscences of James D. Sedinger, Company E, 8th Virginia Cavalry (Border Rangers)*, Charleston, WV, Vol, 51, 1992, 69.
89. *Ibid.*, 69; David L. Phillips, and Rebecca L. Hill, *War Stories: Civil War in West Virginia*, Gauley Mount Press, Leesburg, VA, 1991.
90. Sedinger, 70.
91. *O.R. Vol. 31*, pt. 1, 413.
92. *Ibid.*, 463.
93. *Ibid.*
94. Freeman, *Vol. 3*, 299.
95. *O.R. Vol. 31*, pt. 1, 463.
96. George T. Williams, *Company A 37th Battalion Virginia Cavalry C.S.A.: A History of Its Organization and Service in the War Between the States, 1861–1865*, R. H. Fishburne, Roanoke, VA, 1910, 24.
97. *O.R. Vol. 31*, pt. 3, 875.
98. Lambert, 14.
99. *Ibid.*, 16.
100. James W. Orr, *Recollections of the War Between the States By James W. Orr of Jonesville, Va., 1st Lieutenant, Company E., 37th Virginia Infantry*, Filed with the Southwest Virginia Historical Society by Luther Addington, to whom the original pamphlet was loaned by Miss Josephine Wolfe, 14. http://www.lva.virginia.gov/public/guides/va22_burnedco.htm; Bonnie Ball, "Impact of the Civil War Upon the Southwestern Corner of Virginia," *Historical Sketches of Southwest Virginia*, Publication No. 15, Southwestern Virginia Historical Society, 1982, 3.
101. Williams, 24.
102. *Ibid.*
103. *O.R. Vol. 32*, pt. 1, 59; J.A.G. Wyatt, "The Battle of Jonesville," *Confederate Veteran, Vol. 30*, 1922, 102.
104. *O.R. Vol. 32*, pt. 1, 58.
105. Wyatt, 103.
106. *O.R. Vol. 32*, pt. 1, 64.
107. *Ibid.*, 59.
108. *Ibid.*, 60–64.
109. *Ibid.*, 60.
110. Wyatt, 103.
111. *Ibid.*
112. *Ibid.*
113. *Chicago Tribune*, New York Times Archives, October 2, 1864.
114. *Ibid.*
115. *Ibid.*
116. *Ibid.*
117. *Ibid.*, 83–90.
118. *O.R. Vol. 32*, pt. 1, 60.
119. *Ibid.*, 58.
120. *Ibid.*, 60.
121. Lambert, 93.
122. Williams, 27.
123. Lambert, 94; *O.R.Vol. 32*, pt. 2, 595–596, 612, 613, 634.
124. *O.R. Vol. 32*, pt. 2, 682.
125. Lambert, 98–99.
126. *O.R. Vol. 32*, pt. 1, 411.
127. Lambert, 98.
128. *Ibid.*, 98–99.
129. *O.R. Vol. 32*, pt. 1, 412.
130. *Ibid.* Jones referred to Gibson's Mill which was in proximity to Wyerrman's Mill on Indian Creek.
131. *Ibid.*, 413.
132. Orr, 17.
133. McKnight, 186.
134. Lambert, 112.
135. Lambert, 112.
136. *O.R. Vol. 32*, pt. 2, 73, 74.
137. *O.R. Vol. 32*, pt. 1, 411.
138. National Archives U.S. Military Service Record on Reuben A. Davis, U.S. War Department Special Orders No. 597, dated December 14, 1866, about S.O. Nos. 233 & 303.
139. Lambert, 113. According to Lambert, Davis received a second gunshot wound by James C. Luttrel, a former Confederate and mayor of Pine Knot, Kentucky over an unknown dispute. Davis survived that injury, but the wound at Wyerman's became infected in 1895 ultimately killing him. It was said that his body was so badly bloated, mourners could not nail down the lid on his coffin.
140. *O.R. Vol. 31*, pt. 1, 413.
141. Lambert, 112.
142. *O.R. Vol. 32*, pt. 1 pp. 490–491; Sedinger, 70. Note: Sedinger alleged that Jones' forces captured 100 Federals but not confirmed in the *O.R.*
143. Lambert, 118.
144. Freeman, *Vol. 3*, 336; *O.R. Vol. 33*, 1054.
145. Cole, 74.
146. National Archives, C S Military Service Record on Vincent A. Witcher.
147. Cole, 71.
148. *Ibid.*
149. National Archives, C. S. Military Service Record on Vincent A. Witcher.
150. *Abingdon Virginia,* March 18, 1864.
151. National Archives, CS Military Service Record on Vincent A. Witcher.
152. *Ibid.*
153. *O.R.* Vol. 32, pt. 3, 843.
154. *Ibid.*, 845.
155. *Ibid.*
156. *Ibid.*
157. *Ibid.*, National Archives CS Military Service Record on Ambrose C. Dunn. Dunn was reinstated on June 24, 1864, following the death of W. E. Jones.
158. *O.R. Vol. 32*, pt. 3, 845. The report does not

mention Peters by name but as the commander of the Twenty-first Virginia Cavalry Regiment.
159. *Ibid.*
160. *Ibid.*, 843–845.
161. *Ibid.*, 845.
162. McKnight, 198.
163. James A. Ramage, *Rebel Raider: The Life of General John Hunt Morgan*, The University Press of Kentucky, Lexington, 1986, 211. His source: Kevin H. Siepel, *The Life and Times of John Singleton Mosby.*
164. *Ibid.*
165. *Ibid.*
166. *Ibid.*
167. *O.R. Vol. 37*, pt. 1, 739.
168. McClellan, 320. Note: Stuart had been mortally wounded at Yellow Tavern while attempting to thwart Phillip Sheridan's Richmond Raid on May 11, 1864, during the Spotsylvania Campaign. Stuart died on the following day.
169. *Ibid.*, 321.

Chapter 18

1. *O.R. Vol. 37*, pt. 1, 747.
2. Cecil D. Eby, *A Virginia Yankee in the Civil War: The Diaries of David Hunter Strother*, Chapel Hill, University of North Carolina Press, 1961, p, 215.
3. Scott C. Patchan, *The Forgotten Fury, The Battle of Piedmont, Va.* Sergeant Kirkland's Museum and Historical Society, Inc., Fredericksburg, VA, 1996, 3.
4. *Ibid.*, Boatner, 418.
5. Brice, 13.
6. Boatner, 419.
7. Tucker, 459.
8. Henry Algernon Du Pont, *The Campaign of 1864 in the Valley of Virginia and the Expedition to Lynchburg*, National Americana Society, New York, 1925, 38.
9. Patchan, 1996, 8.
10. *Ibid.*, 9; Brice, 14.
11. *Ibid.*, 1996, 5.
12. Charles H. Lynch, *The Civil War Diary 1862–1865 of Charles H. Lynch, 18th Conn.* Vol's Originally printed from Harvard University, 1915, Published in 1915 by Case, Lockwood and Brainard Co., Hartford, CT, 62.
13. *Ibid.*, 531.
14. *O.R. Vol. 37*, pt. 1, 525.
15. *Ibid.*, 517–518.
16. Eby, 235.
17. *Ibid.*
18. *Ibid.*, 238
19. *Ibid.*
20. *Ibid.*
21. *O.R. Vol. 37*, pt., 1, 161
22. Harry Gilmor, *Four Years in the Saddle*, Harper & Brothers, New York, 1866, 161–162.
23. *O.R. Vol. 37*, pt. 1, 747–748.
24. *Ibid.*, 749.
25. *Ibid.*
26. Brice, 30, His Source: Broadside, Alderman Library, University of Virginia, Charlottesville.
27. *O.R. Vol. 37*, pt. 1, 749.
28. *O.R. Vol. 39*, pt. 1, 76.
29. *Ibid.*, 67.
30. Cole, 81.
31. *O.R. Vol. 39*, pt. 1, 66.
32. Ramage, 215*Ibid.*
33. *O.R. Vol. 37*, pt. 1, 750.

Chapter 19

1. O'Ferrall, 89.
2. National Archives, CS Military Service Record on John N. Opie. His original home was in Jefferson County, WV.
3. Opie, 38.
4. Cullum, 704.
5. National Archives, CS Military Service Record on Richard H. Brewer.
6. *Ibid.*
7. *Ibid.*
8. Patchan, 1996, 44–45.
9. Vernon H. Crow, *Storm in the Mountains, Thomas' Confederate Legion of Cherokee Indians and Mountaineers*, Press of the Museum of the Cherokee Indian, Cherokee, NC, 1982, 13.
10. Crow, 67. His source: Letter from James R. Love to John C. Breckinridge, dated October 15, 1864. William W. Stringfield Collection, 1857–1923, Archives and Special Collections Division, Hunter Library, Western Carolina University, Cullowhee.
11. J. L. Scott, *45th Virginia Infantry*, H. E. Howard, Inc., Lynchburg, VA, 1989, 38.
12. *Official Register of Officers and Cadets*, June 1861.
13. Robert K. Krick, *Lee's Colonels: A Biographical Register of Field Officers of the Army of Northern Virginia*, Morningside Bookshop, Dayton, OH, 1979, 63.
14. *Ibid.*, 43, 45.
15. Patchan, 1996, 91.
16. *Ibid.*, 92. National Archives confirms sixteen Hatfields and nine McCoys served in the Forty-Fifth Battalion Virginia Infantry. Both groups of names showed high rates of absenteeism. Three McCoys were captured by Union forces at Piedmont.
17. Larry Gordon, *The Last Confederate General, John C. Vaughn and his East Tennessee Cavalry*, Zenith Press, Minneapolis, 2009, 90.
18. *Ibid.*, 91.
19. *O.R. Vol. 32*, pt. 3, 845.
20. *Ibid.*
21. Gordon, 93.
22. Patchan, 1996, 227.
23. Scott, 1986, 10.
24. Patchan, 1996, 47.
25. Patchan, 1996, 47--48 His source: National Archives, Major General David Hunter's Report of Service, Record Group 494. Patchan points out that Federal officers found this dispatch on General Jones' body after the battle of Piedmont ended.
26. Brice, 33. His source: Staunton *Vindicator*, July 13, 1894.

27. Tucker, 231.
28. John D. Imboden, "The Battle of Piedmont" (written in 1883), Part 1, *Confederate Veteran*, Vol. 31, Broadfoot Publishing Co., Wilmington, NC, 1923, 459.
29. Imboden, pt. 1, 460.
30. O'Ferrall, 98.
31. Brice, 31-32.
32. *Ibid.*, Oates, 158.
33. Oates, 264.
34. Brice, 30.
35. Patchan, 1996, 43, 227.
36. *Ibid.*, 227.
37. *Ibid.*
38. *Ibid.*
39. *Ibid.*
40. *Ibid.*
41. Eby, 1961, 241.
42. *Ibid.*, 242.
43. *Ibid.*, 242.
44. Patchan, 1996, 67; Eby, 1961, 242.
45. Eby, 1961, 242.
46. Imboden, 1923, 460.
47. *Ibid.*
48. *Ibid.*
49. Brice, 40.
50. *Ibid.*, 69. His reference: *JDI Annals of War*, 174–175., JDI to Marshall McCue, October 1, 1883.
51. Brice, 40.
52. Patchan, 1996, 67.
53. J. l. Henry, "First Tennessee Cavalry at Piedmont" *Confederate Veteran*, Vol. 22 Broadfoot Publishing, Wilmington, NC, 1914, 397.

Chapter 20

1. Imboden, 1923, 460; Eby, 242–243. Francis M. Imboden spent the remainder of the war at Johnson's Island before his release in June of 1865. He lived until 1929.
2. Imboden, pt. 1, 460.
3. *Ibid.*, 461.
4. Imboden, "The Battle of Piedmont" (written in 1883), pt. 2, *Confederate Veteran*, Vol. 32, 1924, 18.
5. *Ibid.*
6. Brice, 56.
7. O'Ferrell, 98.
8. Virginia Historical Society, B. H. Jones, Report on Battle of Piedmont, 1.
9. *Ibid.*
10. Imboden, Vol. 32, 18.
11. *Ibid.*
12. *Ibid.*
13. Lynch, 69.
14. Virginia Historical Society, B. H. Jones Report on Battle of Piedmont, 5.
15. Patchan, 1996, 115.
16. Imboden, Vol. 32, 18.
17. Crow, 73; Stringfield, 747.
18. Stringfield, 747.
19. Brice, 74.
20. O'Ferrall, 99.
21. Brice, 74.
22. Virginia Historical Society, B. H. Jones Report on Battle of Piedmont, 5.
23. Crowe, 73; Stringfield, 747.
24. *O.R. Vol. 37*, pt. 1, 118.
25. Patchan, 1996, 152.
26. Oates, 265.
27. Patchan, 1996, 153.
28. *Ibid.*, 174, 14
29. *Ibid.*, 153.
30. Opie, 203.
31. Patchan,1996, 153.
32. *Ibid.*, 162.
33. Patchan, 1996, 203.

Chapter 21

1. William C. Walker, *History of the Eighteenth Regiment Connecticut Volunteers in The War For The Union*, Published by the Committee, Norwich, CT, 1885, 234.
2. Patchan, 1996, 174.
3. DuPont, 63–64.
4. Ellsworth Eliot, Jr., *West Point in the Confederacy*, G. A. Baker & Co., Inc., New York, 1941, 307.
5. *O.R. Vol. 37*, pt. 1, 151.
6. Patchan, 1996, 154
7. Eby,1961, 246
8. Virginia Historical Society, B. H. Jones Report on Battle of Piedmont, 8.
9. Lynch, 70.
10. Eby, 1961, 247.
11. *O.R. Vol. 37*, pt. 1, 95.
12. Brice, 78.
13. *Ibid.*, 79.
14. O'Ferrall, 101
15. *Ibid.*, 102.
16. *Ibid.*
17. *Ibid.*, 102.
18. *Ibid.*, 103.
19. *Ibid.*, 104.
20. *Ibid.*
21. *Ibid.*
22. O'Ferrall, 104–105. Years after the war, U.S. Congressman O'Ferrall intervened to recognize former Major Otis for valor.
23. *O.R. Vol. 39*, pt. 1, 66.
24. *Ibid.*
25. *Ibid.*, 76.
26. Opie, 202.
27. O'Ferrall, 99.
28. *Ibid.*, 100. Note: New Hope is a town approximately a half mile south of the village of Piedmont. Some historians designated New Hope as the name of the battle.
29. Opie, 203.
30. Milton W. Humphries, *Lynchburg Campaign*, Michie County, Charlottesville, VA, 1924, 51, 53.
31. Eby, 1961, 247.

32. Boatner, 255.
33. Freeman, Vol. III, 565
34. Chancery Records, Washington County, Virginia, Index Record 1906-041, Library of Virginia.
35. Patchan, 1996, 203.
36. Brice, 85. His source: Lynchburg *News*, June 5, 1902.
37. Brice, 137.

Epilogue

1. *O.R. Vol. 37*, pt.2, 367. David Hunter's cousin, Andrew Hunter of Charles Town, was a known secessionist who served as special prosecutor in the trial of John Brown in 1859. Hunter's Special Order No. 128 also ordered the burning of the home of politician and secessionist, Charles James Faulkner in Martinsburg.
2. *Ibid.*, 365-367.
3. Eby, 1961, xx.
4. Cecil D. Eby, *Porte Crayon, The Life of David Hunter Strother*, Greenwood Press, Westport, CT, 1960, 160-161.
5. William S. Dutton, *DuPont, One Hundred and Forty Years*, Charles Scribner's Sons, New York, 1942, 101.
6. *Ibid.*, 161-162.
7. *Ibid.*, 308.
8. National Archives CS Military Service Record on B. H. Jones, 60th Virginia Infantry. He was not released until June 18, 1865.
9. Ella May Turner, *Stories and Verse of West Virginia*, Jim Comstock, Richwood, WV, 1974, 115; Buehring H. Jones, Col., 60th Virginia Infantry *The Sunny Land, Or, Prison Prose and Poetry*, Innes & Co., Baltimore, MD, 1868, VI, Editor's Note, J. A. Houston.
10. C. Stuart McGehee, "The Tarnished Thirty-fifth Star" *Virginia at War, 1861*, Edited by William C. Davis and James I. Robertson, Jr. for the Virginia Center for Civil War Studies, University Press of Kentucky, 2005, 152
11. Turner, 115.
12. William W. Stringfield, "Memoirs of the Civil War, a typewritten copy" McClung Collection, Lawson McGhee Library, Knoxville, Tennessee, 1938, 19.
13. *Ibid.*, 98-99; Stevenson, 94, McKnight, Brian Dallas, *Confederate Outlaw, Champ Ferguson and The Civil War in Appalachia*, Louisiana State University Press, Baton Rouge, 2011, 150.
14. *Ibid.*, 234-236.
15. *Ibid.*, 53.
16. National Archives CS Military Service Record on John N. Opie.
17. Michael, Musick, *6th Virginia Cavalry*, H. E. Howard, Lynchburg, VA, 1990, 143.
18. McDonald, 18.
19. *Ibid.*, 710.
20. National Archives, C. S. Military Service Record on Lt. John Blue.
21. Oates, viii.
22. Festus, Summers, 1962, 108-109.
23. Olson, 31. Note: Chambersburg was burned in spite of Peter's refusal. Colonel Harry Gilmor was a willing party to carry out the order.
24. *O.R. Vol. 43*, pt. 1, 726, 734
25. National Archives, CS Military Service Record on Robert C. Dunn.
26. Catherine S. McConnell, *High on a Windy Hill*, Overmountain Press, Johnson City, TN, 1995, 179.
27. National Archives CS Military Service Record on Vincent A. Witcher. Special Orders # 150.
28. *Ibid.*, Special Order # 187.
29. *O.R. Vol. 43*, pt. 1, 639; *O.R. Vol. 43*, pt. 2, 900.
30. Virgil Carrington Jones, 1944, 266.
31. *Ibid.*, 278-279.
32. *Ibid.*, 299-301.
33. Thomas W. Colley, "Col. W. M. Hopkins" *Confederate Veteran*, Vol. X, September 1902, 421, Alice Roberts, "Col. Warren M. Hopkins"*Confederate Veteran*, Vol. IX, March 1901, Reprinted 1987-1988, Broadfoot Publishing, Wilmington, NC, 1903, 127.
34. Lyon G. Tyler, president of William and Mary College, Editor in Chief, *Men of Mark in Virginia, Ideals of American Life, A Collection of Biographies of the Leading Men of the State*, Vol. III, Men of Mark Publishing, Washington, D.C., 1907, 117.
35. Mosby, 334.
36. Tyler, 117-118.
37. Mahlon R. Robinson, *An Old Man's Memories*, M. L. Robinson, Glade Spring, VA, 1969, 5.
38. Following the fall of Fort Donelson, Floyd received a commission of a Major General by the Virginia Legislature.
39. Thompson, 361.
40. *Ibid.*, 363.
41. *Ibid*.
42. Malsch, 244.
43. Airey, *The Houston Chronicle*, April 19, 1936
44. Tidball, xiii, 494.
45. *Getting Through West Point*, pt. 2, 135.
46. Evan S. Connell, *Son of the Morning Star, Custer and the Little Big Horn*, Harper & Row, New York, 1984, 224; Robbins, 131.
47. Robbins, 131.
48. *Ibid*.
49. *Getting Through West Point*, pt. 2, 135.
50. Kent A Biffle, *A Month of Sundays*, University of North Texas Press, Denton, 1993, 101, Carter, 389.
51. *Getting Through West Point*, pt. 2, 135.
52. Connell, 223.
53. *Ibid*.
54. *Ibid.*, 225.
55. National Archives, CS Military Service Record on James W. Jones.
56. Tucker and Waller, 71.
57. ShEby County, Tennessee Archives
58. Tucker and Walker, 70.
59. Jonathan Kennon Thompson Smith, "Genealogical Abstracts from Reported Deaths," *The Nashville Christian Advocate, 1908-1910*, June 12, 1908, 12.
60. R.C. Jones Family Plot Burial Records, Elmwood Cemetery, Memphis, TN.

Bibliography

Private Collections

Johnston, Steve. Chilhowie, VA.
Judd, Roger J. Fairbury, NE.
Nichols, William. Houston, TX.
Ryburn, Carolyn. Glade Spring, VA.
Smart, Martha. Reference assistant, the Connecticut Historical Society, Library, Hartford, CT.
Wills, Art. Raleigh, NC.

Nonpublished Manuscripts

Eldridge, Charles. *Indianola Letter*, March 30. 1852. University of Texas Archives, Austin.
John C. Tidball Papers. United States Military Academy Archives, West Point, NY.
Stringfield, William W. "Memoirs of the Civil War, a Typewritten Copy." McClung Collection, Lawson McGhee Library, Knoxville, TN. 1938. Tidball, John C. *Getting Through West Point by One Who Did and for Those Who Want to Know.* New York. 1895.

Public Records

Bexar County, San Antonio, TX, Deed Book. 1890.
Calhoun County, Port Lavaca, TX, Deed Books, 1848, 1868. 1875.
Calhoun County, Port Lavaca, TX, Marriage Licenses 1847–1890.
DeWitt County, Cuero, TX, Deed Books, 1988. 1901.
Gonzales County, Gonzales, TX, Deed Books, 1852, 1855
Gonzales County, Gonzales, TX, Register of Marriage License. 1852.
Guadalupe County, Seguin, Texas, Deed Book. 1881.
Shelby County Marriage Licenses, Shelby County Archives, Memphis, TN.
Washington County, Virginia, 1850 Census, Agricultural Schedule, 67th District, Abingdon, VA.
Washington County, Abingdon, VA, Deed Books 1820. 1876.

Newspapers and Periodicals

Abingdon Virginian. Abingdon, Virginia, 1861–1864
America's Civil War. Weider History Group, Inc. Clearwater, FL, July 2007.
Civil War Times Illustrated. Historical Times, Inc., Gettysburg, Pennsylvania, June 1968.
Confederate Veteran. S. A. Cunningham, Nashville, Tennessee, Reprinted 1987–1988, Broadfoot Publishing, Wilmington, N.C 1893–1932.
Galveston *Civilian and Gazette.* Galveston, TX, June 16, 1857, Vol. XX.
Galveston Weekly News. Galveston, TX, September 27. 1875.
Houston Chronicle. Houston, TX, April 19. 1936.
Indianola Bulletin. Indianola, Texas, April 1. 1852.
The Nashville Christian Advocate. Nashville, TN. 1908.
Victoria Advocate. Victoria TX, Obituary Records, 1885–1887.
Washington County News. Abingdon, VA, February 20. 1969.

Institutional Special Collections

Connecticut Historical Society, Hartford.
Duke University, Marshall McDonald Papers, 1777–1926. Perkins Library, Durham, NC.
Gilder Lehrman Institute. William E. Jones Collection, New York.
"Hermesian Society Literary Minutes, 1854–59, Constitution, Members, 1841–53; Chickasaw." Emory & Henry College Archives, Emory, VA.
Historical Society of Washington County, Virginia. "Unfiled Court Records, Washington County, Virginia. Compiled by D. E. Brown, Deeds, 1782–1875, Abingdon, VA.
Historical Society of Washington County Virginia, Abingdon, VA, "Mcthenia Papers,"
Historical Society of Pennsylvania. Gratz and Dreer Collections, Philadelphia.
University of North Carolina, Chapel Hill. Charles

William Dabney Papers (#1412), General Manuscripts, Manuscripts Department, Wilson Library.
United States Military Academy, West Point, NY.
University of Texas at Arlington Archives.
University of Texas Archives, Austin.
Virginia Military Institute Archives, Lexington.
Virginia Historical Society, Richmond.
West Virginia Humanities Council, Charleston.

United Kingdom Government Materials

British Office of Patents

United States Government Materials

National Archives and Records Administration, Washington, D.C.
Official Register of the Officers and Cadets of the U. S. Military Academy. West Point, NY, June 1844, 1845, 1846, 1847, 1848, and 1851.
United States Geological Survey Historical Topographical Map Collection. USGS Clarence King Library in Reston, VA.
United States Patent Office. "William E. Jones of the United States Army, Saddletree." Specification of Letters Patent No. 11,068, dated June 13. 1854.
United States War Department. *The War of Rebellion: A Compilation of the Official Records of the Union and Confederate Armies.* Prepared under the direction of the secretary of war by Robert N. Scott, Government Printing Office, Washington, D.C., 1880–1900.

Books, Articles and Theses

Abraham, Lorraine Netrick. "Levi Sheftall D'lyon, a Preliminary Biography." A paper submitted to Dr. Roger K. Warlick, In fulfillment of the class requirements of History 450/650, Savannah, GA, Armstrong State College, May 1992.
Airey, J. W. E. (Lifetime Chaplain of the National Frontiersmen's Association).
Allardice, Bruce S. *Confederate Colonels, a Biographical Register.* University of Missouri Press, Columbia. 2008.
Allen, Theodore, Edward S. McKee, and J. Gordon Taylor. *Sketches of War History 1861–1865, Papers Prepared for the Commandery of the State of Ohio, Military Order of the Loyal Legion of the United States 1903–1908,* Volume VI. Monfort & Co., Cincinnati. 1908.
The Appomattox Roster: A List of the Paroles of the Army of Northern Virginia Issued at Appomattox Court House on April 9. 1865. Antiquarian Press, New York. 1962.
Armstrong, Richard L. *7th Virginia Cavalry,* 1st Edition. H. E. Howard, Inc. Lynchburg, VA. 1992.
Arnold, J. Barto, III. *A Matagorda Bay Magnetometer Survey & Site Test Excavation Project.* Texas Antiquities Committee Publication No. 9, Austin. 1982.
Ball, Bonnie. "Impact of the Civil War Upon the Southwestern Corner of Virginia." *Historical Sketches of Southwest Virginia.* Publication No. 15, Southwestern Virginia Historical Society, Wise, 1982
Barbe, Waverly Wilson, annotator, and Mrs. Shelby Ireson Edwards. *1850 Census of Washington County, Virginia Annotated.* Holston Territory Genealogical Society, Inc, Bristol, TN/VA. 2000.
Baughman, James P. *Charles Morgan and the Development of Southern Transportation.* Vanderbilt University Press, Nashville, TN. 1968.
Baylor, George. *Bull Run to Bull Run Or, Four Years in the Army of Northern Virginia.* B. F. Johnson Publishing Co., Richmond, VA.1900.
Biffle, Kent, *A Month of Sundays.* University of North Texas Press, Denton, TX. 1993.
Bigelow, John, Jr. *The Campaign of Chancellorsville: A Strategic and Tactical Study.* Yale University Press, New Haven, CT. 1910.
Black, Robert W. *Cavalry Raids of the Civil War.* Stackpole Books, Mechanicsville, PA. 2004.
Blackford, William Willis. *War Years with Jeb Stuart.* Charles Scribner's Sons, New York. 1946.
Blair, Jayne E. *Tragedy at Montpelier: The Untold Story of Ten Confederate Deserters from North Carolina.* Heritage Books, Westminster, MD. 2003.
Blakemore, John A. *Buchanan, a Genealogical History.* Quality Printers, Bristol, VA. 1978.
Boatner, Mark Mayo III. *The Civil War Dictionary.* David McKay Co., New York. 1959.
Bond, Frank A. "Storming Blockhouse at Greenland Gap." *Confederate Veteran*, Vol. XVII, January 1909 to December 1909. Reprinted 1987–1988, Broadfoot Publishing, Wilmington, NC.
Boney, F. N. *John Letcher of Virginia: The Story of Virginia's Civil War Governor.* University of Alabama Press, Tuscalusa. 1966.
Brice, Marshall M. *Conquest of a Valley.* University Press of Virginia, Charlottesville. 1965.
British Office of Patents, no. 1892. George Edward Eyre and William Spottiswoode, Printers to the Queen's Most Excellent Majesty. 1858.
Brown, D. E. *The Marriages of Washington County, Virginia 1781–1853.* Indexed and published by Historical Society of Washington County, Virginia, Abingdon, VA. 1999.
Brown, John Henry. *Indianola Bulletin,* Vol. 1, No. 8, April 1. 1852.
Carter, Robert Goldwaite. *On the Border with Mackenzie or Winning West Texas from the Comanches.* Antiquarian Press, New York. 1961.

Chaltas, David, and Richard Brown. "Battle of Jonesville, the Frozen Fight, January 3. 1864." www.bencaudill.com.

Coale, Charles B., and George R. Barr. *Abingdon Virginian*, Abingdon, Virginia, October 16. 1863.

Cole, Scott C. *34th Battalion Virginia Cavalry*, 2nd Edition. H. E. Howard, Inc. Lynchburg, Virginia. 1993.

Colley, Thomas W. "Brigadier General William E. Jones." *Confederate Veteran*, Vol. XI, January 1903 to December 1903, Broadfoot Publishing Co., Wilmington, NC. 1903.

Colley, Thomas W. "Col. W. M. Hopkins" *Confederate Veteran*, Volume X, January 1902 to December 1902, Reprinted 1987–1988, Broadfoot Publishing Co., Wilmington, NC. 1902.

Collins, Darrell L. *The Jones-Imboden Raid: The Confederate Attempt to Destroy the Baltimore & Ohio Railroad and Retake West Virginia*. McFarland & Co., Jefferson. North Carolina. 2007.

Confederate Military History, Vol. III. "West Virginia." Broadfoot Publishing, Wilmington, NC. 1987.

Confederate States Almanac for the Year of Our Lord 1862. Being the Second After Bissextile, or Leap Year, the Eighty-Sixth of American Independence, & the Second of the Confederate States. Southern Methodist Publishing House, Nashville, TN. 1862.

Connell, Evan S. *Son of the Morning Star, Custer and the Little Big Horn*. North Point Press, New York. 1984.

Cooling, Benjamin Franklin. *Jubal Early's Raid on Washington. 1864*. The Nautical & Aviation Publishing Co. of America, Baltimore, MD. 1989.

Cothern, John W. *Confederates of Elmwood: A Compilation of Information Concerning Confederate Soldiers and Veterans Buried at Elmwood Cemetery, Memphis, Tennessee*. Heritage Books, Westminster, MD. 2007.

Cox, William E., historian, Kings Mountain National Military Park. *Battle of Kings Mountain Participants*. Eastern National Park & Monument Association, reprinted by permission to Historical Society of Washington County, Virginia Abingdon, VA. 1972.

Crimmins, M. L. *The Southwestern Historical Quarterly*, Volume 51, July 1947 to April 1948, "Notes and Documents, W. G. Freeman's Report on the Eighth Military Department." The Texas State Historical Association, Austin. 1948.

Cross, Osborne. *March of the Mounted Riflemen to Oregon 1849*. Ye Galleon Press, Fairfield, WA, 1967

Crow, Vernon H. *Storm in the Mountains, Thomas' Confederate Legion of Cherokee Indians and Mountaineers*. Press of the Museum of the Cherokee Indian, Cherokee, North Carolina. 1982.

Cullum, George W. *Biographical Register of the Officers and Graduates of the U.S. Military Academy at West Point, NY Since Its Establishment in 1802*. Riverside Press, Cambridge, MA. 1891.

Dary, David. *The Oregon Trail: An American Saga*. Alfred A. Knopf, New York. 2004.

Davis, Burke, *J.E.B. Stuart: The Last Cavalier*. The Fairfax Press, New York. 1988.

Davis, William C. and James I. Robertson, editors. *Virginia at War 1861*. University Press of Kentucky, Lexington. 2005.

Dickinson, Jack L. *8th Virginia Cavalry*. H. E. Howard, Inc., Lynchburg, VA. 1986.

Divine, John E. *35th Battalion Virginia Cavalry*. H. E. Howard, Lynchburg, Virginia. 1985.

Douglas, Henry Kyd. *I Rode with Stonewall*. Mockingbird Books, Marietta, GA. 1993.

Dowdey, Clifford, editor and Louis H. Hanarin, associate editor. *The Wartime Papers of Robert E. Lee*. Da Capo Press, Boston. 1961.

Draper, Lyman C. *King's Mountain and It's Heroes: History of the Battle of King's Mountain, 1780, and the Events Which Led to It*. Peter G. Thompson, Cincinnati, OH. 1881.

Driver, Robert J., Jr. *1st Virginia Cavalry*, 1st Edition. H. E. Howard, Inc., Lynchburg, VA. 1991.

Du Pont, Henry Algernon. *The Campaign of 1864 in the Valley of Virginia and the Expedition to Lynchburg*. National Americana Society, New York. 1925.

Dutton, William S. *Du Pont, One Hundred and Forty Years*. Charles Scribner's Sons, New York, 1942.

Eby, Cecil D., Jr., editor. *A Virginia Yankee in the Civil War: The Diaries of David Hunter Strother*. The University of North Carolina Press, Chapel Hill. 1961.

Eby, Cecil D., Jr., editor. *"Porte Crayon": The Life of David Hunter Strother*. Greenwood Press, Publishers, Westport, CT. 1960.

Eggleston, George Cary. *A Rebel's Recollections*. Louisiana State University Press, Baton Rouge, LA. 1996.

Eggleston, George Cary. *Southern Soldier Stories*. SCS Publication, Arlington, VA. 1998.

Eldridge, Charles. Manuscript: *Indianola Letter*, University of Texas, Archives, Austin, Texas, Note: This is an unpublished and untitled manuscript dated March 30. 1852. *Independence* passenger, Eldridge of Mt. Carmel, Illinois wrote a personal eyewitness account of the wreck in a letter to his friends. Although untitled, The University of Texas Archives did so for filing purposes. He also joined his brother in law, John Henry Brown as a co-source to the *Indianola Bulletin* account of the ship wreck.

Eliot, Ellsworth, Jr. *West Point in the Confederacy*. G. A. Baker Company, New York, 1941

Ewing, G. D. "Battle of Rogersville or Big Creek,

Tn." *Confederate Veteran,* Vol. 30, January1922 to Decmeber 1922, Reprinted 1987–1988, Broadfoot Publishing Co., Wilmington, NC. 1922.

Freeman, Douglas Southall. *Lee's Lieutenants,* Volumes I, II, & III. Charles Scribner's Sons, New York. 1945.

Frye, Dennis. *12th Virginia Cavalry.* H. E. Howard, Lynchburg, Virginia, 1988

Gibson, Langhorne, Jr., *Cabell's Canal, the Story of the James River and Kanawha.,* Commodore Press, Richmond, VA, 2000

Gilmor, Harry. *Four Years in the Saddle.* Harper & Brothers, New York, NY. 1866.

Gordon, Larry. *The Last Confederate General: John C. Vaughn and His East Tennessee Cavalry.* Zenith Press, Minneapolis. 2009.

"Grumble Jones, a Personality Profile." *Civil War Times Illustrated.* Harrisburg, PA, June 1968.

Guthrie, Keith. *Texas Forgotten Ports, Mid-Gulf Coast Ports from Corpus Christi to Matagorda Bay.* Eaken Press, Austin. 1988.

Handbook of Texas Online. https://tshaonline.org/handbook.

Henderson, George Francis Robert. *Stonewall Jackson and the American Civil War.* Grossett & Dunlap, New York. 1943.

Henry, J. L. "First Tennessee Cavalry at Piedmont." *Confederate Veteran*, Vol. 22. Broadfoot Publishing, Wilmington, NC. 1914.

Hervey, Thomas Kibble. *The Devil's Progress: A Poem.* Lupton Relfe, London. 1849.

Holston Territory Genealogical Society. *Families of Washington County and Bristol, Virginia, 1776–1996.* The Society, Bristol. 1996

Hopkins, Luther W. *From Bull Run to Appomattox: A Boy's View.* Fleet-McGinley Co., Baltimore, MD. 1914.

Hout, Steve (State Marine Archeologist). *Current Archeology in Texas,* Volume 7, Number 2, November, 2005, Texas Historical Commission.

Humphreys, Milton W. *A History of the Lynchburg Campaign.* The Michie Company, Charlottesville, VA. 1924.

Imboden, John D. "The Battle of Piedmont" (Written in 1883) Part 1. *Confederate Veteran*, Vol. 31, Broadfoot Publishing, Wilmington, NC. 1923.

Imboden, John D. "The Battle of Piedmont" (Written in 1883) Part 2 pt. 2. *Confederate Veteran*, Vol. 32. 1924.

Johnson, Andrew. *Pardons by the President, Final Report of the Names of Persons Who Lived in Alabama, Virginia, West Virginia, or Georgia, Were Engaged in Rebellion and Pardoned by the President, Andrew Johnson.* Heritage Books, Inc., Bowie, MD. 1986.

Johnson, Clint. *Touring Virginia's and West Virginia's Civil War Sites.* John F. Blair, Winston Salem, NC. 2011.

Jones, Buehring H. *Report on the Battle of Piedmont.* Virginia Historical Society, Richmond. Not dated.

Jones, Buehring H. *The Sunny Land, Or, Prison, Prose and Poetry, Containing the Productions of the Ablest Writers in the South, and Prison Days of Distinguished Confederate Officers.* Innes & Co., Printers, Baltimore, MD. 1868.

Jones, Virgil Carrington. *Gray Ghosts and Rebel Raiders.* Gallahad Books, New York. 1956.

Jones, Virgil Carrington. *Ranger Mosby.* The University of North Carolina Press, Chapel Hill, NC. 1944.

Jones, Virgil Carrington. *The Hatfields & the McCoys: The Bloodiest Family Feud in American History.* Mockingbird Books, Marietta, GA. 1974.

Kieffer, Chester L. *Maligned General: The Biography of Thomas Sidney Jessup.* Presidio Press, San Rafael, CA, and London, 1979.

Keifer, Joseph Warren. *Slavery and Four Years of War, Vol. 1-2—A Political History of Slavery in the United States Together—With a Narrative of the Campaigns and Battles of the Civil War—War in Which the Author Took Part: 1861-1865.* Filquarian Publishing, Lexington, KY. 1899.

Kielman, Chester V. *The University of Texas Archives: A Guide to the Historical Manuscript Collections in the University of Texas Library.* University of Texas Press, Austin. 1967.

Krick, Robert K. *Lee's Colonels: A Biographical Register of the Field Officers of the Army of Northern Virginia.* Morningside Press, Dayton, Ohio. 1979.

Lambert, Dobie Edward. *Grumble, the W. E. Jones Brigade 1863-64.* Lambert Enterprises, Wahiawa, HI. 1992.

Lehigh County Pennsylvania Historical Society. *History of Lehigh County, Pennsylvania and a Genealogical and Biographical Register of Its Families.* Lehigh Valley Publishing Co., Allentown, PA. 1914.

Longacre, Edward G. *Lee's Cavalrymen: A History of the Mounted Forces of the Army of Northern Virginia. 1861-1865.* Stackpole Books. 2002.

Lowry, Thomas P., M.D. *The Story the Soldiers Wouldn't Tell: Sex in the Civil War.* Stackpole Books, Mechanicsville, PA. 1994.

Lynch, Charles H. *The Civil War Diary of Charles H. Lynch, 18th Conn. Vol's.* Case, Lockwood and Brainard Co., Hartford, CT. 1915.

Ludeman, Annette Martin, *La Salle County, South Texas Brush Country, 1856-1975.* Texas County History Series, Nortex Press, No. Quanah, TX. 1975.

MacKinnon, William P. *Kingdom in the West, the Mormons and the American Frontier, Volume 10,* at Sword's Point, Part I, a Documentary History of the Utah War to 1858. The Arthur H. Clark Co., Norman, OK. 2008.

Malsch, Brownson, *Indianola: The Mother of Western Texas*. State House Press, Austin. 1988.

Marcy, Randolph B. *The Prairie Traveler, a Handbook for Overland Expeditions*. Harper & Brothers, New York. 1858.

Marvel, William. *Southwest Virginia in the Civil War: The Battles for Saltville*. H. E. Howard, Inc., Lynchburg, VA. 1992.

Mays, Thomas D. *The Saltville Massacre*. Ryan Place Publishers, Fort Worth, TX 1995.

McAlister, Wayne H, and Martha K. *A Naturalist Guide to Matagorda Island*. University of Texas Press, Austin. 1993.

McClellan, Henry B. *I Rode with Jeb Stuart: The Life and Campaigns of Major General J.E.B. Stuart*. Indiana University Press, Bloomington. 1958.

McConnell, Catherine S. *High on a Windy Hill*. Overmountain Press, Johnson City, TN. 1995.

McDonald, William N. *A History of the Laurel Brigade, Originally the Ashby Cavalry of the Army of Northern Virginia and Chew's Battery*. Edited by Bushrod C. Washington. John Hopkins University Press, Baltimore, MD. 2002.

McGehee, C. Stuart. "The Tarnished Thirty-Fifth Star." *Virginia at War, 1861*. Edited by William C. Davis and James I. Robertson, Jr. for the Virginia Center of Civil War Studies, The University Press of Kentucky, Lexington. 2005.

McKnight, Brian D. *Contested Borderland: The Civil War in Appalachian Kentucky and Virginia*. The University Press of Kentucky, Lexington. 2006.

McNeil, John A. "The Imboden Raid and Its Effects" *Southern Historical Society Papers*. Volume XXXIV, Richmond, VA. 1906.

McVey Multimedia, Inc. *Freedom* (movie). Bristol, Virginia, DVD. 2007.

Miller, John A., *The Battle of Monterey Pass, Pennsylvania's Second Largest Battle, July 4th–5th. 1863*. (no publishing info on the pamphlet).

Moffett, George H. "The Jones Raid Through West Virginia." *Confederate Veteran*, Vol., XIII, S. A. Cunningham, Nashville, TN. 1905.

Morrison, Michael A. *Slavery and the American West, the Eclipse of Manifest Destiny and the Coming of the Civil War*. University of North Carolina Press, Chapel Hill. 1997.

Mosby, John Singleton. *Mosby's Memoirs*. J. S. Sanders & Co., Nashville, TN. 1995.

Mosgrove, George Dallas. *Kentucky Cavaliers in Dixie: Reminiscences of a Confederate Cavalryman*. University of Nebraska Press, Lincoln. 1999.

Musick, Michael P. *6th Virginia Cavalry*. H. E. Howard, Lynchburg, Virginia. 1990.

Myers, Frank M. *The Comanches: A History of White's Battalion Virginia Cavalry, Laurel Brig., Hampton's Div., A.N.V.C.S.A.* Kelly, Piet & Co., Baltimore, MD. 1871.

Neese, George M. *Three Years in the Confederate Horse Artillery*. The Neale Publishing Co., New York, and Washington. 1911.

Nelson, Truman. *The Old Man John Brown at Harpers Ferry*. Haymarket Books, Chicago, IL. 1973.

O'Ferrall, Charles T. *Forty Years of Active Service; Being Some History of the War Between the Confederacy and the Union and of Events Leading Up to It*. The Neal Publishing Co., New York and Washington. 1904.

Oates, Dan, editor. *Hanging Rock Rebel, Lt. John Blue's War in West Virginia and the Shenandoah Valley*. The Burd Street Press, Shippensburg, PA. 1994.

Official Register of the Officers and Cadets of the U.S. Military Academy. United States Military Academy. West Point, NY, June, 1844 to June, 1851.

"Old Grumble Jones Could Cuss and Fight." *Washington County News*. Annual Historical Edition, Vol. XXII, No. 8, Thursday, February 20. 1969.

Olson, John E. *21st Virginia Cavalry*. H. E. Howard, Lynchburg, VA. 1989.

Opie, John N. *A Rebel Cavalryman with Lee, Stuart, and Jackson*. W. B. Conkley Co., Chicago. 1899.

Orr, James W. *Recollections of the War Between the States 1861–1865*. Filed with the Southwest Virginia Historical Society by Luther F. Addington to whom the original pamphlet was loaned by Miss Josephine Wolfe, Written 1909, Price 25 Cents. Proceeds to be used in erecting a Monument to the Memory of Confederate Soldiers of Lee County, Virginia, on the Public Square, at Jonesville, VA.

Parker, Michael P. *President's Hill, Building an Annapolis Neighborhood 1664–2005*. The Annapolis Publishing, Annapolis, MD. 2005.

Patchan, Scott C. *The Battle of Piedmont and Hunter's Raid on Staunton: The 1864 Shenandoah Campaign*. History Press, Charleston, SC, and London. 2011.

Patchan, Scott C. *The Forgotten Fury, the Battle of Piedmont, Va*. Sergeant Kirkland's Museum and Historical Society, Inc., Fredericksburg, VA. 1996.

Pendleton, William Cecil. *History of Tazewell County and Southwest Virginia: 1748–1920*. W. C. Hill Printing Company, Richmond, VA. 1920.

Petruzzi, J. David, "Annihilation of a Regiment." *America's Civil War*. Weider History Group, Inc. Clearwater, FL, July. 2007.

Phillips, David L., editor, and Rebecca Hill, chief researcher. *War Stories: Civil War in West Virginia*. Gauley Mount Press, Leesburg, VA. 1991.

Pinnegar, Charles. *Brand of Infamy: A Biography of John Buchanan Floyd*. Greenwood Press, Westport, CT. 2003.

Powell, Diana. *Pioneer Families of Washington County, Virginia*. 2005-2013. www.ramblingroots.com:

Ramage, James A. *Rebel Raider: The Life of General John Hunt Morgan*. The University Press of Kentucky, Lexington. 1986.

Ransom, John L. *John Ransom's Andersonville Diary: Life Inside the Civil War's Most Infamous Prison*. Berkley Books, New York. 1986.

Richardson, Frank. *From Sunrise to Sunset, Reminiscence*. King Printing Co., Bristol, TN. 1910.

Roberts, Alice. "Col. Warren M. Hopkins." *Confederate Veteran*, Vol. IX, Broadfoot Publishing, Wilmington, NC. 1901.

Robertson, James I, editor. *Soldier of Southwestern Virginia, [The Civil War Letters of Captain John Preston Sheffey]*. Louisiana State University Press, Baton Rouge. 2004.

Robertson, James I, Jr. *Stonewall Jackson, the Man, the Soldier, the Legend*. Macmillan, New York. 1997.

Robins, James S. *Last in Their Class: Custer, Pickett, and the Goats of West Point*, Encounter Books, New York. 2006.

Robinson, Mahlon R. *An Old Man's Memories*. M. L. Robinson, Glade Spring, VA. 1969.

Rosenberg, Charles E. *The Cholera Years: The United States in 1832, 1849, and 1866*, University of Chicago Press, Chicago. 1962.

Sayers, Elizabeth Lemmon. *Smyth County, Pathfinders and Patriots, Prehistory to 1832*, Volume I. Edited by Joan Tracy Armstrong, Smyth County Historical and Museum Society, Inc., Marion, VA. 1983.

Scott, J. L. *36th and 37th Battalions Virginia Cavalry*, 2nd Edition. H. E. Howard, Inc. Lynchburg, VA. 1986.

Scott, J. L. *36th Virginia Infantry*. 1st Edition, H. E. Howard, Inc., Lynchburg, VA. 1987.

Scott, J. L. *45th Virginia Infantry*. H. E. Howard, Inc., Lynchburg, VA. 1989.

Scott, J. L. *60th Virginia Infantry*. H. E. Howard, Inc., Lynchburg, VA. 1997.

Scott, Sameul W. and Angle, Samuel P., *History of the Thirteenth Regiment Tennessee Volunteer Cavalry, U.S.A.*, P. W. Ziegler & Col, Philadelphia, PA, Reprinted 1977 by Don Crow and Harold Lingerfelt.

Settle, Raymond W., editor. *The March of the Mounted Riflemen from Fort Leavenworth to Fort Vancouver, May to October, 1849 as Recorded in the Journals of Major Osborne Cross and George Gibbs and the Official Report of Colonel Loring*. University of Nebraska Press, Lincoln. 1968.

Shaffer, Michael K. *Washington County in the Civil War*. The History Press, Charleston, SC. 2012.

Smith, Jonathan Kennon Thompson. "Genealogical Abstracts from Reported Deaths." *The Nashville Christian Advocate, 1908-1910*.

Smith, Thomas T. *The Old Army in Texas: A Research Guide to the U.S. Army in Nineteenth-Century Texas*. Texas State Historical Association, Austin. 1950.

Stanton, Henry T., *Poems of the Confederacy, Being Selections from the Writings of Major Henry T. Stanton of Kentucky*. John P. Morton & Co., Louisville, KY. 1900.

Steffen, Randy, *United States Military Saddles, 1812-1943*. University of Oklahoma Press, Norman. 1973.

Stevenson, George J., *Increase in Excellence: A History of Emory & Henry College 1836-1963*. Appleton-Century-Crofts Division of Meredith Publishing, New York. 1963.

Stringfield, W.W. "Sixty-Ninth Regiment" *Histories of the Several Regiments and Battalions from North Carolina in the Great War 1861-1865*, Vol. III. Edited by Walter Clark. Nash Brothers, Goldsboro, NC. 1901.

Stubbs, Mary Lee, and Stanley Russell Connor. *Army Lineage Series, Armor-Cavalry, Pt. 1, Regular Army and Army Reserve*. Office of the Chief of Military History, United States Army, Washington, D.C. 1969.

Summers, Festus P. *The Baltimore and Ohio in the Civil War*. Stan Clark Military Books, Gettysburg, PA. 1993.

Summers, Festus P., editor. *A Borderland Confederate*, Greenwood Press, Westport, CT. 1973.

Summers, Lewis Preston. *History of Southwest Virginia, 1746-1786 and Washington County, 1777-1880*. J. Hill Printing Co., Richmond, VA. 1903.

Terraserver Satellite and Aerial Imagery, Raleigh, NC.

Texas Parks & Wildlife, *Port O'connor Photochart, Espiritu Santo Bay, Pass Caballo*, Houston, Texas. 1994.

Thomas, Emory M. *Bold Dragon, the Life of J.E.B. Stuart*. University of Oklahoma Press, Norman. 1999.

Thomason, John W., Jr. *Jeb Stuart*. University of Nebraska Press, Lincoln, Nebraska 1994.

Thompson, Jerry. *Henry Hopkins Sibley, Confederate General of the West*. Texas A&M University Press, College Station. 1996.

Tidball, Eugene C. *No Disgrace to My County: The Life of John C. Tidball*. The Kent State University Press, Kent, OH. 2002.

Tucker, Mabell Abbott, and Jane Warren Waller. *Lincoln County, Tennessee Bible Records*, Volume II.

Lincoln County, Tennessee Pioneers, Batavia, IL. 1971.

"Tragic Drowning of Two Women at Old Indianola Enshrouded in Mystery." *The Houston Post*, April 19. 1936. This was part of a series of articles commemorating Texas pioneer families in celebration of the state's centennial. Mildred Minot Cummings of Houston provided information about this source.

Tucker, Spencer C. *Brigadier General John D. Imboden: Confederate Commander in the Shenandoah.* The University Press of Kentucky, Lexington. 2003.

Turner, Ella May. *Stories and Verse of West Virginia.* Jim Comstock, publisher, Richwood, WV. 1974.

Tyler, Lyon G., editor in chief. *Men of Mark in Virginia, Ideals of American Life: A Collection of Biographies of the Leading Men of the State*, Volume III. Men of Mark Publishing Co., Washington, D.C. 1907.

von Borcke, Heros, and Scheibert Justus. *The Great Cavalry Battle of Brandy Station, 9 June. 1863.* Translated from the German, with historical commentary by Stuart T. Wright and F. D. Bridgewater. Palaemon Press, Winston-Salem, NC. 1976.

Waddell, Joseph A. Member of the Virginia Historical Society. *Annals of Augusta County with Reminiscences Illustrative of the Vicissitude of Its Pioneer Settlers, Biographical Sketches of Citizens Locally Prominent and Those Who Have Founded Families in the Southern and Western States, a Diary of the War, 1861–'5, and a Chapter on Reconstruction.* W. M. Ellis Jones, Richmond, VA. 1886.

Walker, Gary P. *Hunter's Fiery Raid Through Virginia Valleys* (Re-titled from—*Yankee Soldiers in Virginia Valleys: Hunter's Raid*). A & W Enterprise, Roanoke, VA 1989.

Walker, William C., *History of the Eighteenth Regiment Connecticut Volunteers in the War for the Union.* Published by the Committee, Norwich, CT. 1885.

Wallace, Lee. *A Guide to Virginia Military Organizations 1861–1865.* H. E. Howard, Inc., Lynchburg, VA. 1986.

The War of Rebellion, a Compilation of the Official Records of the Union and Confederate Armies. United States War Department. Prepared under the direction of the secretary of war by Robert N. Scott, Government Printing Office, Washington, D.C. 1880–1900.

Warner, Ezra. *Generals in Gray: Lives of Confederate Commanders.* Louisiana State University Press, Baton Rouge. 1959.

Weaver, Jeffrey C. *45th Battalion, Virginia Infantry, Smith and Count's Battalions of Partisan Rangers.* H. E. Howard, Inc., Lynchburg, VA. 1994.

Webb, Jim. *Born Fighting, How the Scots-Irish Shaped America.* Broadway Books, New York. 2004.

Wessels, William L. *Born to Be a Soldier: The Military Career of William Wing Loring of St. Augustine, Florida.* Texas Christian University Press, Fort Worth. 1971.

West Virginia History, Vol. 51. State of West Virginia, Charleston. 1992. This contains the diary of James D. Seddinger.

"William E. Jones of the United States Army, Saddletree." United States Patent Office. Specification of Letters Patent No. 11,068, dated June 13, 1854.

Williams, George T. *Company A, 37th Battalion Virginia Cavalry C.S.A.: A History of Its Organization and Service in the War Between the States 1861–1865.* R. H. Fishburne, Roanoke, VA. 1910.

Wilson, Mark R. "The Extensive Side of Nineteenth-Century Military Economy: The Tent Industry in the Northern United States During the Civil War." *Enterprise and Society 2*, Oxford University Press, USA. 2001.

Wittenberg, Eric J., and J. David Petruzzi, and Michael F. Nugent. *One Continuous Fight: The Retreat from Gettysburg and the Pursuit of Lee's Army of Northern Virginia, July 4–14, 1863.* Savas Beatie, New York and California. 2008.

Wooster, Robert, *Soldiers, Sutlers, and Settlers: Garrison Life on the Texas Frontier,* Number Two. Texas A&M University Press, College Station. 1987.

Yancey, Dwayne. "Rebel First of the Slick Fighters." *Roanoke Times & World News*. Roanoke, VA, January 31. 1991.

Index

Numbers in *bold italics* indicate pages with illustrations

Abingdon, Virginia 82, 83, 87, 88, 89, 176, 180, 181, 182, 183, 195, 203, 209, 245, 246
Abingdon Virginian 1, 180, 181, 199, 200
Academy of Medicine, Abingdon 245
Adams, John Quincy 206
Aldie, Virginia, cavalry engagement 157
Allen, Theodore 189
Altamont, Maryland 133, 135, 136, 137, 144
American Falls, Idaho 38
American Literary, Scientific and Military Academy *see* Norwich University
American Revolution 5, 6, 10, 84, 101, 213
Andersonville, Georgia 187, 235; *Andersonville Diary* 187
Annandale, Virginia 94
Anti-Slavery Society 76
Antietam, Campaign 109, 113, 117, 129, 212
Appomattox Campaign/Courthouse 235, 241, 242, 244, 245, 247
Armistead, Lewis 227
Ashby, Richard 102, 104
Ashby, Turner 101-105, 107-113, 117-118, 127, 178, 242
Ashby Gap 101, 159, 161
Ashland, Virginia 90
Asra, steamship 77
Augusta County, Virginia 5, 116, 238, 240; battery 209, 219; reserves 209, 219, 220, 225, 227
Augusta High School, Maine 1
Averell, William 202-203, 212, 216

Balder, Christian 162
Baltimore, Maryland 68, 124
Baltimore & Ohio (B & O) Railroad 114, 115, 117, 118, 119, 121, 123, 125, 128, 129, 133, 140, 144, 160, 245
Baltimore Light Artillery 129
Banks, Nathaniel 103, 108, 202

Baylor, George 130, 131, 242
Bealeton, Virginia 98
Bean Station, Tennessee 180, 192
Beattie, Fountain 9
Beauregard, Pierre Gustave Toutant 90, 92, 93, 102
Beckley, Henry 215, 218
Bedford County, Virginia 182
Beeres, Charles 194, 195, 198
Belle Island 187, 189
Benicia, California 39
Berryville, Virginia 122
Beverly, (West) Virginia 140-141, 145
Beverly's Ford 151, 152
Big Creek, Tennessee 184, 185, 186
Black Fox Ford 191
Blackford, William Willis 82, 83, 86, 92, 97, 98, 99, 100, 245
Blair, Hugh 24
Blair, Montgomery 235
Bleeding Kansas 73, 74, 76, 80
Blountville, Tennessee 88, 176, 179, 184, 187, 188, 189
Blue, John 106, 107, 126, 136, 149, 165, 166, 218, 242
Blue, Monroe 218, 227, 230, 242
Blue Springs, Tennessee 179
Bolivar Heights 102
Bond, Frank A. 126, 136, 137
Boone, Daniel 193
Boonsboro, Maryland 169, 171 201, 202, 212, 215, 216, 217
Border Rangers Militia 181
Border State Conventions 85
Boteler, Alexander Robinson 123, 125-126
The Bower 109-111, 170
Bragg, Braxton 174, 176, 179, 180, 184, 190, 191, 201, 209, 213, 233
Brandy Station 2, 106, 147-157, 159, 170, 172, 178, 242, 247
Breckinridge, John C. 83, 202, 205, 207, 208, 209
Brewer, Charles, Dr. 213
Brewer, Richard Henry 212, 213, 216, 219, 223-225, 227, 230
Brewster, H.P. 71

Brice, Marshall Moore 237
Bridgeport, (West) Virginia 138, 140
Bridger, Jim 75
Bristol, Virginia & Tennessee 83, 176, 179, 180, 184, 195, 199, 200
Bristol Courier 86
British Patent No. 1892 (Jones Saddle) 68
Brown, John, abolitionist 2, 80, 81, 82, 84, 87, 88, 91, 92, 102, 116
Brown, Ridgley 129, 132, 133, 135
Browne, William Henry 214, 218, 225, 230
Bryan, Thomas A. 214, 218, 234
Buchanan, James, President 32, 66, 67, 68, 70, 73, 80
Buchanan, John A. 237
Buchanan, Virginia 216
Buchanan County, Virginia 200
Buck, William Alexander 132
Buckhannon, (West) Virginia 140, 141
Buckner, Simon Bolivar 201, 210
Buford, John 151, 152, 157, 167, 168, 169, 247
Bull's Gap, Tennessee 180, 187
Burning Springs, (West) Virginia *see* Oiltown
Burns, William Wallace 70, 71, 73, 78, 246
Burnside, Ambrose P. 16, 34, 97, 118, 140, 177, 179, 186, 190, 193
Butler, Benjamin Franklin 120, 202
Buttermilk Falls, NY 21, 26, 27, 29, 30
Byars, William 10
Byrd, William 5

Cabell, Henry Coalter 121
Cabell County, (West) Virginia 181
Calhoun County, Texas 45, 52
Calliopean Literary Society 13
Camp Clinton, West Point 18, 19, 23, 27
Camp Crawford, New Mexico 64

279

Index

Camp Sumner, Kansas 36
The Campaign of 1864 in the Valley of Virginia and the Expedition into Lynchburg 240
Campbell, Jacob. M. 227, 230
Campbell, William 6, 84
Campbell Saddle 68
Carpenter, Daniel A. 186
Carr, Albert. A. 189
Carrick's Ford, West Virginia 116
Carter, James 219
Carter Valley Road 185, 186
Carter's Station, Tennessee 190
Cashtown, Pennsylvania 161, 163, 168
Cecil County, Maryland 5
Cedar Creek, Virginia 205, 207, 208; battle of 235
Cedar Mountain, battle of 108
Cemetery Ridge, Gettysburg 161
Centerville, Virginia 93, 96
Central Depot (Radford), Virginia 202, 213, 214, 215, 216
Chambersburg, Pennsylvania 110, 111, 113, 181, 235, 243
Chambersburg, Raid of *see* Stuart-Chambersburg Raid
Chambliss, John Randolph 157, 158, 160, 169
Chancellorsville, Virginia 141, 146, 147, 148; campaign of 146, 147, 158
Chantilly, Virginia battle of 109
Charles I, King 77, 101
Charles Town (West) Virginia 81, 109, 170, 239, 243
Charleston Mercury 154
Charlottesville, Virginia 104, 206, 212, 214, 215, 216, 217, 219
Chattanooga, Tennessee 176, 179, 180, 190, 191, 192
Cheat Mountain, battle of 97, 115
Cheat Mountain District 116, 119, 121
Cheat River Bridge/Viaduct, Rowlesburg 128, 130, 132, 133, 134, 139
Cherokees, Indian Tribe 5
Chester County, Pennsylvania 5
Chew, Preston 102, 150, 152; Mounted (Horse) Artillery/Battery of *see* Virginia Troops
Chicago Tribune 195
Chickamauga, Georgia, battle of 176, 177, 179, 206
Chilton, Robert H. 172, 175
Chrisman, George 20
Claiborne, James R. 192
Clarksburg, (West) Virginia 115, 138, 140
Cleburne, Patrick 176
Cleveland, Grover 243–244
Clinch, District of the 196
Clinch Mountain 192
Clinch River 191, 194
Clinton, schooner 51
Cloyd's Mountain, battle of 202, 212, 214, 215
Cluseret, Gustave Paul 119, 120

Cobden, John C. 77
Cold Harbor, Virginia, battle of 232, 237
College of St. James 168, 169
Collins, Charles 10, 12, 13
Columbia River 35, 38, 39
Columbian College of the District of Columbia 136, 242
Comanches *see* Virginia Troops, Thirty-Fifth Battalion Virginia Cavalry, AKA White's Battalion
Confederate Congress 99, 117, 120, 181, 206
Confederate Veteran 52, 223
Conklin, Effie 29
Connecticut Troop Units:
 Eighteenth Connecticut Infantry 207, 226, 231
 First Connecticut Cavalry 170
Conscription Act 117, 182
Cook, Alphonso 201
Cook, William 60
Cooke, Phillip St. George 91
Cooper, Samuel 108, 111, 177, 203
Corns, James M. 182, 188, 196, 201
Corpus Christi, Texas 54
Corse, Montgomery D. 184
Craig, Robert 237
Cranberry Summit (Terra Alta) 135, 136, 137, 144
Crawford, Edward, Reverend 10
The Crisis 118
Crittenden County, Arkansas 41, 43, 63, 248, 249
Crockett's Gap 203
Crook, George 202, 203, 206, 207, 212
Cross, Osborne 37, 38
Cross Keys, Virginia, engagement 104
Cross Road at Piedmont **221** 224, 228
Culpeper, Virginia 108, 157; county 148, 149, 170, 171; courthouse 147, 148, 149, 150, 151, 154, 159, 171, 172
Culp's Hill 156, 160
Cumberland Gap 176–177, 180, 183–184, 191–197, 199
Cumberland River 196
Cumberland Valley 148
Curtin, Andrew Greg 140–141
Cushing, Alonzo 214
Custer, George Armstrong 2, 164–165, 214, 227, 248

Dabney, Robert Lewis 175
Dailey, John 136
The Dalles, Oregon 38
Damascus, Virginia 240
Darkesville, (West) Virginia 110
Davidson College 11
Davis, Alexander 219
Davis, Jefferson 34, 61, 64, 66, 70, 71, 84, 85, 86, 90, 94, 101, 104, 117, 118, 125, 154, 172, 173, 176, 177, 184, 187, 201, 213, 233, 240, 244
Davis, Reuben A. 197–198

Davis, Sturgess 211, 219, 223
Day, George W. 219
Derby & Miller, publisher 77
Deshler, David T. 23, 176
Deshler, James 176
D'Lyon, James W. "Buck" 30
Dodd, Mead & Company 246
Doyle, Robert 229, 233
Dred Scott Decision 6
Dublin Depot/Station, Virginia 176, 177, 179, 181, 201
Duffie, Alfred 150
Dulaney, Richard H. 129
Dunn, Ambrose C. 183, 201; Dunn's Partisan Rangers *see* Virginia Troops
Dunn, Eliza *see* Jones, Eliza "Pink" Margaret Dunn
Dunn, Emily J. 55
Dunn, Florence Virginia 51
Dunn, Jane Beattie Ryburn Edmundson (Edmiston) 42, 52, 55, 58
Dunn, Robert Campbell 182, 243
Dunn, Samuel 42, 55, 58
Dunn, William Logan 42, 89, 91, 245
Dunn family/section, Old Glade Presbyterian Church Cemetery 236, 243, 245
DuPont, Henry Algernon 207, 226, 230, 233, 234, 240

Eagle Pass, Texas 63
Eakin, William L. 219
Early, Jubal Anderson 1, 168, 235; Early's Washington Raid 235, 237, 239, 240, 241, 242, 243
East Road, Piedmont *see* Staunton Road
East Tennessee & Virginia Railroad 180
Echols John C. 205
Edmiston/Edmondson, family name 5
Edmondson, Andrew "Jolly Andy" 41
Edmondson, Arkansas 41
Edmondson, Eliza Kennedy 6, 42
Edmondson, Henry A. 183
Edmondson, John 5
Edmondson, Margaret Montgomery 6, 42
Edmondson, Robert Buchanan 8, 9, 11, 42, 43, 51, 89
Edmondson, Samuel 5
Edmondson, Thomas Benjamin Estill 43, 51, 89, 245
Edmondson, Thomas Tate 43
Edmondson, William, Colonel 5, 6, 42
Eggleston, George 90, 93, 95, 96
El Paso & Fort Yuma Wagon Road 71
El Paso del Norte, Texas 63
Eldridge, Charles W. 45, 46, 47, 48, 49, 50, 51, 52
Eldridge, Hannah Mitchell Avery 45, 47, 48, 49

Ellicott, George M. 208
Elmwood Cemetery, Memphis, Tennessee 249
Emack, George M. 164, 165, 166, 167
Emancipation Proclamation 109, 114, 120, 123
Emory & Henry College 9, 10–15, 26, 89, 91, 182, 213, 240, 245
English Civil War 77, 101
Evans, Thomas 227, 230
Evansville, (West) Virginia 135
Ewell, Thomas 54
Ewell's, Richard, Corps 103, 156, 158, 160, 161, 164, 166, 157, 168, 207
Ewing, Hugh B. "Monk" 30
Exeter Hall, London 76–77

Fairfax County, Virginia 93, 96, 97
Fairfield, Pennsylvania, battle of 162–163, 169, 173
Fairfield Gap 163, 164, **167**
Fairfield Hagerstown Road 164
Fairmont, (West) Virginia 138–140,144 146, 241
Falcon, Atlantic steamship 40
Falling Waters, (West) Virginia 170
Fauquier, Francis 6
Fauquier County, Virginia 98, 101, 158, 160; County Rangers 102
Ferguson, Champ 241
Fife, William Estil 215, 218
Fillmore, Millard 53, 57
Fincastle County, Virginia 6; militia 6
Fire Eaters 76
First Brigade, C.S. Army of the Valley District 214, 218, 225, 226, 234, 240
First Bull Run/Manassas Campaign 92–97, 102, 117, 215, 247
First CSA Engineers Regiment 129
Fisher's Hill 208; battle of 240
Fishersville, Virginia 230, 232
Five Forks, battle of 235
Fleetwood Heights/Hill 151–152
Flournoy, Cabell E. 151, 162
Flournoy, Thomas 107
Floyd, John Buchanan 67, 71, 73, 74, 75, 78, 80, 81, 246
Floyd County, Virginia 182
Flynn, James M. 123–124, 133
Fort Belknap, Texas 70–71
Fort Bliss, Texas 63
Fort Boise, Idaho 38
Fort Bridger, Wyoming 38
Fort Delaware 242
Fort Donelson 97, 215, 246
Fort Duncan, Texas 63
Fort Ewell, Texas 53–54, 56, 58–60
Fort Hall, Idaho 38
Fort Kearny, Nebraska Territory 37
Fort Laramie, Wyoming 37, 73
Fort Leavenworth, Kansas 30
Fort Loudon, Tennessee 190

Fort Merrill, Texas 52–54, 60
Fort Riley, Kansas 70–71
Fort Sanders, Tennessee 190
Fort Sumter 80, 86, 90, 215
Fort Vancouver, Washington 38–39
Fortress Monroe 97
Forty Years of Active Service 241
Franklin Academy, Jonesville 194
Franklin & Nashville Campaign 246
Frazer, John W. 193
Fredericksburg, Virginia 103, 118, 147, 150; campaign of 120, 121, 158
Freeman, Douglas Southall (D. S.) 102, 245
Freeman, W.G., Colonel 54, 58
Fremont, John 66
French and Indian War 5, 101
Front Royal, Virginia 103, 122
Frozen Fight *see* Jonesville, battle of
Fulkerson, Samuel Vance 88–89
Fulkerson's Mill 285
Funkstown, Maryland 169

Galveston, Texas 44–46, 60
Garnett, Richard 108
Garrard, Israel 184–188, 191
Garrard, Theophilus Toulmin 196–198
Gauley River 143, **145**
Geary, John White 70
George Washington University *see* Columbian College of the District of Columbia
Georgetown University 34
Georgia Troop Units: Sixteenth Georgia Cavalry 184, 215
Gettysburg, Pennsylvania 111, 160, 161, 171, 173, 174, 178; campaign of 2, 106, 111, 155–183, 211, 242, 247; raid *see* Stuart's Gettysburg Raid
Gilmor, Harry L. 208
Giltner, Henry Lyter/Brigade 179, 184, 185–188, 190
Glade Spring Depot 6, 31, 42, 43, 61, 63, 78, 85, 87, 89, 175, 177, 203, 210, 212–213, 214, 235, 243, 245, 249
Glenville, (West) Virginia 143
Gonzales, Texas 45, 51, 247
Gordon, John B. 237
Gordonsville, Virginia, Gordonsville Loop 105, 107, 206
Gorgas, Josiah 121
Grafton, (West) Virginia 116, 128, 138–140
Grand Review, First 149–150; Second 150
Grant, Ulysses S. 33, 34, 97, 171, 174, 179–180, 190, 191, 202, 204–205, 206, 208, 235, 239, 244, 246; *Personal Memoirs* 33
Grant County, West Virginia 130
Green, John Shac 129, 134, 139

Greene, Charles W. "Geographic" 30
Greene County, Tennessee 179, 181
Greenhow, S.C. 66
Greenland Gap 130–133, 137
Greer, Jefferson 41, 43, 63, 248–249
Greer, Sarah Eliza Jane *see* Redman, Sarah Eliza Jane Jones Greer
Greer, Virginia 249
Gregg, David McMurtrie 151–152, 157
Grimsley Saddle 61, 68
Gus's Point, Hudson River 23

Haden, Benjamin 94
Hagerstown, Maryland 163–164, 166–169, 171, 235
Halleck, Henry Wagner 116, 124–125, 138–141
Hampden-Sydney College 175
Hampshire County, West Virginia 218, 230, 242
Hampshire Review 242
Hampton, Wade, Cavalry 110–111, 149, 152, 155, 157, 158, 160, 169, 173, 174, 180
Hampton Roads 61
Hancock, Winfield S. 18
Hancock County, Tennessee 193
Hanover, Pennsylvania 160
Hanover County, Virginia 90
Hanover Junction *see* North Anna River
Harlow, William T. 12
Harman, Asher Waterman 122, 129, 133, 135–142, 170, 218
Harman, William Henry 218–219, 225
Harney, Selby 186
Harnsberger, H.B. 209, 219
Harper, Adam 118
Harper, Kenton 209
Harper's Augusta and Rockbridge Reserves *see* Virginia Troops
Harpers Ferry, (West) Virginia 2, 80–81, 84, 90–91, 102, 109, 114, 116, 118–119, 124, 127, 161, 170, 180, 243
Harper's Monthly 239
Harrisonburg, Virginia 209, 217
Havana, Cuba 40
Havens, Benjamin J. "Benny," tavern 21, 26, 28
Hayes, Rugherford B. 239, 244
Hays, Harry Thompson 173
Henderson, John 139
Herbert, James R. 129
Hermesian Literary Society 13
Hervey, Thomas Kibble 143
Heth, Henry 173
Hill, Ambrose Powell (A.P.): Corps 105, 156, 157, 163–164, 212–213
Hoboken, New Jersey 45
Hollingsworth Hotel, Woodstock 208
Hollywood Cemetery, Richmond 240–241

Holston, River 185–186, 191–192; middle fork 6, 7, 63, 210; valley 180
Holston Conference 9–10, 213
Hood, John Bell: Division of 147
Hood's Mill, Maryland 160
Hooker, Joseph 120, 129, 146, 148, 150–151, 156, 161
Hope Saddle 68
Hopkins, George Washington 13
Hopkins, Luther 161, 165–166
Hopkins, Warren M. 113, 155, 186, 244–245
Horrell, Mr. 47–48
Horton, Lewis 200
Houston, Sam 33
Hovey, Hubble 47–48, 51
Humphreys, Milton Wylie 234
Hunter, Andrew 239
Hunter, David 205–209, **206**, 211, 216–217, 219–222, 224–226, 231–235, 237, 239–240

Illinois Troop Units:
  Second Illinois Artillery 184
  Sixteenth Illinois Cavalry 194
  Twenty-Third Illinois Infantry (Irish Brigade) 130
Imboden, Francis Marion 211, 223
Imboden, George W. 211, 219
Imboden, John D. 116–120, 128–129, 140–141, 143, 145–146, 148, 163, 168, 183, 205, 208–211, 216–227, 229, 231, 233–235, 240
Immortals, West Point vernacular 20–21
Independence, Missouri 34
Independence, (West) Virginia 135, 137, 144
Independence Rock, Oregon Trail 38
Independence, steamship 45–51, 61, 247
Indian Creek, Virginia 197
Indiana Troop Units:
  Ninety-First Indiana Infantry 197–198
Indianola, Texas 44–45, 247
Indianola Bulletin 52
Irish Brigade *see* Illinois Troops, Twenty-Third Illinois Infantry
Irving, Charles 96

Jackson, Alfred E. "Mudwall" 179, 235
Jackson, Cummins Edward 141
Jackson, Mississippi 174
Jackson, Thomas Jonathan "Stonewall" 17, 19, 21–23, 26, 34, 55, 88, 90, 93, 102–105, 107–109, 11–112, 114, 118, 119, 122–123, 125, 141, 143–144, 146, 148, 175, 179, 180, 199, 204 Shenandoah Valley Campaign 102–105, 113, 116–117, 205–206, 218, 229, 237, 242, 246
Jackson, Thomas K. 23
Jackson, William L. 216
Jackson's James River 90, 114, 202

Jackson's Mill, (West) Virginia 141
James River and Kanawha Canal 61
Jefferson, Thomas 15, 35
Jefferson Barracks 35–36, 40–41
Jefferson College *see* Washington & Jefferson College
Jefferson Medical College of Pennsylvania 245
Jenkins, Albert Gallatin 169, 181–184, 200, 202, 208, 214, 21
Jesup, Thomas Sidney 61, 70,-71, 73–75
John Red, prize stallion 199
Johnson, Andrew 239, 241
Johnson, Bradley T. 245
Johnson's Island, Ohio 218, 240, 242
Johnston, Albert Sidney 75, 212
Johnston, James W. 218
Johnston, Joseph Eggleston (Joseph E.) 70, 90, 92–94, 102, 117, 174, 202, 235
Jones, Beuhring H. (B. H. Jones) 214, 218, 225, 231, 240
Jones, Catherine Moffett Edmondson 6–8, 10–11, 41, 43, 63, 248
Jones, David R. 7–8
Jones, David Rumph 25
Jones, Eliza "Pink" Margaret Dunn 42–43, 45, 47, 51–52, 61–63, 182, 236, 247
Jones, Henry 6
Jones, Henry S. 7, 11, 41
Jones, James W. 7, 41–43, 63, 248
Jones, Martha 6
Jones, R. (Roger), Adjutant General 43
Jones, Robert 7–8, 10, 15, 41–43, 63
Jones, Robert Campbell 7, 24, 41–43, 237, 248–249
Jones, Samuel (Sam), Major General 176–177, 179, 181, 183–184, 196
Jones, Sarah Eliza Jane *see* Redman, Sarah Eliza Jane Jones Greer
Jones, Virgil Carrington 244
Jones and Imboden West Virginia Raid *see* West Virginia Raid
Jones Jonathan S. 7–8
Jones Saddle 68, 94
Jonesville, Virginia, battle of 193–199, 201–202; "Frozen Fight" 195

Kanawha County, (West) Virginia 214
Kanawha District, Army of the Kanawha 202–203, 207, 220, 234
Kanawha Valley 182
Kansas border disturbances 91, 184, 246
Kansas Territory 91
Kaufman, M.R. 122–123
Kelley, Benjamin 118–119, 124–125, 128, 130, 133, 138
Kelley's Island 102

Kellogg, Horace 118
Kelly's Ford 151–152, **153**, 158
Kentucky Troop Units (CS):
  Fourth Kentucky Cavalry 179, 183–184
  Tenth Kentucky Cavalry 184, 194
Kernstown, Virginia, battle of 103, 108, 119, 126
Kerr, R. Hulton 49
Kershaw, Joseph Brevard 173
Khedive of Egypt 246
Kilpatrick, Judson, Cavalry Division 152, 157, 160, 164–169
Kings Mountain, Campaign of 5–6
Kingsport, Tennessee 185
Kingston, Jamaica 45
Kingwood, (West) Virginia 135–136
Knoxville, Tennessee, campaign for 176, 179–180, 184, 190–193, 199, 203, 213, 215

La Salle, County, Texas 54
La Salle, René-Robert Cavelier, sieur de 44
Lacey & Phillips, Saddlers 68
Lacey Spring, Virginia 128–129, 209
Landell, John H. 71, 75, 78
Lane, Joseph 35, 39
Laurel Brigade, moniker 178, 242–243
Laurel Hill, (West) Virginia 116
Leach, James B. 71
Lee, Edwin G. 230
Lee, Fitzhugh (Fitz) 63, 99–100, 110, 125, 127–128, 157–158, 160, 169, 173–174
Lee, Robert E. 34, 63, 66, 70, 76, 80, 83–84, 87–89, 91, 97, 104–105, 108–112, 114–116, 118–121, 124–129, 134, 139, 144, 146–148, 150, 152, 154–155, 157–163, 169–177, 180, 199, 202, 204, 207, 208–210, 220, 232, 235, 241–244
Lee, Stephen D. 176
Lee, William Henry Fitzhugh "Rooney" 110, 152, 157
Lee County, Virginia 193–194, 196–197, 199–200, 202
Lemert, Wilson C. 194–195
Letcher, John 86–90, 98, 120, 235
Lewinsville, Virginia 94, 97
Lewis and Clark Expedition 35
Lewisburg, (West) Virginia 143, 181; battery *see* Virginia Troops
Lexington, Kentucky 203
Lexington, Virginia 82, 114, 116, 235, 239
Libby Prison 187, 189, 195
Life and Campaigns of Lieut. Gen. Thomas J. Jackson (Stonewall Jackson) 175
Lincoln, Abraham 2, 33, 79, 83–84, 86, 103, 105, 109, 114–116, 118, 123, 129, 138, 140–141, 163, 170–171, 188, 195, 206, 232, 237, 239, 244

Lincoln County, Tennessee 41
Litterell, Ewing 197
Litterell, William 197
Little Big Horn 227, 248
Little Kanawha River 142
Little Round Top 156, 160
Little War Gap 195
Live Oak, County, Texas 54
Lodi, Virginia 6
Lomax, Lunsford Lindsay 129
Long Shoals, Tennessee 185
Longstreet, James 34, 109, 119–120, 147, 156–157, 159, 161, 164, 172, 174, 176, 184, 190–193, 195–197, 199, 213, 215
Loring, William Wing 34–36, 38–39, 54, 56–57, 64, 66, 172, 246
Loudon, Tennessee 90
Loudon County, Virginia 105, 157–158
Louisiana, U.S. Mail steamer 46, 49, 51
Love, James R., Jr. 213, 219, 241
Lynch, Charles H. 207, 226, 231
Lynchburg, Virginia/campaign 61, 182, 202, 206, 212–217, 219, 231, 234–237, 241, 243
Lynchburg & Danville Railroad 245

Magruder, John Bankhead 97
Mahan, Dennis Hart 28
Manassas Gap Railroad 90
Manassas (Junction), Virginia 90, 92, 97
March to Oregon Expedition *see* Oregon, march to, expedition
Marion, Pennsylvania 163
Marion, Virginia 89, 234
Marion County, (West) Virginia 138, 141
Marquis, James C., Marquis Augusta (Boy) Battery *see* Virginia Troops
Marshall, Thomas A. 106–107, 131, 169
Marshall, Virginia 160
Martha Washington College 89
Martin, J.G. 181
Martin, Walter K. 204, 228
Martin, William Thompson 192
Martinsburg, (West) Virginia 109–110, 127, 202, 205, 208–208, 218–219
Maryland Troop Units (CS):
  Baltimore Light Artillery 129
  First Maryland Cavalry Battalion 121, 126, 129, 131, 136, 140, 164
  First Maryland Infantry Battalion 121, 129
Maryland Troop Units (U.S.):
  First Maryland Cavalry Regiment 106
Mason, John Young, Sec. of Navy 19
Mason Dixon Line 164, 166–167
Massachusetts Troop Units:
  Thirty-Fourth Massachusetts 227, 228

USS *Massachusetts*en}40
Matagorda Bay 44, 46, 49, 51
Matagorda Island 44, 51, 61, 246–247
Matagorda Peninsula 44
McCausland, John C. 215, 235, 243
McClanahan, John H. 211, 219, 223, 224, 229
McClellan, George B. 22, 34, 68, 97, 99, 100, 102–103, 105, 109–111, 115–116, 154
McClellan, Henry B. 95, 175, 195
McClellan Saddle 68
McConnell, Sylvester P. 183
McDonald, Angus W. 102
McDonald, Edward H. 133, 135–136
McDonald, William N. 130, 139, 178
McDowell, Irvin 90 92, 103
McDowell, Virginia 103, 209–210
McKay, Donald 45
McKay, Lauchlan 45, 4
McLean, Nathaniel 23
McLean, Thomas Frelinghuyson McKinney "Old Bison" 16–17, 22–30, 39–40, 247–248
McNeil, John Hanson 128, 133, 135
Meade, George 34, 163, 168–171, 174
Mechling, William L. 22
Meigs, John Rogers 207
Memphis, Tennessee 36, 41–43, 52, 56, 63, 71, 237, 248–249
Mercer Institute/Mercer University 11
Merrill, Moses, Captain 54
Mexican War/Cession 26–27, 29, 32–35, 39, 41, 44, 53–54, 56, 60–61, 67, 88, 93, 116, 181, 203, 206, 215, 218, 246
Michigan Troop Units:
  Fifth Michigan Cavalry 164
  Ninth Michigan Cavalry 187
Middle River 221–222, 224–225, 229
Middleburg, Virginia 157
Middletown, Virginia 126
Milbourne, Andrew 195
Milburn, William H. 9
Milroy, Robert Huston 115–129, *116*, 156, 178, 207
Minot, Louisa Papley "Lucy" 45, 48, 51
Minot, Stephen, family of 45, 47–48, 51, 247
Missionary Ridge 179, 184, 190
Mitchell, Lucy 45, 47
Mocks Mill 240
Moffett, George 142
Monocacy Bridge 129
Monongahela River 138–140, 144, **145**
Monongalia County (West) Virginia 136–138
Monterey, Mexico 33
Monterey Hotel 165
Monterey Pass, engagement 163–168, **167**

Montgomery, Alabama 84, 86
Montgomery County, Virginia 182
Montpelier Station 173
Moorefield, (West) Virginia 116, 119,-121–123, 125, 129–130, 133, 243
Morgan, Charles 44–45
Morgan, George 46–48
Morgan, John Hunt 203–204, 208–210, 233, 243–244
Morgan County, (West) Virginia 123–124, 241
Morgan Steamship Line 44–45
Morgan's Farm 199
Morgantown, (West) Virginia 133, 135–140, 242–243
Mormon Church, settlement 35, 73, 244
Morris, William Hopkins 26–27, 30
Morristown, Tennessee 180, 186–187, 190–191
Morse, Samuel 19
Mosby, John Singleton 3, 52, 83–84, 86, 88–94, 96–98, 100, 244–245; *War Reminiscenes* 244
Mosby, Pauline Clarke 83; death 244
Mosgrove, George Dallas 179–180, 183
Mount Crawford, Virginia 146, 148, 208–209, 211, 216–***221***
Mount Jackson, Virginia 208–210
Mount Sidney, Virginia 220–221
Mowery, George 220
Mowery's Hill 220–224, 232–233
Mulligan, James Adelbert 132, 135, 139
Munford, Thomas Taylor 109–112

Nat Turner's Rebellion 80
Nebraska Territory 34, 37
Neese, George M. 150
Nelson County, Virginia 83, 96, 182
New Creek, (West) Virginia 127, 130, 138
New Creek Mountain 130
New Hope, Virginia 220, 222, 229–230, 232, 234
New London Academy 182
New Market, Virginia 119, 205, 27–209, 211, 217–218, 227, 231, 237
New Orleans, Louisiana 40–41, 43–44, 45, 63
New River 6, 8, 183, 202–203, 212–216
New York, New York 26, 30–31, 44, 51, 67, 70, 78–79, 171, 246
New York Troop Units:
  Fifteenth New York Cavalry 220
  Fifth New York Cavalry 106
  First New York Cavalry 126
  Twenty-First New York Cavalry 232
Newtown, Virginia 207–208
Nichols, W.A., Major, Assistant Adjutant General 64

284 Index

Nichols, William 46–49, 51, 247
Norfolk & Western Railroad 245
North Carolina Troop Units (CS):
  Fourth North Carolina Cavalry Regiment 164
North Carolina Troops (U.S.):
  Second North Carolina Infantry 197–198
North Fork of the Red River, battle of 248
Norwich University AKA American Literary, Scientific, and Military Academy) 115
Nueces, River 33, 53–54, 59, 60, 63

Oakland, Maryland 128, 133, 135–137, 144
O'Ferrall, Charles T. 123–124, 143, 158, 211, 217–218, 232–234, 241
Ohio County (West) Virginia 137
Ohio River 115, 118, 140, 142
Ohio Troop Units:
  One Hundred and Tenth Ohio Regiment 123
  One Hundred and Twenty-Third Ohio Regiment 118
  Seventh Ohio Cavalry 180, 184, 186, 189
  Twenty-Second Ohio Battery 194
Oiltown, (West) Virginia 142–144
Old Baptist Cemetery Annex 245
Old Glade Presbyterian Church Cemetery 51, 61, 89, **236**, 243, 245
Old Glade Spring Depot, Virginia *see* Glade Spring
Old Night Hawk, moniker 123, 194
Opequon Creek 114, 119, 243
Opie, John Newton 134, 142, 144, 158, 211, 223, 233–234, 241
Orange & Alexandria Railroad 149
Orange County, Virginia 105, 171, 173–174
Orange Courthouse 147, 172, 175, 242; engagement 106–108
Ordinance of Secession 86, 102, 115
Oregon, march to, expedition 2, 36–39, 57
Oregon City 38–39
Oregon Territory 2, 33–35, 38–40, 53, 58
Oregon Trail 34–35, 37–38
Oregon Treaty, boundary dispute 32–35
Otis, Charles 232–233

Palmetto, steamship 44, 46
Panama, Isthmus of 40, 56
Parkersburg, (West) Virginia 138, 140–141
Parrett, Solomon 71
Parsons, Job 118
Partisan Ranger Act 117
Pass Caballo, Texas 44–46, 49
Patten, George 71, 74

Patterson, Robert 90, 92
Patterson Creek 130–131
Paxton, Elisha Franklin 146
Peaks of Otter 235
Pelican Island **50**
Pender, Dorsey 176, 212–213
Pennsylvania Troop Units:
  Fifty-Fourth Pennsylvania Infantry 227–228, 230
  Thirteenth Pennsylvania Cavalry 126
Peters, William Elisha 182, 201, 243
Petersburg, (Hardy/Grant County, West) Virginia 116, 119, 121, 129–130
Petersburg Campaign 242
Pettigrew, James Johnson 170
Philippi, West Virginia 115–116, 140
Pickett, George E. 21–22, 34, 147
Pickett's Charge 156, 161, 163, 227
Piedmont, Virginia 216, **221**–243, **228**
Pierce, Franklin 61, 66
Pierpont, Francis H. 115, 128, 139, 140–141, 144–145, 239, 241
Pittsylvania County, Virginia 182, 244
Platte River 37–38
Pleasanton, Alfred 18, 151, 154, 157–158
Point Lookout, Maryland 218, 242
Polk, James K. 20, 32–33
Polk, Leonidas 212–213
Pope, John 105, 108–109, 120
Port Republic, Virginia 104, 220, 222–223
Powder Spring Gap 192
Powell Mountain 194
Pratt and Hunt 75
Preston County, (West) Virginia 130, 133, 135
Price, Joseph H. 26
Pridemore, Auburn L. 194–196, 199

Radford, Virginia *see* Central Depot
Ramseur, Stephen Dodson 173
Randolph, Beverly 209
Randolph, George Wythe 98–99, 113, 117
Randolph County, Missouri 16
Ransom, John L. 187
Ransom, Robert, L. Jr. 184, 187–188, 201–202, 213, 215–216, 235
Rapidan River 106–108, 171–172, 174, 202
Rappahannock River 114, 119, 146–149, 151, 153–154, 156–157, 171–172
Rasin, William I. 137
Rayburn, steamship 48–51
Red Eye, celebrated thoroughbred 199
Redman, Reuben T. 248
Redman, Sarah Eliza Jane Jones Greer 7, 41–42, 63, 248–249

Regiment of Mounted Rifles *see* U.S. Troops, U.S. Mounted Rifles
Reynolds, Joseph J. 115
Rhode Island Troops:
  First Rhode Island 157
Richmond Dispatch 99, 154
Richmond Enquirer 154
Richmond Examiner 154
Richmond Medical College 245
Richmond Whig 154
Ringgold Barracks, Texas 60–61
Rio Grande, River 33, 53, 59, 61, 63, 91
Rio Grande City, Texas 61, 63
Rives, Tom 90
Roberts, Benjamin S. 138, 140
Robertson, Beverly H. 104–105, 107–109, 111, 148, 152, 157–159, 161, 172–173
Robertson, Frank 150
Robertson, William J. 83
Robertson, Wyndham 82
Rockbridge County, Virginia 5
Rockfish Gap 230, 232
Rockingham County, Virginia 128, 143, 146, 241
Rogersville, Tennessee, battle of 55, 180, 184–192, 194–196, 201–202
Romney, (West) Virginia 102, 118, 125, 127
Rose Bank 101
Rosecrans, William Starke 176
Rosser, Thomas Lafayette 102, 178, 214, 242–243
Rowlesburg, (West) Virginia 128, 130, 133–134, 139, 143
Russell, William 186
Russell County, Virginia 13, 87, 182, 200–201
Russell Courthouse 209

Saint George, (West) Virginia 118
St. James Church 151
St. Louis, Missouri 35–36, 41, 47, 56, 75
St. Louis Republican 248
St. Paul, Minnesota 75
Salem, Virginia 212, 214–216
Salem Depot, (Marshall) Virginia 160
Salt Lake City, Utah 35, 37
Saltville, Virginia 176, 182–183, 200, 202–204, 209–210, 212–214; first battle of 241
Saluria, Texas 51, 55, 246–247
San Antonio, Texas 54, 58, 64, 66
San Francisco, California 39–40, 244
San Jacinto, battle of 33
Santa Anna, Antonio Lopez de 33
Santa Fe, New Mexico 57
Sayler's Creek 235
Schenck, Robert C. 124–125, 138–139
Scott, Winfield 33
Scott County, Virginia 87
Second Brigade, C.S. Army of the

Valley District 112, 214, 218, 224–226
Second Bull Run/Second Manassas campaign 108–109, 111, 113, 116, 212
Seddon, James 120–122, 125–128, 187, 208, 233, 244
Seminary Ridge 160–161, 163
Seminole War 34, 54
Seven Days Battles 104–105, 214
Seven Pines, battle of 213
Shackelford, James M. 180, 192
Sheffey, John P. 201
Sheffey family cemetery 243
Shelby County, Tennessee 41, 43, 63, 248
Shenandoah County, Virginia 119
Shenandoah Mountain, (West) Virginia 118
Shenandoah River 103, 114
Sheridan, Phillip H. 235, 237, 239–240–243; Shenandoah Valley Campaign of 235, 237, 240–241, 243
Sherman, William T. 30, 174, 191, 202
Sherman Silver Purchase Act of 1893 243
Shrady, John, Dr. 188
Sibley, Charlotte 78–79
Sibley, Henry Hopkins 2, 68–75, 78–80, 246
Sibley, Tent 68–75, 78–81, 180, 246
Sigel, Franz 108, 205, 207–208
Simonson, John Smith 54
Sim's Mill 194
Sixty-Ninth North Carolina Infantry (Sixty-Ninth North Carolina Infantry, AKA Thomas Legion of Cherokee Indians and Western North Carolina Highlanders) 188, 213, 216, 219, 225, 226–227, 229, 240
Smyth, Tobias 10
Smyth County, Virginia 176–177, 182, 199–202
Snake River 38
South Mountain 163–164, **167**, 169
Southampton County, Virginia 80
Southern Pacific Railroad 244
Southern Soldier Stories 95–96
Sperry, J. Austin 86
Spotsylvania Courthouse 204, 245
Sprole, W.J., Reverend 28
Stanton, Henry T. 187
Starr, Samuel "Old Paddy" 162
Starr County, Texas 61
Staunton, Virginia 114, 116, 119, 121, 125, 129, 133, 205–207, 209, 211–212, 214–218, 220–222, 230–232, 234–235, 241
Staunton Road AKA East Road **221**, 224–226, **228**, 229
Steel, John 6
Stevensburg, Virginia 151
Stevenson, George J, Dr. 13
Stoddard, Charles 45–46
Stoneman, George 22
Stowe, Harriet Beacher 76

Strasburg, Virginia 90, 103, 122–123, 205
Strawberry Plains, Tennessee 190, 213
Stringfield, William W. 188, 213, 226, 240–241
Strother, David Hunter 207, 219, 231, 239
Stuart, Flora 99
Stuart, James Ewell Brown 1–2, 13, 52, 80, 83, 90–100, 102, 108–113, 128, 146–160, 164, 168–170–179, 182–184, 199, 204, 213, 237, 241, 244–246; Stuart's Chambersburg Raid 110–111, 113, 159, 178; Stuart's Gettysburg Raid 159–161, 173
Sullivan County, Tennessee 184
Summersville, (West) Virginia 141, 143
The Sunny Land 240
Surgoinsville, Tennessee 185
Sutter's Mill, California 34
Swan, Robert 93, 95

Taylor, W.E.S. 174
Taylor, Zachary 33, 53
Tazewell, Tennessee 194, 196
Tazewell County, Virginia 182, 200, 214
Tennessee Troop Units (C.S):
 Fifty-Ninth (59th) Tennessee Mounted Infantry 215
 First (1st) Tennessee Cavalry 184, 215
 Forty-Third (43rd) Tennessee Mounted Infantry 215
 Sixteenth (16th) Tennessee Cavalry 215
 Sixtieth (60th) Tennessee Infantry 215
 Sixty-First (61st) Tennessee Infantry 215
 Sixty-Second (62nd) Tennessee Infantry 215
 Third (3rd) Tennessee Mounted Infantry 215
 Thirty-Ninth (39th) Tennessee Mounted Infantry 215
 Twelfth (12th) Tennessee Cavalry 215, 229
Tennessee Troop Units (U.S.):
 Eleventh (11th) Tennessee Cavalry 197
 Second (2nd) Tennessee Mounted Infantry 180, 184, 186, 188
 Third (3rd) Tennessee Infantry 199
Texas Rangers 58
Texas War for Independence 33
Thayer, Sylvanus 15
Thomas, Charles 75
Thomas Legion *see* North Carolina Troops, (CS), Sixty-Ninth North Carolina Infantry Regiment
Thomason, John W. 52
Thompson, John B. 183

Tippett, Thomas E. 132
Tom's Brook, engagement 235
Treaty of Guadalupe Hidalgo 29, 33–34, 53
Twiggs, David E. 36
Tygart Valley River 140

Uncle Tom's Cabin 76
Underground Railroad 189
Union, Virginia (Changed to Unison) 157
Uniontown, Pennsylvania 137
United States Military Academy at West Point AKA West Point 1, 13–32, 35, 39–40, 55, 60–61, 64, 70, 81, 83, 87, 89, 91–92, 94, 97, 101, 104–105, 107, 111, 151, 175–176, 184, 205–207, 212, 214, 230, 247–248
United States Troops:
 Eighth (8th) Army Corps 124
 First (1st) U.S. Regiment of Dragoons 39
 Sixth (6th) U.S. Cavalry 169
 U.S. Dragoons (Old Army) 2, 68–69
 U.S. Mounted Rifles AKA Regiment of Mounted Rifles (Old Army) 31, 34–40, 52–54, 57, 59–61, 91, 94
University of Berlin 182
University of Indiana at Bloomington 116
University of Virginia 82–83, 104, 136, 182, 241, 243
Upperville, Virginia, engagement 157–158, 211
Utah Expedition/War 73–75, 91, 246

Vaughn, John C. 196, 215–217, 219–220, 225–227, 229–230, 232–235, 24
Vermont Troops:
 First Vermont Cavalry 106
Vicksburg, Mississippi 174, 215, 246
Victoria, Queen 29, 68
Vilmorin Andrieux & Company, Paris 77
Virginia Central Railroad 105, 205, 212
Virginia Convention 83, 85–86
Virginia General Assembly 85, 115
Virginia House of Delegates 241
Virginia Military Institute (VMI) 55, 88, 90, 102, 205, 215, 235, 237, 239
Virginia Polytechnic Institute 245
Virginia School for the Deaf 116
Virginia State Line 182, 215
Virginia Troop Units:
 Augusta Reserves, battery 219, 220
 Boy Battery *see* Marquis Battery
 Chew's Battery/Horse Artillery 102–103, 112, 121, 129, 150–152, 161–162, 164
 Comanches *see* Thirty-Fifth Battalion AKA White's Cavalry
 Dunn's Partisan Rangers *see*

286 Index

(Virginia Troop Units, *continued*)
Thirty-Seventh Battalion Virginia Cavalry
Eighteenth (18th) Virginia Cavalry Regiment 211, 219, 223
Eighth (8th) Virginia Cavalry Regiment 181–182, 186, 188, 201
First (1st) Virginia Cavalry Regiment 91–100, 104, 113, 117, 172, 245
First (1st) Virginia Partisan Rangers 117–119
First (1st) Virginia Regiment of Engineers 129, 245
Forty-Fifth (45th) Battalion Virginia Infantry
Forty-Fifth (45th) Regiment Virginia Infantry 214–215, 225
Forty-Third (43rd) Battalion Virginia Cavalry 215, 225
Harper's, Augusta and Rockbridge Reserves 209, 218–219, 225, 227
Lewisburg Battery 214, 218, 225, 234
Marquis's Augusta Battery AKA Marquis "Boy Battery" 209, 219, 225–226
Rockbridge Reserves 209, 219, 227
Second (2nd) Virginia Cavalry Regiment 103
Seventeenth (17th) Battalion Virginia Cavalry 112
Seventh (7th) Virginia Cavalry Regiment 101–108, 110–111, 113, 129, 131–132, 152, 158, 161–162, 164, 169, 173, 178, 245
Sixth (6th) Virginia Cavalry Regiment 103, 106–107, 112, 121, 129–130, 134, 138, 140–141, 151–152, 161–165, 169, 173, 211, 218, 241
Sixtieth (60th) Virginia Infantry Regiment (AKA Wise Legion) 214, 225, 227
Sixty-Fourth (64th) Virginia Mounted Infantry Regiment AKA Sixty-Fourth Virginia Cavalry 194, 199
Staunton Artillery 116–117
Thirteenth (13th) Virginia Infantry 94
Thirty-Fifth (35th) Battalion Virginia Cavalry (AKA White's Battalion, AKA the Comanches 112, 123, 129, 132, 152, 156, 161
Thirty-Fourth (34th) Battalion Virginia Cavalry (AKA Witcher's Battalion) 129, 142, 182–183, 186, 197, 200, 210
Thirty-Seventh (37th) Battalion Virginia Cavalry 181–183, 186, 192, 201
Thirty-Seventh (37th)Virginia Infantry 88
Thirty-Sixth (36th) Battalion Virginia Cavalry 182–183, 186, 197, 214
Thirty-Sixth (36th) Virginia Infantry Regiment 214–215, 225, 227
Twelfth (12th) Virginia Cavalry Regiment 112, 121–123, 130, 133, 135–136, 142, 152, 158, 161, 170, 211
Twenty-Fifth (25th) Virginia Cavalry Regiment 245
Twenty-First (21st) Virginia Cavalry Regiment 182, 198, 201, 243
Twenty-Seventh (27th) Battalion Virginia Cavalry 182–183, 186, 197, 199
Twenty-Third (23rd) Virginia Cavalry AKA Robert White's Cavalry 211, 217, 223, 241
Virginia Volunteers 87–88; Wise Legion *see* Sixtieth (60th) Regiment Virginia Infantry; Witcher's Battalion *see* Thirty-Fourth (34th) Battalion Virginia Cavalry

Walker, Henry Harrison 173
Walker, Thomas, Dr. 193
Walker's Ford 191
Wallace, Martin 130–133
War of 1812 21, 54, 101
Warm Springs, Virginia 143
Warrenton (Junction), Virginia 97–98, 244
Washington & Jefferson College AKA Jefferson College 181
Washington & Lee University AKA Washington College 116, 235, 241
Washington College *see* Washington & Lee University
Washington County, Virginia 1–2, 5–6, 8, 10, 14–15, 26, 31, 41–43, 51–52, 55, 58, 61, 63, 67, 71, 75, 78, 83, 86–89, 100, 113, 167, 175, 181–182, 199, 237–238, 240, 245–246
Washington Peace Conference of 1861 84–85
Waynesboro, Virginia 219–220, 235
Waynesboro-Emmitsburg Turnpike 164–165
Waynesville, North Carolina 213
Weems, O.T. 134
West Union, (West) Virginia 141–142
West Virginia Constitutional Convention of 1872 240
West Virginia Raid AKA Jones Imboden West Virginia Raid 128–146, 148, 158–159, 174, 178, 182–183, 211, 241–243
West Virginia Troop Units:
First (1st) West Virginia Cavalry 165
Fourteenth (14th) Regiment of (West) Virginia Volunteers 130
Sixth Regiment (6th) West Virginia Volunteer Infantry 138
Twelfth (12th) West Virginia 227
West Virginia University 136, 242–243
Western State Lunatic Asylum 234
Westervelt & Mackay Shipyard 45
Westminster, Maryland 160
Weston, (West) Virginia 140–141
Wharton, Gabriel C., Brigade 184, 205, 21

Wheeler, Joseph A. 190, 213
Wheeling, (West) Virginia 115, 128, 137–138, 140, 144, 146
Whig Party 116
White, Elijah V. "Lige" 112, 123, 132, 156, 161
White, Robert 211, 217, 223
White Slaves of England 77
White Sulphur Springs, (West) Virginia 176; battle of 182
White's Cavalry *see* Thirty-Fifth Battalion Virginia Cavalry, AKA Comanches
White's Ford 111
Whitman, Marcus, Dr. 35; Whitman Massacre 35
Wilcox, Cadmus Marcellus 22, 173
Wilderness Road 193, 197
Wiley, Ephraim E. 12
Wiley Hall 10, 241
Wilkinson, Nathan 138
Willey Waitman T. 136
Williams, Charles 123
Williams, George 196
Williams, John S. "Cero Gordo" 179, 181, 183–184
Williams, S.B. 66
Williamson, William G. 129, 139–140
Williamsport, Maryland 109, 163, 167–170, 211
Wilmington & Northern Railroad 240
Wilson, John 60
Wilson, William Lyne 122, 135–136, 138, 242–243
Wilson-Gorman Tariff Act 243
Winchester, Virginia 90, 103–104, 109, 111, 119–123, 125–129, 156, 170; second battle of 207, 235; third battle of 235, 240
Winford, John G. 12
Wise, Henry A. 81
Wise County, Virginia 200
Wise Legion *see* Sixtieth Virginia Infantry, Virginia Troop Units
Witcher, Vincent Addison 129, 142, 182–183, 186, 200–202, 210, 243–244
Withers, Henry H. 119–120
Wolf's Craig 101
Woodstock, Virginia 103, 119, 123, 126, 208
Wyerman's Mill 197–200, 202
Wyoming, Territory of 35, 37–38, 73
Wyoming County, (West) Virginia 215
Wythe County, Virginia 176, 193, 199, 202–203, 210, 214
Wytheville, Virginia 202–203, 210

Yancey, William L. 86
Yellow Store, Tennessee 186
Yorktown, Virginia 97, 99, 117
Youghiogheny River, Bridge 135–136
Young, Brigham 73

www.ingramcontent.com/pod-product-compliance
Lightning Source LLC
Chambersburg PA
CBHW081543300426
44116CB00015B/2732